Teaching in the Secondary School

SEVENTH EDITION

Tom V. Savage

Santa Clara University

Marsha K. Savage

Santa Clara University

David G. Armstrong

Boston   Columbus   Indianapolis   New York   San Francisco   Upper Saddle River
Amsterdam   Cape Town   Dubai   London   Madrid   Milan   Munich   Paris   Montreal   Toronto
Delhi   Mexico City   Sao Paulo   Sydney   Hong Kong   Seoul   Singapore   Taipei   Tokyo

Vice President, Editor in Chief: Paul A. Smith
Senior Acquisitions Editor: Kelly Villella Canton
Editorial Assistant: Annalea Manalili
Senior Marketing Manager: Darcy Betts Prybella
Production Editor: Renata Butera
Editorial Production Service: Rakhshinda Chishty
Manufacturing Buyer: Renata Butera
Electronic Composition: Aptara®, Inc.
Cover Designer: Bruce Kenselaar
Creative Art Director: Jayne Conte
Cover Photo: © moodboard/Alamy

Photo Credits: Critical Thinking box photo © Thinkstock

Credits and acknowledgments borrowed from other sources and reproduced, with permission, in this textbook appear on appropriate page within the text.

Library of Congress Cataloging-in-Publication Data

Savage, Tom V.
   Teaching in the secondary school / Tom V. Savage, Marsha K. Savage, David G. Armstrong.—7th ed.
     p. cm.
Includes bibliographical references and index.
ISBN-13: 978-0-13-210152-3 (alk. paper)
ISBN-10: 0-13-210152-1 (alk. paper)
1. High school teaching—United States.   2. Education, Secondary—United States.
I. Savage, Marsha Kent, 1952-   II. Armstrong, David G.   III. Title.
LB1737.U6A75 2012
373.1102—dc22
                         2011008015

2 3 4 5 6 7 V069 20 19 18 17 16 15

www.pearsonhighered.com

ISBN-10:   0-13-210152-1
ISBN-13: 978-0-13-210152-3

Contents

Part II Preparing for Teaching   97

Chapter 5

What Should Students Learn? Defining the Curriculum   98

Chapter 6

Learning Assessment: Making Data-Driven Decisions   122

Chapter 7

Planning Units and Lessons   148

Chapter 8

One Size Does Not Fit All: Differentiated Instruction   169

Contents

Preface

People entering the field of secondary teaching are facing exciting opportunities as well as numerous challenges. There may be more proposals for changing secondary education than ever before in the history of U.S. education. Some of these proposals offer exciting new opportunities to meet the needs of students. Other proposals, however, appear to be based on flawed assumptions that could be detrimental to the education of our most valuable resource, our children. Navigating through these waters requires informed professionals with a clear understanding of the teaching and learning in secondary schools.

The seventh edition, like the previous editions, of *Teaching in the Secondary Schools* provides information for those who are interested in the rewarding yet sometimes frustrating role of secondary school teacher. It addresses the proposals for change in secondary education and how those changes would affect secondary teachers and their students. The text covers the wide range of responsibilities of secondary teachers, including lesson planning, unit planning, assessment of learning, meeting the needs of a diverse student population, developing a repertoire of teaching strategies, and engaging in professional growth.

We, the authors, recognize the enormous changes that are taking place. Thus, we do not try to provide answers for all of the challenges that a teacher might face. In addition, our intent is neither to persuade individuals to choose a career in secondary education nor to dissuade them from doing so. Our intent is to provide perspectives and information that will help readers make informed decisions. We have attempted to do this through our many years of teaching as well as our years working with secondary school teachers and student teachers. We hope that these perspectives will provide a useful lens through which individuals can obtain understanding about the past, the present, and the future of secondary education.

New to This Edition

Each chapter in this edition has been revised and updated. No chapter exists exactly as it appeared in the sixth edition. New features that are especially noteworthy include the following:

- *The chapter on assessment has been totally revised and moved to a new location.* The revised chapter places more emphasis on formative assessment. In addition, a section on diagnostic assessment was added. The chapter was moved up in the chapter sequence in order to model the backward design model. It is placed directly after the chapter on content selection and the development of objectives. Therefore, after identifying the end point of instruction, assessment should be designed and used as guidelines for the selection of teaching approaches and the design of lessons.

- *Revised sample unit.* To keep the chapter content more in line with the emphasis on the backward design model, we revised the sample unit in Chapter 7 to reflect this change in emphasis.

- *New content of Race to the Top and other reform proposals.* Chapter 1 has been substantially changed to reflect new trends in school reform. The Race to the Top initiative of the Obama administration is discussed as a key reform proposal.

- *New content on writing.* A new section has been added to the chapter about reading across the curriculum to address writing in the content areas. This is in response to the growing awareness that teachers in all content areas need to address the critical topics of reading and writing.

- *New content on bullying and cyberbullying.* Several tragedies have led educators to consider seriously the role of the school and the teacher to address bullying and cyberbullying. The chapter on management and discipline has been revised to include this content and recommendations on how to address these important concerns.

- *New content on professional development opportunities.* The Internet provides some excellent opportunities for professional development. Teachers no longer need to spend time and money to travel to conferences and workshops. Many excellent opportunities exist for teachers to work at their own pace from their home to design personalized professional growth plans. This new content has been added to the final chapter on professional growth.

Organization of This Text

Organizing a text on the topic of secondary teaching can be a challenge because of the variety of approaches to secondary teaching used in preparation programs. Earlier editions of *Teaching in the Secondary Schools* have been used in courses such as secondary methods, introduction to teaching, and issues in education. Sometimes the course is designed to prepare secondary teachers in a specific content area; other times, the course is a more generic one that includes prospective teachers in several subject areas. Therefore, we have designed the text to be flexible so that users can organize and use the text in ways that best fit their needs.

The organization that we have chosen includes four basic parts. Part 1 addresses the societal context of secondary education. We focus on current reform proposals, a brief history of secondary education so individuals can understand how we got to this point in time, information about the diversity of the school population, and information about how schools are attempting to meet contemporary challenges.

The focus in Part 2 is on preparing for teaching in the classroom. We highlight the importance of individuals becoming reflective teachers. We believe that all teachers need to learn how to reflect on their own teaching and perform self-evaluations. We have also used the backward design model as a guide for organizing the chapters. For example, the backward design approach emphasizes that the beginning point for planning involves the identification of the end points of instruction. Therefore, we have placed a chapter on understanding the nature of content and the selection of big ideas as the end point of units of instruction. The next step in the model includes defining how teachers know that students have learned the big ideas or generalizations. Therefore, the development of assessment procedures is the next step in the planning process. After the end points of instruction have been identified as well as how student learning will be assessed, then attention focuses on planning units and lessons and differentiating instruction to meet the needs of all students.

In Part 3, we focus on the instructional act. We provide information on different teaching approaches, including direct instruction, teaching for higher-level outcomes, and small-group and cooperative learning. We also address the importance of teaching reading across the curriculum. Secondary school teachers often have little preparation for helping students read. However, every subject in the curriculum requires some reading, and student failure can often be traced to the inability of students to comprehend the material they read. Finally, we also address the critical aspect of classroom management and discipline. There are two major tasks that all teachers face: presenting lessons and maintaining control of the classroom. These two tasks are related because well-planned and exciting lessons lead to fewer management problems, and good management keeps students on track. As one of our friends, a secondary school principal, states, "You can't teach unless you can manage the classroom."

Part 4 focuses on the professional content of teaching. One of the professional responsibilities of teachers is to understand their legal obligations and their legal rights. Teaching can be perilous for those who do not understand the legal dimensions of their teaching role. As with other aspects of the law, ignorance of the law is not an excuse when a problem occurs. Finally, we conclude the text with a chapter on professional growth. We are constantly amazed at how many teachers we encounter who are unaware of the many opportunities that exist for teachers to engage in exciting professional growth. We (the authors) have all reached our professional levels by first engaging in professional growth opportunities that then opened new doors and additional professional growth. Today Internet opportunities such as webinars and online courses open professional development to all teachers regardless of where they teach.

Special Features of This Text

Several features of *Teaching in the Secondary School* will help readers maximize their comprehension and understanding. Those features include the following:

- *Graphic organizers.* At the beginning of each chapter, we have provided a graphic organizer. The purpose of the graphic organizer is to provide a visual display that can serve as an advance organizer for the content of the chapter.

- *Chapter introduction.* The introduction for each chapter helps set the stage for the content of the chapter. It is intended to raise questions and create a reason for learning the content of the chapter.

- *More from the Web.* In most chapters, we have listed websites that provide more information or enrichment for the content of the respective chapter.

- *Bulleted objectives.* At the beginning of each chapter, we have stated objectives that help the reader define important material that should be learned.

- *For Your Portfolio.* We have linked the content of most chapters to the Interstate New Teacher Assessment and Support Consortium (INTASC) standards for beginning teachers. In those chapters, readers are challenged to select material that demonstrates their understanding of the INTASC standards for inclusion in a professional portfolio.

- *Critical Incidents.* In many chapters, we present critical incidents to help readers engage in thinking about how they would respond to situations that teachers face in the classroom. These incidents are based on experiences we have observed or encountered in classrooms.

- *What Do You Think?* This feature provides opportunities for readers to examine personal beliefs and convictions regarding important issues.

- *Figures.* In some key places, figures are used to reinforce content or illustrate relationships.

- *Key Ideas in Summary.* This feature completes the instructional cycle that begins with the advance organizer. The graphic organizer provides an overview and advance organizer for the chapter content; the key ideas are provided to help readers review important points in the chapter content.

- *Reflections.* These sections at the end of several of the chapters engage the readers in thinking about the content of the chapter and how it relates to their understanding and beliefs.

- *Learning Extensions.* These exercises are intended to provide readers with suggestions on how they can continue their learning on key issues discussed in the chapter.

- *References.* The references direct readers to source material the authors have used.

Supplements

An **Instructor Manual/Test Bank,** downloadable from our password-protected Instructor Resource Center, is available to adopters of this text. If you are already registered, log in at www.pearsonhighered.com/irc or visit this URL to request access, which will be granted after Pearson verifies instructor status. The manual contains chapter overviews and outlines, key terms, guiding questions, a test bank of multiple choice, true/false, short answer and discussion questions, and additional class activities for each chapter.

Acknowledgments

Many individuals are involved in the development of any book. We are grateful for contributions of numerous individuals who provided assistance in the development of this manuscript.

The following individuals reviewed the previous edition of the text and provided many helpful suggestions: Sharon M. Hunter, North Carolina A & T State University; Cathy May, Southwestern College; David D. Victor, Elmhurst College; Cynthia Cole Robinson, Purdue University–Calumet. In addition, we want to thank our students at Santa Clara University. They let us know what is useful and where improvements are needed.

Finally we want to thank the helpful staff at Allyn & Bacon. We especially want to thank our editor, Kelly Villella Canton, and her assistant, Annalea Manalili, for the time they have spent helping make this edition a reality.

TVS
MKS

Teaching in an Age of Change

Bob Daemmrich Photography

The Changing World of Teaching

Objectives

This chapter will help you

- identify changes that are likely to occur in secondary education
- clarify reasons for becoming a secondary school teacher
- trace the historical roots of secondary education practices
- define the difference in philosophy between the middle school and the junior high school

- state the potential impact of Race to the Top on secondary school teachers
- define the implications of reform trends for teachers
- explain the rationale for standards-based education and common standards
- state the arguments for and against high-stakes testing
- define the impact of accountability on teacher practices

Bob Daemmrich Photography

Graphic Organizer: Chapter 1

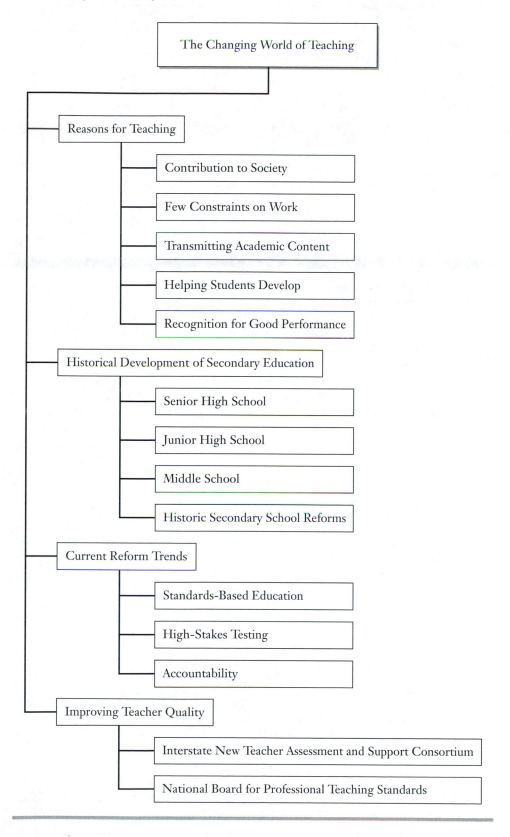

The Changing World of Teaching

Reasons for Teaching
- Contribution to Society
- Few Constraints on Work
- Transmitting Academic Content
- Helping Students Develop
- Recognition for Good Performance

Historical Development of Secondary Education
- Senior High School
- Junior High School
- Middle School
- Historic Secondary School Reforms

Current Reform Trends
- Standards-Based Education
- High-Stakes Testing
- Accountability

Improving Teacher Quality
- Interstate New Teacher Assessment and Support Consortium
- National Board for Professional Teaching Standards

Introduction

Traveling across the United States, one is struck by the great diversity of the nation. There are huge forests nourished by cool days and abundant rainfall in the Northwest. Traveling across the Southwest, one encounters vast deserts with low humidity and miles upon miles of sweeping vistas of sagebrush and cactus. The Southeast offers warm, humid days and prolific vegetation. The Great Plains are covered with miles of crops irrigated by central pivot sprinklers. Great cities with high population densities are teeming with people and traffic. In contrast, small hamlets offer a personal touch where everyone seems to know each other. The harsh climates of the upper Midwest and Alaska contrast with the perpetual summers of Hawaii, Florida, and southern California. This diversity is an interesting and appealing feature of the nation.

This fascinating diversity extends beyond the physical environment to the human inhabitants. There is cultural and ethnic diversity wherever you go. Even in small towns, you will find restaurants featuring ethnic dishes. Widely scattered hogans of the Navaho in the Southwest contrast with high-density condominiums in metropolitan centers. Tibetans are living in Minnesota, and Vietnamese are living in Texas.

However, there is a common feature that can be found in all of these places. One does not need to look hard to find a secondary school. In fact, as you enter many small towns across the nation, you are greeted with signs proclaiming the accomplishments of the local high school, from athletic championships to academic decathlons and marching band awards.

The secondary school, an institution that was once primarily an institution for the elite, has now become a vital institution for all of society. A common concern of citizens, wherever they live, is the quality of the local schools. Businesses seeking a new location and families looking for a new home are vitally interested in the quality of the local secondary schools.

At the state and national level, politicians proclaim that a quality secondary school education is essential for the future of the nation. They express concern about how well the schools are performing and have found that educational issues resonate with the voters.

Nearly everyone accepts the premise that future citizens will need to know how to respond to an increasingly complex and rapidly changing world. There is much controversy, however, concerning how well secondary schools are performing and preparing students to take their place in this complex new world. There is considerable debate concerning what these future citizens should know and be able to do.

Some data reinforces concerns about secondary education. For example, Wise (2010) claims that every available indicator suggests too many secondary students drop out and too many are unprepared for college or employment. His contention is that the goals of education have changed profoundly, yet the basic structure of secondary education has remained very much the same. Therefore, current secondary schools were not designed to meet contemporary demands.

Darling-Hammond and Friedlaender (2010) reinforce this perspective. They contend that the "factory model" for high schools, one designed to process large numbers of students efficiently while supporting only a few for "thinking," is still the pervasive model for secondary education. However, this model is not appropriate to meet the changing goals of secondary education.

As a result, secondary education has become a topic of much discussion and controversy. Issues relating to the quality of secondary education are being debated from the highest levels of government to dinner tables in homes. Newspapers that once contained little more than information about school board meetings and the lunch menu of the local high school now regularly feature front-page articles about educational issues. Statewide rankings of schools command considerable space in local newspapers when they are released. Other "hot" political topics that regularly make their way to the nightly news and to regular articles in popular periodicals include school funding priorities, school budgets, national curriculum standards, international comparisons of student achievement, accountability, high-stakes testing, teacher quality, tenure, turning around low-performing schools, merit pay for teachers, charter schools, vouchers, and Race to the Top. To be sure, education is receiving considerable attention. The results are likely to be fundamental changes in secondary education and the role of teachers.

On an individual level, nearly all of us have vivid memories of our secondary school experience. Some of the memories are good, some are not. This is because secondary education occurs at a critical time in the lives of individuals. It is a time of seeking independence, developing self-concept and identity, and basically coming of age. It is a time of life when the decisions made have lifelong consequences.

Some of us developed interests through special programs such as athletics, debate, drama, and music that continue to influence and enrich our lives. Many of us encountered a special teacher or coach that influenced our lives in dramatic ways. In fact, many people choose to be secondary school teachers because of the influence of a special teacher.

For many students, however, the secondary school experience is not viewed positively. For them, the experience was one that was impersonal and irrelevant. A significant number do not believe that their teachers were interested in their success (MetLife Survey, 2010). The National Commission on the High School Senior Year (2001) found that students who did not demonstrate prowess in academics, athletics, or music went through school with no counselor, teacher, or adult knowing him or her well. Their high school experience was impersonal and irrelevant to their lives, and they became disengaged and alienated from the school. While this is not a new phenomenon, the concern is that the nation can no longer afford the consequences of a significant number of low-achieving, disengaged, and alienated students. Contemporary society demands large numbers of well-educated individuals in order to meet contemporary challenges.

Change is a reality that must be faced by anyone contemplating a career in secondary education. The role that you think you will play might not be consistent with the secondary school of the future. Our challenge to you as you proceed through this text is to think deeply about your decision to enter the world of secondary education. What are your assumptions about the role of a secondary teacher? Are you willing to challenge your assumptions and change them? What is most attractive to you in choosing secondary education as a career? Are those features you find attractive likely to persist in the face of proposed change?

Entering the world of secondary teaching presents many challenges. It is not an easy job nor is it one where you will reap abundant monetary rewards. Some of your family and friends will scoff at your choice. It is easy to become discouraged when your efforts are not recognized and your profession is frequently criticized. Are you up to this challenge? Will you be discouraged or challenged when you face students who do not share your enthusiasm and commitment to education and to the subject you teach? Will you be frustrated when you face a lack of resources as school budgets are slashed to balance state budgets? Will you be angered by proclamations of policy makers who have never been in classrooms as they blame teachers for the failures of the society? This, too, is part of being a teacher.

However, secondary teaching can be immensely satisfying and rewarding. There are few things more exciting than seeing the light in the eyes of a student when something becomes clear. The enthusiasm of the youth is contagious. It is deeply satisfying when you see students grow and develop, and you know that you have had an impact on them. It is very rewarding when you receive notes from former students. These are the things that attract most secondary school teachers.

You must start the journey to teaching in the secondary school by understanding that you need to become a reflective teacher. Reflective teachers think about their experience and continually learn from their successes and failures. A successful secondary teacher cannot expect to learn everything they need to know in their preparation program. They must be lifelong learners, and reflection is a key component of lifelong learning.

A good place to start your journey of reflection is with a self-assessment. What do you find rewarding? What are your ambitions and goals? Are you being honest as you consider your strengths? Where do you need to grow? How do your values and priorities square with

---

Box 1-1 Self-Assessment

PRIORITIES FOR CHOOSING TEACHING

Individuals' reasons for choosing a career in secondary teaching vary. A few reasons that people sometimes mention are included in the statements that follow. What priority would you assign to each?

Priority

High	Medium	Low	
___	___	___	Making a contribution to society
___	___	___	Enjoying the freedom to work with few constraints

High	Medium	Low	
___	___	___	Working with youth
___	___	___	Transmitting academic content
___	___	___	Having secure employment
___	___	___	A work schedule that provides blocks of time off
___	___	___	Helping students develop as individuals
___	___	___	Being recognized and rewarded for good performance

---

the realities of teaching at the secondary level? To gain a personal perspective on these issues, spend some time being totally honest with yourself and complete the "Self-Assessment Ranking Exercise" (see Box 1-1). Your answers may tell you something about your priorities.

Reasons for Teaching

Unfortunately, many individuals enter teaching, soon become discouraged and leave. One study found that 33% of teachers leave within the first three years of teaching and 46% leave within the first five years (Moulthrop, Calegari, & Eggers, 2006). There are some unique reasons for this high turnover rate. For example, teaching, compared to many other professions, attracts a large percentage of young women who often step out of teaching in a few years to raise a family. Some teachers continue their education and in about five years are ready to move into nonteaching roles such as administration and counseling. Some teacher recruitment programs view teaching as something akin to a service commitment and ask individuals to commit to just a couple of years of teaching before they move on to other careers.

However, a number of individuals leave because they become disillusioned with teaching. They entered with unrealistic expectations that were not realized. Their views of the role of the teacher were not based on reality. Some discovered that they did not have adequate preparation for the complex task of teaching secondary-level students, and they were unable to experience the rewards associated with teaching. The number of teachers who leave in the first few years is a serious issue. It is difficult to build quality schools if nearly half of the teaching force needs to be replaced every five years. Individuals choosing secondary teaching need to enter teaching with a realistic understanding of the challenges posed by the changing world of secondary teaching.

Given the challenges, why do teachers remain in teaching? The top three reasons given by teachers for remaining in teaching were (1) they enjoy working with young people, (2) they feel education is important, and (3) they have a deep interest in their subject (Moulthrop, Calegari, & Eggers, 2006). Let's dig a little deeper into some of the reasons that people enter the field of teaching.

Making a Contribution to Society

Did you rank this option high on your priority list? If so, you have lots of company. Many people are motivated to teach because they believe they will be doing "something important." One study indicated that 52% of those polled cited this as a major reason for choosing teaching (Ornstein & Levine, 2003).

Certainly, few people challenge the point that education is critical to health and survival of society. In addition, it is widely recognized that a quality teacher in the classroom is the key ingredient for quality education. Therefore, good teachers certainly do make an important and lasting contribution to society.

However, this by no means suggests that educators are members of a profession that enjoys high status. Although it is common for members of society to proclaim the importance of teaching, it is often not backed by action. An alarmingly low percentage of people do not bother to vote in elections involving school issues, few parents attend school functions, and educational budgets are often one of the first to be slashed when budgets are tight. You might be surprised at the number of individuals who assert that teaching demands quite low levels of intelligence and skill. For example, one of our students recounted being told, "You're a bright girl. Be something; don't be a teacher." Another student who was interested in changing her major from business to one leading to a secondary teaching credential came to our office. As we concluded the conference, she stated, "Don't tell my dad. He'll be upset." The lack of respect and status awarded to teachers often has such a demeaning impact on teachers that when they are asked about their profession, they respond, "I am *just* a teacher!"

In summary, many teachers have a deep commitment to teaching and believe what they do is important. They know they are making an important contribution to society even though they may not have status appropriate for their contributions. As a teacher you need to realize that you will probably not get much recognition from society, and you may need to rely on the personal satisfactions you get from working with young people.

Freedom to Work with Few Constraints

In the not too distant past, teachers enjoyed considerable autonomy. When a teacher walked in the classroom and closed the door, it was the teacher's domain. Although there was a defined curriculum and an occasional visit from an administrator, few questioned what teachers did in the classroom. While teachers, still enjoy some freedom of action, the days of absolute teacher decision-making are quickly fading.

There are more limitations on what you can teach. You may teach in a state or school district that requires teachers to follow a detailed curriculum. Criticism of teaching in recent years has led to more emphasis on "scripted lessons" that teachers are expected to follow. The increased use of high-stakes standardized tests have placed pressure on teachers to teach to the test and require that they spend more time on content that will be tested rather than on content they believe is important. Some school administrators require teachers to justify every lesson and to stick to a strict plan of content coverage and to a pacing schedule.

It is fair to say that contemporary teachers enjoy less freedom of action than those who taught just a few years ago. This has caused dissatisfaction among experienced teachers and has led some to leave teaching or to seek teaching positions in places where they have more input into decision-making.

On the other hand, when you are in front of a classroom interacting with students, you are still the one making the decisions. The unpredictability of classroom environments and the reality of unexpected events make your decision-making essential. You need to use all of your knowledge and creativity to create a productive learning environment and to meet unpredictable challenges. Authors of scripted lessons cannot anticipate what will happen in a given classroom, and they cannot tell you how to respond.

Lessons are your personal creations. Students are not inert raw material waiting to be processed. They are human beings! They have hopes and fears, interests, and aspirations. They are the product of past successes and failures. They come from incredibly diverse backgrounds and have different strengths and weaknesses. Some come to school ready to learn; others come to school with poor nutrition and in poor health. Some are excited to be there, while others are only in school because they are required to attend. Regardless of their qualifications or their good intentions, individuals far removed from your unique classroom simply cannot prepare lessons that will meet the day-to-day realities.

Realizing that lessons must be your personal creation is both challenging and exhilarating. It is exhilarating when a lesson goes well and you observe the success and the excitement of the students. That is your creation!

It can be discouraging and frustrating, however, when it does not go well. You put forth considerable effort and feel like you failed. A teacher evaluator once explained that one of the most difficult dimensions of evaluating teaching was this personal involvement in lessons. He noted that criticizing a teachers' lesson is like saying, "My you have an ugly baby!"

Yes, teachers still have a good measure of freedom when they are in the classroom. Teaching is one of the few occupations where you still have the ability to make significant changes if you are unhappy with what is happening in your working environment. However, if you lack initiative, if you are insecure and need someone to tell you what to do next, if you become defensive when critiqued, if you have difficulty responding to the unpredictable, if you need lots of public affirmations of your abilities, then teaching is probably not for you.

Transmitting Academic Content

Are you excited about the subject or subjects you want to teach? As indicated above, this is one of the top three reasons whey teachers stay in teaching. Enthusiasm about a subject is a great asset in the classroom. Enthusiasm conveys to students that you believe what you are teaching is valuable and, even more important, that you derive some real satisfaction from knowing the subject. Your personal interest can ignite a commitment to your subject even among students who, initially, may express little enthusiasm for what you are teaching.

It can be very rewarding to work in a job that allows (even requires) lifelong learning of a subject that interests you. We have certainly enjoyed the opportunity to continue to learn in our content areas throughout our careers. Interest in what you are doing is a key element of job satisfaction in any job. Some teachers find it exciting to attend workshops, take additional college coursework, and engage in various forms of professional growth. It might be said that some individuals choose to be teachers because they enjoy being students! To them this is one of the most appealing aspects of being a secondary school teacher.

On the other hand, when you begin working with a class of students, you need to understand that some of them will not share your enthusiasm for the subject. It can be discouraging to a teacher, especially a new teacher, when students demonstrate a lack of student enthusiasm, or even open hostility, toward his or her subject. One of the most common complaints that we hear from student teachers and new teachers is that students don't seem interested in learning. That is why some new teachers express an interest in teaching advanced placement classes. They assume that advanced placement students will be more interested in the subject.

However, it is very rewarding to spark an interest in a subject in reluctant and unmotivated students. It is exciting when they see the usefulness of the subject and expend time and energy outside class to pursue additional knowledge.

Teaching involves more than just transmitting information. Wiggins and McTighe (2010) remind us that the goal of education is not just to cover content. Rather, the goal is to help students become thoughtful about the content. The goal is not to help them be good at school, but rather to prepare them for the world outside school. This requires more of teachers than just knowing information. It requires a different perspective on content than simply passing along information.

Helping Students Develop

Sure, it can be fun to continue to grow in knowledge of your subject and discuss it with others. Yes, it is nice to be working in a profession where there is freedom to inject your skill and creativity. But helping students grow and develop as individuals is at the core of teaching. This is one of the most popular reasons individuals gave for choosing teaching as a career.

In one survey, helping students grow and learn was cited as a major reason for teaching by 90% of the respondents (Ornstein & Levine, 2003). All of us want to believe that what we are doing in life is important. Some second-career individuals choose to move into teaching because they want to do something for society rather than just earn a salary.

However, it is also demeaning when influential and powerful members of society continually claim that teachers are academically weak, that they put forth minimal effort, and that they are in teaching because they have favorable daily working hours and they get summers off (Moulthrop, Calegari, & Eggers, 2006).

One of the realities that you will confront when you are a teacher is that everyone is an "expert." Nearly everyone has attended a school, and many of them have "the answer" to what exactly needs to be done to improve education. Notice how at social gatherings everyone has an answer for what is needed to improve education! This "expert" perspective includes policy makers who have no experience teaching, who have seldom visited classrooms, and who have no reluctance in mandating solutions to complex educational problems.

Sometimes debates about school issues seem strangely disassociated from the real human beings the schools serve. Prescriptions for "improvement" tend to focus on test scores and other issues tied closely to the content-transmission goal of public education. The students, as human beings, when mentioned at all, often appear to be viewed as passive objects who are just waiting to be "improved."

Being Recognized and Rewarded for Good Performance

There is intrinsic satisfaction in knowing that you are doing a good job. However, everyone likes to be recognized for their efforts. While there will be students, parents, guardians, and members of the general community who are appreciative of your efforts, you must realize that, as a teacher, you work in an environment that has a high degree of anonymity. It seems strange that this would be true when you may be in front of 100 or more students every day. However, parents almost never see you teach. It is rare for other teachers or even school administrators to observe in your classroom. Secondary students are often so consumed with finding their own identity and with adolescence egocentrism that they seldom consider the needs of teachers. They can be thoughtless and can easily offend overly sensitive teachers. Therefore, extrinsic rewards and recognition for your efforts is likely to be quite rare.

It is a mistake to assume that everyone will applaud what you do or that you will be quickly lauded for your efforts. If you are expecting accolades from others, it might not happen very often. You will need to rely on self-evaluations of your performance. You need to gather good and reliable data regarding your teaching success and be willing to reflect honestly on what you are doing and on your successes and failures. You may need to be satisfied with personal indicators that you are doing a job well.

Another issue related to gaining recognition for your efforts is that people vary enormously in their beliefs about what constitutes "good" educational practice. For example, you may be a strong believer in the worth of inquiry and problem solving in engaging students' higher-level thinking skills. However, you may well encounter parents who think that it is a waste of time and want you to spend more time preparing students for high-stakes assessments. No matter how hard you work developing and implementing engaging lessons, these parents may not regard you as an effective teacher. What all this means is that different people apply different criteria in determining whether the job you are doing is acceptable. You need to understand that people who define quality instruction differently than you do may not be impressed by your instructional practices. For example, one of our former students, an individual who had chosen teaching after a successful career in business, took a teaching position in a highly ranked secondary school. After two years of teaching, he visited us to explain that he was leaving the school because he could not tolerate parents who constantly questioned what he was teaching and how he was teaching.

One of us remembers, not so fondly, the time we taught a successful and engaging lesson that was observed by the school administrator. At the end of the observation, the administrator commented that the blinds on the windows at the back of the room were not all open at the same angle!

Recognition for a job well done is scarce, and it easy to become discouraged. Moulthrop, Calegari, and Eggers (2006) note that teachers are highly educated professionals who want to be recognized and valued. They want to be involved in the direction of education and to lead reform movements. However, they are often treated as little more than babysitters and civil servants with a salary schedule that reinforces this perception.

In summary, teaching is both highly rewarding and highly frustrating. Like most professions, it has highs and lows. It is a role that is recognized, as least verbally, by society as extremely important. It calls for high levels of teacher commitment and involvement. In the final analysis, you will be the one who will have to base your rewards and recognition on the progress you see in students. The students do provide most of the satisfactions. It is always rewarding, and a bit sad, to watch students you have seen grow and mature cross the stage at graduation time.

Historical Development of Secondary Education

Some of the issues that are being addressed in proposing reforms for secondary education have their roots in history. Evaluating why schools operate the way they do and proposing changes is enhanced by understanding the historical roots. For example, many calls for reform seem to imply that at some point in our history there was a "golden age" of secondary education when there were few problems. Schools all had high achievement levels, all teachers were dedicated and qualified, and all students were motivated to learn. These critics contend that education has lost its way and needs to return to those glory days. An understanding of the history of secondary education can reveal the validity of that argument.

The Senior High School

The importance of a high school education is a relatively recent phenomenon. In the early colonial period of our nation, education was restricted to instruction in the basic skills. Education beyond the basic levels tended to be restricted to the sons of the elite. The curriculum was largely classical in nature, and the goal was to prepare these boys for leadership. However, this narrow application of secondary education was questioned.

Thomas Jefferson argued for a broader distribution of education by pointing out that democracy required an educated citizenry. In addition, as middle-class merchants and other practical occupations became more prevalent, they challenged the idea of a curriculum composed of Greek, Latin, and the classics. Some private secondary schools, however, such as the Franklin Academy; Philips Academy at Andover, Massachusetts; and Philip Exeter Academy at Exeter, New Hampshire, emphasized the idea that secondary education was important.

The first public high school established in the United States in 1821 was the Boston English Classical School. The name was soon changed to the English High School. The program of study emphasized what was then defined as useful and practical subjects as opposed to subjects that appeared to have no clear connection to daily living. However, there was not an overwhelming response to the high school as an institution.

As late as 1860, there were only about 40 public high schools in the entire country (Barry, 1961). One of the barriers to the spread of the high school was money. Public financial support for elementary education dated back to colonial times. However, the high school was not viewed as useful for everyone. Those who attended secondary school still tended to be the upper classes and those preparing for higher education. There was doubt about the legality of using tax money to support secondary schools for this limited population. A landmark case in this area was the famous Kalamazoo case of 1874 [*Stuart v. School District No. 1 of the Village of Kalamazoo*, 30 Mich.69 (1874)], which supported the right of state legislatures to pass laws permitting local communities to levy taxes to support secondary as well as elementary schools.

Once the legality of public funding was established, the number of secondary schools increased rapidly. By 1900, there were over 6,000 high schools serving half a million students. However, in 1900, only 50% of the children were in school, and they received an average of only five years of schooling. Only 6% of the 17-year-olds were high school graduates (Bernard & Mondale, 2001).

Great debates developed concerning the purpose of secondary education. The debate centered on whether the secondary school should prepare students for the world of work or for the academic world of higher education.

In the 1890s, the National Education Association's Committee of Ten issued a report suggesting that the high school should be almost exclusively devoted to preparing students for higher education. The committee recommended that all students take Latin, Greek, English, a modern non-English language, mathematics, the sciences, natural history, history, civil government, political economy, and geography (National Education Association, 1893).

However, this view came under attack as high schools grew to include a broader spectrum of the general population. By 1920, school budgets had grown and high school graduation rates had climbed to 17% of the 17-year-old population. Child labor laws restricted the employment opportunities of youth, and new laws made school attendance compulsory. A report of the National Education's Committee of Nine issued in 1911 suggested that the high school had a responsibility to produce "socially efficient" individuals. These were individuals who were committed to fundamental American values and were capable of making real contributions to the technical and social development of the nation (National Education Association, 1911).

In 1918, a compromise was reached by the National Education Association's Commission on the Reorganization of Secondary Education (Commission on the Reorganization of Secondary Education, 1918) in what has been widely regarded as a seminal document on the development of the American high school. The commission suggested that the high school should be "comprehensive" and should serve multiple purposes. These broad purposes were expressed in the Cardinal Principles of Secondary Education. These principles promoted that the following goals be developed:

1. Health

2. Command of fundamental processes

3. Worthy home membership

4. Vocational preparation

5. Citizenship

6. Worthy use of leisure time

7. Ethical character

These cardinal principles guided the development of secondary school throughout the 20th century. Even today, their influence can be seen in the purposes and the curriculum of the school.

The Junior High School

Junior high schools were not established until the early years of the 20th century. As large numbers of public high schools began to emerge, their academic programs were generally quite demanding compared to the basic education offered in the elementary schools. Some individuals saw the need for a school that would help prepare students for the rigors of high school.

Increased interest in child growth and development led others to conclude that children were not simply "miniature adults" but proceeded through developmental stages. This led some to the idea that a special school was needed that could respond to the unique physical and emotional needs of preadolescents and early adolescents. The views of those who saw the need for a school to prepare students for the rigors of high school often conflicted with those who wanted an institution that met the developmental needs of children. This debate has continued unabated since the first junior high school was established in Berkeley, California, in 1909.

The organizational pattern followed in Berkeley was copied by large numbers of school districts throughout the country. This was a 6-3-3 pattern that featured a six-year elementary school, a three-year junior high school, and a three-year senior high school. Junior high schools in this pattern usually involved Grades 7, 8, and 9. However, there were other patterns. A common one was a two-year junior high school that served Grades 7 and 8 and left Grade 9 in the senior high school.

By the end of World War I, the debate over the purpose of the junior high school had largely been won by the partisans of academic preparation for high school. Most of the teachers hired for the junior high school had preparation that was oriented toward teaching in the high school. Many of the junior high teachers had aspirations to "move up" to the high school. Ever sensitive to negative comments that might come their way from teachers at the senior high school, many junior high school teachers worked hard to prove that there was nothing "academically soft" about junior high school programs.

As a result, attention was not focused on the specialized needs of junior high students. This continued to bring criticism from people concerned about the growth and development issues. Over time they began to win support. Drawing on the work of developmental psychologists as an intellectual rationale, critics of the traditional high school began proposing in the 1960s the establishment of school with a different emphasis. They proposed that this school be called a middle school, a term borrowed from European education.

The Middle School

The middle school concept began to catch on in the 1960s. In general, middle schools were organized to include at least three but not more than five grades that must include Grades 6 and 7 (Lounsbury & Vars, 1978). What was more important was the middle school philosophy. The middle school was to be developed around the special emotional and developmental needs of students in the 11–14 age range. Since middle schools first began to appear in the 1960s, their popularity continued to increase so that they became the dominant type of intermediate school.

As originally conceived, middle schools were supposed to be schools heavily oriented toward serving the unique developmental needs of students. Many institutions called middle schools do reflect this philosophy. However, there are others that reflect the academic orientation that differs little from the junior high school programs that initially prompted the establishment of middle schools. It is common to hear middle school proponents refer to a school as "a middle school in name only."

Similarly, some junior high schools have developed student-oriented programs and curricula that are every bit as responsive to the developmental needs of students as similarly oriented middle schools. It is simply an overgeneralization to state that "middle schools care about students," and "junior high schools care about subjects."

There are many challenges as well as rewards in teaching students in the intermediate years. Individuals teaching at this level must have an appreciation of the special needs of students at this level. The students are active and can display great maturity one moment and tremendous immaturity the next. They are often not afraid to get excited about things and will often do things that are not "sophisticated" enough for high school students.

There is no doubt that these middle years are crucial years when many students either develop a positive self-concept and move toward success, or begin the downward spiral toward failure. Because this age is the turning point for those who eventually drop out of school, the need for committed and understanding teachers at this level is great.

More from the Web

The following are three websites where you can explore issues and trends in secondary education.

EDUCATION COMMISSION OF THE STATES (ECS)
URL: http://www.ecs.org

The Education Commission of the States has an extensive website that covers a broad range of issues in education. Clicking on the issue "high school" brings up a wealth of information on reports, research, and contemporary issues in high school education. Numerous other issues such as testing and accountability are also linked to excellent reports and research.

THE NATIONAL MIDDLE SCHOOL ASSOCIATION
URL: http://www.nmsa.org

This organization provides a wealth of information about middle school education. Current events, conferences, professional development opportunities, research summaries, and links to other sites are listed at its website.

NATIONAL ASSOCIATION OF SECONDARY SCHOOL PRINCIPALS
URL: http://www.nassp.org

This website contains excellent information on issues, trends, research, and publications relating to secondary schools.

Historic Secondary School Reforms

The role of the secondary school has been challenged throughout history. There has never been a "golden age" when everyone agreed with the priorities of secondary education and believed that secondary education was functioning properly. This lack of agreement has led to several reform eras. We are currently in an era where reform is very strong. Reform of secondary education is being advocated by a wide range of individuals and organizations. Many of these reform proposals have their roots in the past. Some have been tried before and are now getting renewed attention.

From the earlier origins of the modern secondary school at the beginning of the 20th century to the 1950s, there has been tremendous growth in the number of students attending secondary school. Around 60% of the age-eligible students were attending secondary schools by the 1950s (Bernard & Mondale, 2001). However, there were great inequities based on gender, color, and ethnicity. African American students were segregated by law in 17 states. The opportunities for girls were limited, the average number of years of attendance for Mexican American students was 5.6 years, and 72% of children eligible for special education were not even enrolled in school (Bernard & Mondale, 2001). While some groups were doing well in secondary schools, a substantial segment of the population was not being well served.

A number of events quickly changed the educational scene. *Brown v. Board of Education of Topeka* in 1954 overturned the "separate but equal" policy and moved the schools toward integration. This development was not well received by all citizens. There was some movement toward private schools and growth of de facto segregation. Criticism of education in general was accelerated with the Soviet launching of the earth satellite *Sputnik* in the fall of 1957. The event was a severe blow to American pride, and people wanted explanations about why the nation had lost its technical and scientific superiority.

The schools became the target of the criticism. A number of popular books were published that were critical of the schools and contended that the basic purposes of secondary education were misguided and that the curriculum was out of date and weak. Individuals who disagreed with the progressive school movement had been claiming that the schools were focusing too much on student needs and interests and were attempting to make school "fun" and "meaningful." They seized on the launch of *Sputnik* as evidence that American schools were too soft and had moved away from intellectual rigor. In 1958, the National Defense Education Act was passed and emphasized a subject matter–centered curriculum. Science and mathematics, areas that were viewed as critical to national defense, were the first areas of the curriculum addressed by the new act. Much of the curriculum development was turned over to subject specialists and academics in the content areas. New curricula were developed for high school physics, biology, chemistry, and mathematics. A nationwide network of summer institutes for teachers was launched in an effort to improve the quality of instruction.

Toward the end of the 1960s, other social problems such as widespread poverty, racial unrest, the Vietnam War, and a rebellious youth culture shifted attention from the space race. Once again the schools became a target. This time a more liberal segment of the population depicted schools as joyless, oppressive, and inhumane places. This shifted the focus of the schools from the more conservative subject-matter emphasis that followed *Sputnik* to a student-centered, open approach allowing high degrees of student freedom. A variety of alternative high schools were developed in many regions of the nation. Some allowed students to choose what they wanted to study and how they wanted to study it.

Toward the end of the 1960s, another issue that was to have long-term impact on the schools came to the forefront. Advocates for the special needs of students followed the civil rights lead of an earlier era and began a campaign requiring the inclusion of special needs students in public education. By the mid 1970s, Public Law 94-142 was passed. That law required that public schools be responsible for the education of handicapped students from the ages of 3 to 21. In addition, it required that, where feasible, handicapped students should be taught in regular classrooms. This changed the student composition of regular classrooms, required additional education for classroom teachers, and resulted in large expenditures for school districts.

By the late 1970s, new concerns about the student-centered emphasis of the past decade began to surface. The publication in 1983 of the National Commission of Excellence in Education report, *A Nation at Risk,* began a new reform movement. This reform movement was triggered by the economic success of other nations such as Japan. These nations were growing in economic power and were challenging the industrial leadership of the United States. Much like the reaction to *Sputnik* 25 years before it, this report placed primary responsibility on the schools. The report claimed that the schools were failing and this failure threatened survival of the nation because of its inability to compete with other nations (Hlebowitsh, 2001)!

Given that the challenge addressed by *A Nation at Risk* was an economic one and that many of those who crafted the report had business backgrounds, it is not surprising that the report signaled the ascendancy of a conservative philosophy emphasizing that schools needed to be operated like a business. The report called for more rigorous graduation standards, the development of national standards against which school performance could be measured, more emphasis on academic subjects like math and science, more teacher and school accountability, more parental choice, longer school days and longer school years, and revised preparation programs for teachers that emphasized academic rigor rather than teacher education. The Japanese educational system was held up as a model that the nation should emulate.

Many questioned the data upon which these reforms were based (Astuto et al., 1994; Berliner & Biddle, 1995). They pointed out that the American schools were a great success. More students from more diverse backgrounds had been educated to higher levels in the United States than any other society in the world (Ryan & Cooper, 2004). Significant improvements had been made in the educational attainments of minority populations, dropout rates were low, and more students were graduating from high school and contemplating higher education than ever before. Actually, the SAT scores for every subgroup had improved over the years, even though the overall score had dropped, because more students from traditionally low-performing groups were taking the test (Berliner & Biddle, 1995).

However, *A Nation at Risk* was a public relations success, and large segments of society were convinced that education was failing. The reforms mentioned in the report continue to guide educational policy almost 30 years later. The impact of *A Nation at Risk* continued into the 21st century, and many of the reform proposals were implemented in the No Child Left Behind (NCLB) Act of 2001 (P.L. 107-110) signed into law in 2002. This act was a reauthorization of the Elementary and Secondary Education Act first passed in 1964 as part of the Johnson administration's "war on poverty." No Child Left Behind was another expansion of federal influence and focused on the establishment of state academic standards, assessment, accountability, and improved teacher quality. This legislation signaled a major change in the educational landscape by increasing federal involvement in educational policy-making.

Current Reform Trends

Many of the current reform trends have their origin in these earlier reform proposals. Current reform proponents advocate three components to successful reform: curriculum standards, frequent assessment to provide data for decision-making, and teacher and administrator accountability (Ornstein, 2003). These three components reflect the business model of resources allocation and efficiency applied to education. Setting standards is the educational equivalent of setting production or sales goals, assessment is intended to provide concrete data focus on the accomplishment of the goals, and accountability assigns rewards or sanctions to individuals based on goal attainment.

Standards-Based Education

Policy makers have been frustrated with previous educational reform efforts. There seemed to be lots of action, but with disappointing results. States would adopt new books and curricula, yet classrooms would continue pretty much as they had in the past. School districts would reorganize and develop new mission statements but fundamental change did not occur. Money would be spent on professional development and technology but with little impact on teaching practice.

As a result, the focus of educational reform shifted from changing the "inputs" (money, curriculum, resources) to evaluating outcomes (student achievement). Standards-based education became the foundation for educational reform movements across the nation.

There are positive dimensions of clearly stated content standards. Many secondary school teachers, even after having completed a college major in a subject, are left wondering what parts of that content need to be taught to a specific group of students. Clear content standards can help teachers conceptualize the essential elements of a subject that should be taught to students. They can be very useful in planning for teaching. In the past, the decision about what to teach was based on the content of the textbook. However, textbooks have an uneven quality and reflect the decisions of the authors as to what is important. Standards can be a more comprehensive and reliable guide.

One argument made by supporters of standards-based education focusing on good standards places the focus on what students should learn. This provides the foundation for developing measurements of these educational outputs. In addition, measurement of clear standards can provide for meaningful comparisons among schools. These comparisons would allow parents, guardians, and policy makers to make judgments about individual schools and would increase competition between schools that would lead to school improvement.

Content standards describe what elements of a content area teachers are supposed to teach and students are expected to learn. Many national subject-area organizations recognized the importance of clear content standards and developed content standards defining what the experts in the content area defined as essential. National content standards were developed for subjects such as mathematics, English language arts, history, civics and government, science, and geography.

While the content standards established by national organizations defined what the "experts" believe is important, they did not overcome the political necessity for states to define their own standards. Defining the curriculum is a state responsibility, and state standards form the legal basis for the curriculum in a given state. No Child Left Behind required that states develop these standards to qualify for federal funds.

While states have always been responsible for curriculum within the state, the guidelines have usually been general ones that were then used by local school districts to guide the development of what was taught in the classrooms. This focus on state standards represents a fundamental shift in the traditional ways educational decisions have been made. The establishment and enforcement of state content standards on all districts in a state effectively removed control of the curriculum from local authorities. Proponents of common standards contend that high mobility of the population makes it important that there be some consistency of expectations across school districts.

However, the establishment of state standards raises a couple of critical questions. Who should determine the content standards for the schools and therefore for all students? And how is achievement of the standards to be measured?

Those controlling the establishment of standards can exert a tremendous impact on what students learn. Fear of political influence on what students learn has led to reluctance to place curriculum decisions too far away from the local community. One example of this fear has been the actions of the committee in Texas that establishes social studies standards for the state. This elected group with a conservative orientation developed standards that clearly emphasized a political agenda. Should politicians such as the president, governors, or legislators decide what students should know? Should leaders in business and industry define what students should learn? Perhaps academic professors in universities should make the decision. Consider the possible agenda of each of these groups and how the standards would be different based on who developed them.

It can be argued that the goal of the reform movement to standards-based education has largely been accomplished. States have developed content standards as required in No Child Left Behind. However, some critics pointed out that the standards adopted by different states are uneven and some are much less demanding than others. The call now is for common national standards. This has been a major provision of the Obama administration's Race to the Top program.

The other major issue relates to how the standards are assessed. If the assessment process is flawed and the data gathered is invalid, then data about student achievement is relatively worthless. This then undercuts the argument that data would better inform the public and policy makers and would provide the foundation for better decisions.

Are current approaches to assessment adequate? Are they providing useful data regarding student achievement and teacher performance? The quality of the assessments is key to achieving the goals of the reform movement. If the emphasis is changed from "inputs" to "outcomes," then good assessment of the outcomes is required. However, there is widespread concern that current assessments of student performance are inadequate at best and are generally flawed and misleading. Because this is such an integral part of education reform, it is curious that there have been few efforts directed at improving the quality of educational assessment.

High-Stakes Testing

The reform movement focuses on identifying how well students are achieving and how well teachers and schools are performing. This information is used to make important decisions such as the allocation of resources, teacher evaluation, school rankings, and whether students are allowed to move to the next grade or to graduate. These decisions have important consequences. Tests that gather data to be used in making these important decisions are called high-stakes tests.

The most prevalent approach to testing is the use of standardized tests. A standardized test is usually one that has been developed by a professional testing company. The test items are developed and tested on a group of students. Test items are revised as needed and norms are established based on the scores of the group. Standards are then established for the administration of the test so that all students taking the test will do so under similar conditions. This process then allows for comparisons of student scores from across the nation based on the established norms or proficiency levels.

The testing associated with standards-based assessment presumes that the testing program will be well matched to the instructional program. In reality this is not always the case. The simple fact that standardized tests are usually developed by large, for-profit companies intent on selling tests to the widest possible audience means that tests cannot focus on the standards for different states. The result is that the test will not measure all of the standards of a given state. In addition, it is likely that because of state-to-state differences, some of the content measured on a given standardized test may not have even been taught in a particular state. In these instances, using test results as a valid measure of students' learning of content standards makes little sense.

High-stakes testing has fueled intense debate. Critics of high-stakes testing point out that such testing practices narrow the curriculum to those things included on the tests. Because lower-level content is easier to test, that is the content that will be emphasized. In addition, because high-stakes tests are so important, great amounts of instructional time are spent teaching to the test rather than teaching important content. Basing decisions solely on the content of a high-stakes test also runs the risk of misidentifying good teachers and good schools (Popham, 2001).

The issue of the alignment of the tests with content standards brings about another concern. Because there is seldom a strong alignment between tests and standards and because teachers are teaching to the tests, defining what should be taught is influenced more by those writing the tests than by those defining the standards.

Because of concern over the possible misuse and the negative consequences of high-stakes tests, several professional organizations have issued position statements. One such statement was developed by the prestigious American Educational Research Association (July 2000). This position statement included the following points:

1. Decisions that have important educational consequences should not be based solely on the basis of test scores.

2. The content tested must be incorporated into the curriculum and the materials prior to administering the test to students.

3. High-stakes tests should not be limited to the portion of the curriculum that is easiest to measure.

4. Sound procedures must be followed in establishing proficiency levels and passing scores.

5. The validity of the tests needs to be established and reported.

6. Attention needs to be given to language differences and students with disabilities.

7. The reliability or the precision of the test scores must be established.

8. The intended and unintended consequences of high-stakes tests needs to be subjected to ongoing evaluation.*

In summary, many of the reform proponents have emphasized high-stakes testing as the only way to bring about educational reform. High-stakes testing is an important

*Source: American Educational Research Association (2000). AERA position statement concerning high-stakes testing in preK–12 education.

What Do You Think?

High-Stakes Testing

This is one of the most debated issues in contemporary education. There are intense feelings on both sides of the issue. Some believe that high-stakes testing is essential to the improvement of education, and others see the movement as a serious detriment to quality education.

Questions

1. After reading the previous section, what is your position on high-stakes testing?

2. Do you agree that only high-stakes testing will motivate students and teachers to do better?

3. Which arguments do you find most compelling both for and against high-stakes testing?

4. What are the alternatives to high-stakes testing?

component of the reform movement and is likely to be a feature of education in the years to come. However, the goal of having well-crafted tests is one about which there is considerable debate. Most of the critics of high-stakes testing contend that the majority of the tests are not well crafted and do not adequately indicate successful learning of standards. These individuals point out that high-stakes testing has the potential for serious harm. Educators need to understand the issues involved and be prepared to take a stand (Savage, 2004). See Box above for some questions to think about.

Accountability

The third component of educational reform is that of accountability. Accountability is directly tied to the standards movement and to high-stakes testing. Accountability in education means holding teachers and schools responsible for what students learn. Accountability is closely related to issues such as the financing and control of education, and it developed in response to several concerns. One was the cost of education. Educational expenditures are a significant portion of the budget of any state. As costs have increased, policy makers have insisted that schools be held accountable for spending money in ways that result in improved student learning.

Few educators disagree with the concept of "fair accountability." However, several issues relate to questions of what teachers should be accountable for, what data is useful for accountability, and whether the accountability process is fair. Is accountability fair if it is based on the results of one test that is given over one or two days once a year? Should teachers be held accountable only for how well students score on tests? Is it fair to hold teachers accountable when they have no control over a number of variables that influence student achievement, such as the quality of the learning materials, language differences, learning disabilities, and the home environment of the students?

Some experts point out that real educational reform is time consuming and costly. It requires reorganizing schools and classrooms, expanding tutoring programs, lengthening the school day and the school year, reducing class size, changing teaching and learning conceptions, and confronting the societal problem of poverty (Ornstein, 2003).

Other critics point out that there needs to be better data gathered from a variety of sources in order to reflect fairly on the accomplishments of the schools and teachers. They suggest that data on topics such as dropout and graduation rates, college acceptance rates, follow-up studies of high school graduates in the years following graduation, and teacher turnover rates are examples of data that need to be considered when making valid determinations of school and teacher accountability.

The problem is that gathering this data is difficult, time-consuming, and expensive. However, if critics are interested in fair accountability and true educational reform, then a broader definition of accountability to include multiple data sources must be considered.

In summary, accountability is an important concept that is here to stay. Teachers will need to gather data that indicates that students are learning. However, the idea of "fair accountability" is still an ideal. Educators must be knowledgeable and make sure that accountability does not continue to be defined in narrow terms that simplify the complexity of teaching and learning. Fair and useful accountability will mean that teachers, parents, and students all must be involved (Ornstein, 2003).

Improving Teacher Quality

The teacher is central to any attempt to reform secondary education. Thus, a focus on improving teaching quality is a component of nearly all reform proposals. Your own teacher preparation program may well include components that have been added in response to some of these improvement initiatives. Ideas put forward by the Interstate New Teacher Assessment and Support Consortium (INTASC) and the National Board for Professional Teaching Standards (NBPTS) have been particularly influential.

Interstate New Teacher Assessment and Support Consortium (INTASC)

The Interstate New Teacher Assessment and Support Consortium (INTASC) was established about 20 years ago as an alliance among state education leaders, colleges and universities, and national groups with interests in promoting educational improvement and development of high-quality educators. INTASC defines quality teachers differently than No Child Left Behind. INTASC has promoted teacher preparation programs that ensure teachers leave their preparation programs knowing both the subjects they will teach and methods for transmitting content that will enable all students to learn. To achieve this end, INTASC has developed a guiding set of principles that are known as the INTASC Model Core Standards. They represent features of teaching and teacher performance that should be present regardless of subjects taught or the age and grade level of students. Many state-level departments of education and teacher preparation programs in universities have used the INTASC standards as guidelines.

The Model Core Standards are listed in Box 1-2. At the end of many of the chapters in this text, you will find an exercise titled For Your Portfolio. This provides you with an opportunity to put information you have learned into a professional-development portfolio. You will be asked to cross-reference materials you include to one or more of the Model Core Standards. To do this, you will want to refer back to the standards provided in Box 1-2.

National Board for Professional Teaching Standards (NBPTS)

In 1987, the Carnegie Forum on Education and the Economy supported establishment of the National Board for Professional Teaching Standards (NBPTS). NBPTS's governing board includes teachers, administrators, members of the public, and other stakeholders in education. The organization operates as a private, nonprofit group that receives financing from foundations, grants from large businesses, and funding from certain federal sources.

NBPTS seeks to improve education by promoting the development of teachers who:

- are committed to students and their learning,
- know the subjects they teach and how to teach those subjects to students,
- are responsible for managing and monitoring student learning,
- think systematically about their practice and learn from experience, and
- are members of learning communities. (NBPTS, 1999)

Box 1-2   INTASC Model Core Standards

1. The teacher understands the central concepts, tools of inquiry, and structures of the discipline(s) he or she teaches and can create learning experiences that make these aspects of subject matter meaningful for students.

2. The teacher understands how children learn and develop, and can provide learning opportunities that support their intellectual, social, and personal development.

3. The teacher understands how students differ in their approaches to learning and creates instructional opportunities that are adapted to diverse learners.

4. The teacher understands and uses a variety of instructional strategies to encourage students' development of critical thinking, problem solving, and performance skills.

5. The teacher uses an understanding of individual and group motivation and behavior to create a learning environment that encourages positive social interaction, active engagement in learning, and self-motivation.

6. The teacher uses knowledge of effective verbal, nonverbal, and media communication techniques to foster active inquiry, collaboration, and supportive interaction in the classroom.

7. The teacher plans instruction based on knowledge of subject matter, students, the community, and curriculum goals.

8. The teacher understands and uses formal and informal assessment strategies to evaluate and ensure the continuous intellectual, social, and physical development of the learner.

9. The teacher is a reflective practitioner who continually evaluates the effects of his or her choices and actions on others (students, parents, and other professionals in the learning community) and who actively seeks out opportunities to grow professionally.

10. The teacher fosters relationships with school colleagues, parents, and agencies in the larger community to support students' learning and well-being.

Much of the work of NBPTS has been dedicated to identifying high standards related to what teachers should know and do to help students achieve. NBPTS has established a certification process for the purpose of identifying teachers who meet these standards. If you seek a National Board Certificate after beginning your career as a teacher, you will undergo a rigorous set of assessments. You will be observed in your own classroom and in special situations that are developed for candidates at NBPTS assessment centers. You will also be required to prepare an extensive portfolio to document your instructional procedures and their effectiveness with learners.

National Board Certificates do not replace teaching credentials, certificates, or licenses that states issue. What they do is provide formal recognition of teachers who have met much higher standards. National Board Certificates provide evidence that holders have met rigorous criteria that clearly identify them as outstanding classroom practitioners.

Not everyone approves of NBPTS. A few critics argue that the practice of applying national standards and awarding certificates to people who meet them challenges the tradition of certifying teachers at the state level. Even though National Board certification does not replace state certification, some people suggest that it is a step in that direction. Supporters point out that the high NBPTS standards may encourage states to adopt more rigorous certification requirements that, in time, will improve the quality of teachers everywhere.

For additional information, visit the National Board's website at http://www.nbpts.org/

Race to the Top

The Obama administration continued federal involvement in education and educational reform with the establishment of a program called Race to the Top (RTTT). RTTT is a $4.35 billion incentive program designed to stimulate educational change across the nation. It was designed by the United States Department of Education and included as part of the American Recovery and Investment Act of 2009 (U.S. Department of Education, 2009). This act provides for competitive grants to states that embarked on a reform agenda. It includes several features of the educational reform agenda that the Obama administration feels is key to the improvement of schools. RTTT is viewed as an effort to prompt some educational reforms that have been difficult for states to address.

The RTTT competition focuses on 19 criteria identified for awarding grants (United States Department of Education, 2009). These 19 criteria relate to four central themes. The four themes require that states (a) develop internationally benchmarked curriculum standards; (b) develop a statewide data system that can be used to track student progress; (c) improve the recruitment, retention, and rewarding of educators; and (d) turn around low-performing schools.

The development of internationally benchmarked curriculum standards is focused on getting states to agree to a common set of national standards. This addresses the concern that the quality of state standards is uneven and some are of inferior quality. The intent is to hold all states and all schools accountable for achieving rigorous standards that will keep students competitive with other nations.

To comply with the RTTT criteria, many states have adopted common standards. However, this focus also results in considerable concern. Some states contend that their standards are more rigorous than the common standards and therefore adopting common standards is a step backward. Other states cite concern about federal intrusion into their state affairs.

The theme related to the development of a statewide data system for tracking students continues a reform emphasis on "data-based decisions." Proponents of educational change have long been critical of the absence of good data for assessing education within states. In many states, good data cannot be found that actually indicate how many students drop out of school. Students are not tracked from school district to school district. Many students get lost in the system and their progress cannot be determined. This lack of data is a significant barrier in identifying what needs to be done to improve education in a state.

The need to attract and retain good teachers and principals has long been a major concern. As noted earlier in the chapter, there is a significant attrition rate for teachers, with nearly half of them leaving within the first five years of entering the profession.

Some experts have suggested that a contributing factor to teacher attrition is found in teacher compensation. They contend that the common salary based on the amount of education of the teacher and years in service does not provide rewards for good teachers. In addition, some educational reform proponents believe that we would see dramatic improvement in student achievement if we simply based teacher salaries on student achievement data.

Therefore, this theme of RTTT focuses primarily on tying teacher and principal salaries, at least in part, to student test scores. This emphasis continues the focus on accountability. In essence, it assumes that differences in student achievement are directly linked to teacher performance. While RTTT does not mandate that all teacher and administrator pay rates tie directly to student test scores, it still promotes considerable opposition.

Critics of this theme point out the widespread agreement that current tests of student achievement do a poor job of assessing student achievement and generally focus on limited topics and low-level educational outcomes. They say that it doesn't make sense to base important decisions such as teacher and administration compensation on these inadequate assessments of student learning. Other concerns relate to the underlying assumption that teacher performance is the major factor influencing student test scores. While teachers are important, there is also an important relationship between student achievement and the socioeconomic level of the students.

Some skeptics point out that teachers do not choose who they will teach. If student performance has a significant impact on something as important as their salary or their employment evaluation, should they not be allowed to have some voice in whom they teach? In addition, if teacher pay is to be linked to student scores, will they be willing to seek teaching positions in those schools where bringing about change in student scores is most difficult?

Another assumption behind merit or performance pay is that monetary incentives are needed to motivate teachers to do a good job. While there is no doubt that teachers would enjoy the opportunity to make more money, it can be questioned that this is their primary motivation for teaching. As the study cited at the beginning of the chapter indicates, salary did not rank in the top three factors influencing teacher motivation.

In fact, it can be argued that, unlike many businesses, there is a built-in incentive for teachers to do well. In many other occupations, the goals of the employer and the employees are in opposition. The employer wants to maximize effort from employees in order to achieve a profit. However, employees want to expend a minimum amount of effort. Therefore, incentives are needed to get employees to increase the amount of effort they expend in helping the employer achieve production goals.

However, good teaching itself provides an incentive for teachers because good teaching makes the job easier. It results in fewer problems and increased social and emotional rewards. Therefore, increased effort usually pays dividends without other incentives. Most teachers contend that increased pay would not increase their performance because they are now expending maximum effort. Therefore, there is considerable doubt that significant improvements in student performance will occur by basing teacher pay on student test scores. Rather, merit pay based on student test scores will only accelerate the focus on "teaching to the test" and the narrowing of the curriculum to information likely to be on the test. Another outcome, one that has already been seen as a result of No Child Left Behind, is that the most effort will be directed to those students who are most likely to improve with the least amount of effort. Those students near the top, where there is little room for improvement, and those at the bottom, where considerable effort would be required to improve achievement, would be largely ignored. The majority of the effort would be directed toward those students at about the median because increased effort is most likely to have the largest payoff in terms of improved class averages.

This emphasis in RTTT led to opposition from teacher associations. Some states have dropped out of the competition for RTTT funds because of the controversial aspects of this emphasis.

The fourth emphasis in RTTT is on turning around low-performing schools. This emphasis focuses on those schools across the nation identified as the nation's worst performing schools. These are the schools with the highest dropout rates and lowest achievement scores. Four different options were specified as acceptable in turning around these low-performing schools.

One option requires that the school completely transforms itself. In this option, the school needs to be reorganized and restructured. Teachers and administrators are often required to reapply for teaching positions in the school. Options include lengthening the school day and adding days to the academic calendar. Typically the school is reorganized with different schedules and groupings of students. The intent is to provide an opportunity for the school to engage in innovative practices and to reconstitute the teaching staff. One criterion associated with this option requires states to create conditions that facilitate the success of innovative and charter schools. This might mean changing state regulations, teacher contracts, and tenure provisions.

A second option calls for the removal of the school principal and at least half of the teachers if the school does not make significant improvement. President Obama indicated that schools should be given an opportunity to improve. If they show no signs of improvement, however, then there needs to be some accountability (Rowland, 2010). Related to this option is a requirement about the assignment of teachers and principals. This requirement takes into account findings that low-performing schools usually have more new teachers and fewer credentialed teachers than do more successful schools. The intention is to encourage the assignment of high-quality, experienced teachers and principals to the school. This provision of RTTT is controversial. Teacher associations interpreted it as making teachers scapegoats rather than focusing on the conditions and tools needed to facilitate success (Rowland, 2010).

A third option is for schools to close and reopen under new management. Along with this option is the requirement that states lift limits on charter schools, which are publicly funded but privately run. Several states responded to this option by increasing or eliminating limits of charter schools within the state (Toppo, 2009). However, the critics of this option point out that, at best, the research on charter schools is mixed. There has been no definitive indication that charter schools are a superior option to more traditional schools. There are some good charter schools and some poor charter schools. Simply focusing on opening more charter schools is not a prescription for success.

The fourth option is simply to close the school for good. This drastic option accepts the contention that there are some schools for which there is no hope. States need to close them and consider other options for meeting the educational needs of students in those communities.

In addition to the four central thrusts of RTTT, criteria for funding the competitive state grants are identified. One of the criteria is that the state has to obtain the cooperation of teacher associations in the state. This has led to the elimination of some state efforts to obtain the funds because the teacher associations do not agree with the provisions of RTTT. In some states, some school districts agreed to participate and some did not.

RTTT has continued to promote several key components of the reform agenda. It has stimulated considerable action at the state level. Several states made fundamental changes to their education code. However, many of the larger states and those with strong teacher associations have not participated. In the first round of the competition, only two states, Tennessee and Delaware, were awarded grants.

RTTT has the potential to make significant changes in education. The provisions may significantly alter the way schools are operated and the role of teachers. Anyone entering education ought to understand the reform agenda and the potential changes that they may confront as they enter teaching.

Key Ideas in Summary

- New challenges and trends are changing the face of secondary education. If you want to play a role in shaping your profession, you need to become familiar with arguments of both proponents and opponents of school change and reform proposals.

- The basic reasons people give for choosing teaching as a career include making a contribution to society, pleasant working conditions, transmitting academic content, helping students develop, and being rewarded for good performance. Of these reasons, helping students develop is cited by 90% of those preparing to be teachers as a major factor.

- The senior high school became a major component of education during the 20th century. In 1900, only about 6% of the 17-year-old population graduated from high school. However, in 2002–2003, approximately 87% of the population graduated from high school in California. This graduation rate would be similar to that of the nation as a whole.

- The junior high school was originally developed as an intermediate-level school to prepare students for high school.

- The middle school is a recent development with a philosophy that focuses on the unique developmental and intellectual needs of preadolescents. It is fast becoming the dominant intermediate school pattern.

- Standards-based education seeks to provide clear descriptions of what teachers should teach and students should learn. The idea is to provide clear "targets" for instruction.

- High-stakes testing is the use of standardized tests to measure student achievement of standards and the implementation of serious consequences for schools, teachers, and students who do not meet the standards.

- Accountability is a key ingredient in many reform proposals. It is the desire to hold educators accountable for students' learning. It changes the focus of education from "input" or what is put into education to "outputs."

- Two important efforts to improve the competence of classroom teachers have been mounted, respectively, by the Interstate New Teacher Assessment and Support Consortium (INTASC) and the National Board for Professional Teaching Standards (NBPTS). INTASC has identified a list of capabilities that new teachers should have. Many teacher preparation programs now are designed with a view to preparing candidates who meet these standards. NBPTS has developed a system of issuing National Board Certificates to experienced teachers whose performances measure up to rigorous standards.

- Race to the Top, the Obama administration plan to reform education, contains four basic components. These components implement elements of the reform agenda. It contains several controversial components. However, it has had an impact on state policies.

Reflections

1. Have your reasons for choosing teaching changed as a result of the information contained in this chapter? If so, explain.

2. How does an understanding of the history of secondary education relate to some of the current issues?

3. What is your response to proposals to reform secondary education?

4. What is your reaction to high-stakes testing and teacher accountability based on student test scores?

5. Review the INTASC standards. Which ones do you think are your strengths? Which ones will require additional learning and experience?

Learning Extensions

1. Conduct a poll of secondary teachers about their reasons for choosing teaching as a career. Also ask them the extent to which teaching has met their expectations. Note any patterns that emerge from your poll. Is there a difference between high school and middle or junior high school teachers? Are there gender differences? Are there differences according to years of teaching experience? How do you account for the differences?

2. Together with several others in your class, organize a symposium on this topic:

   "The 10 Most Likely Changes in Secondary Education during the First Quarter of the 21st Century"

   Present findings to your class and invite follow-up comments at the end of the presentation.

3. Review professional journals for articles focusing on standards-based education, high-stakes testing, and accountability and RTTT. List the claimed advantages and disadvantages. Define your own position based on the information you have gathered.

4. Interview some of the faculty members in your teacher preparation program to determine how well your program matches the INTASC standards. Conduct a self-evaluation. Which of the standards do you think you can meet and where do you need additional growth?

References

American Educational Research Association. (2000, July). AERA position statement concerning high stakes testing in preK-12 education. Retrieved from http://www.aera.net/about//policy/stakes.html

Astuto, T., Clark, D, Read, A. M., McGree, K., & Fernandez, L. (1994). *Challenging the roots of reform: Challenging the assumptions that control change in education.* Bloomington, IN: Phi Delta Kappa Educational Foundation.

Barry, T. (1961). *Origin and development of the American public high school in the nineteenth century.* Unpublished doctoral dissertation. Stanford University.

Berliner, D., & Biddle, B. (1995). *The manufactured crisis: Myths, fraud, and the attack on America's public schools.* Reading, MA: Addison-Wesley.

Bernard, S., & Mondale, S. (2001). *School: The story of American public education.* Boston: Beacon Press.

Commission on the Reorganization of Secondary Education. (1918). Cardinal principles of secondary education. Washington, DC: U.S. Government Printing Office.

Darling-Hammond, L., & Friedlaender, D. (2010). Creating excellent and equitable schools. *Educational Leadership, 65*(8), 14–21.

Hlebowitsh, P. (2001). *Foundations of American education: Purpose and promise* (2nd ed.). Belmont, CA: Wadsworth/Thomson Learning.

Interstate New Teacher Assessment and Support Consortium. (1999). Interstate new teacher assessment and support consortium. Washington, DC: Council of Chief State School officers. Retrieved from http://www.ccsso.org/intasc.html

Lounsbury, J., & Vars, G. (1978). *Curriculum for the middle years.* New York: Harper & Row.

Moulthrop, D., Calegari, N. C., & Eggers, D. (2006). *Teachers have it easy: The big sacrifices and small salaries of America's teachers.* New York: The New Press.

National Association of Secondary School Principals. (2004) *Breaking ranks II.* Reston, VA: NASSP.

National Board for Professional Teaching Standards (NBPTS). (1999). The five propositions of accomplished teaching. San Antonio, TX: NBPTS. Retrieved from http.//www.nbpts.org/nbpts.standards/five-props.html

National Commission on Excellence in Education. (1983). *A nation at risk: The imperative for educational reform.* Washington, DC: U.S. Department of Education.

National Commission on the High School Senior Year. (2001). *Raising our sights: No high school senior left behind.* Princeton, NJ: Woodrow Wilson National Fellowship Foundation.

National Education Association. (1893). *Report on the committee of ten on secondary school studies.* Washington, DC: National Education Association.

National Education Association. (1911). Address and Proceedings. Washington, DC: National Education Association.

Ornstein, A. (2003). *Teaching and schooling in America: Pre and post September 11.* Boston: Allyn and Bacon.

Ornstein, A., & Levine, D. (2003). *Foundations of education* (8th ed.). Boston: Houghton Mifflin.

Popham, W. (2001). *The truth about testing: An educator's call to action.* Alexandria, VA: Association for Supervision and Curriculum Development.

Rowland, K. (2010). Obama offers cash for turnaround schools. *Washington Times.* Retrieved June 30, 2010, from http://www.washingtontimes.com/news/2010/mar/2/

Ryan, K., & Cooper, J. (2004). *Those who can, teach.* Boston: Houghton Mifflin.

Sacks, P. (1999). *Standardized minds: The high price of America's testing culture and what we can do to change it.* Cambridge, MA: Perseus Books.

Savage, T. (2004). Assessment and quality social studies. *The Social Studies, 94*(5), 201–206.

Stuart v. School District No. 1 of the Village of Kalamazoo, 30 Mich. 69 (1874).

Toppos, G. (2009). Race to the top educational grant propels reforms. *USA Today.* Retrieved July 6, 2010, from http://usatoday.com/news/education/2009-11-04-obamatop04-st-N.htm

United States Department of Education. (2009). Race to the Top executive summary. Washington, DC: U.S. Department of Education.

Wiggins, G., & McTighe, J. (2010). Put understanding first. *Educational Leadership, 65*(8), 36–41.

CHAPTER

2

Students and Schools

Objectives

This chapter will help you

- identify the racial and ethnic characteristics of the current student population

- describe the relationships between poverty and academic success

- state the types of special needs students in secondary classrooms and the policy debates that have accompanied their inclusion in regular classrooms

- define competing views of excellence in education

- explain the principles of secondary education included in the Coalition of Essential Schools

- compare the recommendations of Breaking Ranks with those of the Coalition of Essential schools

- explain the changes that would occur if the recommendations of Accelerating the Agenda were adopted

- state the recommendations for change that are most consistent with your views of a quality education

Bob Daemmrich Photography

Graphic Organizer: Chapter 2

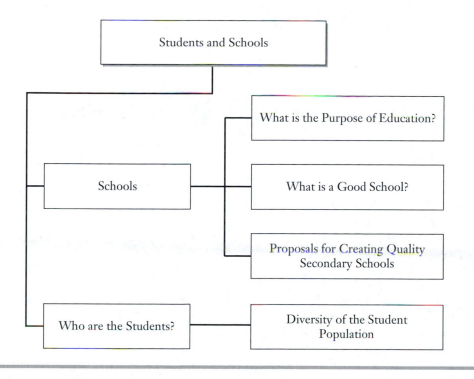

Introduction

As you contemplate a career as a secondary teacher, how do you envision your role? What will a typical day look like? What will be your major responsibilities? What will the school be like? What are the characteristics of the students you will teach?

Many of those choosing to teach in a secondary school anticipate that the future will be a continuation of the past. They think they have a good grasp on the roles and responsibilities of a teacher because they were participants in the K–12 educational system for a number of years. Past teachers have served as models, and people considering the teaching profession have observed their actions, successes, and frustrations. In summary, they believe their prolonged contact with many teachers over a number of years has provided them with knowledge of teachers and schools. They expect that their role will be much like those they observed as a students.

However, there are some challenges to this assumption. While it is true that the operation of schools as institutions has resisted massive change for decades, there are many indicators that this is changing. These calls for change are coming from many different groups. Federal intervention in education has reached a new high. Questions about school practice are commonplace in the media, with popular newsmagazines including lead articles questioning education performance and practice. Significant figures such as Bill Gates have funded foundations designed to change current educational practice. The inertia of the past may well be broken, and it is highly likely that the schools of the future will be quite different from those of the past.

In this chapter, we will investigate secondary schools both as they are and as they might become. Special consideration will be given to students. As teachers, our main concern should be the students. Many educators point to changing demographics, changing cultural values, and the influences of technology as variables that make contemporary students fundamentally different from those in the past. If student needs, backgrounds, aspirations, and motivations have changed, then schools must change.

A major emphasis on students is also needed in order to respond to proposals for change. Unfortunately, many proposals to change or "reform" secondary education seem to overlook the students. Some proposals seem to view students as inert organisms that all respond in predictable ways. The success of change in secondary education requires that the needs of students be addressed, or the changes are doomed to failure.

The following section will discuss schools and proposals for change. Then we will turn our attention to the diversity of the student population.

Schools

"America's high schools are obsolete." That was the conclusion of Bill Gates. He further concluded that contemporary schools are the wrong tools for the time and that they simply cannot teach students what they need to know (Gates, 2005).

Complaints about secondary schools have always been part of the educational landscape. Perhaps this is the result of a diverse nation where there are numerous views about what schools ought to do. However, what is new is that these complaints are now coming from interest groups that have the power to change the nature of secondary education substantively.

The most powerful voice that is changing educational practice is the federal government. While education has been primarily a state responsibility and federal involvement has been relatively minor, there are now powerful forces at the national level advocating a dominant federal role. They claim that education is too important for the health of the nation to leave the decisions in the hands of the various states. Others claim that states have not done an adequate job of responding to change and the needs of the nation. They realize that an educated populace is vital to the future of every nation. Therefore, they look at education as vital for the health of the United States and are advocating more centralization and standardization to meet the needs of the nation rather than the narrower interests of the states.

Indeed, data seems to support the contention that contemporary secondary schools are not fulfilling their mission. For example:

> 1.2 million students drop out of high school every year. That breaks down to about 6,000 students a day.
>
> 25% of high school students don't graduate on time.
>
> 70% of eighth-graders cannot read at their grade level.
>
> (Zhao, 2009)

In addition, some advocates for reform point out that about 30% of the first-year students in postsecondary institutions need to take remedial courses to learn material they should have mastered in high school, and approximately 30% to 40% of recent graduates claim that their secondary education did not prepare them for life beyond high school (Northwest Education, 2008). Others point to disappointing student scores on international achievement tests, concerns about student misbehavior and violence, and a persistent achievement gap between students of different socioeconomic and racial groups as indicating a need for change.

While some of the conclusions about the perceived failure of secondary education might not be warranted by a closer look at the data, there is no doubt that these concerns have prompted widespread call for change. These proposals come from different groups that make a variety of recommendations. Some of these groups have considerable influence, and their recommendations have a good chance of being implemented.

While many disagree about the data that supports the various recommendations, they all agree that changes are needed. There *will be* changes in secondary education. In fact, the secondary school that has existed for nearly a century is changing (Daniels, Bizar, & Zemelman 2001). The crucial, most discussed issue currently is that of assessing the impact of the proposed changes on students and the quality of their education. What changes are best for the development of citizens who will need to compete in a world of rapid globalization, technological innovations, and changing labor markets? How can we educate individuals to be informed citizens in a complex democratic society (Miller, 2009)?

As we evaluate all of the proposals for change, we must answer several critical questions. How do these proposals address these issues? Who will the proposals benefit and who might be harmed? Finally, and most important, when data is cited to support a specific change, is it critically evaluated to make sure it is valid, not "manufactured" in order to advance narrow special interests rather than broad societal needs?

What is the Purpose of Education?

A beginning point in reviewing proposals for change in secondary education is the question, What are the purposes and goals of secondary education? Should a primary purpose of secondary education be that of preparing students for higher education, or should it be preparing individuals for the world of work? Should secondary schools be preparing students to meet present needs or should they focus on 21st-century skills? Is there a common body of knowledge that all students should learn, or should schools promote diversity of knowledge and skill? Some voices claim that the role of education ought to be that of creating a common culture in order to develop a cohesive society, while others claim that diversity is a strength that should be preserved. Only after the purposes of secondary schools have been clearly defined and prioritized can we address the question: What is a quality secondary school?

Any effort to improve secondary education must also consider the students. Too often policy debates ignore the nature of students. Depending on the metaphor, students are the clients or the raw material of the schools. It would be unthinkable for a business to consider how to improve without thinking about the clients they serve or the nature of the material that is available to them. Students do not come to the secondary school as a blank slate ready to be processed and transformed. They come with a variety of ambitions, goals, talents, fears, and frustrations. Proposals for changing secondary schools sometimes neglect to consider that education is one of the few enterprises where success is dependent on the cooperation of the "raw materials." The students must choose to be changed. If students reject what is being done to them, no amount of money or effort will bring about change to the schools.

Many of the differences in proposals to reform secondary education are the result of differences in understanding regarding the purposes of education. There is no national consensus regarding the purposes of education. Even within a community there is a variety of opinions regarding what secondary school should be doing. Consequently, reaching agreements about change is extremely difficult.

The current patterns of secondary education have been greatly influenced by recommendations and understandings that were at the forefront of educational reform about a century ago. One of the most influential was the Commission on the Reorganization of Secondary Education. This report outlined what came to be known as the Cardinal Principles of Secondary Education. These cardinal principles established a direction for secondary schools that came to be known as the comprehensive high school, a high school that had a curriculum under the same roof for both vocational students and those bound for higher education. In other words, it was a school that was charged with meeting the needs and interests of all students. This was viewed as the democratic thing to do. The children of the poor and the wealthy, and those of diverse backgrounds were to come together in the secondary school. This contact in the school was thought to establish a foundation of equality and respect for individuals living in a diverse democracy.

Is this model of the comprehensive high school still a viable one? Is it really possible to be everything for all students? There have been critics of the comprehensive secondary school from the beginning. Currently, some contemporary proposals for reforming secondary education reject the idea of the comprehensive school. Perhaps it is this model that Bill Gates and others view as obsolete.

Some of the proposals for reform focus primarily on the preparation of students for higher education. Over the past century, higher education has become more universal, and higher percentages of students have continued their education beyond high school. Therefore, many contemporary reformers place preparation for higher education as the priority for secondary education. This is interpreted to mean that the secondary school curriculum must be a rigorous one for every student, not just for the college-bound. The result has been that more math, more science, and more English courses are required for all students. Some critics question the place of vocational programs in secondary school. They view vocational preparation as the province of postsecondary schools, such as trade schools and community colleges.

What do you think? What do you see as the purposes of secondary education? How does your teaching area meet the purposes of secondary education? Do you think that we need new models of secondary schools? What would those models look like? These questions are important for you to contemplate as you consider a career as a secondary school educator.

What is a Good School?

What are the characteristics of a high-quality school? If you asked a cross section of people, you might or might not find patterns of agreement. If respondents spoke only about very general characteristics of good schools, you quite probably would find wide agreement on a number of points. For example, you might hear comments such as these:

"Good schools prepare students for a rapidly changing world."

"Good schools prepare individuals to succeed in life after high school."

"Good schools prepare students so that our nation will remain strong in the face of international competition."

"Good schools allow the unique talents of all students to develop."

"Good schools help students develop tolerance for others."

"Good schools produce students who are committed to democratic decision-making."

"Good schools promote the idea that citizens should work together for the good of the total community."

On the other hand, if you pressed people to elaborate on the meaning of phrases contained within these broad statements, you might be surprised at the different, and often conflicting, answers. People with different life experiences, with different cultural backgrounds, and from different social groups bring widely varied perspectives to bear when they consider qualities associated with good schools (Oakes, Quartz, Ryan, & Lipton, 2000). Conflicting views about what constitutes excellence mean that different people apply different standards when they are asked to rate the relative excellence of a program at a particular school.

As with the purposes of education, there is no consensus regarding what constitutes a quality school. Currently, the emphasis tends to define quality in terms of student achievement as measured by standardized tests on a narrow range of subjects. For example, the No Child Left Behind (NCLB) Act of 2001 placed major emphasis on English, math, and science. The definition of a good high school promoted by this act is that quality is defined by good scores on standardized tests in selected subjects. Not everyone agrees with this definition of quality, however, and other proposals start with different definitions of a quality school.

Proposals for Creating Quality Secondary Schools

In spite of the difficulties associated with bridging widely divergent views about what constitutes excellent education, several have attempted to describe the characteristics of high-quality schools. Consequently, many of these discussions, combined with much of the research on quality schools, have prompted educators to recommend and/or develop a variety of distinctive programs.

Coalition of Essential Schools   One program that has received considerable attention is the Coalition of Essential Schools (CES), which is based on the ideas of Theodore Sizer (visit the website at http://www.essentialschools.org). Sizer, a former headmaster of Phillips Academy in Andover, Massachusetts, and a former dean of the Graduate School of Education at Harvard, established CES. Sizer promoted several basic principles in a series of books that challenged some of the basic assumptions of traditional secondary schools. For example, CES challenges the concept of the comprehensive high school. The focus in CES is on the intellectual purposes of education. The argument is that the comprehensive high school presents students with disjointed courses, an arrangement that stands in the way of deep and coherent learning.

Another idea promoted by CES is that of smaller schools. Large high schools are seen as a product of the factory model that promotes economies of scale rather than personalized learning. The contention is that students may go through large high schools without ever becoming well acquainted with individual teachers who could mentor them.

Ten common principles not only outline how CES defines quality schools but also guide their reform efforts. These principles are intended to promote personalized, equitable, and academically challenging schools (Coalition of Essential School, 2009).

Learning to use one's mind well   The central purpose of school is intellectual. The major priority of secondary schools should be to "learn how to learn" and to develop thinking skills and habits of the mind. While other reform proposals also support the emphasis on intellectual development, they tend to focus on traditional measures of school achievement as indicators that students have learned to use their minds.

Less is more, depth over coverage   Rather than emphasizing content coverage and adding more content to the curriculum, CES schools emphasize that each student should learn to master a limited number of essential skills and knowledge. The knowledge they should learn is drawn primarily from traditional academic disciplines. However, the curriculum should be interdisciplinary rather than comprising many separate courses. This principle is considerably different from many other current reform proposals. Other reform proposals often call for more courses and more depth in subject areas rather than more interdisciplinary programs.

Goals apply to all students   There is no choice in what students should learn. The goals should be the same for all students, and the goals should all address essential questions. However, instruction should be differentiated to meet the needs of the students. Therefore, while the goals are the same for all students, the means to accomplish these goals should be different for different groups or classes of students. While the concept that all students should meet the same goals is another common theme in reform proposals, most reform proposals call for the same curriculum for all students.

Personalization   Personalization could be seen as contradictory to the principle that the goals should apply to all students. However, personalization refers to using different content for different students while holding the goals constant.

Personalization should be applied using several approaches. One approach is to develop culturally responsive pedagogy or to alter the teaching methods so that they take into account the culture of the student and alter both the content and the teaching approach in ways that relate to the cultural background of the student. Students coming from different backgrounds respond differently to different types of instruction. This principle emphasizes that one approach does not fit all.

Allowing students different means to accomplish common goals is yet another approach to personalization. Different teaching material and even different content can be used to help students reach common goals. Therefore, decisions about the choice of teaching materials and specific teaching strategies should be kept in the hands of the teachers and the principal rather than dictated by those outside the classroom or the school.

An interesting dimension of personalization included in the CES standards is related to teacher–student ratios. Rather than focusing on class size, CES indicates that no teacher should have direct responsibility for more than 80 students in secondary schools. This is intended to provide better opportunities for teachers to get to know students and to mentor them.

Student-as-worker, teacher-as-coach   The major thrust of this principle is that the traditional role of the teacher as a dispenser of information is rejected. The teacher is viewed as a coach who is helping students learn how to learn. The role of the students is to be totally engaged in the process of learning. In other words, they are to be doing the work of learning rather than having knowledge and information handed to them. This principle is related to the principle of helping students learn how to use their minds. They are active seekers of knowledge rather than passive recipients. They are challenged by essential questions and then engage in the work of gathering the data and finding answers.

Demonstration of mastery   This principle is directed mainly at student assessment. Rather than assessing student learning using standardized paper-and-pencil tests that report success depending on how students compare to others, students are expected to demonstrate mastery by their performance on "real" tasks. Rather than one test and one source of evidence, CES calls for multiple forms of evidence to assess student understanding and mastery. In addition, students should have an opportunity to demonstrate mastery to a wide audience, including parents and the community. This results in increased family and community engagement in education.

Another element of this principle is that the school is not age-graded: Students do not receive credits and promotion is not based on the amount of time they spend in a class. Students are promoted when they present "exhibitions" that demonstrates their mastery of the goals established for that grade level.

A number of secondary schools outside CES have applied this idea. They require students to develop a project or an exhibition that is presented to a panel that includes parents and community members as well as teachers. This panel then evaluates the student exhibition and helps make the determination about whether the student has demonstrated a sufficient level of mastery to be promoted to the next level.

A tone of decency and trust   This principle focuses on the school culture or climate. The school culture should be one that stresses the value of trust, fairness, and generosity. Students are held to high expectations without being threatened. They are to be trusted until they abuse the trust. Parent involvement in the school is emphasized in order to develop the trust between the school and the parents.

Commitment to the entire school   This is another principle that runs counter to some current secondary education reform proposals. In the CES, the principal and the teachers perceive themselves as generalists first and subject matter experts second. Their broader knowledge base facilitates interdisciplinary learning and allows them to fulfill multiple obligations, such as those of teacher, counselor, and manager. The intent is for teachers to understand that they have responsibility for learning across the school and not just in the particular subject they teach.

Many current proposals focus much more attention on the subject-matter specialization of the teacher. For example, No Child Left Behind requires "quality" teachers in every classroom. Quality is defined as possessing a major or the completion of a rigorous subject-matter examination in the subject that teachers teach. The CES proposal addresses the claims of some critics who contend that lack of specialized content knowledge by teachers is a critical weakness in secondary education. Specifically, they point out that a considerable percentage of teachers teaching in mathematics and science do not have college majors in those subjects.

Resources dedicated to teaching and learning   A common complaint of teachers is that too many resources are spent on things outside the classroom. CES agrees with this concern and places priority on allocating resources to the classroom first. In addition, CES emphasizes the development of professional learning communities. This implies that teachers should be collaborating and continuously learning. As a result, budget priorities should focus on lowering the number of students that each teacher handles so that personalization can occur and on providing time for collective planning and collaboration by teachers. To accomplish these tasks and not exceed traditional school budgets by more than 10%, CES admits that some services may have to be reduced or eliminated.

Democracy and equity   This core principle emphasizes that the school should be nondiscriminatory and inclusive. Diversity should be honored and considered a strength. Democratic principles and practices should guide the operation of the school. On the one hand, this principle seems to honor the historic idea that diverse students should be educated together in the same building. On the other hand, the principle seems to call for a change from the autocratic, top-down style of authority that has been common in secondary education to one of shared decision-making.

In summary, the common CES principles define a quality school as one where the emphasis is on thinking and learning. The focus is relatively narrow with a major emphasis on all students working toward the same goals. Students are held accountable, not for passing standardized tests and exit exams, but for demonstrating knowledge on interdisciplinary projects or exhibitions. Students are not age-graded, and progress is not determined simply by the amount of time spent in a given classroom. Teachers should be working with other teachers across disciplines and accept responsibility for the success of the school rather than just the subject they teach.

The CES proposal does call for substantial changes in secondary education. In fact, the Bill and Melinda Gates Foundation initially provided some funding to CES to assist in the development of schools that followed these principles. However, several of the principles run counter to proposals put forth by other power groups. Because they do not focus on accountability measures that can be used to compare students and schools, it is unlikely that the CES principles will be widely adopted as a model for quality secondary education.

Breaking Ranks: A Field Guide for Leading Change   A powerful group that has developed a proposal for reform is the National Association of Secondary School Principals. The reform proposals have grown out of a study of schools entitled *Breakthrough High Schools* (2004). This publication identified 12 high schools that were labeled as "exemplary." One criterion used to define "exemplary" was a student population of at least 50% minority students and 50% students qualified for free and reduced priced meals. Therefore, they highlighted high schools that had very diverse student populations rather than those typically found in affluent communities. In addition to demographic diversity, the exemplary schools had to be academically successful. The criterion used in defining academic success was that 90% of the students graduated and were accepted into college. An analysis of these schools was conducted and common themes identified.

A series of publications grew out of this analysis including, *Breaking Ranks II: Strategies for Leading High School Reform* (2004), and *Breaking Ranks in the Middle: Strategies for Leading Middle Level Reform* (2006). In 2009, *Breaking Ranks: A Field Guide for Leading Change* was published to assist secondary school principals in reforming schools by following the lessons learned from the "exemplary" schools. Given that these proposals were developed by the National Association of Secondary School Principals, there is a high probability that they will have a widespread impact on secondary schools and therefore they need to be understood. The themes that form the basis for the reform proposals contained in *Breaking Ranks* are described in the following subsections.

Creating a safe and orderly school environment   The analysis of the schools that met the criteria of an exemplary school revealed that there were consistent standards of behavior understood by everyone in the school. There was zero tolerance for some activities and issues, such as weapons, drugs, or gang-related behavior, and there were consequences for inappropriate behavior. However, students were given a voice regarding discipline codes, and structures existed to help students solve problems. Diversity was celebrated and students felt free to risk taking more advanced courses. The schools had developed a sense of family or community; as a result, the schools had become a place where students felt safe.

The topic of school discipline and student behavior was not directly addressed in the principles of the Coalition of Essential Schools. However, good discipline is consistently identified as a characteristic of a quality school. It is a major concern of both parents and teachers. There is some overlap with the CES proposal for developing a personalized learning environment where there was a sense of community and where students felt safe.

Having shared values and a vision focused on high achievement for all students
The importance of having shared values and a clear vision is that both communicate common expectations to the entire school community. Students are then socialized into a culture that supports the mission of the school. Many of these missions focus on the idea of high standards, high expectations, and success for all students.

While this theme is stated somewhat differently, it appears to be in line with the basic principles of CES. CES also holds high expectations for students and implies a clear vision by having a clear focus on a relatively narrow curriculum and educating students for mastery.

Holding high expectations for students and staff members   High expectation is a theme that runs through nearly all reform proposals. The exemplary schools studied in this report emphasized that the standards needed to be clear, easy to understand, and applied to all students. However, just having high expectations is not enough. Meeting the expectations is the responsibility of the students, the staff member, and the students' families. A strong culture of support must exist so that everyone can work to ensure high performance for all students.

While somewhat different from the CES principle of everyone having a commitment to the entire school, it does indicate that everyone in the school, from the custodian to the school principal, needs to be held accountable for meeting high expectations. Everyone in the school, as well as the parents, must understand the goals of the school and work consistently to achieve them.

Supporting a personalized learning environment   Making the secondary school personal has increasingly been emphasized in secondary school reform proposals. For example, the National Commission on the High School Senior Year (2001) noted that those in the bottom third of the class reported that no teacher, counselor, or other adult in the school environment knew him or her well.

The *Breakthrough High Schools* report emphasized the importance of personalizing the secondary school. They indicated that much of success in secondary schools was related to establishing relationships. They pointed out that secondary school students need to feel that they belong, are valued, and are respected and that their opinions matter. Supportive relationships that help the students during this critical stage of development were viewed as essential. In addition, these supportive relationships also helped teachers identify warning signs of students in trouble.

The aspect of personalization included in CES focusing on culturally responsive pedagogy and a more personalized curriculum is somewhat different than this definition of personalization. However, the concept of a reduced student–teacher ratio is very consistent with this theme.

Shared leadership, decision-making, and problem solving   It seems clear from this report and other recent studies of effective schools that the model of autocratic leadership, with decisions coming from the top down, is no longer appropriate. Successful schools as well as businesses have recognized that there must be shared decision-making. School principals need to be viewed as leaders, but they must realize that they do not work in isolation. They need to be willing to involve others and give credit to others for success. Teachers and staff members must be empowered to suggest solutions to problems. Members of the community should have a sense of ownership and input into decisions. This allows the school to develop a culture of risk-taking.

This theme is very consistent with the principle of democracy and equity found in the CES principles. However, this theme does not appear to be consistent with some proposals, often originating with business and political leaders, emphasizing top-down management. They advocate national and state-mandated actions that are then applied at the local level. In some instances, teachers are required to use scripted curriculum and lesson plans so that there is little teacher responsibility and power. Some teachers report that they feel as if many educational decisions have been taken from them.

Making decisions based on data   This theme is different from any CES principle and identifies a new emphasis that has become a focus in many schools: data-based decision-making. This emphasis has been facilitated by the heavy reliance on standardized testing. That trend, coupled with the availability of modern technology, has made more data available to more people than ever before. It is now possible to gather, analyze, and disseminate significant data about schools. In *Breakthrough High Schools*, data about attendance rates, in-school illness, and other school issues allowed school officials to identify problems and to respond in a timely manner.

This proposal for making decisions based on data does provide a solid basis for identifying problems and evaluating actions. The emphasis on data-based decisions has spread to decisions about the curriculum, student grades, student promotion, graduation, teacher compensation, teacher effectiveness, and school effectiveness.

While the use of data in decision-making is important, the rush to data-based decision-making runs the risk of obscuring some dimensions of education that are important but difficult to measure. Education involves an infinite variety of humans with a broad range of characteristics. Thus, those interested in improving education need to remember that not every important variable can be measured, and every measured variable is not important. There is certainly a danger that students and teachers can be reduced to a set of numbers and that some important dimensions of successes and some critical problems can be overlooked simply because they are not amenable to data collection.

In summary, the CES and the *Breaking Ranks* proposals have identified a number of dimensions that they believe constitute a quality secondary school. Some of these characteristics are having an impact and can be found in secondary schools across the nation.

Keep in mind that, for the most part, these recommendations come from within the education community and provide insight into what educators define as a quality school. Others, however, do not believe that educators can be trusted to change themselves and that change needs to come from outside the educational community. The political and business communities usually take this stance.

Action Agenda for Improving America's High Schools   A proposal for change that originates from outside the education community is one proposed by state governors. In 2005, the National Governors Association held an education summit on high schools and published their conclusions in *Action Agenda for Improving America's High Schools*. Because progress had been slow in implementing the action agenda, in 2008, the National Governors Association joined the National Conference of State Legislatures, the Council of Chief State School Officers, and the National Association of State Boards of Education to review the action agenda and to recommend new steps. They published *Accelerating the*

Agenda: Actions to Improve America's High Schools (National Governors Association, 2008). Because these four groups represent the major political powers in the various states, their recommendations are showing up in various forms in numerous states.

As might be expected, the recommendations contained in *Accelerating the Agenda* approach secondary school reform from a direction quite different from that taken by the Coalition of Essential Schools and *Breaking Ranks*. One of the major reasons is that these groups started with different criteria for defining quality secondary education. This report did not emphasize criteria such as decency, trust, democracy, equity, or personalization. Rather, the major criteria related to economic factors. In particular, the concern driving *Accelerating the Agenda* was the perceived competitiveness of U.S. students when compared with those around the world. In particular, the report contends that the United States position as a world leader is threatened by the low performance of high school students on international tests of achievement. The report states, "Improvements in student learning can dramatically boost economic growth. Overhauling today's high schools offers U.S. policymakers a potent starting point" (p. 3).

The report contends that students are exiting high school with weaker skills than they were 20 years ago and concludes, like Gates, that "outdated high schools built for a past era are yielding graduates unprepared for today's knowledge-driven economy" (p. 1). The prescription for improvement is making secondary education more academically rigorous and in providing several pathways for both college-bound and career-oriented individuals to achieve these rigorous goals. This coalition defines several actions that they believe will result in a stronger secondary education. The basic points of the proposal are described in the following subsections.

Restore value to the high school diploma   The report begins with the conclusion that the high school diploma has lost its value. It states that the diploma offers little evidence that graduates are ready for college or for work. As evidence, the report states that 42% of community college freshmen and 20% of freshmen at four-year colleges are placed into at least one remedial course (National Governors Association, 2008, p. 7).

Restoring the value of the high school diploma involves adding more academically rigorous courses and implementing quality control measures to make sure students are learning the course content. States should develop a common set of standards that clearly specifies what every student must do in order to graduate. Standardized tests should be administered to make sure that students have mastered the course content. In addition, course content should emphasize information reading over reading literature and emphasize persuasive writing over narrative writing (National Governor's Association, 2008, pp. 7–8). In addition, the contention is that state standards allow teachers to pick and choose those topics within courses that they deem important. State leaders are encouraged to limit the standards so that there is more consistency in what is taught.

The goal is defined as that of the states taking responsibility for defining the curriculum by setting standards while allowing schools and teachers the flexibility to determine how to engage students and address different learning styles (p. 9). This is in direct contrast to CES and *Breaking Ranks* principles that focus on shared decision-making and less top-down management.

The National Governors Association does view the role of the secondary school as one of meeting the needs of all students and not just those who are college bound. The report calls for the development of high-quality career technical programs (CTPs). These programs should focus on high-skill, high-wage programs for 21st-century industries such as biotechnology rather than typical vocational courses such as carpentry. These CTP courses are viewed as integrating academic rigor so that those completing these courses could also qualify for admission to higher education systems.

In summary, *Accelerating the Agenda* does share with CES and *Breaking Ranks* the recommendation of high expectations. However, in *Accelerating the Agenda,* the state sets the expectations and holds the teachers and administrators accountable for implementing them. It is a "top down" that removes decision-making from the local school district and the teachers about what students should learn in a particular subject. In fairness to this proposal, we want to point out that, in some of the states, teachers and administrators serve on panels that write, review, and revise the standards.

Redesign high schools   *Accelerating the Agenda* makes a number of innovative suggestions for redesigning secondary schools. Like other reports, this proposal rejects the idea of the comprehensive high school as an appropriate model for all secondary schools. Instead, the reports calls for a "portfolio" of secondary schools that vary from large comprehensive high schools to career-themed learning communities focusing on a special topic, career technical centers, virtual high schools, and early college high schools. It is clear that an increase in charter schools is viewed as a major component of the reform process. Because charter schools are also a major dimension of the Obama administration's plans to improve education, it is likely that there will be considerable growth in the number of charter schools across the nation.

The idea of a virtual high school grew out of ideas of using technology to meet needs. *Accelerating the Agenda* points to the rapid increase of students taking courses online. The contention is that this number will continue to increase dramatically in the future. The report maintains that, by 2019, nearly 50% of all high school enrollments will be in online courses (p. 14). These virtual schools are a means for delivering advanced, specialized classes such as physics to rural schools and schools with small enrollments. Virtual schools are also a means for creating new courses in technical education that can better prepare students for high-paying occupations.

Early college high schools are those that blend the last couple of years of high school with postsecondary courses. The proposal is to enable 11th- and 12th-grade students to complete a high school diploma and two years of transferable university credit with just one additional year of study. The report cites that, in places where these schools have been implemented, there has been an increase in the number of low-income minority students who continue on to college. In addition, the report indicates that this model saves money.

Like *Breaking Ranks,* this proposal also calls for data-based decision-making. The proposal suggests that states should develop comprehensive data systems so that early warning signs can be noted, and those schools and programs that need academic support, such as remedial instruction, personalized learning, and dropout prevention, can be targeted.

Dropouts, alienated students, and those who do not complete high school on time are identified as critical issues that need to be addressed in the redesign of secondary schools. The report calls for more incentives and new alternative school models to address these needs. The key proposal is to base credits on performance rather than time spent in class and to increase the age where the state will continue to provide support for individuals to complete a high school diploma.

Accelerating the Agenda provides an interesting array of alternatives for education reform. Rather than settling on one model, several models are proposed. Elements of several of these models are now in place in different states across the nation. It will be interesting to see if states can overcome tradition and political battles and implement these models on a widespread basis.

Improve schools by providing excellent teachers and principals   There is no disagreement among reform proposals that the most important element in improving education is the teacher. However, the CES and *Breaking Ranks* do not specifically address this aspect of reforming education. The most logical reason this recommendation appears in the proposal is because the state agencies are responsible for credentialing of teachers and administrators.

Accelerating the Agenda identifies several dimensions to help improve teachers and principals. The report suggests the first step as that of identifying workforce needs. Once that is done, the states should strengthen teacher preparation programs, design alternative routes to teaching, retrain teachers and administrators, improve working conditions, and develop new compensation models.

None of these recommendations are new and several have been implemented in one form or another. However, elements of these recommendations make them different from earlier attempts. For example, the report continues the practice of numerous reform proposals that criticize the quality of teacher preparation programs and call for improved teacher education programs. The report contends that traditional teacher education programs have low standards, an inadequate curriculum, and faculty members who are disconnected from the K–12 system. These criticisms have been cited for decades. However, a new element in the proposal is that of linking the evaluation of teacher preparation programs with the performance of the students taught by their graduates. In other words, how well the students you teach do on standardized tests would be used to evaluate the quality of your teacher preparation program.

While some intuitive connection seems to exist between how well your students do and your preparation, a number of variables influence the achievement test scores of secondary students. The teacher preparation program has little or no control over these variables. For example, teacher preparation programs have no control over who gets hired, where they are hired, whether they are appropriately placed in a teaching situation, the type of instructional materials available to them, or the type of curriculum they are required to use. To hold teacher preparation programs accountable for outcomes related to variables over which they have no control breaks down the logic of this approach. One might ask if medical schools should be held accountable for the health of the patients treated by their graduates or law schools held accountable by the number of cases won by their graduates. It is important, though, that teacher education faculty members stay current, spend considerable time in the schools, and monitor the quality of the graduates they produce. By doing so, schools of education will perhaps be viewed with more respect, which is currently the case in areas where schools of education work closely with local school districts to provide the type of preparation that schools need.

Because of these variables, a simplistic approach that focuses on K–12 student achievement data for holding teacher preparation programs accountable has the potential of drawing erroneous conclusions that actually may be doing more harm than good. For example, one outcome might be that teacher preparation programs would discourage their students from seeking teaching positions in difficult and low-achieving schools, the places where excellent teachers are most needed.

The recommendation also calls for more alternative routes to teaching. These alternative routes are intended to attract talented individuals with little or no educational background to teaching. The recommendation suggests that online courses and credential courses at community colleges would attract these talented individuals to teaching. It is also noted that they would save the state money. Alternative routes to teaching are not new; many have been around for decades. Programs such as "Troops to Teachers" and "Techs to Teaching," a variety of internship programs, and allowing individuals to test out of credential programs have been developed in many states. However, there is scant evidence that these programs have had a positive impact on the quality of the teaching force. The turnover percentage of individuals entering teaching through these routes remains high. However, *Accelerating the Agenda* contends more such programs are needed.

Other recommendations for improving the quality of the teaching force are consistent with the data-driven decision-making recommendation of *Breaking Ranks*. Teacher evaluations should be based on student achievement data, as should decisions about professional development programs. These recommendations seem to continue the high-stakes standardized testing emphasis of No Child Left Behind.

Another recommendation, one that will be politically controversial, calls for providing more power to school principals in the hiring and firing of teachers. This recommendation seems to be directed at reducing the power of teacher associations. Over the years, teacher associations have been successful in getting legislation enacted that places limits on the power of administrators to reassign and fire tenured teachers. These regulations usually define a process to be followed, and many administrators are reluctant to take actions that require these time-consuming, and sometimes costly, processes.

Teacher compensation is cited as another important variable in attracting excellent teachers and administrators. There is widespread agreement that improving compensation plans would have a positive impact on attracting individuals to education. The recommendation contained in *Accelerating the Agenda* calls for changing teacher compensation plans so that teacher compensation is based on student performance. The effectiveness of this proposal has been questioned. Critics of the proposal point out that the focus of No Child Left Behind on student achievement data has led to some negative consequences.

Accelerating the Agenda also calls for redefining the role of the school principal. The report states that current school administrators are so caught up in administrative trivia that they have little time for instructional leadership. The report calls for the creation of another administrative position to address this administrative role so that principals will have more time to provide instructional leadership.

The recommendations included in this aspect of *Accelerating the Agenda* are among the most controversial. If implemented, they would have a dramatic impact on the quality of teachers and administrators. It appears that this report has defined excellence in teaching and quality schools as those who obtain high test scores. The other reports take a much broader definition of quality teaching and quality schools. In addition, some critics contend that there are unintended consequences to these actions and that the outcomes are just as likely to be negative as they are to be an improvement.

Set goals, measure progress, and hold high schools and colleges accountable

This aspect of secondary school improvement emphasizes holding schools and colleges accountable. However, the report notes that about half of the state-mandated tests do not align with state standards. The report calls for aligning achievement tests with state standards and for developing accountability systems that measure more than low-level skills. The report recommends developing formative assessment and more frequent end-of-course exams rather than the once-a-year standardized tests. The report emphasizes that, for assessment outcomes to be useful, they must be benchmarked against rigorous external standards. This means that the tests and test results must be standardized so that students can be compared across districts and states. Other indicators such as on-time graduation, the number of students who complete college-ready and career-ready programs, the number of students who complete industry-recognized skill credentials, and the number of students needing remediation at four-year colleges should also be factored into the assessment program.

In correlation with the earlier proposal to develop early college high schools, this proposal also calls for more collaboration between high schools and colleges. Aligning graduation standards with college admissions requirements and providing financial incentive for colleges to work with secondary schools are proposals for increasing collaboration. One recommendation that many states are developing is a K–16 database so that student progress can be followed from kindergarten through college.

This report also recommends that state leaders should be willing to close low-performing schools, which is similar to aspects of No Child Left Behind. In addition, the report recommends the development of zones that would be used to allow low-performing schools to become flexible by freeing them from many regulations and to allow them to develop partnerships with external agencies in order to redesign the low-performing schools.

Improve education governance
The final recommendation of *Accelerating the Agenda* focuses on developing a comprehensive longitudinal database. This database would supply information that would then be used to make educational policy decisions.

Another key recommendation is that of developing preK–16 councils that would be able to better coordinate educational efforts from preschool through college. This is viewed as a critical link in developing collaboration among all sectors in education and in making students college-ready and career-ready. It is hoped that these councils would reduce conflicts among various sectors in the educational community and could result in more stable funding. This is a proposal that is different from those proposed by CES or *Breaking Ranks*. This recommendation would probably have the least impact on teachers in the secondary schools.

In summary, these three proposals for reform in secondary education have many common elements; however, they also differ in some important ways. Each reform proposal reflects the background and the philosophy of the groups involved in developing the proposal. What these proposals do indicate is that change in secondary education is coming. As you prepare for a career in secondary education, you need to reflect on how these proposals would affect your role as a teacher. Which of these proposals are consistent with your beliefs? Which of these proposals would be difficult for you to accept? The answers to these questions will affect the decisions you make about your career as a secondary school teacher.

Who are the Students?

As you consider a career in teaching in secondary schools and as you reflect on the merits of various reform proposals, you need to focus on the needs of students. Those entering the teaching profession tend to think that most of the students in the schools are just like them. When they enter the fieldwork portion of the preparation program, however, they usually discover that this generalization is of questionable validity.

The characteristics of the student population at the secondary school level have changed dramatically and become incredibly diverse. You will have students in your classes that come from all parts of the world, and some will come from families where English is not spoken at home. Others will come from homes where parents do not value education. The characteristics of students' homes have changed, and the probability is high that both parents are working or that students will have only one parent. In fact, a significant percentage of the students you will be teaching may be working. There will be students in your class that just a few years ago would have dropped out or would have been placed in a special school or special classroom. Indeed, the profile of a typical secondary school student is far different from what it used to be, and the students will exhibit a wider range of beliefs, values, and needs than did those of past decades.

There are some common characteristics, however; the basic characteristics of adolescents today are not that much different from the way we were when we were in secondary schools. They exhibit the same patterns of intellectual and social development. Their basic social and intellectual needs are much the same, and many of them echo the same concerns about themselves and their future that we expressed as we progressed through this very difficult age.

In Chapter 1 we noted that, although it sometimes appears that they are forgotten, the students should be at the center of education discussions. A large part of your success in teaching will depend on your understanding of the student. Be forewarned, however, that one of the good news/bad news aspects of secondary teaching is the unpredictability of secondary students. The good news is that each student and each group of students will be different and will react differently to your instruction. Secondary classrooms are unpredictable places and you never know what may happen. Each day and each group will be different and this keeps teaching interesting and exciting. The bad news is that the students are different and unpredictable and you never know how they will react. This creates anxiety and tension. Understanding some basic characteristics of students can help you reduce some of the negative elements of the unpredictability and allow you to capitalize on the excitement and freshness that can come from being a secondary school teacher.

Diversity of the Student Population

One dimension where students today are considerably different from those of recent generations is in the composition of the student population. The student population today includes considerably more cultural, racial, and ethnic diversity than the secondary schools of the past. In addition, many of the students in the schools are living below the poverty level. Because of legislation, students with disabilities, who in the past had been excluded from many secondary schools, are now present in the classrooms. These various elements all contribute to a much more heterogeneous population than ever before. We challenge you to consider your assumptions about the nature of the students you will be teaching in order to be better prepared to address the challenges of teaching.

Racial and Ethnic Diversity   One of the most dramatic differences in students is their diversity. Between 1972 and 2007, the percentage of public school students who were white decreased from 78% to 56% (National Center for Educational Statistics, Indicator 7, 2009). A large percentage of this change involved the growth in the percentage of Hispanic students. In 2007, the percentage of Hispanic students represented about 21% of the school population. This was an increase of 11% from 1987 (National Center for Educational Statistics, Indicator 7, 2009). The growth of racial and ethnic diversity occurred in all regions of the United States. This means that no matter where you teach, you will see a racial, linguistic, and culturally diverse student population.

Language is another important dimension of student diversity. In 2007, about 20% of students between the ages of 4 and 17 spoke a language other than English at home. This translates into 10.8 million students. Of this group, about 5% spoke English with difficulty (National Center for Educational Statistics, Indicator 8, 2009). This is a large segment of the population, and their needs cannot be ignored. For those students who learned a language other than English as their first language, problems with English may contribute to difficulties at school. As a teacher, you will need to consider the special needs of this segment of the student population as you interact with students and their parents, make reading assignments, and consider that the students may not always be able to obtain assistance at home with homework.

When you think of students with limited English proficiency, you may be inclined to think of students whose first language is Spanish. While Spanish is the most common first language among students with a home language other than English, schools today enroll students who speak many other languages at home. In fact, even medium-size school districts often report that they have a student population where more than 20 languages other than English are spoken at home. In metropolitan school districts, the number often exceeds 60.

Many educators believe our increasingly multicultural society will be well served if the educational system reflects this diversity and continues the practice of the comprehensive high school principle of educating diverse students in the same school and classroom. Even though there has been an overall increase in the diversity of the school population, this diversity may not be reflected in some schools. Because of residential patterns, some schools in a given area have significant numbers of students from a single racial or ethnic group. Therefore, if population data is viewed as a whole, it appears that the schools are becoming more racially diverse; however, large numbers of individual schools have become less diverse. This pattern acts to increase isolation of members of one racial group from another.

One major concern in secondary education is the school dropout rate. As discussed earlier in the chapter, the dropout rate is a major concern of those proposing secondary school reforms. Traditionally, members of some ethnic minorities, particularly African Americans and Hispanics, have dropped out of school at much higher rates than white students. Although calculating the actual dropout rate is difficult because of the way different states record data, one survey did identify the percentages of school dropout rates for individuals aged 16 to 24. In one recent year, 7.6% of the white students, 13.4% of the African American students, and 25.3% of the Latino students had dropped out (Wirt & Snyder, 1999). Over the last 30 years, dropout rates of African American students, though still higher than those of white students, have declined significantly; however, the number of Latino students dropping out remains very high. Dropout rates of Latino students who were born outside the United States are especially high, at 38.6% (Wirt & Snyder, 1999).

What can be done to improve this situation? The gap in test scores and the dropout rates between majority and minority students is related to a complex set of variables. Some critics contend that many of the reform movements have failed to address these complex variables; as a result, they have focused on the wrong issues and have resulted in proposals that are likely to have little impact on the quality of education.

One criterion that can be used to assess the recommendations for improving secondary education is the extent to which they respond to the needs of ethnic minorities. Some of the data used to justify reform movements have failed to take this criterion into account (Zhao, 2009). For example, there is some indication that education has been making progress in addressing the needs of minority students. One measure of this change is a record of improvement of minority students' scores on National Assessment of Educational Progress tests. Scores of African American and Latino students have greatly improved over the past 20 years on tests of reading, writing, mathematics proficiency, and science performance. While these scores still lag behind those of white (non-Latino) students, the gap has become much smaller. This difference in achievement has prompted an improvement in the rate at which minority students take sophisticated courses.

Poverty and Success at School   One of the variables that significantly affects the success of students is poverty. Many students you will teach will come from families living below the poverty level. The United States has the highest rate of child poverty among developed nations (Zhao, 2009). In 2002, one out of every six children below the age of 18 was living in families with incomes below the poverty line. More children are living in poverty today than 25 or 30 years ago. Although the poverty rates are higher for Hispanic and Black students, there are actually more White Non-Hispanic children living in poverty (Children's Defense Fund, 2003).

Young people from poor families face many challenges during the years they are in school. Among other things, these students are at great risk of dropping out before completing high school. Some of these other differences between poor young people and nonpoor young people include the following:

- Poor young people are much less likely to enjoy excellent health than nonpoor young people.
- Poor young people are twice as likely as nonpoor young people to be in the lowest 20% of the student population in terms of their height.
- Poor young people are more likely to have a learning disability than are nonpoor young people.
- Poor young people are twice as likely to repeat a grade in school as are nonpoor young people.
- Poor, young, teen females are nearly three times as likely as a nonpoor female teenager to give birth to a child out of wedlock.

(Brooks-Gunn & Duncan, 1997)

Schools in low-income areas usually have fewer resources to provide technology resources, libraries, and enrichment activities for students and to offset budget cuts. There is considerable evidence indicating that schools in high-poverty areas have the least prepared teachers. Critics of some of the reform proposals, especially those like *Accelerating the Agenda,* contend that the data used to justify large changes in secondary education ignore the fact that the major problem is poverty and not a failure of education. They point out that there is considerable evidence that even a small reduction in family poverty significantly improves school behavior and student performance (Zhao, 2009). Holding schools and teachers more accountable and spending considerably more time and money on tests limits the search for improvement.

Students with Disabilities   More secondary students with disabilities of all kinds are now enrolled as members of regular middle school, junior high school, and senior high school classes. Federal legislation and supportive laws and regulations enacted by individual states have increased a commitment to inclusion, which means that these young people are included in regular class activities and that instructional services need to be delivered to them in an appropriate manner by regular classroom teachers. Federal legislation requires states each year to report numbers of special education students falling within each of the following 13 categories:

1. specific learning disability

2. speech or language impairment

3. mental retardation

4. serious emotional disturbance

5. multiple disabilities

6. hearing impairment

7. deafness

8. orthopedic impairment

9. other health impairment

10. visual impairment or blindness

11. autism

12. traumatic brain injury

13. deaf-blindness

The percentage of students receiving special services has increased nearly every year since 1976. In 1976, about 5% of the population between the ages of 3 and 21, or about 3.7 million students, were receiving Individuals with Disabilities Education Act (IDEA) services. In 2007, this number had grown to about 9%, or about 6.7 million students between the ages of 3 and 21 (National Center for Educational Statistics, Indicator 9, 2009). Of those receiving services, more students were receiving special education services for specific learning disabilities than for any other type of disability. In 2007, about 40% of the students receiving special services had specific learning disabilities. Specific learning disabilities is defined as a disorder in one or more of the basic psychological processes involved in understanding or using language that may manifest itself in an imperfect ability to listen, write, read, speak, spell, or do mathematical calculations (National Center for Educational Statistics, Indicator 9, 2009).

Other disabilities, such as emotional disturbance, mental retardation, and autism, accounted for between 4% and 10% each. Recent studies suggest that the number of students with autism seems to be growing, and it is likely that the percentage of students in this category will be increasing. Students with needs such as multiple disabilities, deafness, blindness, orthopedic, or brain injury accounted for less than 2% of the students with disabilities (National Center for Educational Statistics, Indicator 9, 2009).

Student Mobility   One dimension of the student population that is often overlooked is the increased mobility of students as they move from one school to another. The probabilities are great that a number of students will leave and enter your classroom during a school term. More than half of the student population moves from one school to another at least once during their school years. In addition, between 15 and 18% of the student population moves from one school to another school during the school year (Rumberger, 2002).

High rates of student mobility do affect student learning. Students who move from school to school frequently tend not to do as well academically and have more behavior problems than those who move less frequently. High school students who move frequently have lower rates of high school graduation than those who rarely change schools.

As a teacher, you will experience several challenges when new students enter your classroom at various times throughout the year. It is important to develop rapport with these students and win their trust. You have to discover if they possess the prerequisites to be successful in your classroom, assess whether they have a clear understanding of your academic and behavioral expectations, and help them become part of the classroom group. To the extent possible, you need to try and learn about the previous educational experiences of these new students. You may need to design some learning materials for each transfer student so that they can develop the prior knowledge they need to be successful in your classroom.

Remember that many of these students feel insecure and are often suspicious of their new teachers and classmates. They may not want to be in the new school. If they feel threatened with failure or feel alone and left out, they are not likely to become enthusiastic and cooperative learners. It is in your best interest to find ways of quickly inducting these new students into your classroom culture.

Implications for Teachers   So what are the implications of diversity for you? A number of years ago, a businessperson stated to one of us, "What is so difficult about teaching? All you need to be able to do is read the teacher's guide." Unfortunately, there are too many individuals who believe that teaching is a simple process and that there is one magical process that fits all. While there might be one standard practice for producing widgets or selling a product, there is no one standard practice that meets the needs of all students. Even the very best teacher's guide cannot anticipate the diversity that you will encounter in the classroom. That diversity will change with every class you teach!

There is no doubt that classrooms are becoming more diverse, and diversity is likely to continue to increase. The students you encounter will not be unformed chunks of clay that are passively waiting for you to form them. Each one has different needs, aspirations, hopes, and dreams. Every day you will stand in front of each class you teach and be faced with the daunting but exciting task of trying to figure out how to reach students and help them learn.

Understanding the diversity that is likely to be present in your classroom is a critical ingredient in helping you understand how to bridge the gap between the curriculum you are expected to teach and your students. You will need to know how poverty and hunger might affect student attention and motivation, how culture forms a filter through which individuals process the information they receive, how individuals with limited English proficiency can be assisted in learning without falling further and further behind, and how individuals with varying disabilities can achieve success.

Perhaps the major factor in helping you achieve success in today's diverse classrooms is your attitude. Your attitude needs to be one of celebrating diversity and believing that this diversity enriches the classrooms and adds to the wonderful satisfaction that comes from seeing students learn and change.

Developing a Sense of Teaching Efficacy   In this chapter, we have discussed some of the learner characteristics that you will encounter in the classroom. We have also identified reform proposals and some of their implications for teachers. For you to achieve success and move toward the rewards that teaching has to offer, you need to develop your own professional sense of efficacy (Phelps, 2006). This means that you need to develop confidence in your ability to teach and the ability of the students to learn. Questions such as the following can help you consider your present strengths and weaknesses and assist you in taking actions during your preparation program that will give you confidence and competence:

- What are the special characteristics of the students you are likely to encounter in the classroom?

- What is your attitude toward teaching a diverse student population? Is it something you fear or something you embrace?

CRITICAL INCIDENT

WOULD A HIGH-QUALITY SCHOOL SUPPORT THIS APPROACH TO TEACHING?

Pam Estaban, principal at Mossman Middle School, believes that she heads a particularly outstanding school. She believes her teachers do an excellent job of presenting content in ways that engage students' interests and build their general enthusiasm for learning. She is especially pleased with the work of teachers in the math department.

However, not everyone shares her pleasure. Rose Larsen, mother of sixth grader Judith Larsen, made these comments recently during a conversation with Edwin McKenna, one of Mossman's math teachers:

Mr. McKenna, I'm quite unhappy about what is going on in your classroom. I have to admit that Judith doesn't share my concerns. In fact, you're one of her favorite teachers . . . and, I'll have to agree, you have done a good job of helping her develop a good attitude about mathematics.

But your approach bothers me. I keep hearing about all the time students spend working in groups and helping one another. Now, I know Judith is capable, and I think she likes being looked at as "the expert" when you involve the class in cooperative work. But I don't think this is good either for Judith or for the other students in the long run. It is making the slower kids too dependent on the brighter ones. It tends to hold back the bright people because they have to spend too much of their time assisting those who "just don't get it."

As you know, I'm an engineer. I hope Judith will think about this career when the time comes. I had to struggle through sophisticated mathematics courses to get my degree. Frankly, I had to do this by myself. In high school and college, there is none of this group-hand-holding business. I'm afraid that Judith is going to lack the personal study habits she is going to need once she gets to high school. In addition, because this group arrangement fails to encourage her to master content beyond what is expected of everyone in the group, she's not going to enter high school as intellectually equipped as she should be.

I'm here to ask you to give up this cooperative business and get back to teaching these students as individuals. This emphasis on process at the expense of substance has got to go. These kids need more "meat."

■ ■ ■

What are some values that are especially important to Judith's mother? How do these values shape her views of what should go on at a high-quality school? What things do you think are highly important to her? Given her priorities, do her comments make sense?

What are some priorities that you can infer from the decision of Mr. McKenna to use a lot of group work in his classes? What might be his motives for this approach? What do his actions suggest about the kinds of things that are important to him?

Are there ways in which differences in the perspectives of Rose Larsen and John McKenna can be bridged? Is there an accommodation that might be made that takes into account important values of each? What are some of your suggestions for responding to this situation? What do your proposed solutions reveal about your own values and priorities?

- Do you have realistic ideas about where you will teach and the types of students you will teach?

- What is your comfort level in teaching students in a diverse classroom? Which characteristics do you feel most prepared and least prepared to address?

- What do you need to learn in order to feel prepared to respond to a broad range of student needs and differences?

Addressing these and other questions as you progress toward teaching will assist you in developing an increased sense of professional efficacy. Approaching the classroom with realistic expectations and understandings can give increased confidence and competence and can help you enjoy the rewards of teaching.

Key Ideas in Summary

- Not everyone supports the comprehensive high school model. One reform group that poses alternatives to the comprehensive high school is the Coalition of Essential Schools. This group contends that the comprehensive high school presents students with fragmented, disjointed academic experiences. It makes a case for less is more, arguing that students should pursue a more limited number of subjects in much more depth.

- The National Association of Secondary School Principals investigated 12 exemplary high schools and identified several characteristics of these schools that it named Breakthrough High Schools. It followed this with specific recommendations for changing secondary schools in their publication *Breaking Ranks*. The actions that it proposes in reforming secondary education include creating a safe school environment, having a common message, holding high expectations, personalized learning, shared leadership, and data-based decision-making.

- A powerful group that has proposed changes in secondary education is a coalition of political groups including the National Governors Association, the National Conference of State Legislatures, the Council of Chief State School Officers, and the National Association of State Boards of Education. Their recommendations for change are included in the publication, *Accelerating the Agenda: Actions to Improve America's High Schools*. Because of their potential political power, it is likely that many of the recommendations will be enacted in states across the nation.

- The specific recommendations of *Accelerating the Agenda* reflect the political roots of the group that wrote it and are based on the assertion that reform is necessary if the United States is to prepare students who are competitive with students from around the world. The group's specific recommendations include restoring the value of the high school diploma, redesigning the high school, providing excellent teachers and principals, setting goals, measuring progress and holding high schools and colleges accountable, and improving educational governance.

- The various reform proposals are already changing educational practice across the nation. Individuals who are anticipating a career in teaching need to consider how these proposed changes affect the role of secondary teaching. The array of proposals from a variety of groups means that the status quo is not an option. Change will occur, and secondary teachers need to understand the implications of proposed changes.

- The word *diversity* applies well to today's secondary schools. Today's students reflect the spectrum of differences found throughout our society. Students vary in terms of their physical characteristics, aspirations, intellectual abilities, interests, and values.

- Educators today are challenged to develop school programs responsive to the needs of students in these groups who, traditionally, have not done as well at school as white, non-Latino students. The number of students whose native language is not English is increasing in secondary school classrooms. Though their achievement scores relative to white, non-Latino students have been improving, educators still have much work to do to close the gap.

- Young people from economically impoverished families face many difficulties during their school years. They are less likely than other students to enjoy good health. They are more likely to have a learning disability. They are twice as likely as nonpoor young people to repeat a grade in school.

- Today's students fall into one of 13 special education categories identified by the federal government. The category with the largest number of students includes young people with specific learning disabilities.

Learning Extensions

1. To help you learn more about today's diverse student body, invite a secondary teacher to your class who teaches a course that draws a typical cross section of students. (Classes that are required for high school graduation tend to do this.) Ask the teacher to describe the variety of interests, abilities, and attitudes of individuals in one of his or her classes. You might also wish to ask this teacher about specific instructional modifications that are made to respond to the needs of diverse learners.

3. Do some additional reading on Theodore Sizer's ideas for reforming secondary education. Your library will likely have some information. You might also consider writing to the Coalition of Essential Schools. Once you feel you have a good understanding of Sizer's ideas, interview a secondary school principal. Ask him or her to comment on difficulties that might be encountered in an effort to incorporate Sizer's ideas into his or her school. Present a report of your interview to your instructor or to the class.

References

Brooks-Gunn, J., & Duncan, G. J. (1997). The effects of poverty on children. *Children and Poverty, 7*(2), 55–71.

Children's Defense Fund. (2003). *2002 Facts on child poverty in America.* Retrieved from http://www.childrensdefense.org/familyincome/childpoverty/basicfacts.asp

Coalition of Essential Schools. (2009). The CES common principles. Retrieved October 21, 2009, from http://www.essentialschools.org

Daniels, H., Bizar, M., & Zemelman, S. (2001). *Rethinking high school: Best practice in Teaching, learning and leadership.* Portsmouth, NH: Heinemann.

Gates, W. (2005). Remarks at the national Education Summit on High Schools. Retrieved October 15, 2009, from http://www.admin.mtu.edu/ctlfd/Ed%20Pshch%20Readings/Dillgate.pdf

Miller, M. (2009). Teaching for a new world: Preparing high school educators to deliver college- and career-ready instruction. November Policy Brief. Washington, DC: Alliance for Excellent Education.

National Association of Secondary School Principals. (2004). *Breaking ranks II: Strategies for leading high school reform.* Reston, VA: Author.

National Association of Secondary School Principals. (2006). *Breaking ranks in the middle: Strategies for leading middle level reform.* Reston, VA: Author.

National Association of Secondary School Principals. (2009). *Breaking ranks: A field guide for leading change.* Reston, VA: Author.

National Center for Education Statistics. (2009). The condition of education. Retrieved from http://www.nces.ed.gov/programs/coe/2009 (accessed December 16, 2009).

National Commission on the High School Senior Year. (2001). *The lost opportunity of senior year: Finding a better way.* Princeton, NJ: Woodrow Wilson National Fellowship Foundation.

National Governors Association. (2008). *Accelerating the agenda: Actions to improve America's high schools.* Washington, D.C.: Author.

Northwest Education. (2008). Helping high schools achieve. Retrieved July, 21, 2009, from http://www.nwrel.org/nwedu/13-02/achieve.php

Oakes, J., Quartz, K. H., Ryan, S., & Lipton, M. (2000). Becoming good American schools: The struggle for civic virtue in education reform. *Phi Delta Kappan, 81*(8), 568–575.

Phelps, P. (2006). The three R's of professionalism. *Kappa Delta Pi Record, 42*(2), 69–71.

Public Law 107-110. (2002, January 8). No Child Left Behind Acts of 2001. *Statutes at Large* (115 Stat. 1425).

Rumberger, R. W. (2002, June). *Student mobility and academic achievement.* Urbana-Champaign, IL: ERIC/EECE Publications-Digests. http//ericeece.org/pubs/digests/2002/rumberger02.html

Wirt, J., & Snyder, T. D. (1999). *The condition of education, 1999.* Washington, DC: National Center for Education Statistics.

Zhao, Y. (2009). *Catching up or leading the way: American education in the age of globalization.* Alexandria, VA: Association for Supervision and Curriculum Development.

CHAPTER 3

Understanding Diversity

Objectives

This chapter will help you

- discuss the importance of responding to the special needs and perspectives of all students

- identify planning perspectives that can be helpful in developing instructional programs well suited to the needs of the different ethnic, cultural, and language groups enrolled in your classes

- describe teacher actions that can help students with different disabilities succeed in the classroom

- explain changes in approaches to working with students who have disabilities and the implications of these changes for regular classroom teachers

- describe characteristics of gifted and talented students and suggest ways that their needs can be accommodated in the classroom

Bob Daemmrich Photography

Graphic Organizer: Chapter 3

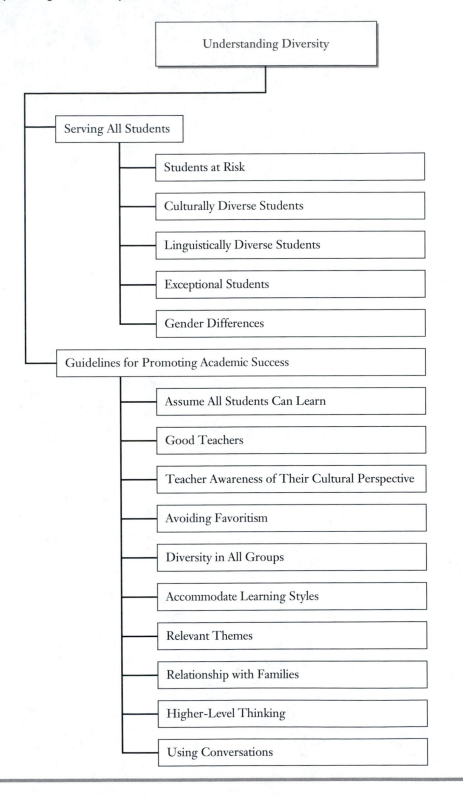

Introduction

In the previous chapter, we identified some of the major categories of diversity. In many ways, however, all students are different. Even students coming from the same family will have different skills, interests, and aspirations. For example, anthropologists note that more diversity exists within cultures than between cultures. The challenge for all teachers is to respond to the needs of all students. Teachers need to be cautious about forming generalizations about a particular group and culture and assuming that there is one best instructional approach for all of the members of that group. What is needed is a classroom environment that is based on the principle that all students are individuals, and teachers' instructional choices must account for these differences. (Chapter 8 addresses the need to consider individuals differences when delivering instruction.)

Serving All Students

Regardless of your cultural background, you need to understand that there are no universally applicable generalizations about teaching individuals from different backgrounds. Some general principles derived from research can be useful, however, in planning for these students with special characteristics. These principles can be used as a starting point in reaching these students.

Students At Risk

All schools have students who are at risk. *At risk* refers to those students who are failing or who are at risk of dropping out of school. Secondary reform proposals frequently target these at-risk students for intervention. For example, the *Accelerating the Agenda* report states that less than three out of four students graduate on time. They estimate that the cost of dropouts to the nation in terms of lost wages, taxes, and productivity is more than $320 billion (National Governors Association, 2008, p. 1). The estimated cost for the daily operation of K–12 education across the nation is $400 billion a year (National Center for Educational Statistics, 2005). Therefore, the estimated economic loss for dropouts is almost as much as the cost for education! Given this enormous cost, addressing the needs of at-risk students is a high priority.

Although a number of variables contribute to students being at risk, ethnicity, poverty, and having a primary language other than English are prominent ones. Experts who have studied the achievement of students in schools have identified several risk factors that are characteristic of students who do not do well. Among these risk factors are the following:

- lives in a single-parent family
- family receives public assistance
- primary language other than English
- brother or sister dropped out of school
- mother not a high school graduate
- attended five or more schools during lifetime
- less than one hour per week spent on homework
- spends no time each week reading for fun
- watches television more than five hours a night
- little communication with parents about things studied at school
- over the age for grade level by at least one year (Gleason & Dynarksi, 1998)

Individuals having a single risk factor may not necessarily experience difficulty in school. Researchers have determined that students having two or more risk factors, however, are particularly likely to do poorly. Responding to these risk facts usually requires a commitment on the part of the entire school. An individual teacher can take some actions, including the following, that will help these students:

- become engaged with the students
- make the content of the curriculum meaningful
- emphasize success

Become Engaged with the Students   These students often lack role models and frequently feel lonely and forgotten. Greeting these students each day, showing an interest in them as a person, asking them about things outside the classroom, and finding out what matters to the students communicates a sense of acceptance. If they see the school as a place that cares about them and is interested in them, students are less likely to drop out.

Make the Content of the Curriculum Meaningful   Too often, teachers make assumptions that these students need low-level, remedial instruction. In fact, many at-risk students are very capable of attacking high-order tasks if they perceive those tasks to be meaningful and important. This means bridging the gap between what the school expects and what the students see as important. Over the years, numerous books and movies, such as *Stand and Deliver* and *Freedom Writer's Diary*, have illustrated what can happen when this gap is bridged.

Emphasize Success   A typical response to this action is "But what if they are never successful?" It is true that some secondary students have had such a history of failure that they have given up. This requires that the teacher spend considerable time identifying where a particular student can have success. This is not an easy task and may take considerable effort. However, persistence and providing small doses of success can begin to change the attitude of any student. Once students begin to believe that you are an advocate rather than a threat and that they are capable, the changes can be remarkable.

Student failure is sometimes related to circumstances rather than ability. Some might not have a place to do homework. They might not have anyone in their lives to help them with difficult assignments. Perhaps they have not had anyone model how to approach tasks. Listening to these students, rather than judging them, and identifying the barriers that hinder their success is extremely important. When the barriers to success are indentified, encouraging success may not take a great deal of effort. For example, assigning tasks that take into account their special circumstances, helping them learn to focus on one task at a time, providing them with time and a place to do homework, and simply making yourself available to talk to the students are relatively simple actions that change school from a threatening environment to a supportive one.

Culturally Diverse Students

A historic goal of education has been that of getting culturally diverse students to fit into the dominant culture. This view was reinforced by several historical perspectives of the difficulties experienced by culturally diverse students.

An early explanation for minorities' failures to excel in school was the genetic deficit view (Freeman & Freeman, 2001; Savage & Armstrong, 2004). The premise of this position was that some minority groups do better than others because of genetic makeup. This was ascribed to their status as sons and daughters of individuals who were not particularly bright. This view was reinforced when it was found that some cultural groups did poorly on standardized intelligence tests. Hence, it was argued, an insufficient capacity to learn was passed on to their children. This mistaken belief provided a perfect rationale for schools to do little or nothing to improve instruction directed at minority students. Why, it was argued, should the schools commit scarce resources to programs designed to serve individuals who lacked the capacity to learn?

The genetic deficit view had fallen from favor by the middle of the twentieth century. In the 1960s, a new deficit view, the cultural deficit position, enjoyed some currency for a time (Erickson, 1987). Individuals who were impressed by this idea felt that school problems of many culturally different students could be traced to their homes. They alleged that the homes provided an intellectually sterile background that failed to give them attitudes and aptitudes needed for success in school. The cultural deficit argument allowed school leaders, who were reluctant to commit serious resources to programs designed to help culturally different students, to blame the home for failure of these young people to learn. Because many of these students came from impoverished home backgrounds, variables related to poverty and culture were often confused.

Another explanation for student failure that provided a rationale for school inaction was the communication process position. Proponents of this view blamed poor student performance on language differences separating students and their teachers. They alleged that these differences were so profound that many culturally different students could not understand what was said in the classroom or what was expected of them at school. Their failure was attributed to this communication gap. Critics of this position pointed out that some culturally different students did extremely well in school despite economic and social backgrounds very similar to those who did poorly.

Unfortunately, you will still hear some of these views recited to support particular political and economic decisions. However, most responsible educators now reject these theories. They recognize that culture does play an important role. Not only might the curriculum of the school not take into account different cultural backgrounds, it is also the case that the home values may conflict with school values and may lead to confusion regarding appropriate behavior (Rothstein-Fisch & Trumball, 2008).

The contemporary view is that it is the responsibility of the school to meet the needs of all students, regardless of their cultural or linguistic background. An understanding of the two broad cultural value systems will help clarify this viewpoint. These two systems are based on the emphasis a given culture paces on individual versus group well-being. One system might be labeled that of "individualism" and the other "collectivism" (Rothstein-Finch & Trumbull, 2008).

The basic values of the individualism orientation include the following:

- the well-being of the individual and responsibility for one's self
- independence and self-reliance
- the accomplishments of the individual
- the importance of self-expression and a willingness to take independent positions
- a primary focus on task completion
- self-esteem and the self-importance of the individual
- emphasis on cognitive ability and intellectual attainment

The collectivism cultural orientation includes the following values:

- the well-being of the group is primary and the responsibility of the individuals is to preserve the group
- cooperation and working interdependently with others
- emphasis on the accomplishments of the group above those of the individual
- modesty in individual accomplishments and respect for the accomplishments of others
- a priority on preserving the social organization of the group as opposed to putting the task first

■ emphasis on social skills and social intelligence (adapted from Rothstein-Fisch & Trumbull, 2008, p. 9)

In general the majority culture of the United States tends to reflect more of the values of the individualism system, whereas numerous immigrant groups, as well as Hispanics, Native Americans, and African Americans, tend to favor collectivism values (Rothstein-Fisch & Trumbull, 2008).

Ignoring these two basic orientations can lead to difficulties. Teachers who are unaware of the cultural perspectives of others may well plan classroom activities and emphasize approaches that place students in the awkward position of choosing school over their family and culture. For example, teachers might emphasize self-expression and independence, while parents might have emphasized the importance of quiet listening and respect for authority.

The current position is that all students have the ability to learn if the educational experience takes into account the unique differences of all students (Tomlinson & Imbeau, 2010). Most of the suggested practices for taking into account the cultural differences of students are simply good teaching practices that benefit all students, including the following:

■ Use culturally responsive pedagogy.

■ Accept all learners' experiences, values, and tastes.

■ Select instructional materials that relate to the experiences and needs of the students.

■ Acknowledge the cultural heritage of all cultural groups.

Use Culturally Responsive Pedagogy   Different cultures may emphasize different goals and attitudes. For example, some cultures place group cohesion ahead of individual accomplishments. Other cultures place more emphasis on individual responsibility and individual accomplishments. This has implications for the classroom. Individuals whose culture values group cohesion might be uncomfortable learning in an environment that emphasizes competition between individuals. On the other hand, those who come from groups that emphasize individual accomplishments may feel approaches such as cooperative learning are unimportant.

The major point to keep in mind is to remember that different cultures may have different norms and values. Culturally responsive pedagogy requires some cultural understanding so that students are not placed in situations where they have to make a choice between school and deeply held cultural values and practices.

Accept All Learners' Experiences, Values, and Tastes   There is an ethnocentric tendency to think that our cultural values and interpretations of reality are the "natural" or "normal" ones. Those who have different cultural interpretations or experiences are viewed as "strange." Not accepting the cultural values and experiences of another culture communicates a rejection of that culture. Teachers need to understand how their background influences how they view and interpret events. They then need to understand that there may well be alternative interpretations. Accepting that others may place different interpretations on actions and events is important for teachers to accept the culture and the background of students. In essence, teachers need to "pull back their cultural blinders" and take a broader view of the world. Not only is this beneficial in teaching, it often leads to new learning!

Select Instructional Materials That Relate to the Experiences and Needs of the Students   Over the past couple of decades, it has been recognized that there are many pathways to achieving important educational goals. All of us like to feel valued and important. If our heritage is ignored or absent from the curriculum, we reach the conclusion that we are not important or valued. If our heritage is included, however, we are more motivated and more likely to get involved. In addition, we recognize that the experiences of secondary students are not the same across the nation. The experiences of secondary students living in New York City are certainly different from those living in Des Moines, Iowa, or Laredo, Texas. Instructional materials that are based on the experiences of one group may be viewed by others as "strange" and unimportant. This has led educators to increased attention on the importance of instructional materials that include a variety of experiences and perspectives. There is a wealth of instructional materials and books that can be used to relate school objectives to different groups.

Acknowledge the Cultural Heritage of All Cultural Groups   There has been some debate in recent years around something called the cultural wars. Some groups believe that schools should emphasize the heritage of our nation and choose material that largely reflects the Western European tradition. Others point out that all cultures have validity and have made important contributions to humankind. They believe that providing multicultural perspectives is not only useful for culturally diverse students, it is useful for all students. While there is value in making sure that students encounter and understand the unique heritage of our nation, this should not preclude the inclusion of the important contributions of others. Once again, removing our cultural blinders may actually assist us in the search for solutions to persistent problems.

Linguistically Diverse Students

As noted in Chapter 2, the number of students who spoke a language other than English at home had increased from about 3.8 million (9% of school population in 1979 to 10.8 million (20% of school population) in 2007 (National Center for Educational Statistics, Condition of Education, Indicator 8, 2009).

These students often face special challenges. The classroom is a very language-oriented environment. A great deal of the time in a typical classroom is devoted to spoken language. Many secondary teachers rely on textbooks as a major element in delivering the curriculum. Students who are English language learners (ELLs) are beginning with a handicap. These students want to do well and have the same aspirations of other students. Some assistance in helping them cope with the heavy language demands of the typical classroom can result in some great benefits. Actions that you can take to assist these students achieve success include the following:

- Use nonverbal communication to support the verbal.
- Utilize group learning.
- Use student volunteers to help the student comprehend the verbal messages.
- Be patient!

Use Nonverbal Communication to Support the Verbal   Teachers need to make sure that they deliver their verbal communications with smoothness and clarity. Taking time to make sure that verbal communication is logically connected, with few digressions, makes it easier for ELL students to follow the verbal message. Attention should be given to the words that are used. Words that have more than one meaning need to be explained and clarified. Frequent checks for understanding can make sure that the ELL students are receiving the information clearly. For example, an ELL friend of ours tells of the worry and effort he expended when a teacher casually mentioned "Scooby Doo" in his college classroom. Being afraid to speak up in class, he went to an English language dictionary and an encyclopedia before he got the courage to ask another student about this mysterious term. He was then relived to discover it was a cartoon character! How many of our students have been frustrated because they didn't understand the vocabulary?

Simplifying the message and making sure that the rate of speech is not too rapid is also useful in increasing the comprehension of students. Other techniques that can be useful in increasing clarity include using diagrams, outlines, photographs, and other visual material, which can help connect elements of the verbal message.

In addition, homework directions should be written, not just delivered orally. Remember that the students may not be getting help at home. With written directions, they may be able to seek help from others in understanding what is required.

These suggestions are elements of good teaching! They are useful for planning and delivering instruction for all students, not just ELLs.

Utilize Group Learning ELL students need to learn to use English. Because of their limited English abilities, however, they are often reluctant to speak in front of the whole class. As a result they are not getting the practice that they need. Many ELLs are more likely to speak up in small groups. Teachers who use small-group learning provide ELLs more opportunities to use language and allow them to improve faster. In addition, students in small groups are usually willing to take time to explain things to ELLs and help clarify misconceptions.

Use Student Volunteers Who Can Help the Students Comprehend the Verbal Messages There may be students in your class with the same primary language as the ELLs but who have more advanced English comprehension. These students can help clarify phrases and words for the ELL students. Or maybe other students in the school or some adults in the community might volunteer to assist the students in comprehending the material and successfully completing assignments. One teacher had an ELL student in his classroom who spoke a language not common in the schools. However, he identified another, more proficient student who spoke the same language in the school. They made a daily appointment so that they could review all assignments with the ELL student. This small bit of assistance was all that was needed to help the student quickly become successful.

Be Patient! Provide more time for ELL students to respond. Be willing to slow down and repeat directions. Remember, many of these students have to translate and process the information they are receiving in English. It simply takes them more time. Impatient teachers may make them feel ashamed and cause them to be reluctant to participate.

Exceptional Students

There are great differences among exceptional students. Sometimes the term *special education* is used as a general descriptor for individuals who have learning disabilities, physical problems, or emotional and behavioral difficulties that deviate markedly from the norm. Exceptional students also include those identified gifted-and-talented learners whose intelligence and/or skill levels have been found to be well above those of their age or grade peers. And as mentioned earlier in this chapter, English learners can fall into either of these categories. (Unfortunately, they are too often placed automatically and erroneously into special education programs.) The inclusion of exceptional students in the classroom is not a school or a teacher choice. There are legal mandates that must be followed.

The inclusion of exceptional students in regular classrooms is governed by several pieces of complex legislation. Among these laws are (1) the Education for All Handicapped Children Act, which was first passed in 1975 as Public Law (P.L.) 94–142 and renamed the Individuals with Disabilities Education Act in 1990 (P.L. 101–476); (2) the Individuals with Disabilities Education Act of 1997 (P.L. 105–117); and (3) the Jacob K. Javits Gifted and Talented Students Act of 1994 (P.L. 100–297).

When the Education for All Handicapped Children Act was enacted in 1975, both supporters and critics predicted that it would change the face of education in the United States (Heward, 1996). This proved to be true. The updated version of this legislation, the Individuals with Disabilities Education Act, mandates the following six basic principles first articulated in the original 1975 legislation:

- *Zero rejects.* Schools must enroll every child regardless of the nature or severity of the disability. Implementing this principle has been expensive. Many school districts have had to increase their budgets to provide educational services for some students who, previously, were excluded from schools.

- *Nondiscriminatory testing.* Multiple indicators must be used to determine whether an individual has a disability and whether special services are needed.

- *Appropriate education.* Schools must develop and implement an Individualized Education Plan (IEP) for each student with a disability.

- *Least restrictive environment.* A student with a disability is to be educated in the setting that is the least restrictive for that individual. Often this has involved placement (or mainstreaming) of students with disabilities in regular classrooms for at least part of the school day. This provision has changed the nature of the student population served by regular teachers in traditional classrooms. Students with disabilities, who formerly were segregated into special education classrooms, now are interspersed with so-called regular students in traditional classrooms.

- *Due process.* The rights of students and their parents in planning and placement decisions must be protected by due process procedures.

- *Parental participation.* Parental participation in the decisions made regarding the education of the student is mandated.

The Individuals with Disabilities Education Act of 1990 added an important new principle. It required schools to provide transition services for students with disabilities (Heward, 1996). Transition services are identified as a coordinated set of services designed to help the student make the transition from high school to postschool activities such as college, vocational training, employment, and independent living or community participation. This addition to the original legislation was adopted in response to studies that revealed educational programs were doing a poor job of preparing students with disabilities for life after high school.

Public Law 105–117, the Individuals with Disabilities Education Act of 1997 broadened existing requirements tremendously to serve learners with disabilities in regular classrooms. In part, this expansion stemmed from strong legislative support for the principle of *inclusion*. Inclusion represents a commitment to the idea that students, regardless of unique personal characteristics (including, for example, disabilities of all kinds), not only have a legal right to services in a regular classroom but are also welcomed and wanted as members of these classes. Some schools now pride themselves on being *full inclusion* environments. In these schools you will find almost a total absence of special education classrooms for learners with disabilities. Almost all services are provided to these students in regular classrooms.

Advocates of inclusive education claim several key advantages for this approach (Smith, Polloway, Patton, & Dowdy, 1996). Among their points are the following:

- It is possible for special education students to receive an appropriate education in the regular classroom.

- Educating special students in the regular classroom reduces the stigma that sometimes has been attached to them when they have been taught in separate special education classes.

- Because teachers in regular classrooms expect students to have varied abilities, there is less likelihood of any individual student being permanently mislabeled as a "special education" student and provided with an instructional program inappropriate for his or her needs.

- In a society that includes incredible diversity, there are benefits for both special education students and regular classroom students when they are taught together. This kind of association can promote tolerance of individual differences and recognition of the point that all people have personal strengths and weaknesses.

- All students benefit when teachers make efforts to individualize their instruction to meet individual student needs. When special education students are included in regular classrooms, teachers have more incentive to individualize their teaching.

The Individuals with Disabilities Education Act of 1997 put important new legal muscle behind the view that learners with disabilities should be taught, to the fullest extent possible, as members of regular school classes. Some important new requirements of this legislation include the following:

- A student's regular classroom teacher *must* be involved in the development of a student's Individualized Education Plan (IEP) and must participate in IEP planning.

- Parents and guardians have the right to be involved in *all* decisions regarding their children's eligibility for and placement in programs designed to serve them.

- Information about learners with disabilities' achievement must be included in regular public reports on test scores.

The Jacob K. Javits Gifted and Talented Students Act of 1994, unlike the others discussed in this section, did not mandate specific services but provides incentives for state and local education agencies to address the specific needs of individuals with this exceptionality. It allocates money for the identification of gifted students and the professional training of teachers. Money made available as a result of this legislation also supports the National Center for the Education of the Gifted. The Javits Act was adopted out of a recognition that gifted and talented students have special needs and that they may require additional support and services if they are to reach their potential.

Special Needs Students   Suppose you find yourself with a number of students with disabilities in your classroom. To help them learn, first of all, you must have an accepting attitude toward these young people. You don't want to approach teaching these students with a mistaken preconception that working with learners with disabilities will be a frustrating and unrewarding experience. On the contrary, you are likely to derive considerable satisfaction from helping these special young people as you see them begin to develop academically and socially, establish rapport with others, increase their self-confidence, and overcome emotional problems.

The world of teaching has changed dramatically in the past few years. As a secondary school teacher, you are increasingly likely to be involved with groups of professionals. For example, your school may have specialists who work with language minority students as well as students with disabilities. Some schools will have intervention-assistance teams whose members will be available to help you adapt and deliver instruction for exceptional students. A resource teacher may also be available for some portion of the day to assist you in working with students with disabilities. This team approach requires that you prepare yourself to work with all of the individuals interested in the welfare of your students. You may well find yourself involved in collaborative activities such as the following:

- *Participating in the IEP meetings.* As a teacher, you will be expected to attend and make contributions during these meetings and to understand the specific objectives for the student as prescribed in the IEP.

- *Communicating with specialists in the education of students with disabilities concerning the objectives and the content of the classroom.* Discrepancies between expectations and the abilities of the students are a major cause of failure of students with disabilities who are taught in regular classrooms (Smith, Polloway, Patton, & Dowdy, 1996). Discussions you have with professionals who have special training in working with students with disabilities can help you work effectively with these young people.

- *Informing the special needs student about behavioral and academic expectations.* A lack of understanding on the part of students regarding the expectations and demands in the regular classroom is frequently the cause of much frustration and anxiety and can lead to acting-out behavior. You need to take care that these students understand what they are expected to do.

- *Monitoring student progress.* It is especially important that you assess the progress of exceptional students frequently. This helps the team members make adjustments in the delivery of services to the special education students. In addition, celebrating success is important in building students' self-esteem.

- *Communicating openly with specialists about any concerns and fears you have about teaching these students.* If you do not deal with these concerns and fears, you may communicate nonacceptance to the students with disabilities who are members of your classes.

- *Learning the unique characteristics of each student.* It is important to find out from specialists information about issues such as the distractibility of individual students, including details about issues such as learning rates, specific difficulties in processing information, and the nature of any special learning aids you need to provide.

Your objective is to provide opportunities for students with disabilities to succeed. This requires modifying your instruction so that these students have a legitimate opportunity to learn and grow (Smith, Polloway, Patton, & Dowdy, 1996). At the same time, you need to guard against making too many accommodations. Many of these learners can do much of the work teachers ask of students without disabilities. You want to be sure that students with disabilities feel that they are a legitimate part of the regular classroom group. You should encourage them to participate and interact with regular students so they will not be isolated and separated from the normal activities of the classroom.

Your work with specialists in the education of students with disabilities should not be restricted to planning for classroom instruction. For example, together you may also want to spend time identifying appropriate post–high school academic or vocational training opportunities for these students. Learners with disabilities represent a group that particularly benefits from adult support as they think about what to do with their lives. Teaching self-advocacy is a key to helping them make the transition to life after high school.

Part of your efforts should be directed to helping special needs students think about what they need to do to live independently. You can help them make this transition by pointing out practical applications of what you teach in the classroom. Helping them understand how to be organized, how to handle and solve problems, how to establish and maintain social networks, and how to deal with issues such as drug abuse are among the topics that you can cover in the context of your lessons.

Gifted and Talented Students   In a status report prepared more than 20 years ago, the U.S. Commissioner of Education pointed out that only a few specific programs for the gifted and talented existed in the nation's schools. Stimulated by the considerable interest generated by this report, Congress established the Office of Gifted and Talented within the U.S. Department of Education. Sometime later, the Jacob K. Javits Gifted and Talented Students Act of 1994 (P.L. 100–297) provided funds to support programs to identify gifted students and to prepare teachers to respond to their special needs. This legislation also established funding for a National Center for the Education of the Gifted.

At one time, students were selected for gifted and talented programs almost exclusively on the basis of their scores on standardized intelligence tests. Critics charged that gifted and talented people had a wide range of abilities and that intelligence test scores did not appropriately identify many of these. Fears that standardized intelligence tests were culturally biased and, hence, tended to screen out minority group students drew additional negative attention to selection based only on test scores.

Through the years, educators and researchers have broadened the conception of the characteristics of gifted and talented people. The work of Renzulli (1978), a leading expert in the education of these students, was especially important in gaining acceptance for the idea that selection should be based on multiple criteria. Renzulli argued that evidence

What Do You Think?

Students Should Be Placed in Ability Tracks

A critic of present secondary school practices recently made the following comments:

> The presence of less academically able students in secondary classrooms results in a waste of academic talent. Teachers have to gear instruction to the lowest common denominator, which slows down the progress of brighter students and leads to boredom. If we want significant reform in education, we need to remove this handicap and encourage our gifted and talented students. One way we can do this is to follow practices established in some other countries. Students could be tested as they enter high school and assigned either to a general track or a college track. Less able students would take general-track courses and not be asked to compete with brighter students in the college track. Students in the college track could be provided more challenging work. This system would simplify teachers' jobs. They would not have to plan for such a wide range of academic talent as they now must do in classrooms open to all.

Questions

1. Would everyone benefit from this plan? Why or why not?

2. Describe possible positive and negative effects of this idea.

3. What track would you have been in if you had been assigned to either a general track or a college track at the time you completed the sixth grade? Point out the potential impact of this action on your education.

should be gathered in three distinct categories of student characteristics when decisions were being made regarding who should be admitted to gifted and talented programs:

- Intelligence
- Task commitment
- Creativity

Information related to intelligence should be gathered not just from standardized test performance. We should consult other sources, such as grades and comments from individuals who have had opportunities to observe the academic work of students.

Task commitment refers to a person's ability to see through a project or activity to the end. People who are gifted and talented tend to finish things, even when there are frustrations along the way. They are not apt to bounce from one project to another, leaving a lot of loose ends along the way.

Creativity refers to the ability to engage challenges and solve problems in unusual ways. Gifted and talented students tend to look at dilemmas in nontraditional ways and to use innovative (and sometimes surprising) techniques to respond to them.

What are gifted and talented students really like? Certainly there are popular misconceptions. Consider, for example, how some films portray bright students as eccentric misfits. Contrary to this view, most studies have found that gifted and talented students are well accepted by their peers. It is true that these students face some special kinds of pressure from other students. In particular, they may be pressured to do less and thereby keep the teacher from setting expectations too high for the class as a whole (Brown & Sternberg, 1990).

Some gifted and talented students have parents who expect too much of them. This leads some of these students to set unrealistic expectations for themselves and to feel bad when they fail to live up to them. You can help these students by focusing them on their accomplishments, not their shortcomings (Baum, 1990). Teach them that everybody has strengths and weaknesses and that there is nothing to be ashamed of when they are less than outstanding in a given area.

Enrichment and Acceleration   Enrichment and acceleration are the two basic orientations of programs for gifted and talented students. Enrichment programs assume students will remain in the same classes and go through school at the same rate as other students who are not gifted and talented. The expectation, however, is that enriched programs will be provided for them that go well beyond the academic fare served to the other students.

Acceleration programs increase the pace at which gifted learners complete their schooling. In an accelerated program, gifted learners might complete the entire high school program in just two years. There is no attempt to keep gifted learners in classes with learners who are in the same age group. This often means that gifted learners are in classes where most of the students are older than they are.

Though there are loyal supporters of both types of programs, enrichment programs are much more common today than acceleration programs because enrichment programs can be implemented with fewer administrative changes. Also, the possibility that some gifted and talented students in accelerated programs will be in classes with students who are much older than they are is a source of concern to some parents and educators. This concern is a force working against the popularity of the acceleration approach.

When you work with gifted and talented students, you have to ensure that what these students are asked to do is truly different from what is required of other students. It is particularly important that you do not simply ask them to do more of the same. For example, if you ask most of your students to do 10 homework problems, it is a mistake to ask your gifted and talented students to do 15 problems from the same set. If you do this, you will communicate to gifted and talented students that their condition is a burden, and you are punishing them by asking them to do more schoolwork than their classmates. Students are likely to see this as unfair. One result can be a diminished interest in school and a disinclination to stretch academically.

It is important to encourage development of gifted and talented students' creativity. To accomplish this, you can do the following:

- Let your students know that you encourage risk-taking.
- Suggest ways your students might put to use information they might gain as a result of taking risks.

Avoid placing unnecessary limits on gifted students' creativity by laying out hard-and-fast rules regarding how learning will be assessed. You should communicate to them that innovative, creative responses will be all right. You want to challenge them to develop unusual approaches that will stretch their imaginative and creative powers.

Establishing the Personal Importance of Learning   It is important to provide gifted and talented students with opportunities to pursue some issues they select themselves. They should be encouraged to redefine tasks you provide in ways that will make them more personally important. Gifted and talented students are not often motivated to stretch themselves in pursuit of uninspiring academic goals that seem little connected to their own needs or interests. They may see such pursuits as "a stupid game" and simply refuse to play.

However, when these bright learners are encouraged to play an active part in identifying (or at least redefining) the learning task, they will often commit their intellectual and emotional resources to it with great enthusiasm. This kind of commitment is essential. Without it, they may fail to develop their outstanding creative, imaginative, and intellectual powers fully.

General Guidelines for Teaching Exceptional Students   Because of the variety of exceptional students who may be present in a given classroom, specific suggestions for them are related to their unique needs. Many of these students will have Individual Educational Plans (IEPs). As already indicated, legal mandates require that the IEP must be followed. Some general suggestions can be followed, however, that will increase the probability of success for special needs students.

Use Alternative Assignments for Exceptional Students   Students with special needs may not be able to complete work at the same pace as others. This does not mean that they are excused from learning; it just means that they may be given fewer problems to complete or shorter assignments. The technique for doing this is first to identify the essential learning in the lesson, then sample the essential learning. This is done with fewer samples than is required of others in the classroom. This technique allows special needs students to work on the same content, just with a different degree of difficulty. It allows these students the opportunity for success and is likely to increase their motivation.

Gifted and creative students should not just be expected to "do more of the same." In essence, this approach is punishing a student for being gifted or talented. Alternative assignments that focus on the objectives of the lesson but allow these students to complete assignments so that they use their creativity or are challenged by seeking applications of the knowledge are more likely to keep them engaged (Tomlinson & Imbeau, 2010).

Use Peer Tutoring   You will find in most classrooms that other students like to assist students with special needs. Some teachers object that this penalizes the tutor by hindering their learning. However, research has indicated that the person who often learns the most is the person doing the tutoring! Therefore, using peer tutors that are just slightly ahead of the student is a technique for helping both students achieve greater success.

Including gifted and talented students in working with others provides important modeling for other students. When gifted students explain to others how they solve a problem, they often provide a model of thinking that will help other students learn.

Allow Students Choices about How to Complete Assignments   Many assignments can be done in more than one way. For example, some students who have difficulty with writing or language may construct a project or complete a picture or diagram. Giving an oral exam rather than a written one to some students will allow them an opportunity to demonstrate what they have learned.

Gifted and talented students often enjoy the challenge of doing something different. Again, the trick is to keep the focus on the important objectives and intent of the lesson, but to allow the students to use creative ways of demonstrating what they have learned. Conversations with gifted students can allow them to express their ideas and often leads to some interesting alternative assignments that can enrich the entire classroom. Remember that students can demonstrate impressive on-task behavior when they are working on something that interests them.

One word of caution: Some gifted and talented students may not automatically jump at the chance of doing an alternative assignment. Many of them, through several years in education, have learned that having the "right answer" is what pays off. They may be reluctant to engage in an alternative activity for fear that it will interfere with their search for the "right" answer.

Gender Differences

In recent years, the data on gender differences have led to more discussion and action in creating single-gender schools. As students enter the secondary schools, gender differences often become more pronounced. Students are developing their own identities and are very sensitive to how they are viewed by others, especially those of the opposite gender. In addition, teacher expectations are often different for males and females. Males tend to receive lower grades than females, and there may be lowered expectations for females in certain subjects such as science and mathematics.

The problem is even worse for those students who do not have a traditional sexual orientation. They may feel completely out of place and totally friendless at a time when peer support is absolutely critical.

More from the Web

Meeting Diverse Learners' Needs

Educators face challenges in providing instruction that is responsive to the needs of an increasingly diverse student population. This situation has prompted the development of many websites with practical information for teachers. We have selected a few you might want to visit.

DEFINING MULTICULTURAL EDUCATION

http://curry.edschool.virginia.edu/go/multicultural/initial.html

Not all educators agree on the components and purposes of multicultural education. At this website, you will find information from a number of leading authorities in the field. You will also find details related to definitions of the term *multicultural education* and to components, assumptions, goals, and principles of multicultural education programs.

BILINGUAL EDUCATION: FOCUSING POLICY ON STUDENT ACHIEVEMENT

http://www.ascd.org

This website is maintained by the Association for Supervision and Curriculum Development (ASCD), a group dedicated to improving school programming for all learners. If you explore either Education Topics or Issues, you will find information about various approaches to meeting the needs of bilingual students, particularly with respect to some controversies they have engendered and to some research-based findings about approaches that have worked well with students whose first language is not English.

TEACHING DIVERSITY: PEOPLE OF COLOR

http://www.theaha.org/pubs/diversity.htm

Some members of the American Historical Association (AHA) have been concerned that many studies of American history have failed to include references to contributions of certain racial and ethnic groups. In response to this situation, the AHA Committee on Minority Historians has commissioned an essay series. At this website, you will find references to available essays, including topics such as the following: Teaching U.S. Puerto Rican History, Teaching Asian American History, Teaching Asian American Women's History, Teaching African American History, and Teaching American Indian History.

NATIONAL ASSOCIATION FOR MULTICULTURAL EDUCATION

http://www.name.org

This website provides the organization's definition of multicultural education as well as information about issues in multicultural education. You will also find links to state websites.

NATIONAL ASSOCIATION FOR BILINGUAL EDUCATION

http://www.nabe.org

The National Association for Bilingual Education is dedicated to important issues in bilingual education. You will find discussion of policy and legislative issues as well as links to other important websites for organizations that are concerned with bilingual education.

COUNCIL FOR EXCEPTIONAL CHILDREN

http://www.cec.sped.org/

The Council for Exceptional Children (CEC) is a leading professional organization for educators with interests in serving the needs of students with disabilities. You will find much information here about useful approaches to inclusion and to many other topics related to serving these students well in the classroom.

(continued)

FEDERATION FOR CHILDREN WITH SPECIAL NEEDS
>   http://www.fcsn.org/resource.htm

The Federation for Children with Special needs is an advocacy group dedicated to supporting efforts to serve students with disabilities well. You will find links to information sources maintained by state and federal agencies. This is a good source for details about inclusion and other topics related to students with disabilities.

NATIONAL ASSOCIATION FOR GIFTED CHILDREN
>   http://www.nagc.org

The National Association for Gifted Children (NAGC) advocates for programs for gifted and talented students. There are good links at this site to other Web locations where you can find information related to meeting the educational needs of gifted and talented students.

The differences in personalities and dispositions, many of them arising out of gender differences, can be vast. While the teacher has no control over students' personalities and dispositions, the teacher does have a great deal of control over the learning climate. A positive and inclusive learning climate is a critical factor in helping all students develop a sense of psychological security that enables them to overcome many of their interpersonal challenges. Therefore, the learning climate may be one of the most important dimensions of effective teaching.

The learning climate toward which teachers should strive is one that values the strengths and the perspectives of all students regardless of interests, ability, gender, or culture. Teachers should attempt to create a classroom climate that is warm and accepting, but also businesslike. Students need to believe that the classroom is a safe place where they will be protected from psychological as well as physical assault, where they are accepted, and where there is a teacher who is interested in them as a person. However, they also need to enter the classroom knowing that they will be required to work and they will be expected to learn. Teachers who are able to create this type of classroom will find that they have a more exciting and successful teaching experience.

Guidelines for Promoting Academic Success

Experts have developed a number of guidelines to promote better learning and better attitudes toward school for a diverse student population. These guidelines are generally just good teaching principles. However, they are especially important in promoting the success of diverse students. We have included here some recommendations that are reflected in several proposals:

- Assume all students can learn.
- Provide good teachers.
- Insist that teachers become aware of their own cultural perspectives.
- Encourage teachers to avoid favoritism in the classroom.
- Include students from varied ethnic and cultural backgrounds in each group when members of a class are divided into groups for instruction.
- Vary teaching methods to accommodate different learning styles.
- Organize curriculum around relevant themes.
- Develop close working relationships with students' families.
- Emphasize development of higher-level thinking skills.
- Use conversations to uncover ways to contextualize instruction.

Assume All Students Can Learn

As a teacher, you will find minority group students (and, indeed, students in general) very sensitive to how you view them. If minority group students feel that you have little confidence in their abilities to learn, they will be inclined to "live down" to your expectations. Under the best of circumstances, the middle school, junior high school, and senior high school years are emotionally trying for young people. The last thing you want to do is to reinforce any feelings of personal inadequacy.

In addition to the negative impact on students' self-concepts that can result if your actions suggest to them that they cannot learn, such an attitude can affect how you interact with these learners. There is evidence that teachers' beliefs about the learning potential of students influence their commitment to prepare good lessons and deliver high-quality instruction. In other words, your conviction that your instruction can make a difference motivates students to do their best. In the absence of this motivation, the quality of your instruction is likely to suffer and, as a result, your students will not achieve a high level of academic success.

When you think about your students, remember that there is great diversity within any group of people. You want to avoid concluding that information that may well describe certain individuals who are African American, Latino, Native American, or Asian generalizes to all people who belong to one of these groups. This kind of stereotyping distorts reality.

This diversity implies a need to have a depth of understanding about those you teach and to vary your instruction to meet their needs. You need to resist searching for a single teaching approach that will respond well to the characteristics of every student you teach. This mistaken approach is akin to a futile search for an instructional holy grail. "It risks becoming a sacred calling that consumes resources in the search for an illusory panacea for complex social and educational ills" (Lomawaima, 1995, p. 342).

Provide Good Teachers

It seems redundant to state that diverse students need good teachers. All students deserve good teachers. It is particularly critical, however, that minority students be taught by teachers who are sensitive to their special ethnic and cultural perspectives, respectful of them as individuals, and strongly committed to the view that they can and should learn. Regrettably, considerable evidence indicates the neediest students tend to get the least prepared teachers and large numbers of minority students are not being taught by good teachers.

In many places with large minority student enrollments, turnover rates of teachers are high. This means that many minority students are taught by teachers who are either relatively new to the profession or relatively new to the school where they are presently employed. Many of these teachers also are people who are teaching outside their major field of preparation. Minority students also have a higher than average probability of being taught by teachers holding only an emergency or substandard teaching credential.

Be Aware of Students' Cultural Perspective

Individuals tend to consider their experiences as normal. Their ethnocentric perspectives lead them to conclude that their worldview is the normal and natural one. As a result they often do not recognize that their worldview may differ from that of members of other cultural and ethnic groups. In truth, all people are to a great extent conditioned to make sense of the world in ways consistent with the perspectives of the people with whom they interact. This suggests that you need to think clearly about your own assumptions and to reflect on how actions you take might be viewed by students in your classes with different assumptions about what is "right" and "normal." You need to consider answers to questions such as the following:

- What are my views about what the curriculum ought to be?
- How do I think individuals learn in the classroom?

- What do I consider to be appropriate behavior in the classroom?

- What assumptions am I making about the previous experience and the background my students bring to school?

- To what do I attribute lack of school success of students who are members of certain groups?

- Where did I get my ideas about good educational practice?

- How are my ideas influenced by the community I lived in and the schools I attended when I was a student?

Honest answers to these questions can help you think about the appropriateness of decisions you make about working with students from cultural and ethnic groups that differ from your own.

To enhance your success, consider drawing on some practices of cultural anthropologists: Become a participant-observer in the community where you teach. Take part in cultural events sponsored by different ethnic and cultural groups. Note carefully the worldviews, values, norms, cultural practices, and rituals of those you teach and use this information to develop programs that will provide a culturally responsive education for your students.

If you fail to recognize that there are multiple perspectives and interpretations of events and actions, you may erroneously assume that your own worldview is the only one (or at least the only "correct" one), and you may make assumptions about others that will hinder your ability to understand them and effectively communicate with them. In turn, your actions might be misinterpreted by your students. They may then respond to you in ways that seem puzzling.

CRITICAL INCIDENT

"MR. HOBBS, YOUR HISTORY IS IRRELEVANT."

Nolan Hobbs teaches U.S. history at Lee High School. He is also occasionally called on to teach economics classes and sociology classes. Recently, he shared the following comments with Rafaela Sanchez, vice principal for academic programs at Lee High School.

Things have gone just great this year. Well, that's generally the case, but there is a student in my fifth-period class who has become a bit of a thorn in my side. I'm talking about Cassiella Birdsong. You'll remember she was in talking to you a few weeks ago about getting some bulletin board space in the hall for the African American Students Association.

Well, anyway, Cassiella has convinced herself that I have absolutely nothing to teach her. She told me this morning that our history book was "filled with a bunch of lies about dead white guys." Even though I go out of my way to include information about contributions of African Americans, she still has it in her head that my whole course is dedicated to imposing a point of view she wants no part of.

I know she's bright, and I am concerned that she's just not working up to her potential. I'm getting pretty frustrated with her telling me every day how "irrelevant" everything in my course is. Her attitude is beginning to have a bad influence on some of the other students as well.

■ ■ ■

How might you explain Cassiella's point of view? What do these views tell us about her values? Is her reaction something Mr. Hobbs should be concerned about? What does Mr. Hobbs believe to be important? What should he do next? In addition to the vice principal, who else might he consult for advice? What specific advice would you provide to Mr. Hobbs and/or to Cassiella?

Avoid Favoritism

By the time they arrive in secondary schools, many minority group students may have had experiences in school and elsewhere that have led them to conclude that sometimes members of minority groups are treated differently than members of the white, non-Latino majority. Nearly all students are concerned about the general issues of consistent and appropriate treatment. Your credibility definitely will be at risk if your students suspect you are not fair.

One way to demonstrate fairness is to avoid favoritism in the classroom. It is particularly important that minority group students sense that, as individuals and as a group, they are being treated as well as others in the class. If your minority students suspect that you single out individuals for negative treatment or comments in a way that seems tied to ethnicity or race, you may find it difficult to maintain their interest and cooperation.

Students often measure fairness by looking at how teachers handle episodes of misbehavior. The general rule you should follow is to respond to a given kind of misbehavior in the same way regardless of the offender. That is, your high-achieving students shouldn't get off more lightly than your low-achieving students, your white students shouldn't get off more lightly than your minority group students, and so forth. When students feel that you dispense justice equitably and hold all to the same standard, their motivation levels increase, your discipline problems diminish, and students' achievement levels improve.

Include Diverse Students in Every Group

When you plan group work, it is important that your groups not serve as a vehicle for re-segregating students on the basis of race or ethnicity. For one thing, individual groups sometimes are asked to do different things. For example, you may assign some groups to work on more challenging academic tasks than others.

There is evidence that some groups are organized by teachers so that racial minorities are concentrated within a few groups (Rist, 1985). This is a mistake. Learners must not see group instructional techniques as subtle covers for an instructional program designed to provide different (and perhaps lower-quality) instruction to minority group students.

An important goal of secondary education is to help students adjust to living in a multicultural society. Given this priority, it makes sense for you to organize groups to encourage personal contacts among students from varying cultural and ethnic backgrounds. Such practices break down group-to-group isolation and provide a way for students to become more familiar with perspectives different from their own.

Respond to Different Learning Styles

Students vary in terms of their preferred learning styles. This means that some individuals learn better when they read about new information. Others learn better when they listen to someone explaining new content. Others are visual learners: people who master new content best when they are presented with examples they can see. Still others need opportunities to touch, handle, and otherwise manipulate physical objects. Preferred learning settings also vary. For example, some individuals prefer to learn alone; others do much better when they are organized into groups.

Researchers have found that students' cultural backgrounds affect their learning styles (Grant & Sleeter, 2007). This does not mean that individuals with similar cultural backgrounds do not vary. Rather, it suggests that more people from one cultural group may have a given learning style than people from another cultural group.

There is evidence that students from African American and Latino backgrounds do better when they are presented with a broad general overview of a situation first and then asked to think about how specific information relates to the general situation (Bowman, 1991). For example, it would be better for you to provide general information about the Civil War and then ask about the relationship of the Battle of Gettysburg to the war in general. Non-Latino white students, however, have been found to do well when complex situations are first broken down into small parts. These small parts are learned one at a time, and only in the end does a general picture emerge. Given this orientation, you might have your class study individual battles of the Civil War one at a time, and then conclude with a description of their cumulative effects on the war in general.

Organize the Curriculum Around Relevant Themes

Students should have an opportunity to study a topic in depth. The more diverse the student population, the more important this idea becomes (Garcia, 2002). Conceptually, this varies from the normal school day where classes are divided into time periods and taught without connections among subjects. Freeman and Freeman (2001) point out that one benefit of this approach is that students develop their academic language more easily. Typically this approach has been more common in elementary classrooms. As middle and high school environments change to adapt to new dynamics, however, the opportunity to develop integrated, thematic instruction is becoming more common.

Develop a Relationship with Students' Families

To the extent possible, you should establish relationships with members of minority group students' families. Although many relatives of minority students are positively disposed toward the school and its programs, this attitude is not universal. Some of them may not have had particularly good experiences in school themselves, and they may be inclined to lump educators into a category that includes indifferent city hall bureaucrats, law enforcement officials, and other establishment figures that, in their view, have not always treated minorities fairly. People with these views may be reluctant to come to the school on open house nights or on other occasions, and you need to make special efforts to contact them.

Students' priorities and general attitudes are strongly influenced by those of their parents, grandparents, and other relatives, especially those living in the same household. If you can establish a common ground with a student's family members that results in a consensus regarding what the student should be doing in school, the student may benefit. In fact, Ogbu (1973) found that "school learning is most likely to occur when family values reinforce school expectations" (p. 27).

Emphasize Higher-Level Thinking Skills

If you have some minority group students who are not doing well, avoid the temptation to lower your instructional expectations. Their academic performance may result from circumstances having little or nothing to do with their real ability levels. Students gain nothing when they are provided with unchallenging classroom instruction. What you need to do is fit instructional tasks to students so that they will be intellectually "stretched" but not to the extent they will be unable to succeed. For learning to take place Vygotsky (1978) suggests that it must take place in a student's zone of proximal development (ZPD). He defines the ZPD as "the distance between the actual developmental level as determined by independent problem solving and the level of potential development as determined through problem solving under adult guidance or in collaboration with more capable peers" (p. 86). Over time, instruction that pushes students to develop sophisticated thinking skills gives them the tools needed for dealing with more complex subject matter. These academic successes build students' confidence and stimulate their interest in the school program.

Use Conversations to Uncover Ways to Contextualize Instruction

As you seek to connect with your students, you need to develop instructional activities that students in your class see relate to their own lives, their families, and their communities (Tharp, 1999). Your aim is to contextualize your instruction, creating teaching episodes that tie closely to the personal experiences of the people who will receive it—your students. Providing good contextualized instruction requires that you know your students well. One useful approach for gaining insights into your students' personal backgrounds involves engaging them in conversations. If you listen carefully and respectfully to what students say, they will reveal a great deal about their personal, family, and community backgrounds. All of this information can be useful as you design lessons that are responsive to the individual circumstances of your students.

Key Ideas in Summary

- Ethnic and cultural diversity among the population of secondary students is becoming more pronounced. In responding to particular needs of minority group students, teachers need to guard against assuming that all students from a given ethnic, racial, or cultural group share common characteristics. There are important within-group differences, and the proper approach is to focus on the characteristics of the individual student rather than the presumed characteristic of the group to which he or she belongs.

- A number of risk factors have been identified that commonly characterize students who drop out of school. These risk factors include the following: (1) living in a single-parent home, (2) being a member of a family receiving public assistance funds, (3) speaking a primary language other than English, (4) having a brother or sister who dropped out of school, (5) having a mother who is not a high school graduate, (6) having attended five or more schools, (7) spending less than one hour per week on homework, (8) spending no time each week reading for fun, (9) watching television more than five hours a night, (10) rarely communicating with parents about things studied at school, and (11) being overage for a particular grade by one year or more.

- In times past, poor performance levels of minority students were attributed such "causes" such as genetic deficit. According to this now discredited view, minority group children lacked the necessary intellectual resources to succeed academically; hence, it made little sense to worry too much about their failure to do well in school. Another outdated view suggested that minority students suffered from a cultural deficit (from intellectually sterile home environments) that failed to prepare them to do schoolwork. Still another view was that minority students suffered a communication process problem. It was suggested that they had language characteristics that made it nearly impossible for them to grasp what teachers expected them to do. The genetic deficit, cultural deficit, and communication process views are now largely regarded as blame-the-victim excuses that allowed schools to avoid their responsibilities to provide quality educational services to minority group students.

- A number of guidelines have been developed to help teachers promote better learning and better attitudes toward schooling among diverse students, including (1) assuming all students can learn, (2) providing minority students with good teachers, (3) insisting that teachers become aware of their own cultural perspectives, (4) encouraging teachers to avoid favoritism in the classroom, (5) including students from varied ethnic backgrounds in each group when students are divided into groups for instructional purposes, (6) varying teaching methods to accommodate different learning styles, (7) organizing curriculum around themes, (8) developing close working relationships with students' families, (9) emphasizing development of higher-level thinking skills, and (10) using conversations to uncover ways to contextualize instruction.

- Provisions for meeting the needs of students with disabilities have changed in recent years. One approach has been that of defining a continuum of services and placing exceptional students in the least restrictive setting. There has been an increasing commitment to the principle of inclusion. Inclusion presumes that (1) to the extent possible, these students should be taught in regular classrooms, and (2) their membership in these classrooms should be expected and welcomed.

■ Recent changes in the delivery of services require that secondary school teachers collaborate with teachers who are specialists in the education of students with disabilities. Among other things, this cooperation can help students with disabilities make the transition to experiences they will face after completing high school.

■ Several legislative mandates must be followed in delivering instruction to students with disabilities. These mandates provide very specific guidelines that school authorities must follow in preparing, delivering, and assessing instructional programs for these students.

■ Teachers today encounter many students with disabilities in their regular classrooms. This means that all classroom teachers must be familiar with various categories of student disability and be able to develop, in cooperation with others, programs of instruction that will be appropriate to the special needs of these learners.

■ Gifted students tend to be selected on multiple criteria, which often include measures of intellectual abilities, creativity, and task commitment (persistence). Despite some popular misconceptions, most gifted and talented students are well adjusted and get along well with other students. These students tend to be served either by enrichment programs or acceleration programs. Currently, enrichment programs are more common than acceleration programs.

Reflections

1. What does the term *exceptional student* mean? What are some categories of exceptional students found in secondary schools?

2. What are some risk factors associated with dropping out of school? Are these risk factors more or less common among minority group students than among the school population as a whole?

3. What are some historic views of minority group students, and how might they have influenced school practices in the past?

4. Why is it important for teachers to appreciate the cultural context that minority group students bring with them to school?

5. Why is it desirable for teachers to approach their instructional tasks with the assumption that all students can learn?

6. Open communication between regular classroom teachers and teachers with special training in the instruction of students with disabilities is critical to the development of lessons that will meet these students' needs. What are some kinds of information that regular teachers and these specialists need to share?

7. What is meant by full inclusion, and how is this concept changing what regular classroom teachers do?

8. What categories of mentally retarded students are you likely to encounter in your classes, and what are some things you can do to help these young people learn?

9. In what ways can you help students with (a) learning disabilities, (b) attention deficit disorders, (c) physical and health impairments, and (d) emotional disturbance problems?

10. Why has selection of gifted and talented students sometimes posed problems? What are some criteria commonly used today to identify these young people?

Learning Extensions

1. Interview a central office administrator from a school district that enrolls a culturally and ethnically diverse group of students. Ask this person to comment on high school graduation rate differences among the major cultural and ethnic groups enrolled in his or her school. Also, solicit comments about any special programs the district has to encourage minority group students to stay in school. Share your findings in an oral report to your class.

2. Read some reports in professional journals (perhaps supplemented by other sources suggested by your instructor) that describe programs that have increased high school graduation rates of minority group students. From these articles, develop a list of features that seem to be associated with the success of these programs. Distribute these lists to others in your class, and use them as a basis for a discussion focusing on the topic Keeping Minority Students in Our Secondary Schools: What Works.

3. Many teachers who work successfully with students from diverse cultural and ethnic groups have taken time to familiarize themselves with how members of these groups see the world. Compile a list of journal articles, books, and other sources of information that might be helpful to non-Latino white teachers interested in learning more about the cultural perspectives of members of selected minority groups. Share your list with others in the class.

4. Invite a panel of five or six secondary school teachers to your class. Have them discuss their experiences working with students with disabilities who are enrolled in their regular classes. In particular, urge them to share ideas about how instruction has been modified to meet these students' special needs.

5. Organize a class debate on this topic: Resolved that programs for the gifted and talented divert scarce educational resources away from other, more deserving students.

References

Baum, S. (1990). The gifted/learning disabled: A paradox for teachers. *Education Digest, 55*(8), 54–56.

Bowman, B. (1991). Educating language minority children: Challenges and opportunities. In S. L. Kagan (Ed.), *The care and education of America's young children: Obstacles and opportunities* (pp. 17–29). Nineteenth Yearbook of the National Society for the Study of Education. Part I. Chicago: National Society for the Study of Education.

Brown, B. B., & Sternberg, L. (1990). Academic achievement and social acceptance. *Education Digest, 55*(7), 57–60.

Erickson, F. (1987). Transformation and school success: The politics and culture of educational achievement. *Anthropology and Education Quarterly, 18*(4), 335–356.

Freeman, D. E., & Freeman, Y. S. (2001). *Between worlds: Access to second language acquisition* (2nd ed.). Portsmouth, N.H.: Heinemann.

Garcia, E. (2002). *Student cultural diversity: Understanding and meeting the challenge.* Boston: Houghton Mifflin.

Gleason, P., & Dynarksi, M. (1998). *Do we know whom to serve? Issues in using risk factors to identify dropouts.* Princeton, NJ: Mathematica Policy Research, Inc.

Grant, C. A., & Sleeter, C. E. (2007). *Making choices for multicultural education: Five approaches to race, class, and gender* (6th ed.). New York: Harper Collins.

Heward, W (1996). *Exceptional children: An introduction to special education* (5th ed.). Upper Saddle River, NJ: Merrill/Prentice Hall.

Lomawaima, K. (1995). Educating Native Americans. In J. Banks & C. Banks (Eds.), *Handbook of research on multicultural education* (pp. 331–347). New York: Macmillan.

National Center for Educational Statistics. (2005). Digest of educational statistics tables and figures. Table 84. Retrieved September 6, 2006, from http//nces.ed.gov/programs/digest/d05/tables/dr05_084asp

National Center for Educational Statistics, Condition of Education. (2009). The condition of education. Retrieved December 16, 2009, from http://www.nces.ed.gov/programs/coe/2009

National Governors Association. (2008). *Accelerating the agenda: Actions to improve America's high schools.* Washington, D.C.: Author.

Ogbu, J. H. (1973). *Minority education and caste.* New York: Academic Press.

Renzulli, J. (1978). What makes giftedness: Re-examining a definition. *Phi Delta Kappan, 60*(3), 180–184, 261.

Rist, R. C. (1985). On understanding the process of school: The contributions of labeling theory. In J. A. Ballentine (Ed.), *Schools and society: A reader in education and sociology* (pp. 88–106). Palo Alto, CA: Mayfield.

Rothstein-Fisch, C., & Trumbull, E. (2008). *Managing diverse classrooms: How to build on students' cultural strengths.* Alexandria, VA: Association for Supervision and Curriculum Development.

Savage, T. V., & Armstrong, D. C. (2004). *Effective teaching in elementary social studies* (5th ed.). Upper Saddle River, NJ: Merrill/Prentice Hall.

Smith, T., Polloway, E., Patton, J., & Dowdy, C. (1996). *Teaching students with special needs in inclusive settings.* Boston: Allyn & Bacon.

Tharp, T. (1999). Vision of a transformed classroom. *Talking Leaves, 3*(3), 1–2. Santa Cruz, CA: Center for Research on Education, Diversity & Excellence, the University of California.

Tomlinson, C. A., and Imbeau, M. B. (2010). *Leading and managing a differentiated classroom.* Alexandria, VA: Association for Supervision and Curriculum Development.

Vygotsky, L. (1978). *Mind in society: The development of higher psychological processes.* Cambridge, MA: Harvard University Press.

Reflective Teaching

Objectives

This chapter will help you

- define reflective teaching
- define constructivism
- describe the four elements of the decision-making processes of reflective teachers
- point out how pedagogical personality, pedagogical assumptions, and pedagogical repertoire affect a teacher's classroom performance
- describe the strengths and weaknesses of various sources of information about effective teaching and learning

- point out some limitations of learning theories as sources of information teachers can use as bases of lessons for students in specific classes
- describe how teachers' expectations of students may influence their instructional practices
- define fluid planning, and state why it is necessary
- explain how professional development portfolios can help teachers to be more effective

David Mager/Pearson

Graphic Organizer: Chapter 4

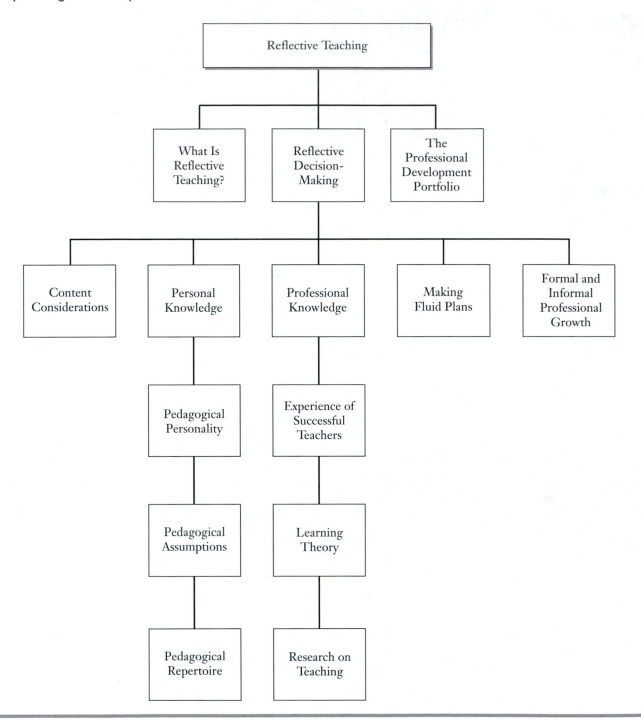

Introduction

Because you are interested in a career as a secondary school teacher, let's focus on teaching. Suppose you have just been employed to teach tenth-grade world history (or math, English, or science—choose your own subject). Where will you begin? How will you approach your task?

Some of you may smile and say to yourself, "I'm an English major. That certainly prepares me to make decisions about what to teach." Being knowledgeable in the subject is certainly an important prerequisite for teaching success, but content knowledge does not provide guidance about where to start, what to include, and how to make your subject meaningful to a particular group of students. What if your students do not have the necessary prerequisite background? What if they don't share your interest and enthusiasm?

Perhaps you will conclude, "In high school, I had an outstanding English teacher. I'll begin by following his or her example." The intent to follow the example of one of your own outstanding teachers may be a good start, but this approach also presents you with certain problems. For one thing, you and your model teacher are different people. You do not share the same experiences, personality, or knowledge. In addition, the students in your classroom may be quite different from those taught by your model. Even in the unlikely event that you were able to follow patterns established by your model teacher perfectly, students you teach may not react to your instruction as you remember yourself and others reacting to your teacher. Your students have different experiences and live in a different time, and their interests are influenced by their social and cultural backgrounds.

If you decide that following the example of one of your own teachers is insufficient, you may decide simply to follow suggestions provided in the teacher's guide that accompanies the text supplied for your class. After all, it is presumed that this textbook was written by knowledgeable individuals and has been reviewed and tested. Shouldn't these experts know how to teach secondary school students? First of all, these assumptions may or may not be valid. In addition, this perspective presumes that "experts" somewhere have discovered the right formula for teaching all students. All you need to do is follow this formula and success will follow.

While some would-be educational reformers seem to think that approach will work and have even developed scripts for teachers to follow, this is not reality. Individuals who wrote the textbook had no information regarding your specific group of students or their backgrounds, interests, strengths, and individual needs. The bracing truth is that not all students are stamped out of the same mold. As Chapter 3 indicated, they possess incredible differences. Veteran teachers emphasize this fact when they point out that the differences are so great that even within a school, what works in one period of the day may not work in another period of the day. Classrooms simply vary too much for a prescription written by someone far removed from an individual classroom to work. The ideas and suggestions provided in a teacher's guide might be important and helpful, but they should not be viewed as a prescription.

When confronted with prescriptive teaching approaches, it is useful to remember that teaching has little in common with work on an assembly line. Students are not inert raw materials who will eagerly and passively await your attempts to "mold" them into predetermined final products. If teaching were like manufacturing, you would reject raw materials (students) with flaws that interfere with your ability to transform the students into educated persons efficiently. As a society, however, we have a compelling interest in educating all individuals. Those who are rejected do not disappear but often become a burden to society for decades to come. As teachers, we have to accept all students regardless of their background, ability, and motivation. It is a violation of professional ethics to deny instruction to individuals who fail to conform to certain expectations or standards. We simply do not discard students who are "different" and do not meet the "norm."

Because of differences among students and because of your obligation to respond to the needs of all of them, simply following suggestions in a teacher's guide will not suffice. Numerous attempts have been made throughout educational history to develop "teacher-proof" programs or prescriptions that, if followed religiously by teachers, would all but guarantee high levels of student learning. Not surprisingly, educational history also indicates that these programs have failed largely because of the differences among teachers, students, and teaching contexts.

It is important to understand that teaching is not a technical act but a professional one. The challenge of becoming a teacher requires that you decide what you value, how you will conduct yourself with students, and the type of teacher you want to be (Goethals, Howard, & Sanders, 2004). It requires that you engage in decision-making based on knowledge that takes into account unique circumstances. You must consider the nature of the students you are teaching, their previous knowledge, their aspirations, their motivations, and their attitudes. In addition, you need to acquire alternative approaches to teaching and know when and how to use them.

It is not surprising that new teachers often feel overwhelmed by the number of decisions and the importance of the decisions they must make every day. This is what makes student teaching and the first years of teaching so stressful. For some new teachers, this is unexpected. As one student teacher who was having difficulty once commented, "But it looks so easy!"

Because of the complexity and the ever-changing nature of students and learning, reflection is an integral component of professional growth. Taking time to reflect deeply regarding your values, beliefs, and aspirations; conducting honest self-assessments of your knowledge and skill; and seeking feedback from others are essential steps in your journey to becoming a teacher (Goethals, Howard, & Sanders, 2004).

The graphic organizer at the beginning of this chapter illustrates that the chapter has three major components: a definition of reflective teaching, the process of reflective decision-making, and the uses of professional development portfolios in the process of reflection. The process of reflective decision-making includes the five areas of professional knowledge, personal knowledge, context considerations, making fluid plans, and formal and informal professional growth. Developing personal knowledge is accomplished by considering the experiences of other teachers, learning theory, and research on teaching. Personal knowledge is developed by reflecting on your pedagogical personality, your pedagogical assumptions, and your pedagogical repertoire.

What is Reflective Teaching?

Borich (2008) defines *reflection* as a teacher's ability to consciously consider his or her professional growth. He suggests that teachers develop reflective habits by developing observational skills that can provide a lens for what goes on in classrooms.

Reflective teaching is based on the psychological model of constructivism. Constructivism holds that humans build or construct knowledge. Knowledge does not consist of a set of facts or concepts to be shoved into predetermined file folders somewhere in the brains of students. Knowledge is created and stored when people seek to bring meaning to their experience (Zahorik, 1995). This means that learning how to teach cannot be reduced to a set of procedures that you can apply effectively in all situations. You bring a set of personal filters related to your knowledge, beliefs, and values through which you process information related to the task of learning how to teach. How you interpret information about teaching will be different from those around you. What you view as relevant may be perceived as irrelevant by another. For you to develop as a professional, you need to be able to reflect on your beliefs and theories and check their validity.

Preparing to teach, then, does not involve collecting a list of how-tos. Rather, preparing to teach includes questioning and reflecting on your experiences so that you can make sense out of them and identify principles that will assist you in making better decisions. New information and experiences should challenge you to test your assumptions and beliefs. If you are open to new information and are willing to engage in reflection, then professional growth is possible.

Because humans construct knowledge, it is conjectural and fallible and grows through exposure. This means that knowledge is never stable. Indeed, it is constantly changing. Your understanding of teaching will be continuously altered as you learn from new experiences. This process of nonstop professional renewal is one that energizes teachers. Members of our profession never know all there is to know about teaching.

Reflective teaching builds on the concept of reflection. As applied to education, reflection refers to your ability as a teacher "to reflect thoughtfully on the conditions at hand and respond appropriately in the best interest of the learner" (Rogers & Freiberg, 1994, p. 349). Henderson (1996) suggests that decision-making processes of reflective teachers include four elements:

1. Decisions are sensitive to the context of the situation. Learning does not take place in a vacuum. It occurs in the context of a specific school in a particular community during a certain time of the year. Schools and parents have expectations. Your students may come from families with few resources or abundant resources. The peer groups within the school have certain norms and sanctions for those who choose to ignore them. The students may be concerned in the fall with trying to become part of a group, while in the spring they might be consumed with thinking about summer vacation. Their moods change according to things they are experiencing in their personal lives. They simply do not leave all of their experiences and emotions at the classroom door.

2. Decisions are guided by a cycle of fluid planning. As a teacher, you face an interesting dilemma. On the one hand, you have to plan to achieve success. On the other hand, you are working with unpredictable human beings. Even your best plans, those that worked last period, may not necessarily work next period.

   What is the solution? It is certainly not to give up planning. Rather, you have to engage in fluid planning. This means that you have to be ready to modify plans when unexpected conditions arise. It is sometimes difficult to see that this is something excellent teachers do routinely. What you are likely to see in a visit to their classrooms is a seamless flow of orderly instruction. What you ordinarily don't see are the minute-by-minute decisions and changes that the teacher is making.

3. Decisions are informed by professional and personal knowledge that is critically examined. To make good decisions, you need to have a good knowledge base. You need to be aware of the possible reasons learning occurs. You need to know about alternative approaches to teaching your content and the possible consequences of these approaches. Beyond just having a lot of background about teaching and learning, however, you have to constantly reflect on or examine your decisions. What were your reasons for making a particular decision? Were they valid? Did you overlook important information that should have been considered? This means that you subject your personal and professional knowledge base to an ongoing critical examination.

4. Decisions are enhanced by both formal and informal professional growth opportunities. As a reflective teacher, you function as a lifelong learner who is constantly seeking new knowledge. You need to discover sources of information that will help you to grow professionally. These might be formal opportunities such as additional coursework, or they might come to you in informal ways. For example, you might gain important insights into your local community by cooperating with area residents on an important neighborhood project.

Judy Eby (1998) proposes a model of reflective teaching based on Dewey's (1933) ideas of reflective thinking. This model focuses on active, persistent, and careful thinking that accounts for evidence that is synthesized into action (Eby, 1998). Specifically, Eby suggests that successful reflective teachers are:

- Active people who energetically seek solutions to problems rather than passive people who ignore them or rely on tradition and imitation as guides to their instructional practices.

- Persistent people who are undaunted in their search for successful responses to instructional challenges and who are not satisfied with superficial or simple solutions.

- Careful practitioners who reflect a commitment to the ethical and moral dimensions of teaching as they keep an unwavering focus on students' needs rather than their own.

- Thoughtful individuals who consider evidence as they review, study, and reconsider what has occurred in the classroom for the purpose of revising practices in ways that will better serve students' needs.

As a reflective teacher, you function as a hypothesis-tester. Based on your own past experiences and your knowledge and intuition about the capacities of your students, you devise an instructional strategy. As you implement it (and after), you check the accuracy of your assumptions. You might ask yourself questions such as the following:

- Were my preconceptions about what might be effective correct? If not, why not?

- Did parts of the lesson work particularly well? If so, how might I capitalize on these successes in preparing other lessons?

- Were there a few weak spots in a generally good lesson? If so, how might I fix them?

This kind of systematic review helps you keep focused on student understanding. Researchers have found that effective teachers spend considerable time thinking about impact-on-student issues as they reflect on their own instructional practices. Less effective teachers tend to focus on issues associated with relatively superficial events that interrupt the flow of their instruction (for example, announcements coming in unexpectedly over a speaker system) rather than on components of classroom instruction that provide important learning benefits to students (Reynolds, 1992). In other words, effective teachers use more important, student-learning-related criteria as they assess the adequacy of their instruction.

A key to your development as an effective reflective teacher is to do something with your conclusions once you have thought carefully about how well a lesson has served your students. You want to put new insights to work as you plan new learning experiences for members of your class. It does no good whatsoever to think carefully about what has happened and then simply repeat instructional practices that did not work particularly well the first time.

A department head one of the authors knows mentioned a comment she made to a particularly ineffective teacher who went through the motions of thinking about how her lessons were being received by students (generally not well), and then making absolutely no modifications in her instructional program. In a conversation with the department head, the teacher said, "I should be getting better. After all, I've had five years' teaching experience." The department head replied, "No, you haven't. You just repeated your first year five times!" This comment may have been a bit harsh, but it underscores the point that simply thinking about your lessons is not enough; to grow as an effective, reflective practitioner, you have to reflect on the impact of your lessons and then act on your conclusions. Such action adds to your professional knowledge base over time and is a key element in your professional growth (Reynolds, 1992).

Reflective Decision-Making

Combining James Henderson's (1996) reflective-teaching decision-making processes with Judy Eby's (1998) reflective-teaching dimensions results in a framework for putting reflective teaching into action. This framework suggests that, as you seek to become a more effective reflective teacher, you need to commit to:

- considering the context
- using personal knowledge
- applying professional knowledge

- making fluid plans
- taking advantage of formal and informal professional growth opportunities

Context Considerations

To achieve success, you need to actively and carefully consider elements of the context that will influence how you teach and how your students learn. Successful teaching requires more than just walking into a classroom and implementing a generic set of lesson plans. The most significant variable of all is the nature of your students.

Students are not empty vessels or blank slates who walk into your classroom eager to be filled with knowledge (Henderson, 1996). Young people in a typical classroom are incredibly diverse. You can expect some who are eager to learn, and some who are not. Certain individuals will have a previous history of success and others a history of failure. Many students will view your subject as relevant; others will think it is boring. Some students may come from homes where they have been provided with considerable support and assistance; others will come from homes where indifference seems to rule. Some students may have an individualism orientation and others may have a collectivism orientation. You will have students with special needs and you will probably have students for whom English is a second language.

As you begin planning, you need to think about your answers to these questions:

- What are your students' hopes, dreams, and aspirations?
- What is their history of success?
- What is their prior knowledge of the subject?
- What are their attitudes toward the subject?
- How powerful are their peer groups and what are the prevailing norms of the peer group about education in general and this subject in particular?
- What are your students' interests, and what motivates them?
- What are their cultural backgrounds?

Actively pursuing the answers to these questions means that you must spend considerable time and energy observing students, speaking to them, diagnosing their background knowledge, conducting interest surveys, reviewing records, and talking with other professionals in the school. You will not be able to gather all of this information before you begin teaching. You will need to continue gathering it throughout your career. Your students will change from year to year. You will even see important student differences in the various classes you teach during a given year.

Another key context variable is the school itself. Characteristics of individual schools vary enormously. Even those in the same district with similar student populations might often provide quite different contexts for teaching and learning. One way to understand these differences is to think about each school as having a unique culture.

Individual schools have their own attitudes, norms, values, beliefs, sanctions, myths, ceremonies, and traditions that influence both the teachers and the students. Barth (2001) notes that every school has a culture. Some are toxic and some are hospitable. He states that the culture in a school wields astonishing power in shaping how people think and act and that the culture is incredibly resistant to change.

Marzano (2003) reviewed research on effective schools and identified several school-level factors that appear to be important in enhancing student achievement. He identified a guaranteed and viable curriculum, challenging goals and effective feedback, parent and community involvement, a safe and orderly environment, and collegiality and professionalism as the school-level factors that make a difference.

A guaranteed and viable curriculum is one in which the school has a central focus on teaching and learning. Teachers are given clear guidance regarding what is expected, and students are provided the time to learn the content.

CRITICAL INCIDENT

"Somehow, I'm Not Connecting"

Jared North, a first-year social studies teacher at Cotton Mather Senior High School, poured a cup of coffee and slumped into a chair in the departmental office. He looked wearily across the room at Ramona Reyes, the long-time head of the social studies department.

"Rough day?" Ramona asked.

"Not one of my greatest," Jared admitted. "You just wouldn't believe some of the answers I got on my short-essay question."

"Right," Ramona acknowledged with a grin. All of us get strange answers from kids all the time."

"Well, okay," admitted Jared, "this may not be all that unusual. But it's discouraging. We've been studying the Civil War and the campaign leading up to the Battle of Gettysburg for a solid week. I just can't understand where some of these kids are coming from. Some of their answers don't make any sense at all."

"Give me a 'for instance'," said Ramona. "Maybe that will shed a little light on what's going on."

"Okay," Jared replied. "I asked a pretty straightforward question: 'Why did Lee take the army into Pennsylvania?' I got some just crazy answers. One kid said that Lee went there because the other Confederate generals were busy elsewhere. Another one said that Lee knew that Quakers who opposed war had settled Pennsylvania and that he felt no one there would fire a shot at his troops once they crossed the Pennsylvania border. Another person said that Lee might have had relatives in Pennsylvania and that he had personal reasons for going there. Someone else actually wrote that fodder for horses was known to be good in Pennsylvania and that's why Lee took his men there."

"And, I take it," Ramona asked, "that these answers don't have much to do with what you were discussing in class?"

"Absolutely nothing!" replied Jared.

"Okay, let's think about these answers. But first of all, tell me something. How did you give your students the question? I mean, did you give it to them orally, or was it written on the board or on a paper that you gave to each student?"

"I wrote it on the board. The students wrote their answers in class on paper I gave them," answered Jared, shaking his head and wondering why Ramona was interested in this issue.

"All right, let's think about this," Ramona continued. "You know, Jared, written language doesn't communicate as clearly as spoken language. It lacks the inflections and emphases we give individual words when we speak that add to the clarity of what we're trying to say. When your students read your question, they probably put their own inflections on your written words. These could have given your question a different meaning than you had intended. There are many ways your question might have been spoken. Let's look at some of these. Now help me out, the exact wording of your question was 'Why did Lee take the army into Pennsylvania?' Is that right?"

"Yes," Jared acknowledged. "That's exactly what I put on the board."

"Here are some different ways individual students might have read your question: '*Why* did Lee take the army into Pennsylvania?' A student who read the question this way probably would have focused on the reasons, motives, and so forth, for Lee's actions. This is probably what you wanted.

"But another student could have read the question as 'Why did Lee take *his* army into Pennsylvania?' Read in this way, the question seems to be asking why Lee, as opposed to someone else, took the army into Pennsylvania. A student who interpreted the question in this way would tend to focus on other people who might have taken the army and why, in the end, Lee led the army to Pennsylvania.

"Still, another student could have read the question as 'Why did Lee take his army into *Pennsylvania?*' Read in this way, your question seems to focus on special characteristics of

Pennsylvania that convinced Lee to take his army there. Again, this interpretation would prompt a student to answer your question in a certain way."

"That just blows me away, Ramona. I thought I was asking a really simple question. So how do I keep this kind of problem from happening again?"

"There's no simple answer. There is no silver bullet out there that will slay every instructional problem. That's one of the difficulties we have in this business that seems to elude politicians and other simplistic reformers. People keep forgetting that we deal with individuals and keep looking for a one-fits-all approach to teaching. What you need to keep in mind is that each of your kids has a special set of prior experiences. You need to be careful about dismissing an answer that you get that seems strange, bizarre, or totally off base. Often there is an internal logic to what students tell us in their answers. But we can't know what this logic is until we really know our students well. That's the real key: Know your kids, how they think, what is important to them, and how they make sense of the world. When you do that, you'll be a lot less astounded by the responses you get on your tests."

■ ■ ■

What steps should Jared take next? How can he find out more about each of his students? Are some students likely to have values that lead them to think some things are not so important (or in some cases, are more important) to them as they are to Jared? If so, what use might Jared make of this information? What does he need to do to make his instruction more responsive to his students' needs? Where should he seek information about possible instructional responses he might make? Who are some other people whose advice he might seek?

Challenging goals and effective feedback refer to a clear specification of goals that are challenging for students. These goals are accompanied with a high expectation that the students will achieve them. In addition, the attainment of the goals is monitored, and effective feedback is provided.

Parent and community involvement focuses on how involved and supportive the parents and the community are in supporting the school. This factor can be identified by considering the effectiveness of the communication between the school and the parents, actual participation of parents and others in the daily operation of the school, and governance structures that allow parents and the community some voice in school decisions.

A safe and orderly school environment is one where both the students and the teachers feel safe. This is related to a clear set of schoolwide rules governing student behavior. There is an emphasis on teaching self-discipline and responsibility to students, and rules are consistently enforced.

The final factors identified by Marzano, collegiality and professionalism, focus on the professional climate of the school. They relate to the manner in which faculty members and administrators interact with each other. Fullan and Hargreaves (1996) define this as authentic interaction that includes openly sharing failures and mistakes, demonstrating respect for each other, and constructively analyzing procedures and practices. In one of our local high schools, a new principal was assigned to a high school that had high teacher morale. Her leadership style, very top-down with little teacher input (sort of "It's my way or the highway" approach), quickly deteriorated the outstanding working relationship that had previously existed between teachers and administrators. By the end of the year, 17 teachers had left for jobs in other schools, the head football coach of a highly successful program left and took other coaches with him, and parents and students filled the seats at school board meetings to complain about the situation. This is what can happen in a short period of time when collegiality and professionalism are nonexistent.

As you reflect on the type of teacher you want to be, you need to consider the context factors and how they will affect you. This can assist you in finding a school with a professional context that can help you achieve success and grow as a professional. Here are some questions you might consider:

- Does the school have a clearly stated set of goals and expectations?
- What is the extent of parent and community participation?
- Is the environment an orderly one that is conducive to learning?
- How do teachers and administrators interact? Is there obvious respect?
- Do teachers in the school believe that they can achieve success with their students?
- What are community perceptions of the school?
- What resources are available for teachers to use to supplement and support their classroom instruction?

Clearly, some answers to these questions can highlight conditions that may make it difficult for you to be successful. For example, it is hard for students to concentrate on learning if they are worried about their safety. If access to the Internet is difficult, then there are constraints on teachers' abilities to plan lessons that depend on information available only through the Internet. The physical environment of the school can also undermine your well-intentioned efforts to serve students well. In places with out-of-date textbooks, leaking roofs, poor lighting, and overcrowded classrooms, students' performance levels are likely to suffer. Finally, if faculty members do not get along or if tension exists between teachers and administrators, issues associated with smoothing difficult interpersonal relations problems may divert attention from providing optimal learning experiences for students.

In addition to parent and community involvement, you should also attend to the community context. Community priorities and values affect the entire educational enterprise. In response to this reality, it makes sense for you to learn as much as you can about the community where your school is located. This task will require some real effort, particularly if you find yourself teaching in an urban school that may be located in an area far removed from your personal residence. Students attending your school may manifest behavior patterns and reflect attitudes that will make sense to you only if you understand the residential patterns, demographics, religious preferences, norms, values, and other characteristics that go together to create the local community culture. You might begin by seeking answers to questions such as these:

- What is the ethnic and socioeconomic composition of the community?
- What are the major opportunities and challenges in the community?
- What opportunities are provided in the community for the students to be involved in local activities?
- What are the expectations of the community for the school?
- Do community members view the school as supportive or threatening?

Careful consideration of these questions can help you understand some of the student attitudes and behaviors you will see in your classes. This information can assist you in the process of making instructional decisions that are appropriate to the needs of your students. Instructional decisions that are made in light of information about community characteristics enhance students' chances for learning. In turn, students who feel good about themselves reflect positive attitudes back to the community and act to enhance your credibility as a professional educator.

Personal Knowledge

Decisions you make as a teacher are filtered through your own values, beliefs, and understandings. You will have developed some of these as a consequence of your fundamental personal values. Others will be associated with some of your general personality characteristics. Still others will tie closely to the particular store of knowledge you have acquired.

Palmer (1998) places great emphasis on personal knowledge. He notes that we often ask the "what," "how," and "why" questions but seldom ask the "who" question. The most important question, he says, is "Who is the self that teaches?" It is imperative that we ask this most fundamental question about teachers and teaching. Palmer further emphasizes that good teachers possess a capacity for connectedness and weave a complex web among themselves, their subjects, and their students. Thus, in becoming a good teacher, it is essential to ask the "who" question.

What should you know about yourself as you consider your role as a teacher? One authority who has investigated this question suggests you should think about information related to the following three categories: pedagogical personality, pedagogical assumptions, and pedagogical repertoire (Millies, 1992).

Pedagogical Personality   *Pedagogical personality* is a term used to refer to your self-concept, confidence, and biases in terms of how these characteristics affect your interactions with students. To gain an appreciation of your pedagogical personality, ask yourself these questions:

- What do I believe about myself and my abilities as a teacher?
- What do I fear?
- What do I find fulfilling?
- What is my view of what a teacher "ought to be like"?

Pedagogical Assumptions   The phrase *pedagogical assumptions* refers to the basic values and beliefs that guide teachers' practices in the classroom. Questions that focus on this dimension include:

- What do I believe is the purpose of education?
- What do I believe about teaching?
- How do I feel about students from different social, economic, and ethnic groups?
- What learning principles are most important and should guide my instruction?

Answers to these questions will help explain how you organize for instruction and interact with students.

Pedagogical Repertoire   The term *pedagogical repertoire* refers to teachers' knowledge of and appreciation for alternative approaches to managing students and introducing content. Questions such as these provide insights into the nature of your own pedagogical repertoire:

- What are the best approaches to managing students in the classroom?
- What alternatives are available to me to teach this content?
- In which instructional approaches do I have the most confidence?
- What are some of my ideas for motivating members of this class?
- With which instructional techniques am I not comfortable?

Answering questions associated with pedagogical personality, assumptions, and repertoire can help you think through alternative approaches to teaching specific content to specific students. Thinking about possible responses challenges assumptions and encourages thought about choices you might make when several options seem to have promise. The hope is that, over time, this process will increase your understanding of yourself and provide the foundation for continual professional growth.

Professional Knowledge

In addition to personal knowledge, reflective teaching requires you to have professional knowledge related to basic principles of teaching and learning. Among the several sources of information about this kind of professional knowledge, you can consult the following:

- Experiences of successful teachers
- Learning theory
- Research-on-teaching studies

Experiences of Successful Teachers   You can sometimes learn about the experiences of successful teachers by consulting them directly. This kind of exchange may well take place during your student teaching, when you have the opportunity to work with one or more especially effective teachers. While you can learn much from the experiences of successful teachers, it is a mistake to rely only on professional judgment as you seek to broaden your knowledge of teaching. For example, some outstanding teachers have developed patterns gradually over the years that have become so embedded in their own personalities that they may be unable to tell you how they operate in the classroom. For example, if you were to ask, "Why did you do that?" they may just respond, "I can't really tell you; it just felt right."

Another obvious limitation on professional judgment as a source of information is that each person has a unique personality and style. Something that works splendidly for another teacher may be a disaster when you try it.

And sometimes professional judgment is just plain wrong. Behaviors that may seem right to a given individual and that may even have a lot of intuitive logic behind them may be undesirable. For example, common sense would seem to dictate that the more praise a teacher gives to a student, the better that student's academic performance will be. Researchers have found that this is not true. In fact, praise that is not tied clearly to a specific correct accomplishment with a given academic task may have little or no impact on students' learning (Good & Brophy, 2007).

In summary, you need to examine and reflect on the advice and practices of other teachers. Uncritical acceptance can lead to frustration and difficulties.

More from the Web

Developing Your Personal and Professional Knowledge Base

These websites provide you with some opportunities to add to your personal and professional knowledge base. On these sites, you will have the opportunity to interact with others, locate notices of professional development opportunities, and find sample lesson plans.

TEACHERS HELPING TEACHERS
http://www.pacificnet.net/~mandel
This website is regularly updated with new information. Among other things, you will find advice from experienced teachers for newcomers. Lesson plans are available. There are excellent links to other educational resources.

DISCOVERY SCHOOL
http://discoveryschool.com/schrockguide/
This excellent website features many links to resources for teachers, including links to tips for teaching individual subject areas, evaluation tools, special education resources, and upcoming professional development seminars.

Learning Theory   Learning theory is another source for information on teaching and learning. Individual learning theories explain relations among variables in the teaching-learning process.

Bigge and Shermis (1999) classify current learning theories into two broad families: the behaviorist family and the cognitive interactionist family. For the behaviorists, learning is defined as a change of observable behavior that occurs as a result of a relationship between stimuli and responses. A great emphasis is placed on making sure that desired responses are reinforced and wrong or undesired responses are ignored so that there is a strengthening of the bond between the stimuli and the desired responses. This increases the probability that the correct or proper responses will occur when the individual is confronted with stimuli.

Cognitive interactionists, on the other hand, view learning as a process of changing insights or thought processes. They see learning as taking place inside the student. They are more interested in helping students reorganize or change their perceptual or cognitive fields in order to gain insight.

It is obvious that your reflections will be guided by your learning theory. If you lean toward the behaviorist approach, you would be interested in the observable actions of the students. Your problem-solving will be directed toward understanding how to reinforce desirable responses and identifying and removing what might be reinforcing inappropriate responses. If you lean toward a cognitive interactionist approach, you will be more concerned with identifying how students view or understand the world and how to help them constantly reorganize this information in order to gain understanding.

Learning theory is not always as helpful as you might think. The theories themselves are grounded in a body of research and analysis that attempts to frame general principles consistent with this scholarly work. However, when dealing with the rapid pace of the classroom filled with unpredictable human beings, it is not always clear which principles apply. Bigge and Shermis (1999) outline three choices that teachers might make:

1. A teacher might try to adhere to one systematic theory as much as possible.

2. A teacher might borrow ideas from different theories and fit them together into a mosaic that can be drawn upon when needed.

3. A teacher might develop his or her own new or synthesized theory by selecting and modifying ideas from other theories.

Not only are your reflections guided by your learning theory, your reflections result in reinforcing or changing your personal learning theory.

Research-on-Teaching Studies   Individual research studies represent another source of information about teaching. There has been an enormous increase in research focused on classroom instruction over the past couple of decades. Organizations such as the American Educational Research Association publish reviews of research in specific areas. One journal that summarizes research on topics of interest to teachers in each issue is the *Review of Educational Research*. It is available in most university libraries and some public libraries, too.

Research rarely speaks with a united voice on a given issue. It is not uncommon for several studies of the same question to come up with quite different results. You need to be especially wary when someone prefaces a defense of a particular instructional practice with the phrase *Research proves*. Research rarely proves just one thing. It is important to know how much research has been done, and the general trend of the findings. (Generally, a trend is all you can hope to find. All studies of a given question almost never yield common results.)

In spite of frustrations you may encounter as you try to find consistent patterns of findings, we highly recommend that you become familiar with professional research literature. This research can be very helpful to you as you reflect on your teaching and can help guide your reflections toward useful solutions for instructional problems.

To give you some sense of trends uncovered by specialists who conduct research on teaching, we have selected some findings that can provide you with information that can be useful when you reflect on your instructional decisions. Information in this section has been divided into these five categories:

- Beliefs about students
- Stimulating student interest
- Using student contributions
- Making wise use of time
- Presenting good lessons

Beliefs about students   The most important variable teachers work with is student characteristics. It makes no sense for you to plan instruction without good information about the backgrounds, abilities, interests, and general behavior patterns of your students. Decisions you make in response to this information will greatly influence the overall impact of your instruction.

Teachers' expectations of individual students are strongly tied to their beliefs about what students can do (Good & Brophy, 2007). These findings suggest that students for whom you hold high expectations will achieve more than students for whom you have lower expectations.

Teachers' expectations result from their analyses of several key variables, including student appearance, intelligence and achievement test scores, and behavior patterns. Some evidence suggests that some teachers even form opinions about how an individual student will perform based on how their older brothers and sisters did in school. If you are not aware of these perceptions and their limitations, you may find yourself interacting with some class members in ways that do not support their maximum personal and intellectual development. Braun (1987) described a cycle of behavior that some teachers develop as a result of their beliefs about what individual students can do:

1. The teacher establishes a level of expectation for a student based on what he or she believes to be true of this individual.
2. Student behaviors are interpreted in light of this expectation.
3. As a result of how the teacher reacts, the student begins to develop a self-concept that is consistent with the teacher's beliefs.
4. As a result, the student's performance begins to reflect the teacher's expectation. This means students for whom the teacher has higher expectations do well, and students for whom the teacher has lower expectations do poorly.

How should you deal with the possibility that your perceptions of individual students may affect how you interact with them? There is no easy answer. It is human nature to make inferences about others. However, self-monitoring efforts can help you check on the accuracy of the inferences you are making and ensure that you are not prompting irresponsible patterns of behavior. Periodic efforts to take stock are often helpful. As part of ongoing reflection, you need to think seriously about any biases you might have that are resulting in unproductive patterns of working with certain individuals.

Stimulating student interest   Disinterested students tend to misbehave and disrupt the learning of others. The key to prompting student interest is to plan learning experiences that connect students' past experiences and views to what is important in the school curriculum. This implies a need to know your students well. You also must know your subject matter well enough so you can adapt and explain it to students in an understandable way (Reynolds, 1992).

What Do You Think?

Have a Teacher's Expectations Ever Influenced You?

Without realizing they are doing so, teachers sometimes communicate to some students that they have little confidence in their abilities. At the same time, they may communicate to others in the class that they expect great academic work from them. Reflect on some of your own experiences as a secondary school student as you respond to the following questions.

Questions

1. Can you recall times when a teacher's actions prompted you to do more? To do less? What happened in each case?

2. Do you recall any students who could have done better work but were turned off by what they perceived to be lack of teacher confidence in their abilities?

3. If you remember times when teachers seemed to have preconceived notions about what individuals could do, how do you think their impressions affected these students' abilities?

It is important to remember that planning for motivation does not occur only at a lesson's beginning. You need to plan for motivation during three distinct phases of a lesson: (1) at the beginning, (2) during lesson development, and (3) at the conclusion of the lesson.

Motivation often occurs when students' curiosity is aroused. Frequently this happens when they are introduced to something unique or novel (at least unique or novel to them). Sometimes students react positively to information regarding the personal importance of mastering the content that is about to be introduced. Variety during the lesson also tends to prompt continued student interest. The same can be said about encouragement. It is especially important for you to take time at the end of a lesson to highlight what students have learned.

Students' confidence grows as they realize they have encountered and understood substantial amounts of new material. Feelings of success and accomplishment build students' levels of self-esteem. As a result, they become more highly motivated to study material introduced in subsequent lessons. Additional information related to motivation is introduced in Chapter 9.

Using student contributions   How should you use student contributions? No answer to this question fits every occasion. The key principle is that your reaction to students' contributions should encourage their continued participation; provide them with appropriate feedback; and, at the same time, ensure that you do not lose the central focus of the lesson.

When should you challenge students' ideas? In general, if a challenge to an idea will cause the students to do more thinking about the issue and develop more sophisticated reasoning skills, the challenge may make sense. However, if students are likely to see your challenge as a put-down, little good will come of it. This is a good time to consider another approach. When you decide challenge is appropriate, you want to deliver it in a tone that implies, "I may disagree with what you have said, but I still think highly of you as a person."

Making wise use of time   Time available for instruction is limited. As a result, you need to use it wisely. Researchers have identified what is called opportunity to learn as one of the most significant variables that accounts for student achievement (Freiberg & Driscoll, 2000). Opportunity to learn refers to the amount of time available to students to learn the content. Not surprisingly, when students have more time to learn the content (more opportunity to learn), they experience higher achievement. Unless you plan carefully, administrative tasks such as roll-taking, distributing and collecting materials, and making announcements can significantly reduce the opportunity to learn. Carefully planning administrative tasks so that you spend only a few minutes each day on them will provide you with many additional hours of instructional time over the academic year. As you consider time management issues, think about three types of time that can help you keep students on task and increase opportunity to learn: allocated time, student engaged time, and academic learning time.

The first, allocated time, is the amount of time you set aside for students to learn specific material. Researchers have found that different teachers allocate very different quantities of time for teaching the same content (Good & Brophy, 2007). Why is this so? In part, this situation arises because of class-to-class differences in students. Another determinant seems to be the teachers' varying levels of personal interest in and feelings of competence with the topic being taught. Teachers tend to allocate more instructional time to topics they like and about which they believe themselves to be particularly well informed. For example, some English teachers who really enjoy teaching literature allocate much more time to teaching literature than to teaching writing. Consider the long-term implications for students who need to master skills in both areas.

To make proper time allocation decisions, you also need to consider the relative importance of each topic as it relates to the major aims of the course. You need to provide sufficient time for students to learn material associated with each topic, but not so much time that they become bored. Just because you allocate a given amount of time for students to work on an assigned task does not guarantee that they will do so.

A second type of time, student engaged time, refers to the portion of allocated time that the students are actually engaged in studying the assigned material. Researchers have observed great classroom-to-classroom differences in the amount of engaged time (Good & Brophy, 2007). Student engaged time is a better indicator of opportunity to learn because it is the time the students are actually interacting with the content. In general, your intent should be to increase the total amount of student engaged time.

A third type of time, academic learning time, is the portion of student engaged time when the students are not only interacting with the material but are also experiencing success. Sometimes even though students are engaged in studying material, they are not experiencing success. Thus, they are not really learning. Our goal then is to maximize academic learning time. One place to begin is to make sure you know your students well. This allows you to match your assignments to the prior knowledge of the students, their interests, and their abilities. You will also need to monitor student progress carefully so that you can quickly step in and help them when they begin to experience difficulty. Then you need to be ready to reteach the lesson or parts of the lesson to help students achieve success.

Presenting good lessons Good planning is a basic characteristic of successful secondary school teachers. Well-planned lessons feature the following:

- Clarity
- Feedback to students
- Good modeling

Clarity Clarity requires a clear and precise use of language and a presentation style that moves logically and smoothly from point to point. There are many threats to clarity. For example, your students may be confused if you use vague and ambiguous terms or if you use vocabulary that is unfamiliar to them. One of the problems you will encounter in teaching secondary school is that specific subjects have content-specific vocabulary that has special meaning. New teachers often assume that students understand these terms. When they do not, confusion and frustration result.

Internal summaries also enhance clarity of lesson presentation. These are stopping points during a lesson when you pause to review with students what you have already covered. These summaries help students focus on key points and see interrelationships among important ideas.

Clarity is improved when your lessons feature a well-organized conclusion. A good conclusion summarizes what you have covered and draws students' attention to important ideas. You will want to repeat key content ideas during this phase of a lesson to help your students retain the new material.

Feedback to Students   Feedback to students involves specific actions you take to communicate information to students about the appropriateness or correctness of their responses. This information helps your students avoid errors and to focus on important dimensions of content.

Praise is often used as part of feedback. Researchers have found that, to be effective, praise should be specific and genuine. It should also be used in moderation (Good & Brophy 2007). The term *specificity*, as applied to appropriate use of praise, means that you need to tell your students what they have done that you have found praiseworthy. The praiseworthy behavior you cite should relate to content you are teaching. If you give general praise that has no clear connection to a desirable academics-related behavior, this action will have little impact on student performance.

Criticism also has its place when you provide feedback to students. Proper criticism focuses on helping a student resolve an academic difficulty. It is designed not simply to indicate student errors, but rather to suggest appropriate ways of correcting mistakes. Good criticism never demeans students as people. It focuses on enhancing their self-esteem by helping them master content.

Modeling   Providing a model for learners during a lesson improves student performance. For example, your personal enthusiasm for a topic often is catching and most likely will increase levels of student interest. Students also benefit when you model thinking processes that are appropriate for a particular task. For example, you might solve a problem similar to ones your students will be asked to solve by thinking out loud with members of the class. ("Now if I found myself faced with this situation, the first thing I would look at would be. . . . Next, I would compare _____ and _____. If they seemed consistent, I probably would decide to. . . .)

You might find it useful sometimes to develop an example of a product of learning similar to what you expect to receive from students. For example, if you want your students to write a short paper comparing and contrasting positions of two individuals, you might prepare a sample of such a paper. When making your assignment to the students, you can share this material, drawing their attention to various features you hope to see in the papers they will be preparing. An example of this kind greatly reduces the possibility that your students will fail to understand your expectations.

Making Fluid Plans

Armed with thoughtful information carefully gathered about the context and your personal and professional knowledge, you will be ready to make fluid plans. Classrooms are unpredictable environments with a rapid flow of events that that often require immediate actions (Doyle, 2006). Secondary school classrooms can be especially unpredictable because you are working with adolescents who often exhibit unpredictable behavior and who often have a knack for getting teachers off track!

Because of these factors, it is difficult to plan for everything that might happen in a classroom. However, this does not mean that planning is unimportant. In fact, planning is probably more important in unpredictable environments. Good, thoughtful planning helps you think through alternatives and allows you to anticipate potential issues. Then, when the unpredictable occurs, you will be better equipped to deal with the event without losing the focus of the lesson. The skill in developing fluid plans is planning in a way that provides you with knowledge that will allow you to get in front of the classroom with confidence, but not planning lessons that are so rigid that unexpected events will totally disrupt the flow of the lesson and the opportunity to accomplish the objective. This is what is called fluid planning.

For example, one of us was observing a student teacher when an announcement was made of an incident that had just occurred in the community. Rather than taking advantage of the event to capture a "teachable moment," the student teacher tried to calm the students so she could continue with the planned lesson.

Fluid plans are those that clearly focus on the objectives and the important outcomes of the lesson. They lay out a logical sequence for reaching the objectives, identify the needed materials, and include opportunities to check the understanding of the students as they proceed through the lesson. However, fluid plans are not inflexible scripts to follow so that the unpredictable event causes the teacher to lose focus. The key to fluid planning is that of keeping the objective of the lesson clearly in mind. Then, when an unpredictable event happens, that event can be evaluated in terms of how it relates to the objective of the lesson. If there is a clear relationship, it can be used to move the class forward. If it is clearly off the topic and does not relate to the objective, then refocusing student attention on the objective and moving forward is the proper course of action.

Inflexible plans function as guides you will use to begin your lessons and that you may modify, as needed, as the classroom interaction takes place. Perhaps an analogy of fluid planning is that of taking a trip. As you are preparing to take a trip you may consult a map to identify the most efficient route to your destination. However, it is also useful to look for alternative routes. Then as you start on the trip, if something unexpected happens, such as an accident or road work, you can consider an alternative route that will help you get around the problem and reach your destination.

As a flexible planner, your teaching is adaptive. You are not limited by just one pathway to the objective. You have given some thought to alternatives and have considered the possibility of unanticipated events and know where your lesson might be changed to accommodate these occurrences. One teacher that was good at flexible planning once stated, "No matter what happens, you don't get upset, you evaluate the potential uses of the event, and you use that as a part of the lesson."

It may well be that your plans unfold just as you anticipated and the lesson flows smoothly from beginning to end. But fluid planning prevents you from getting so locked into one pathway and helps you avoid becoming frustrated if things do not go the way you had anticipated.

One of the most important steps in fluid planning is identifying the objectives for the lesson. When identifying objectives, you need to focus on what you expect the students to know or be able to do as a result of the lesson. Remember the focus is on what the students should be able to do, not on methods they will use to accomplish that objective. For example, a good objective might indicate that the students in the class know relationships in a mathematical equation or why a given chemical reaction occurs rather than "read the chapter," "solve problems," or "conduct an experiment." These are activities to help them achieve the objective, not outcomes themselves. Then, if something occurs, such as textbooks missing or lab equipment that doesn't work, you can still consider alternative routes to help them attain the objective.

Once the objectives are defined, you need think through a logical sequence to move students toward the objective. At critical spots in the sequence, identify places where you can check to make sure the students understand what they have been presented. Flexible planners then consider alternative steps to take if students are having difficulty. What might be alternative examples that will make the content more concrete? Will you need to go back and teach some prerequisite knowledge that students might be missing? This is where teacher problem-solving and reflection is important. Just trying to stubbornly move ahead when students are not learning will only lead to frustration and anger.

In addition, flexible planners need to consider alternatives if some or all of the students quickly attain the objective. This alternative should include enrichment or extension activities that can engage the students in application or enrichment activities. For example, one of us planned a lesson that we thought would be compelling. The lesson began with a question that was designed to provoke student inquiry. It happened that a student in the class had completed a project for another class on that same topic and responded to the question with most of what was to be discussed in the lesson! In essence, the lesson was over, at least for this student and a few others in the first 10 minutes of class. Because the teacher had planned additional activities in case this happened, he was able to move on with the lesson. This example highlights the importance of planning alternatives that can be used to help knowledgeable students apply or extend their understanding.

In summary, fluid planning is applying reflection to the planning process. It means that the planning process involves more than merely putting a plan down on a lesson plan form. It requires anticipation of places where difficulty might arise and reflection on how the plan can be altered if things do not go as planned.

Formal and Informal Professional Growth Opportunities

Your preparation for teaching does not end when you are awarded an initial teaching certificate or license. You will need to continue to develop your personal and professional knowledge throughout your career. You can do this best by pursuing activities that will help you learn what you need to know. Your specific actions will vary depending on your own diagnosis of your personal professional needs. For example, if you need additional knowledge in your content area, you might decide to take additional courses in your subject. If you need to develop a better understanding of your community, then you might consider one or more informal approaches to gaining this information. For example, you might think about volunteering for some community events or taking other actions that will bring you into closer contact with local people, organizations, and neighborhoods.

The Professional-Development Portfolio

By definition, reflective teaching demands reflection. As a means of organizing information to consider as you engage in serious thought about teaching and learning, you may find a professional-development portfolio useful. This kind of a portfolio often includes ideas and thoughts about information or instructional techniques you would like to include in your lessons. You may also want to include materials you actually use in lessons, along with your thoughts about how effective individual lessons were and what you might have learned that will improve your teaching of subsequent lessons. Keeping a professional-development portfolio can be an important aid to your development as a teacher.

Professional-development portfolios can be formatted in a variety of ways. Often, they include (1) information or materials that prompt you to reflect, and (2) written summaries of your reflections.

Individual teachers vary in terms of specific items they put in professional-development portfolios to prompt reflection. After considering your options, you might decide to include the following types of entries:

- Descriptions of procedures for implementing new instructional techniques
- Explanations of special features of your teaching context (nature of the students, noise levels in your classroom, adequacy of learning materials, and so forth)

- Copies of lesson plans you have developed
- General information from a variety of sources that you think might facilitate your development as an effective teacher
- Comments of any observers who may have seen you teach
- Examples of student work

Written summaries of your reflection may take different forms. You might decide to frame your written reactions as answers to questions you might pose, such as:

- How might I actually incorporate some new instructional techniques into my lessons, and what is my rationale for wanting to do so?
- To what extent have context variables helped and hindered the effectiveness of my lessons, and how might I change what I have been doing in light of this information?
- Do lesson plans I have used really emphasize what I want to highlight with my students, and is the presented information optimally organized and sequenced to facilitate learning of all of my students? What specific changes do I want to make when teaching these lessons again?
- How can I move from a knowledge-level understanding of new information I have learned about effective teaching to making this information part of my active teaching repertoire?
- How congruent are comments noted by people who have observed my teaching with my own perceptions about how I have been performing? What thoughts do I have about changing what I have been doing as a result of thinking about their observations and suggestions?
- How pleased am I with the quality of work I am getting from students? What can I do to increase the numbers of students who are achieving high levels of academic success and deriving personal satisfaction from their involvement in my lessons?

Using questions to prompt written summaries of your reflections or using a different approach to recording your thoughts is a matter of personal preference. The critical point is that a professional-development portfolio must include some record of your own reflections about the basic information that is included. Otherwise, preparation of the portfolio amounts to little more than construction of a scrapbook. To have real value as an aid to your professional development, you need to engage the content, mull it over carefully, and give written expression to your reflections. It is the intellectual engagement, not the simple gathering together of included materials, which makes professional-development portfolios credible vehicles for developing teachers' expertise.

You may wish to start a professional-development proposal as you work through this text. At the end of chapters in this text, you will find a For Your Portfolio exercise. This provides you with an opportunity to put information you have learned into a professional-development portfolio. Once you have started a portfolio, you need to review it regularly. You might ask yourself some general questions as you conduct these periodic status checks, such as:

- Does my portfolio reveal that I have been actively engaged in seeking answers for questions and in growing professionally?
- Have I been persistent in seeking knowledge and in finding ways to respond to the challenges of teaching?
- Have I been thoughtful and careful in drawing my conclusions, and have I considered the moral and ethical dimensions of my actions?
- Have I adequately considered the impact of my ideas on my students?

FOR YOUR PORTFOLIO

This is a good time to begin assembling your personal portfolio. This portfolio will be useful to you in establishing a foundation for reflection, providing information about your growth, and providing evidence of your knowledge.

One of the first steps in developing a portfolio is to establish an organizational framework. One we suggest is to establish your portfolio using the Interstate New Teacher Assessment and Support Consortium (INTASC) standards. (There are others that have been developed by individual states. You may want to choose one appropriate for the state where you plan to teach.) There are 10 INTASC standards, so you can begin by establishing 10 sections for your portfolio. In each section, you should provide some material related to each standard as well as your personal reflections about the material you have included.

The content of this chapter relates specifically to INTASC standard nine (A professional educator is someone who is a reflective practitioner). Select two to three items that you will include in your portfolio related to the content of this chapter. You might consider entries that focus on areas such as your pedagogical personality, your pedagogical repertoire, or your personal learning theory.

1. How does this information relate to your ability to reflect and self-evaluate?

2. Write a reflection stating why you chose each entry and what you think it indicates about your ability to be a reflective practitioner.

- Are criteria I have been using to judge my success as a teacher worthwhile and important?

- Does my portfolio reflect changes I have made as I have learned new things about my students, my teaching context, and my subject?

Professional-growth portfolios can provide you with a basis for understanding yourself and for promoting your professional development. You may find yourself looking back at sections of your portfolio completed early in the academic year and observing with real satisfaction some of the changes you have made in working with your students. Portfolio-based documentation of your increasing expertise as a teacher can be a tremendous confidence-builder. A record of past successes will function as an excellent motivator as you begin thinking about ways to become more effective in areas that you believe still need work.

Key Ideas in Summary

- Reflective teaching is an orientation to instruction that will call on you to reflect thoughtfully on the conditions at hand and to vary your teaching responses to serve the needs of students best. Eby (1998) points out that the reflective teacher needs to be active, persistent, and careful, and to consider available evidence while engaging in reflection. The foundations of reflective teaching are found in constructivism, the idea that knowledge does not exist in any abstract sense but that it is "constructed" by individuals as they interact with and attempt to make sense of their environment.

- Reflective teaching involves (1) a sensitivity to content, (2) a willingness to be informed by personal and professional knowledge, (3) an understanding that good instruction is best guided by fluid planning (planning that quickly adjusts to changing circumstances in the classroom), and (4) a commitment to career-long informal and formal professional development.

- Your decisions as a teacher will be influenced strongly by your own personality, biases, and general worldview. This means that you need to develop an awareness of your own personal perspectives. Such awareness will help you avoid making decisions that are too strongly tied to your biases—decisions that, in some cases, may not be best for your students.

■ Researchers have found an important connection between teachers' expectations of students and students' levels of performance. In general, your students will do better when you hold high expectations for them.

■ When you teach, you may find yourself gathering information for decision-making from many sources. Personal experiences of other teachers may provide some useful information. Because of differences in individual teacher personalities, students to be served, and other variables, however, these experiences may not be wholly useful to you. Learning theory offers some guidance. Principles derived from learning theory may not be applicable, however, in every instructional situation. Individual research studies also provide some useful information. Again, studies may yield insights that may not be applicable to the special features of your own teaching setting.

■ Relating the school curriculum to students' needs and interests enhances their levels of interest. Ideally, motivational activities should occur during three distinct phases of a given lesson: the beginning, as new information is presented, and at the end. Researchers have found that using student ideas during a lesson helps to maintain student interest and involvement. You should react to students in ways that (1) encourage their continued participation, (2) provide them with appropriate feedback, and (3) help them maintain a focus on the central content of the lesson.

■ Effective teachers manage time wisely. It is particularly important to maximize the amount of classroom time actually devoted to instruction. This is referred to as opportunity to learn. As students are provided with more time, or more opportunity to learn, achievement increases. Researchers who have looked at the issue of teachers' use of time have identified three important time concepts. Allocated time refers to time set aside for instruction. Engaged time refers to the time students are actually working on an assigned task. Student success rate is the actual time that students are working on a task with success.

■ Good lessons do not happen by accident. They tend to feature recurring patterns of effective teacher behavior, including (1) efforts to ensure clarity of communication, (2) attempts to enhance student achievement through provision of appropriate feedback, and (3) modeling.

■ Understanding your teaching context requires you to gather information about your students, the culture of your school, and the nature of your community. Information about these dimensions can help you reflect on the opportunities and challenges you face in the classroom and assist you as you seek to design more successful lessons.

■ Continued professional growth is a characteristic of successful teachers. This professional growth is best enhanced when you actively pursue formal and informal professional development opportunities.

Reflections

1. Do you consider yourself a reflective person? How do you think your answer will influence your teaching?

2. What personal knowledge do you have about yourself that you think is related to your potential success as a teacher?

3. How would you describe your pedagogical personality?

4. What is your theory about teaching and learning? What are the roots of this theory?

5. What are some research findings on teaching that you find especially useful? Why?

Learning Extensions

1. Several books have been written relating teachers' classroom experiences. Read several teachers' accounts from one of these sources. As you read these accounts of classroom teachers, consider how they address the context, the personal and professional knowledge base, fluid planning, and professional growth. Prepare a report on your reading to share with your class.

2. Much is being published today about reflective teaching. Read four or five journal articles that focus on this subject. Summarize your findings in a short paper. Include comments comparing and contrasting information from these articles to information about reflective teaching introduced in this chapter.

3. Do an informal needs-assessment of your personal and professional knowledge. Identify what you want to know about yourself and what you want to know about teaching and learning. Use this assessment to guide you as you proceed through this book and your teacher preparation program.

4. Teach a lesson to other members of your class and arrange to have someone record your presentation. Review the recording privately and identify aspects of your lesson that you think could have been done better. Prepare a written summary explaining precisely what you would do to improve your overall presentation.

5. Spend some time as an observer in a secondary school. Try to identify and characterize the elements of the school culture. How does this culture seem to influence both teachers and students?

References

Barth, R. (2001). *Learning by heart*. San Francisco, Jossey-Bass.

Bigge, M., & Shermis, S. (1999). *Learning theories for teachers* (6th ed.). New York: Longman.

Borich, G. D. (2008). *Observation skills for effective teaching* (5th ed.). Upper Saddle River, NJ: Pearson/Merrill Prentice Hall.

Braun, C. (1987). Teachers' expectations. In M. Dunkin (Ed.), *The international encyclopedia of teaching and teacher education* (pp. 598–605). New York: Pergamon Press.

Dewey, J. (1933). *How we think* (rev. ed.). Lexington, MA: D.C. Heath.

Doyle, W. (2006). Ecological approaches to classroom management. In C. Evertson and C. Weinstein (Eds.), *Handbook of classroom management* (pp. 97–126). Mahwah, NJ: Lawrence Erlbaum Associates, Inc.

Eby, J. W. (1998). *Reflective planning, teaching and evaluation K–12* (2nd ed.). Columbus, OH: Merrill/Prentice Hall.

Freiberg, H., & Driscoll, A. (2000). *Universal teaching strategies* (3rd ed.). Boston: Allyn and Bacon.

Fullan, M., & Hargreaves, A. (1996). *What's worth fighting for in your school?* New York: Teachers College Press.

Goethals, M., Howard, R., & Sanders, M. (2004). *Student teaching: A process approach to reflective practice* (2nd ed.). Upper Saddle River, NJ: Merrill/Prentice Hall.

Good, T., & Brophy, J. (2007). *Looking in classrooms* (10th ed.). Boston: Allyn and Bacon.

Henderson, J. C. (1996). *Reflective teaching: The study of your constructivist practices* (2nd ed.). Columbus, OH: Merrill.

Marzano, R. (2003). *What works in schools: Translating research into action*. Alexandria, VA.: Association for Supervision and Curriculum Development.

Millies, P (1992). The relationship between a teacher's life and teaching. In W. Schubert & W. Ayers (Eds.), *Teacher lore: Learning from our own experience* (pp. 25–42). New York: Longman.

Palmer, P. (1998). *The courage to teach: Exploring the inner landscape of a teacher's life.* San Francisco: Jossey-Bass.

Reynolds, A. (1992). What is competent teaching? *Review of Educational Research, 62*(1), 1–35.

Rogers, C., & Freiberg, H. J. (1994). *Freedom to learn* (3rd ed.). Upper Saddle River, NJ: Merrill/Prentice Hall.

Zahorik, J. A. (1995). *Constructivist teaching (Fastback 390).* Bloomington, IN: Phi Delta Kappa Educational Foundation.

Preparing for Teaching

PART II

Dennis McDonald/PhotoEdit ($$)

What Should Students Learn? Defining the Curriculum

Objectives

This chapter will help you

■ describe some issues you need to consider when selecting content to introduce to students

■ explain how political influences, standards, frameworks, textbooks, availability of support materials, and teacher background influence your content selection decisions

■ state how the structure of knowledge can help you decide what content to include and exclude in your instructional programs

■ define goals and instructional objectives

■ describe the cognitive, affective and psychomotor domains of learning

Mac H. Brown/Merril

Graphic Organizer: Chapter 5

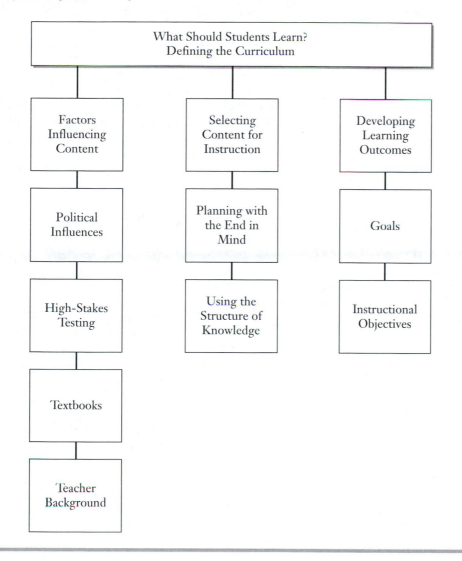

Introduction

In the past, few new teachers gave much thought to the content that they were to teach. Generally, it was expected that new secondary-level teachers had some basic content knowledge about the subject they were teaching as a result of their higher education preparation. Then, new teachers were generally handed a textbook for the year and informed that this was the content they were to cover. In some school districts, a curriculum guide of some sort was available to provide them with a little more guidance.

However, there are some difficulties with these assumptions. For example, it has been noted that a significant percentage of secondary school teachers in some subjects, most notably science, do not have a major in the subject they are teaching. This has been a major concern of some of those individuals advocating reform in secondary education. A number of efforts have been made to make sure that teachers have subject-matter background in the subjects they are teaching. This concern was directly addressed in the No Child Left Behind (NCLB) legislation.

"Qualified" teachers were defined as those with a major in the subject they were teaching or individuals who had passed a rigorous subject-matter examination. As a result many states developed subject-matter examinations that individuals are required to pass before they can obtain a teaching credential. Other efforts have attempted to attract individuals with degrees, often from business and industry, in high-need areas to secondary school teaching.

Using the textbook as the definitive guide for content is somewhat more complicated. Several states, notably Texas and California, have established committees that set content standards for the textbooks to be adopted for use in their respective state. Generally these committees are not selected for their knowledge of the subject area. They may be elected, or they may be political appointees that are subject to political pressures. Because states like Texas and California purchase large numbers of textbooks, publishing companies pay special attention to the standards of these states. Other states may then end up with textbooks that are inconsistent with their values and standards. Therefore, the assumption that primary and secondary school textbooks are written by experts and reflect the best knowledge in the field simply doesn't stand up to scrutiny.

To compensate for some of the deficiencies of a single textbook, some school districts are supplementing traditional printed textbooks with material found online or in computer programs. This practice also raises questions. How does a teacher choose material online that is accurate, up to date, and appropriate for students? A teacher must exercise caution about what is brought into the classroom.

Another issue relates to the relevance of the content for students. It takes time to write and produce a textbook. Because the time between state-level textbook adoptions may be several years, the content of an average textbook may be several years old by the time it is read by students. Because of this time lag, Jacobs (2010) wonders if students feel like they are "time traveling" when they enter the classroom and leave the 21st century and encounter a curriculum based on the past rather than the present.

Finally, content selection needs to take into account state content standards. Currently there is a strong emphasis on holding teachers accountable for student learning. States have developed content standards for many subjects and have developed tests that are used as indicators of student learning. How well students do on these tests is used to evaluate the effectiveness of schools and teachers. Teachers who ignore these content standards when choosing the content of their instruction may find themselves receiving poor evaluations. Because of the importance of these state standards and the accountability process, those being interviewed for a teaching position are often asked about their knowledge of the state standards in the subject they teach.

Keeping these issues in mind, every teacher must address several basic questions regarding the content of the curriculum, including:

- How does my subject contribute to the education of future citizens?
- What is important content in my subject that students need to learn?
- What content is mandated by state standards?
- What content will most likely help students score well on high-stakes tests?
- How does the content relate to student needs and interests?

These are important questions with serious political and social implications. This chapter addresses the important issue of what is taught in the secondary school curriculum and provides you with some guidance in making these important decisions.

Factors Influencing Curriculum Content

The history of education is filled with disagreements about the content of the curriculum. The fact is that education has multiple goals and there is a lack of consensus on the relative importance of these different educational goals. Some individuals and groups have argued that the content is not rigorous enough or that it is not preparing students for the future. Some have complained that too much emphasis is placed on subjects preparing students for higher education and not enough emphasis on preparing them for the world of work. Another group contends that the purpose of education is to develop the unique talents of each student, and therefore the curriculum should be flexible in helping them identify and pursue their own interests. While some individuals warn of the political and social dangers of allowing politicians to determine what is taught, politicians argue that what students learn is too important to be left to states, local communities, or individual teachers. For example, the National Governors Association, in their reform proposal *Accelerating the Agenda,* states that it is the responsibility of the state to determine the curriculum and the responsibility of the teacher to teach it!

Disagreements about the curriculum have been contentious enough to be labeled "culture wars." Various groups want to make sure their values and perspectives are taught to the youth. Business leaders want to make sure that students are prepared to enter the world of work with the skill set they desire. Politicians are concerned that students have content preparation that will allow them to compete with students around the globe. The current push is to have a set of national standards that will be taught in every state and in every classroom and measured by the same tests. In summary, the curriculum of secondary schools has become a political issue that has the potential not only to change what is taught in schools, but also to fundamentally change society.

As indicated in the beginning of this chapter, there are several influences on the curriculum. These influences must be taken into account when you make decisions about what you will teach in your classroom.

Political Influences

Across the nation the battles rage. We have the history wars, the math wars, and the science wars. These are battles over the content of the curriculum. Not too long ago, discussions concerning the content of the curriculum seldom made it out of state- and district-level curriculum committees. Times have changed, however, and the content of the school curriculum regularly makes the news. For example, in 2010, there was much national publicity about the history and social studies curriculum standards in Texas, where curriculum content related to figures such as Thomas Jefferson and Cesar Chavez was deemphasized and content related to more conservative figures such as Newt Gingrich and Phyllis Schafly was increased.

Sometimes the debate over the content of the curriculum has even become part of political platforms. For example, the debate over history standards developed by a national panel reached such a peak during the presidential campaign of 1996 that Robert Dole, the Republican presidential candidate, declared that those who developed the new history standards were worse than the external enemies of the nation (Wineburg, 2001)!

Some argue there should be less emphasis on literature and creative writing in the English curriculum and more emphasis on "practical" documents. Others argue that there is too much emphasis on multicultural themes, while the historic emphasis on the classics of western literature is being ignored. High-level and often acrimonious debates over the science curriculum are taking place in many states as they respond to calls to include "intelligent design" as an alternative theory to evolution. The situation is no different in the mathematics area as groups battle over whether the emphasis should be on problem-solving and mathematical reasoning or on traditional computation and basic skills. In California, the recommendations of teachers and educators regarding the math curriculum were rejected by the state board of education in favor of programs supported by politicians (Jacob, 2001).

There is no doubt about it: The school curriculum has become a hot political issue and there are serious political influences on what is included in the curriculum. Allowing politicians to define what is taught in the schools has some potential dangers. As a teacher, you need to have a solid understanding of your subject so that you can clearly evaluate efforts to change the curriculum in order to further a particular political view.

Standards and Frameworks

In response to pressure from legislation such as No Child Left Behind, most states have now adopted specific content standards that specify the content to be included in the curriculum of secondary school courses. Some local school districts have developed similar requirements and curriculum documents outlining the district response to the state standards.

Similarly, national standards have been developed by various professional groups. Some organizations such as the National Council of Teachers of Mathematics (NCTM) have developed comprehensive standards for their content area. As the Obama administration seeks to shape educational policy at the national level, there is an increased call for national standards rather than state standards. The argument is that the states have been too lax and have not developed rigorous standards that will keep students competitive with the rest of the world.

It is important that you know the content standards in the state where you will teach. These state content standards are legally binding. You are expected to make sure that all students have the opportunity to learn these standards; ignoring them can have legal consequences. To view state content standards for your state, visit the following website: http://www.aligntoachieve.org. This site provides links to all state content standards documents. Alternately, you might also visit the website maintained by your state department of education.

High-Stakes Testing

Results of standardized tests are now regularly reported in local news media and are used as indicators of school quality. Many of these standardized tests are what have been termed high-stakes tests. In other words, they are tests to which important decisions, such as promotion, retention, teacher evaluation, or even the availability of resources, are attached. Schools and teachers whose students score poorly on these tests may come under public criticism or even face the loss of students and money. As a result, administrators in your school district or building may urge you to think about types of information assessed on standardized tests as you make decisions about which content to emphasize.

Popham (2001) contends that this emphasis on high-stakes testing is doing serious educational damage to students. He claims that the high-stakes testing has resulted in a curricular reductionism that has eroded a rich curriculum and is robbing students of important things they should be learning. He concludes that this has led to a distortion of the intellectual fabric of the curriculum and restricts not only the content of the curriculum but also the cognitive operations of the students. When the curriculum is determined by what is tested, the decisions about the curriculum are left to those invisible and unknown individuals who write the tests (Armstrong, 2003). In addition, the tendency is to emphasize content that can be easily measured rather than content that is most important.

Textbook Selection

Teachers have long based curricula decisions on the content included in textbooks. The assumption is that the people writing textbooks and preparing curriculum guides are

CRITICAL INCIDENT

TEACHING TO THE TEST

On a Monday afternoon, Betty Lewis waited with her math colleagues in the faculty lounge for a mathematics department meeting with Ms. Walker, the high school principal. The principal called this special meeting on short notice, and there had been a good deal of talk all day about the agenda.

When a grim-faced Ms. Walker entered the room, it became obvious that she was in no mood for pleasantries. She got right down to business:

"We just received our standardized test scores from the state for the mathematics test our students took in the spring. Our school's average score is down six points from last year. To make it worse, average scores in the other high schools in the district went up. The superintendent was blunt. He said the scores were an embarrassment to the district, and that members of the school board want to know what is wrong with our math department.

The superintendent let me know in no uncertain terms that he expects some immediate action to be taken. In response to his request, I am going to require that each of you teaching students who will be taking the test this year spend a minimum of 15 minutes in each class period drilling students on material likely to appear on the test. I have files of tests from previous years in my office. I want you to study them carefully and identify sample test items you can use to help your students practice for the test they will take in the spring. I will expect a weekly report from each teacher identifying precisely what has been done in every period to focus students' attention on content likely to be included on the standardized test."

Betty Lewis and the other teachers were stunned when they heard this announcement. One veteran teacher looked at Ms. Walker and commented, "Don't you think this policy is a somewhat drastic reaction to a one-year dip in our students' scores? Besides, if we do what you're asking, how will we teach the required course content?"

Another teacher said, "What about our academic freedom? As certified professionals, isn't it our responsibility to teach students what we consider to be important?"

Still another teacher protested, "I question the ethics of taking items from past tests and teaching the students to respond to them correctly. This is 'teaching to the test,' not teaching students how to understand the subject matter. It seems to me this is just plain wrong."

In response to these questions, Ms. Walker said: "I hear what each of you is saying. Let me make some particular comments about the issue of ethics. I would ask you whether it is ethical for our school to be evaluated on the basis of one standardized score. That is precisely what our community is doing to us. We depend on our community for support. We may not like the game that is being played, but that is the reality with which we are faced. Basically, the curriculum is what the community demands. If this means that your academic freedom sometimes has to be compromised, that is just how it is. None of us is happy about all this. But I assure you, the superintendent and board of education members are extremely concerned about the decline in our scores. If our students don't do better next year, even more drastic changes may have to be made."

■ ■ ■

How do you respond to the issue of teaching to the test in an effort to raise scores? What are the pluses and minuses of this practice? What are some values expressed in Ms. Walker's comments? What values are reflected in reactions of some of the teachers? Are there ways in which these divergent views about what teachers should do might be reconciled? What would you do if you were a member of this mathematics department? Do communities unfairly judge schools based on standardized test scores? If so, what might be done about this situation? What is the proper course of action when there is a conflict between community desires and decisions that teachers as professionals want to make?

experts who have the knowledge to make the key content selection decisions. However, several factors call this assumption into question.

First, textbooks are developed by for-profit companies. They are interested in selling the most textbooks and therefore develop books that are likely to appeal to the widest audience. The content of a book usually addresses the content standards of a few "textbook adoption" states that purchase large numbers of textbooks. In reality, the standards of different states are political documents that are derived through compromise.

Second, if you examine several textbooks in a subject you want to teach, don't be surprised if you find that textbook authors do not agree about the content to include or how the content should be divided and sequenced. Your examination may also uncover errors in content. Regular critiques of textbooks point out numerous errors of fact as well as errors of omission.

Finally, you will probably find that the individual texts vary considerably in terms of the depth of treatment given to individual topics. All of these issues call into question the notion that textbooks are the best source of information for curriculum content.

Relying on the text to define the content of the curriculum for you can also lead to instructional difficulties. The characteristics and the prior knowledge of students in every class you teach will differ from the assumptions of the textbook and curriculum document writers. If your students have different prior knowledge than that assumed by the textbook writers, the students may have trouble comprehending the text or may reject the content as unimportant.

In summary, as you consider the text as a source of content, you must weigh all of the above issues. You must also ask yourself whether you want to place the decision making for your curriculum content in the hands of a few publishing companies and authors.

Teacher Background

It is widely accepted that the teacher is the most important variable in providing a quality education. Much attention has been paid in recent years to make sure that high school teachers have strong subject-matter knowledge in the subjects they teach. The basic contention is that a person cannot teach what he or she does not know.

However, teacher knowledge of the content, while it is a necessary condition to quality teaching, is not the entire story. Individuals with an inadequate understanding of how to relate the content to student needs and how to make the content meaningful have difficulty in the classroom (Arrends, 2003). Content knowledge that relates the content of instruction to the needs and interests of students is what has been termed pedagogical content knowledge. This type of content knowledge refers to the ability of a teacher to make knowledge understandable and meaningful to students.

There is much more content in any given subject than there is time to teach it. Therefore, teachers must make decisions about what to teach and what parts of the content will receive the most emphasis. Making decisions about what content to include is related to teacher background. Teachers often choose to emphasize content that they feel most comfortable teaching as well as content they most enjoy. While this is understandable, the needs of the students need to be kept at the forefront. What they need to know should be given priority over what the teacher enjoys teaching.

The focus on the teacher's background raises questions related to the usefulness of those college courses you completed in your undergraduate major. Can you simply look at those notes you took in college courses in order to decide on the content to be included in the curriculum? It would be nice, we agree, but this, too, is no solution. For one thing, the scope of many college and university courses is narrower than the typical secondary school course you will teach. For example, only a small portion of the content presented in a university-level comparative anatomy course is relevant for students in an introductory high school biology course. And the intended audience for university

More from the Web

Content Standards

Content standards are an important consideration when selecting content to be taught. The following websites will provide you with more information about standards.

INTEGRATING NEW TECHNOLOGIES INTO THE METHODS OF EDUCATION
      http://www.intime.uni.edu/model/content/cont.html
This website is sponsored by the University of Northern Iowa. It provides a summary of the background of the standards movement and links to national content organizations and national content standards.

professors' lectures differs considerably from the students enrolled in typical secondary school classes.

Your subject-matter background is an important dimension, however, in helping you make decisions about the content to be included in the curriculum. Your background should help you prioritize the content, evaluate instructional materials, and formulate important questions.

Accommodating these various pressures can frustrate even experienced teachers. How to select important content that is well matched to students' capabilities is one of the challenges you will face throughout your career. Some basic principles can assist you in making these important decisions.

Selecting the Content of Instruction

Although there has been a movement to remove much of the decision making about the content of the curriculum from teachers, you will still have a major impact. You are the person closest to the students. You are most aware of their prior knowledge, their motivations, and their academic strengths and deficiencies. While you will need to consider the standards or frameworks of your individual state, the nature of your standardized testing program, and the influence of textbooks, in the end, *you* are the one in a position to make content decisions that influence what students will learn. Therefore, you need to focus on this important dimension of teaching.

Planning with the End in Mind

A beginning step in content selection and instructional planning is that of first identifying what is desired as the end point of your teaching. For example, in beginning to think about a particular unit of instruction, you need to ask, "What do I want the students to know or be able to do as a result of this unit?" Wiggins and McTighe (2005) state that teachers need to stop, reflect, and engage in what they term backward design before engaging in shortsighted, day-to-day lesson planning. Backward design refers to the process of first developing an understanding of where you want the student to be at the end of a particular unit of instruction and then working from that end point to the beginning of the instructional sequence.

Engaging in backward design helps a teacher relate lessons to each other thoughtfully; plan lessons that follow a logical flow; and ensure that, by the conclusion of the sequence of lessons, the students will possess the knowledge that will be required of them in understanding the subject and in meeting state standards.

A framework that will help you do this is what is termed the structure of knowledge. The structure of knowledge specifies different levels of types of knowledge that individuals need to learn.

Using the Structure of Knowledge

Several levels or types of knowledge are important to consider when defining the curriculum. Understanding these levels can make the content selection easier and increase the probability of significant student learning. Three basic types of knowledge, generalizations, concepts, and facts, need to be defined.

Generalizations and Enduring Understandings

Wiggins and McTighe (2005) state that the beginning point in planning for instruction is to identify the "big ideas" or "enduring understandings" that students should know as a result of studying a particular topic. This focus is important because we want students to learn things that are enduring and will last beyond the study of a single lesson or unit. Education ought to focus on students learning material that will transfer to examples beyond the textbooks and to situations outside the classroom. Having an understanding of big ideas provides an important framework for organizing and making sense of new information.

For example, a common concern of teachers is that they need to teach to the test in order for students to do well on high-stakes tests. This is a legitimate concern. However, studies of content retention indicate that there is a sharp forgetting curve, where forgetting of recently learned information begins almost as soon as we stop studying, and within a few days, a large amount of the new information is forgotten. Therefore, an important issue for those concerned about student performance on high-stakes tests should be on helping reduce the forgetting curve so that students retain a larger percentage of the information they have learned.

How do we reduce the forgetting curve? Retention of new information is increased by relating the new information to something that is meaningful. If new information is related to the learning of a big idea, there is a good probability of increased retention. Thus, teaching in order to learn big ideas is useful in addressing current challenges of the educational reform movement.

The term *big idea* goes by several others names, for example, generalization, proposition, law, or principle. The terminology used to identify these big ideas may vary from subject to subject. For example, the laws of physics are those enduring principles or statements that are almost always true and help us make very accurate predictions. In the social sciences, however, humans are not entirely predictable, so the term *laws* would infer too high a probability that the predictions will come true. In the social sciences, the term *generalization* is more appropriate.

The first step in curriculum selection is that of identifying the enduring understanding or the big ideas that students should know when they have completed a particular sequence of learning activities. Where do you find these big ideas? One source ought to be what you have learned in the classes in your content area that you have taken as part of your preparation. For example, any subject has a relatively limited number of generalizations or principles. An individual who has a good understanding of these basic principles is someone who is an expert in the subject. Too often in our majors, however, we get so caught up in cramming new information for tests, that we miss the big ideas or enduring understandings. This might be the place where those notes from your college classes could be useful. You might review class notes and textbooks and identify the big ideas or the enduring understandings that are the core of what experts in that field know and understand.

Another source of information is textbooks. Textbook authors usually write with the intent of explaining a generalization or principle. Each chapter usually focuses on one or more generalizations or principles. Take the textbooks assigned to the class you are teaching. Read through the chapters, not for specific bits of information, but for the big ideas or generalizations that the author is trying to develop.

Those national and state standards that are now common are yet other sources from which you can derive generalizations or enduring understanding. Good standards are not just statements of facts; they are statements based on big ideas or enduring understandings. The standards may need to be reworded, however, to be useful in your classroom.

The first step in your content selection is to review the standards, review the textbooks, tap your own knowledge of the subject, and identify several generalizations or big ideas that will serve as the focus for your unit. Remember that these are ideas that you want the students to know or understand when they have completed their study of this sequence of learning.

This step is also useful to you in some other ways. For example, let's suppose that the content of a particular chapter of a textbook is not very appealing to a particular group of students. Or perhaps they have difficulty reading the text. By starting with the generalizations or the big ideas, you can ask yourself, Is there some other content that is more interesting to the students that can be used to help them learn the same generalization? This is an important step in differentiating instruction and making it possible for all students in the classroom to achieve success.

Remember that students differ in the abstract-concrete continuum. Although students in your classroom may be of the same age, some will need concrete explanations while others can handle more abstract challenges. Again, beginning with the big ideas can assist you in brainstorming more concrete or more abstract examples that can meet the needs of different students.

Generalizations, principles, and laws are statements that summarize the relationship between two or more concepts. Often the generalizations will have an if-then dimension. In other words, the statement will state that if A happens, then B will result. To give you a feel for the nature of generalizations or principles, the following are some examples drawn from a variety of subject areas. You might try to identify those with an if-then characteristic.

- Inherited characteristics of living organisms do not occur randomly; rather, they follow predictable patterns.

- Increased specialization in production leads to interdependence among individuals, communities, states, and nations.

- Decreasing temperatures result in contraction of objects; increasing temperatures result in expansion of objects.

- Areas and perimeter measurements of polygons do not occur in a random pattern; they can be determined by computations involving linear and angle measurements.

- Compositions of chemical compounds follow predictable patterns that can be discerned through the application of appropriate analytical procedures.

- A force equal to the weight of the dispersed fluid buoys up a body immersed in a fluid.

- Because natural resources are limited and human wants are unlimited, every society has developed a method for allocating scarce resources.

- Different moods of paintings featuring common subjects and symbols result from differences in the sensory and compositional features of the individual work.

Scholars doing research in their individual specialties constantly challenge and test existing generalizations, principles, and laws. Therefore, they should not be introduced to students as definitive answers. Your students need to understand that the search for new knowledge continues and that many of them can look forward to active participation in this exciting process.

Because generalizations, principles, and laws summarize the content of a subject and organize tremendous quantities of information, they function well as content organizers. These broad explanatory statements encourage students to place facts in context and to recognize the importance of understanding relationships among concepts.

Concepts   Once the enduring ideas or generalizations have been identified, the next step in content selection is to identify the key concepts that are imbedded within the generalization. Concepts are usually words, or symbols, that denote a category of items that have common attributes. Concepts are wonderful intellectual tools because they allow us to place lots of information into useful categories. For example, the term *mammal* defines a classification of animals that have common characteristics making them different from reptiles. Therefore, when encountering a new animal, an understanding of concepts helps us in categorizing and identifying it.

The phrase *division of labor* defines an economic or organizational scheme that has certain characteristics regardless of the setting. In learning about any economic endeavor, a person can look to see how labor is divided. Therefore, concepts have wide transfer value.

The defining characteristics of a concept are called attributes. Less complex and simpler-to-learn concepts have relatively few attributes. However, an abstract concept such as democracy has a large number of attributes.

The fewer the number of attributes and the more concrete a concept is, the easier it is for students to learn. More complex concepts require more teaching time than less complex concepts. Thus, a simple concept, such as triangle, with very few well-defined attributes that can be illustrated using concrete examples, might be learned quickly. However, a complex concept like democracy might require several examples and several lessons.

Bruner (1960) stated that any child at any stage of development could learn a concept. He saw the differences in the learning as based on the "concreteness" of the concept, not on the ability to see relationships that form the foundation of concept learning. Younger children, or those with little previous experience in a subject, need to begin with concepts that have relatively few attributes and that can be illustrated using concrete examples. Additional attributes can be added and more abstract applications made as the student learns. For example, teaching a complex concept like democracy to novice learners requires that they begin by encountering very concrete and relatively simple examples of this form of government.

Concepts form an important foundation for any given subject. Students will have difficulty understanding generalizations or principles if they do not have a good grasp of concepts. Teaching concepts and the relationships between concepts should be a major component of your instructional planning.

Once you have identified several key generalizations or principles and selected a few that you expect students to know as a result of your instruction, review those big ideas and identify the important concepts. Making a list of these key concepts will be helpful when you start planning and sequencing individual lessons.

Textbooks frequently identify what the authors believe are the central concepts by highlighting them or including them in vocabulary lists. The information they include in the chapter is usually intended to illustrate or develop these key concepts.

Concepts are organized in the mind into a hierarchy, or schema, that individuals use to store and retrieve information. Some concepts, such as reptile, are broad terms that help organize vast quantities of subordinate information. These large-scale concepts help organize more narrow, related concepts such as snake, turtle, and lizard, which are more limited in scope. Awareness of concept hierarchies and the connections between broad and related, narrower concepts can help you plan and sequence material for students.

Facts   Facts refer to specific circumstances or situations. By themselves, facts have limited transfer or explanatory power. For example, the fact that Mexico City has more inhabitants than New York City is interesting. By itself, however, this fact has little usefulness. Can't you just hear a student asking "Who cares?" Facts derive their importance as concrete examples that can be used to suggest questions that in turn can be used to develop important concepts. For example, the fact that Mexico City is larger than New York City will probably surprise some people and prompt them to ask, "Why has Mexico City grown so large?"

However, simply knowing this fact does not help a person understand the general reasons why cities grow or the economic, political, and social problems of cities. The real value of facts is that they can stimulate questions and hypotheses or can be used to verify hypotheses. In essence, they provide concrete examples around which concepts and generalizations can be formed.

Appropriate selection of facts has long been an issue of concern to curriculum developers. Curriculum specialist John Jarolimek (1990) recommended that, in planning instruction, you should select from among these three types of facts:

- Facts that are likely to remain important over a long period of time
- Facts used frequently in everyday living
- Facts needed to develop or elaborate on important ideas and generalizations

The basic point is that facts do have some value. As teachers, we should recognize that some facts need to be included in the curriculum. However, just the attainment of facts does not mean that a person will be knowledgeable and can use their knowledge base to understand and respond to new situations. Therefore, the facts that are included in the curriculum need to be chosen for a specific purpose.

Understanding the structure of knowledge can help you evaluate and respond to the curriculum wars. For example, during the controversy over the history standards, critics claimed that the new standards were flawed because they did not include certain facts. One such assertion was that the standards did not call for students to know that George Washington was the first president of the United States. However, the developers of the standards pointed out that the new standards asked students to examine major issues confronting the new nation during this era. This would certainly require them to know that Washington was the president (Wineburg, 2001). In other words, the critics of the standards were looking for the inclusion of specific facts, whereas the developers were focusing more on concepts and generalizations. Too often, the curriculum wars have become battles over which set of facts to teach rather than on what concepts and big ideas should be learned.

Understanding the structure of knowledge can help you become a creative teacher. When you understand that concepts and generalizations, rather than specific facts, are the focus, you can begin to brainstorm different ways and different content selections that you can use to teach them. If you are teaching in Wyoming, you might choose different examples for teaching the concepts than someone in Chicago. In both places, however, the key concepts and generalizations could be the same. In addition, when students have difficulty, you don't need to get caught in the trap of just having the student review the same set of facts over and over in hopes that they will somehow now remember them. You can provide them with alternative examples that might be more understandable to them

When presented with the structure of knowledge, one of the first questions asked by teachers focuses on the issue of testing. Teachers understand the wisdom of focusing on concepts and generalizations, but they point out that standardized tests tend to focus on facts. There is some truth to this assertion, although good assessment will focus on key understandings of concepts.

Some successful teachers have found that focusing on concepts and generalizations during the year with a week or two of review of basic facts is an effective strategy for preparing students to take required standardized tests.

Developing Goals and Instructional Objectives

Once you have identified the content to be taught in your classroom, you need to identify your learning outcomes, or what the students should know as a result of your teaching. The learning outcomes take the form of goals and objectives.

Goals

Goals are broad statements that identify what students should learn as a consequence of their exposure to the content. Goals often address the "why" question. If you are teaching students a semester course in biology, why should they learn this content? What do you expect them to know when they have completed the course? The goals might be focused on students understanding and applying the key concepts and generalizations or principles. Other goals might include skills and attitudes you hope the students will acquire as a result of your instruction.

For example, a goal in the skills area might be that the students can identify and use resources on the Web or in the library or that they can give an oral presentation on a topic. An attitude goal might be that the students will develop a positive attitude toward the subject and will be motivated to further study.

In summary, goals are the broad purpose statements that give you a sense of direction and focus, help you select the content, and plan lessons for a unit of study. However, they tend to be somewhat abstract and offer you little day-to-day guidance.

Instructional Objectives

Instructional objectives are specific statements that focus on the daily outcomes of your teaching. They are narrow purpose statements that focus on what students will learn as a result of a given lesson. The basic question you need to ask as you prepare your lessons is, What should students be able to do as a result of this lesson?

In districts with well-developed curriculum guides, new teachers sometimes find that major course topics, generalizations, and concepts have been identified for them. Only rarely, though, are teachers provided with preestablished lists of instructional objectives. Typically, teachers write these themselves.

A well-written objective identifies a specific, observable student behavior that will be an indicator that the student has learned. This behavior should be one that builds student competence toward a broader goal. No specific number of instructional objectives is right or correct for a given goal statement. You must exercise your own judgment in this matter.

Instructional objectives help you in two ways. First, they serve as guideposts for instructional planning. Once a set of instructional objectives for a given unit of work has been prepared, subsequent instructional planning should focus on these objectives. For example, selection of instructional materials is influenced by the expectations of student learning stated in the objectives. If a CD has potential to help students grasp understandings associated with an objective, a good case can be made for including it in the instructional sequence. If the CD is entertaining but has little relationship to the objectives, then it should be eliminated. For example, we can remember some teachers who ordered films that had no relationship to the objectives. It appeared too often that the films were selected because they could be "filler" that would give the teacher relief from planning and teaching. This is professionally irresponsible and a waste of valuable instructional time.

A second advantage that instructional objectives provide teachers is associated with student learning. The use of instructional objectives helps you to be organized and purposeful. There is less confusion about your expectations. This is particularly true when you share instructional objectives with students and make sure they understand what it is they are supposed to be learning (Good & Brophy, 2007).

Development of instructional objectives is a key step in the planning process. It is preceded by identification of topics, concepts, generalizations, and goals. After instructional objectives have been prepared, use them as reference points as you make decisions about instructional techniques, learning materials, evaluation, and other elements. These planning "parts" often are gathered together into systematic instructional units.

An illustration of the relationship of instructional objectives to major concepts, a generalization, a goal, and a topic are presented in Box 5-1. Note the effort to ensure that identified major concepts have been referenced in at least one instructional objective.

A Format for Preparing Instructional Objectives   Of the many formats available for preparing instructional objectives, one we have used for some time is the ABCD format. This scheme presumes that a complete instructional objective includes four elements. Reference must be made in the objective to the audience (A) to be served, to the behavior (B) to be taken as an indicator of appropriate learning, to the condition (C) under which

---

Box 5-1   The Relationship Between Learning Objectives and the Structure of Knowledge

TOPIC: SOLVING EQUATIONS

GENERAL GOAL:

Students will understand the relationship that exists between multiplication and addition as they are exposed to methods for applying this relationship to solving equations.

GENERALIZATION:

The distributive principle states that the product resulting from the multiplication of a given number and the sum of two others equals the product of this given number multiplied by the first of these two numbers plus the product of this given number multiplied by the second of these two numbers. Algebraically, the equality suggested by the distributive principle is depicted as follows:

$$a \times (b + c) = (a \times b) + (a \times c)$$

MAJOR CONCEPTS:

- Simplification
- Equation
- Addition process
- Subtraction process
- Multiplication process
- Division process
- Distributive principle

INSTRUCTIONAL OBJECTIVES:

1. Each student will respond correctly to 8 of 10 true/false questions related to the nature of the distributive principle.

2. Each student will correctly solve at least 7 of 10 equations requiring him or her to use a combination of the addition and multiplication processes.

3. Each student will correctly solve at least 11 of 14 problem equations requiring the use of combinations of the addition, subtraction, multiplication, and division processes.

this behavior is measured (e.g., kind of assessment procedure to be used), and to the degree (D) of competency to be demonstrated before mastery of the objective is assumed. In the next sections we will look at these components of a complete instructional objective one at a time.

A = Audience   The A component of an instructional objective identifies the person or persons to whom the instructional objective is directed. Some individuals leave out this dimension of the objective. We like to include it because it identifies the nature of the individuals who are to be involved in learning. This is especially useful if instruction has been differentiated in the classroom so that different students might be working on different objectives. It can also be useful when other teachers are considering using a teaching approach. The definition of the audience can help them determine if this objective would be appropriate for their class. The audience for a particular objective could be an entire class of students, a group even larger than a class, a small group of students, or even a single student.

Typically, the audience component of an instructional objective will appear as indicated in the following examples:

Each student will. . . .

The literature circle group will. . . .

All students in fourth-period U.S. history will. . . .

Joanne Smith will. . . .

B = Behavior   The B, or behavior, component of an instructional objective describes the observable performance that will be taken as an indicator that learning occurred. This is the heart of an objective. The behavior in an instructional objective must be described in observable terms. This suggests a need to select verbs that describe performance in precise and specific ways and a need to avoid verbs that describe less readily observable kinds of phenomena. To illustrate this distinction, consider the following choices:

Each student will appreciate foreign policy differences of the Republican and Democratic presidential candidates by. . . .

Each student will describe foreign policy differences of the Republican and Democratic presidential candidates by. . . .

In the first example, it is unclear both to the teacher and the student what kind of behavior will be taken as evidence that mastery has occurred. It is not clear what kind of performance signals "appreciation." A student, given an instructional objective with a behavior statement of this kind, might be confused about how he or she should study the material.

The use of the verb *describe* in the second option is much more precise. *Describe* suggests a behavior that is much more observable and specific than does the verb *appreciate*. Students presented with an instructional objective that requires them to describe foreign policy differences can expect to be assessed on their ability to provide some clear indication of a familiarity with key policy points of each candidate. The use of the verb *describe* in the instructional objective suggests to students a need to study carefully specific positions of each candidate. It is true that the verb *appreciate* might suggest a similar activity to some students. But the meaning of *appreciate* is much less precise than *describe*. For example, some students might take the "each student will appreciate" directive to mean that they are to do nothing beyond developing a general knowledge that, indeed, both candidates have differing foreign policy views. For a student who has this impression, there would be no deeply felt need to become thoroughly familiar with the foreign policy positions of each candidate.

Box 5-2   Kinds of Verbs Suitable for the Behavior Component of an Instructional Objective

WHAT DO YOU THINK?
Below is a list of verbs that might be used in writing instructional objectives. Identify those verbs in the list that (1) you think would be suitable for use in an instructional objective and that (2) you do not think would be suitable for use in an instructional objective. Be prepared to defend your decisions.

compute	apply	appreciate	understand
describe	conjecture	comprehend	note
select	solve	demonstrate	judge

In summary, a good deal of ambiguity is removed when verbs used in the behavior component of an instructional objective reference a relatively specific and an observable kind of student performance (see Box 5-2). The following fragments of complete instructional objectives indicate how the behavior component might look:

- Cite specific examples of. . . .
- Describe characteristics of. . . .
- Distinguish between. . . .
- Name. . . .
- List. . . .
- Demonstrate. . . .

C = Condition   The C, or condition, component of an instructional objective describes the condition of assessment. That is, under what condition(s) will the student demonstrate the behavior? Will the students demonstrate the behavior using notes? Will they have to perform something from memory? Will they be expected to demonstrate the behavior under different conditions? For example, a person might be able to correctly select the right response on a multiple-choice question when there are only four choices, but can they actually apply the information when prompts aren't available?

In some instances, the condition might be responding to a formal test of some kind. In other instances, a less formal procedure may be described. The condition component conveys to the student information regarding how his or her learning will be assessed at the conclusion of the instructional sequence. Typically the C component of an instructional objective appears as indicated in the following examples:

- during an oral presentation
- during an open book test
- on a multiple-choice examination
- on a project completed by a small group
- on a formal paper, 6 to 10 pages in length, footnoted properly
- during a game situation

D = Degree   The D, or degree, component of an instructional objective details the minimum level of proficiency that will be acceptable as evidence that the objective has been achieved. The basic question that needs to be asked here is, How proficient does the student need to be? You might expect students just learning the content to perform tasks at a lower level of proficiency than more advanced students. Some tasks require a higher level of proficiency than others. For example, you might require that someone learning basic mathematical operations to perform the operation correctly nearly every time so that she or he will be able to continue with more advanced operations. However, a social studies teacher might not require that a student identify the causes of the Civil War with 100% accuracy because this knowledge is not critical for additional learning. And individuals still argue about the causes of the Civil War.

You can establish the degree or the proficiency level using several different methods. One is to indicate the percentage of the total number of items on an assignment or test that must be responded to correctly. Clearly this procedure does not work for all tasks. On some tasks or assignments, for example, an essay item, the degree frequently might include the number of points made in the essay or the number of errors in the essay.

There is a good deal of teacher artistry involved in describing the degree of competence a student must demonstrate as minimal evidence that a given objective has been achieved. Establishing a proficiency level is a matter of professional judgment. It should be based on the nature of the content you are teaching as well as the prior knowledge and success of the students. In addition, as you gain experience, you will gain additional insight into proficiency levels that are appropriate for students.

The D component of an instructional objective is demonstrated in the following examples:

■ show correct form on at least 8 of 10. . . .

■ in an essay in which specific references are made to (a) motivations for immigration, (b) domestic resistance to immigration, and (c) psychic rewards of immigration. . . .

■ answer correctly 85% of the items on a quiz.

■ will have fewer than 5 mistakes. . . .

Putting It All Together: The ABCD Format

Recall that all complete instructional objectives include references to A, the audience; B, the behavior; C, the condition; and D, the degree. A couple of instructional objectives are listed below. Individual components of each objective have been underlined and labeled.

>   A   B   D   C
> 1. Each student will solve 8 of 10 problems on a weekly quiz featuring questions about right triangles.

>   A   C
> 2. The Swedish immigration group, in an oral presentation
>   B   D
> to the class, will cite at least five reasons supporting and five reasons opposing nineteenth-century Swedish migration to the American South.

Note that the audience, behavior, condition, and degree components may appear in a variety of orders. The order is not critical. What is important is that all four be considered when writing an objective.

In summary, the ABCD format is an easily learned procedure. Instructional objectives containing all four components (audience, behavior, condition, and degree) are capable of conveying a good deal of information to students about a teacher's expectations. For the teacher, they provide a reminder to keep instruction on track so that learning experiences will be consistent with the kinds of expectations reflected in the assessment procedures followed at the conclusion of a given instructional sequence.

Domains of Instructional Objectives   For some years now, educational outcomes have been divided into three basic categories, or domains: (1) the cognitive domain, (2) the affective domain, and (3) the psychomotor domain. In very general terms, the cognitive domain includes what we might call academic or intellectual kinds of learning. The affective domain includes learning related to values, beliefs, and attitudes. The psychomotor domain includes learning related to the sensorimotor system and fine and large muscle control.

Because the general area of concern of each domain has certain unique features, it is not surprising that instructional objectives in each domain tend to be organized in slightly different ways and to be directed toward different purposes. In the sections that follow, some of these differences are introduced.

Instructional objectives in the cognitive domain   The cognitive domain is concerned with rational, systematic, or intellectual thinking. When we think about subject-matter content and our expectation that students will learn it, we have in mind the cognitive domain. The organization of objectives in the cognitive domain stems from the work of Benjamin Bloom and others who, in the mid-1950s, set about the task of developing a system for identifying categories of learning. Out of their deliberations came a ground-breaking educational document, *Taxonomy of Educational Objectives: Handbook I: Cognitive Domain* (Bloom, 1956). Commonly referred to as Bloom's taxonomy, this document suggests that there exists a six-step hierarchy of thinking, ranging from the most elemental thinking processes to the most sophisticated. Ordered in terms from the simplest to the most complex, the elements of Bloom's taxonomy are as follows:

1. Knowledge
2. Comprehension
3. Application
4. Analysis
5. Synthesis
6. Evaluation

For teachers, proposed learning experiences can be categorized by comparing their intellectual complexity with the types of thinking referenced in Bloom's taxonomy. In general, a task demanding knowledge-level performance requires a different type of thinking, often considered low level, than a synthesis-level task, which is considered high level. In thinking about instructional planning, teachers find it useful to know something about the kinds of thinking implied by each level of the taxonomy. When they have made a decision regarding the kinds of intellectual demands they wish to include in their program, they then need to prepare instructional objectives that are clearly directed toward encouraging student performance at the targeted taxonomical level (knowledge, comprehension, application, analysis, synthesis, and evaluation). Let us look briefly at characteristics of each level of the taxonomy.

Knowledge   Knowledge is defined as the recall of a piece of previously learned information. The recall might involve a wide range of material, including the recall of a specific fact or the recall of a whole theory or complex operation. Regardless of the complexity of the recall, however, all that is required is bringing to mind the relevant information. The student is not required to do anything with the information. No manipulation or interpretation is required. The knowledge level is usually considered the lowest level of learning outcomes in the cognitive domain.

Comprehension   Comprehension is a slightly more complex mental operation than knowledge. Comprehension refers to what many call understanding. Comprehension is defined as the ability to understand the meaning of the material. Demonstrating the understanding might be shown by translating the information from one form to another, explaining or summarizing the information, or predicting the consequences of future effects. Comprehension requires that the student do something with the material. Therefore, it is more complex than the knowledge level.

Application   Application refers to the ability to use learned material in a new situation. This is really one of the primary goals of all of education. We expect the students to be able to apply what they learn in school to new situations they encounter in the world outside the classroom. The application might include the application of things such as methods, concepts, generalizations, and theories. The application level is considered more complex than comprehension because it involves knowing the material well enough to know when and to what situations the information can be applied.

Analysis   Analysis requires students to understand the composition of the material well enough so that the component parts and the organizational structure are understood. This might include identifying the various parts of something and the relationship between the parts. The analysis category is considered higher-level thinking because it does require that the student perform some manipulation of the material and to go beyond surface features, such as facts, to get to the underlying structure of the material.

Synthesis   Synthesis requires students to take a number of separate pieces of information and combine them to create knowledge that is new (or, more accurately, knowledge that is new to the student). Synthesis is often viewed as one of the central thinking processes in creativity. This level might include production of something new and unique, like a theme or a speech. Synthesis is considered more complex than analysis because it involves not just understanding the underlying structure of something, but rearranging structure to create a new pattern or a new structure.

Evaluation   Evaluation is the ability to judge the value or worth of something. This level does not just call for opinions. At this level, students are called on to make judgments in light of clearly identified criteria. The criteria for the judgment might come from the students or be given to them. To be at the evaluation level, it is essential for both the element of judgment and the element of established criteria are present. Evaluation never calls on students to engage in simplistic sharing of unsupported personal opinion.

Instructional objectives in the affective domain   The affective domain, as noted previously, concerns people's values, feelings, and attitudes. Clearly in schools we are concerned about the total development of our students, not just with their mastery of academic content. Therefore, we need to consider the issue of students' values, feelings, and attitudes in the instructional planning process.

One framework that has been used to classify objectives in the affective domain is a companion piece to *Bloom's Taxonomy*. This is the *Taxonomy of Educational Objectives: Handbook II: Affective Domain* (Krathwohl, Bloom, & Masia, 1964). This taxonomy was developed on a continuum relating to the internalization of an attitude or a belief. It begins with the level of simply being aware of an issue or phenomenon and moves to the place that the value or belief becomes part of the individual's outlook on life.

The affective taxonomy identifies five levels according to the level of internalization:

1. Receiving (or attending to something)
2. Responding
3. Valuing
4. Organization
5. Characterization by a value or a value complex

Receiving (Attending)   Receiving refers to the willingness of a student to attend to a particular stimulus. Individuals cannot begin internalizing a value unless they are first willing to attend to something new. For teachers, this is the task of getting or directing the student's attention. Receiving might range from just an awareness that something exists to selective attention on the part of the student. For example, it might be getting students to attend to a book, music selection, or a value position that may be different from their own. Receiving does not require any overt response on the part of the students other than attending to something. Receiving is the lowest level of the affective domain.

Responding   The next step in the internalization process requires that the students have some active participation. At this level, students are not only attending to a phenomenon, they react in some way. For example, if we are interested in developing student interest in reading literature, students would respond at this level by actually reading a piece of an literature.

Valuing   At this level, the students have moved beyond just being aware of something or engaging in some form of active participation. The students attach some worth or value to a particular object, activity, or behavior. At this level, we would expect the students' overt behavior to demonstrate internalization of the value. For example, they would choose to spend their time, energy, or money to further their interest.

Organization   Once individuals have attached value to something, they then need to bring together different values, reconcile conflicts between values, and develop a hierarchy of values. In other words, they need to organize an internally consistent value system. This is a complex and sophisticated task that requires analyzing, comparing, and synthesizing values.

Characterization by a Value or a Value System   The highest level of internalization of a value is when values have become so ingrained that they influence behavior in ways that others can see. The behavior is so pervasive and consistent that others can identify what the individual values or believes. No discrepancy exists between what the individual says and what she or he does.

It is best to view the cognitive and the affective domains together. They overlap in several ways. Success in the affective area often associates with success in the cognitive area; in other words, students who like and feel good about what they are doing in school tend to do better in their academic courses than do those who are unhappy in school. Those students who have developed a clear value are more likely to be motivated and pursue additional cognitive learning in the area.

Teachers who demonstrate concern for students' values, feelings, and attitudes direct their energies toward helping students develop an emotional as well as an intellectual dimension to what they are learning in school. The goal of supporting each student's growth toward self-confident and mature adulthood is consistent with an instructional program that makes heavy cognitive demands on students. The critical variable is not the difficulty of the work but rather whether the instructional system has been designed so that each youngster has a realistic chance for success. As long as students feel that they are succeeding, their attitudes toward school and the teacher generally remain positive. Success in academic work can itself be an important contributor to students' developing sense of self-worth.

The affective domain involves all areas in which the general emphasis is on values, attitudes, and feelings. But when you are planning instructional objectives, you face some special concerns.

Recall that instructional objectives identify observable student behaviors. This aspect of objectives can be something of a problem when we are dealing with the affective area.

There is a heavy-handed, possibly authoritarian, ring to the suggestion that a given instructional program is dedicated to shaping students' values in a given way. Certainly in a society that values open discussion and democratic decision-making, we have no business establishing instructional objectives that seem to say to students that certain values, attitudes, and feelings are right whereas others are wrong. A teacher who tries to do this is asking for trouble.

When developing instructional objectives in the affective domain, we must ask ourselves this question: In what area(s) do teachers have a legitimate need to know about students' values, attitudes, and feelings? Perhaps there are several answers to this question, but the one that has always made the most sense to us is that teachers have a need to know how students are feeling about the instruction to which they are being exposed. For example, do they like the topics selected? How do they feel about the various school subjects? If we accept the premise that students who feel disposed toward what is going on in their classes do better in those classes and thus may grow in terms of their own feelings of competence and self-worth, then we have every reason to make some deliberate efforts to gather information that will tell us something about these kinds of student feelings.

Instructional objectives in the psychomotor domain   The psychomotor domain includes behaviors that require coordination of the body's muscular system. Specific behaviors in this area can range from activities such as running that require intensive use of large muscles to precision-drawing activities that require good control of the body's fine muscle systems. The degree to which an individual teacher may need instructional objectives in the psychomotor domain depends on the extent to which intended learning outcomes require students to demonstrate motor control (control of the body's muscular systems).

The psychomotor domain has not been as well defined as the cognitive and affective domains. We have developed our own framework that we have used. Our framework contains four stages:

1. Awareness

2. Performance of individual components

3. Integration

4. Free practice

Awareness   The simplest of these stages is the level of awareness. Somewhat akin to the cognitive level of knowledge, awareness demands only that a student be able to describe correctly the movements that must be made to complete a muscular activity properly.

Performance of Individual Components   At this level, the student is able to correctly demonstrate individual parts of a complex muscular activity.

Integration   At this level, the level of integration, the student can perform the entire muscular activity, including all necessary components, with some teacher guidance.

Free Practice   At the final level, the student can perform the muscular activity correctly, in numerous settings, and without any prompting from the teacher. In general, students who achieve level 4 of the psychomotor objectives can be thought of as having complete mastery of the targeted muscular behavior.

Teachers who wish to prepare objectives in this area need good diagnostic information about students' levels of psychomotor development. If students are asked to perform at levels that are far in excess of their ability levels, many will refuse to try out of a belief they are "beaten before they start."

In summary, developing your curriculum requires that you identify the content that you will be teaching and your learning targets. Your learning targets include long-term

---

Box 5-3   Samples of Instructional Objectives

The following are some sample instructional objectives relating to the different domains of learning.

COGNITIVE DOMAIN
Comprehension Level:
Each student will provide literal translation from Spanish to English for 10 sentences, making no errors in at least 8 of the sentences.

Application Level:
Using a tape measure and a 22-inch globe, ninth-grade geography students will correctly compute the distances between 10 pairs of world cities with less than a 50-mile error allowance.

Evaluation Level:
Each student will compare, contrast, and critique the plays of Racine and Corneille in terms of their adherence to the "rules" of classical drama.

AFFECTIVE DOMAIN
Receiving Level:
When opportunities develop, students will seek additional information on a controversial political issue.

Valuing Level:
Students who take a stand on an environmental issue will demonstrate a commitment to that issue by joining an environmental organization, spending time volunteering, or making a monetary contribution to an organization furthering that issue.

Organization Level:
Each social studies student will identify at least two value priorities that were given precedent over others by the signers of the Declaration of Independence.

PSYCHOMOTOR DOMAIN
Awareness Level:
Each student will describe to the teacher the correct finger placement on a violin for a chord named by the teacher.

Performance of Individual Components Level:
In front of the instructor, each student will demonstrate, with 100% accuracy, the proper body posture and the steps for a beginning dive.

Integration Level:
Each art student, with no assistance from another person, will raise a clay pot of at least eight inches using the potter's wheel.

---

goals and short-term objectives. Your instructional objectives should include aspects of both the cognitive and the affective domains and, where appropriate, the psychomotor domain. It is also important to understand the hierarchy of levels in each of these domains so that students are provided with instruction that goes beyond the lowest levels of learning. See Box 5-3 for some examples of different instructional objective.

FOR YOUR PORTFOLIO

Knowledge of content standards, knowledge of the content you will teach, and the ability to write objectives are often topics that are discussed in job interviews. In addition, Interstate New Teacher Assessment and Support Consortium (INTASC) Standard 1 states that the professional educator understands the central concepts, tools of inquiry, and the structures of subjects taught. Therefore, this chapter provides key information about materials you should select for inclusion in your portfolio.

1. Select up to three items to be included in your portfolio. Develop a rationale for including these specific items and how they relate to INTASC Standard 1.

2. What materials can you include in your portfolio that will demonstrate your understanding of the central concepts of your subject? How can you display these materials so that you clearly communicate your understanding to others?

3. What can you include in your portfolio that illustrates your understanding of the content standards in your content area?

Key Ideas in Summary

- The content of what is taught in schools has been the focus of intense debate in recent years, with little general agreement. A variety of forces are shaping what is being taught in the schools.

- Some of the key forces shaping the curriculum are standardized tests and state standards. These forces are replacing textbooks and teacher decisions about what should be taught.

- When selecting content to be taught, teachers should first identify important outcomes. This is called planning with the end in mind. Identifying the outcomes then provides criteria for selecting content that is most appropriate to assist students in achieving these end points.

- The structure of knowledge provides a framework for defining the outcomes of instruction. These outcomes are often called enduring outcomes, principles, or generalizations. The structure of knowledge consists of three levels: facts, concepts, and generalizations.

- Once decisions have been made about the content to be taught, instructional targets need to be developed. Goals are long-range targets that state what students should learn over an extended period of time. Instructional objectives are specific statements of observable student behaviors that are the focus of an individual lesson.

- Well-written instructional objectives help teachers focus on what they are teaching and serve as indicators that learning has occurred. They are useful to students because they clearly communicate learning expectations and what they will be expected to do. Four dimensions can be addressed in writing clear instructional objectives: the audience, the behavior, the conditions, and the degree of learning.

- Three domains of learning should be considered when selecting content and developing goals and objectives: the cognitive, affective and psychomotor domains. Each one of these domains is organized into different levels, moving from simple to more complex behaviors.

Learning Extensions

1. Obtain a current textbook in your subject area. Analyze its content. Is the content consistent with what you think should be taught? Can you identify the key concepts and generalizations? In general, how could the content selection and sequencing be improved? Present your reactions to your instructor in a short paper.

2. Obtain the content standards developed by the national organization in your content field and the content standards adopted in your state. Perform a content analysis of the two documents and identify the differences and similarities between the two sets of standards. Compare these standards to the content included in the textbook you selected in Learning Extension 1.

3. Interview a secondary school teacher about how he or she selects specific content to be taught. Ask this teacher whether he or she places more emphasis on certain topics than others and, if so, why. Ask how standardized testing has affected the content selection decisions of the teacher.

4. Identify a body of content that you would like to teach. From that body of content, develop several enduring understandings, principles, or generalizations that would be suitable as the end points of a unit of instruction.

5. For the body of content you would like to teach, write at lest two instructional objectives in the cognitive domain; one in the affective domain; and, if appropriate, one in the psychomotor domain.

References

Armstrong, D. G. (2003). *Curriculum today*. Columbus, OH: Merrill/Prentice Hall.

Arrends, R. I. (2003) Instructional strategies. In J. W. Guthrie (Ed.), *Encyclopedia of education* (2nd ed., pp. 1178–1186). New York, Macmillan.

Bloom, B. (Ed.). (1956). *Taxonomy of educational objectives: Handbook I: The cognitive domain.* New York: David McKay.

Bruner, J. (1960). *The process of education.* Cambridge, MA: Harvard University Press.

Good, T., & Brophy, J. (2007). *Looking in classrooms* (10th ed.). New York: Longman.

Jacob, B. (2001). Implementing standards: The California mathematics textbook debate. *Phi Delta Kappan, 83*(3), 264–272.

Jacobs, H. H. (2010). *Curriculum 21: Essential education for a changing world.* Alexandria, VA: Association for Supervision and Curriculum Development.

Jarolimek, J. (1990). *Social studies in elementary education* (8th ed.). New York: Macmillan.

Krathwohl, D., Bloom, B., & Masia, B. (1964). *Taxonomy of educational objectives: Handbook II: Affective domain.* New York: David McKay.

Popham, W. (2001). *The truth about testing.* Alexandria, VA: Association for Supervision and Curriculum Development.

Wiggins, G., & McTighe, J. (2005). *Understanding by design.* Alexandria, VA: Association for Supervision and Curriculum Development.

Wineburg, S. (2001). *Historical thinking and other unnatural acts.* Philadelphia, PA: Temple University Press.

6

Learning Assessement: Making Data-Driven Decisions

Objectives

This chapter will help you

- identify the relationship among assessment, evaluation, and grading
- state basic principles of assessment
- identify assessment options
- write test items and construct a test

- define authentic, natural assessment
- construct a rubric
- understand the uses of standardized assessment
- define norm-referenced and criterion-referenced evaluation and grading
- establish a grading plan

Graphic Organizer: Chapter 6

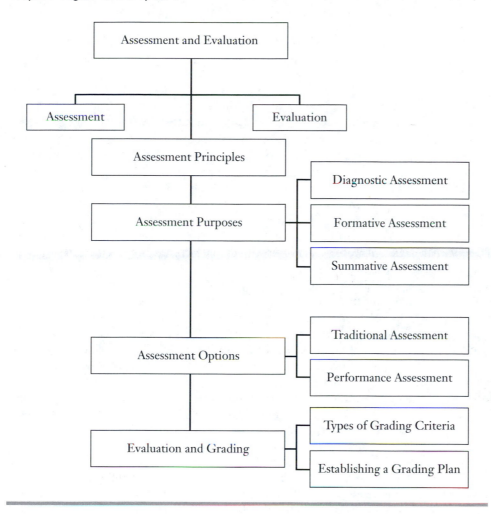

Introduction

In keeping with our emphasis on the backward design model (Wiggins & McTighe, 2005), we present this chapter on assessment at this point in the text so that you might consider its relationship to planning and teaching. Assessment is a topic that is not high on many teachers' list of favorite topics. It is often viewed as a necessary but difficult dimension of being a teacher. Few teachers enjoy constructing and grading tests and assigning grades, the by-product of assessment. In addition, some teachers see the process of grading as something that disrupts student–teacher relationships.

However, assessment is a central component to a successful learning process and involves much more than grading. Understanding the usefulness of assessment can be enhanced when you realize that there is assessment "for" learning as well as assessment "of" learning. Assessment "for" learning is the process of seeking evidence for use by learners and teachers to decide where learners are in their learning and where they need to be in order to achieve success. Assessment "of" learning involves determining what students have accomplished at the conclusion of an educational sequence.

Assessment "of" learning has taken center stage in recent years as educational reformers have called for increased accountability and the standardizing of education across districts and states. Policy makers have clamored for evidence indicating that students in a given class or a given school are learning. They contend that this evidence is important in making wise allocations of scarce resources, identifying good teachers, and making sure that students are staying competitive with other nations.

This has led to a current "hot topic" in education: data-driven decisions. The issue of data-driven decisions is addressed in many professional publications, and testing companies willingly supply schools with pages of test score data. As politicians face the funding requests for education, they want data to support the requests. Teachers are also interested in making good instructional decisions. Good instructional decisions actually make teaching easier and more rewarding.

It is not that teachers are in the habit of making uninformed decisions. Generally teachers rely on professional judgment to inform their decisions. Professional judgment bases decisions on the knowledge, experience, and skill of the teacher. It is useful and is used by individuals in many professions. Few individuals make decisions based entirely on data. Teachers have spent many hours as observers of teaching and actually teaching. They understand that classrooms are very diverse and unpredictable environments. They have professional preparation that helps them interpret events and make informed predictions. They share their experiences and examples with other teachers. Through these experiences, teachers may encounter a good idea, or an approach that seems to be sensible and worthwhile. They may use this information to make a professional judgment about the usefulness of the approach for their students. However, professional judgment can be flawed. We may overlook important variables, and what worked for another teacher might not be as successful when we try it. Therefore, our professional judgment needs to be validated. Good assessment is central to gathering useful data that informs our decisions.

The fact is that policy makers are no longer content to accept the professional judgment of teachers and administrators. They want to see the evidence. However, data can be gathered inappropriately or can be misinterpreted. Therefore, data-driven decisions can also be flawed. The issue should not be one of attempting to replace professional judgment with data. Rather the issue should be one of how to use data to complement professional judgment.

Data-driven decisions are often based on data gathered through standardized, high-stakes assessment procedures. High-stakes assessments are called just that because the data supplied by these assessments are used to make decisions that have important consequences for students, teachers, and schools. Performing poorly on these high-stakes assessments can lead to sanctions imposed on schools, loss of local control of the school, and the firing of the administrator and of teachers!

Unfortunately, this emphasis on assessment "of" learning has diminished the emphasis on assessment "for" learning. Evidence still indicates, however, that more improvement of education results from an emphasis on assessment "for" learning (Stiggins, Arter, Chappuis, & Chappuis, 2004).

In the rush to gather student achievement data, the quality of the data may be overlooked. As Popham (2009) points out, not all test scores are worthy of analysis. They do not provide data that informs educational decisions. If the desire is to make wise decisions about the expenditure of scarce resources and the identification of successful educational change, then valid and reliable data is absolutely essential.

Making useful data-driven decisions requires that teachers and policy makers possess what might be termed assessment literacy. Assessment literacy requires an understanding of how data is gathered and how to make sense of it.

Popham (2001) contends that assessment "illiteracy" has led to the use of unsound assessment procedures and flawed interpretations that have actually harmed learning rather than enhanced it. Assessment illiteracy leads to major mistakes, such as wasting money on programs that do not work and incorrectly labeling students, teachers, and schools.

At the classroom level, the importance of assessment literacy is addressed by Wiggins and McTighe (2005). They place the need to determine acceptable evidence that the students have learned as the second step in the planning process. They note that a course of study should not be just a sequence of learning activities.

Placing assessment early in the planning process ties assessment to important learning outcomes and provides data for making instructional decisions. Indeed, the usefulness of assessment in providing valuable data about student learning is compromised if what is assessed is trivial or not important.

When properly used, assessment is a natural part of the learning process and can result in improved teaching and learning, increased student confidence, better decisions about the allocation of resources, and increased confidence by the public in the performance of teachers and schools. When used improperly, assessment trivializes education, interferes with good teaching and learning, misdirects scarce resources, discourages students and teachers, and leads to a lack of confidence in teachers and schools.

Assessment and Evaluation

Several terms related to assessment are often used synonymously. While some may view the definitions as unimportant or trivial, not understanding the differences between these terms leads to confusion and misplaced emphases. Two of the key terms are *assessment* and *evaluation*. Assessment and evaluation are related but refer to very different processes that require the application of different principles. For example, if principles of good assessment are ignored, then the data gathered may be useless in making sound judgments. On the other hand, if principles of sound data-gathering are followed but good principles of data interpretation are ignored, the evaluation is likely to be misleading or simply wrong.

Assessment

Assessment refers to the process of gathering information or measuring the presence or absence of a quality or trait. Generally, two types of assessment are particularly important for teachers: large-scale standardized assessment and classroom assessment (Stiggins, 1997).

Large-scale standardized assessment usually takes the form of standardized tests that are given to large groups of students. The purpose of these assessments is to gather data that can be used as benchmarks, or indicators of how well students are doing when compared to predetermined standards. Large-scale assessments are usually developed by "testing experts" and are typically administered only a few times during the year, often only once. Today, these large-scale assessments provide the foundation for accountability. The evaluation of schools and teachers is usually based on large-scale, standardized assessments. Teachers need to have an understanding of large-scale assessment practices because their survival as teachers may depend on it.

Classroom assessments are those assessments that teachers administer in the classroom in order to serve instructional and student needs. These assessments form the basis for the decision-making process that teachers go through regarding instructional planning, pacing, and grading. Classroom assessments may be formal assessments (written tests) or informal assessments (observations). They are usually developed by the teacher and may be administered on a frequent basis. Teachers need to have competence in classroom assessment because it leads to improved teaching and learning.

To be useful and valid, both large-scale assessment and classroom assessment should follow rules and principles of evidence-gathering. These rules focus attention on the type of evidence gathered, the conditions under which the evidence was gathered, and whether there is a sufficient sample. Unfortunately, these rules are often violated or misunderstood. For example, large-scale assessments, because they are designed to assess large numbers of students, may not assess what has been given priority in a particular school or classroom. In addition, because large-scale assessments are administered infrequently, they sample student performance at that specific point in time under highly controlled conditions. If other events are occurring at that specific time, for example, a student is ill, then the accuracy of the assessment for that particular student may be compromised. In addition, taking the standardized assessment may not indicate if the student understands when to apply his or her knowledge to real-world situations.

Another possible difficulty is related to the frequency of the assessment. Because large-scale assessments are given infrequently, they simply cannot measure all of the standards in a given subject. To do so would simply require an enormous expenditure of time. Therefore, large-scale standardized assessments are based on limited samples of the content. Making inferences from this limited sample of content is questionable. For example, inferences about students' total knowledge and ability in science because of their responses to a couple of hours of multiple-choice items at one point during the year have a high probability of being flawed.

Classroom assessments may also violate important assessment principles. Classroom assessments too often do not focus on the most important and complex outcomes. Test items may be poorly constructed and designed to "trick" students rather than identify what they know and can do. More frequent assessments usually focus on what has actually been taught in the classroom, but if the data is not based on important learning outcomes, the evaluation is also flawed.

Evaluation

Evaluation is the process of interpreting and making judgments about the evidence gathered in the assessment process. Evaluation is more subjective than is assessment. The same assessment data may lead different individuals to different conclusions about the degree of student learning.

Important questions must be considered when performing evaluations: Is the data gathered focused on important outcomes? What criterion or standard is being used to make the judgment? Is the judgment free of bias? Is there a sufficient sample to warrant a valid judgment? Is the evaluation actually based on the evidence?

The consequences of poor evaluations can be devastating. Student motivation can be diminished; students can be labeled; learning can be stifled; and, in some situations, students may not pass or graduate. This can have important lifelong consequences. For example, one of our colleagues relates how a group procedure based primarily on socioeconomic data rather than achievement data was devastating to him and his fellow students when they entered junior high school (Powell et al., 2001, pp. 54–56).

Few of us would be comfortable with a physician who diagnosed an illness or prescribed medication in the absence of data or based on questionable data. Similarly, we would be uncomfortable if we knew certain medications were prescribed based on some extraneous variable such as the attractiveness of the packaging. Unfortunately, similar practices occur in education all too frequently.

Assessment Principles

The key to competency in a subject is understanding the major principles of the subject. In assessment, several basic principles lead to quality assessment and evaluation regardless of the grade level or subject area. The following are a few of the basic principles that can get you started.

1. Assessment should focus on the measurement of important and worthwhile goals and objectives. This is the basic reason why assessment should be addressed early in the planning process. Although this principle might seem obvious, it is frequently violated. There are a couple of reasons why this is so. First, too many teachers perform assessment as an afterthought. As the end of a unit of instruction approaches, they realize they need some data to use for evaluation. They quickly develop a classroom assessment or test without giving much thought to important outcomes. They tend to focus on what is easy to assess. This tends to emphasize the trivial over the important.

2. Effective assessment requires the use of a variety of assessment tools. The goals of education are complex. Among the many goals of education are for students to learn

how to apply principles and concepts, become creative problem solvers and decision makers, develop lifelong learning habits, become productive citizens, and develop prosocial behaviors. It is unreasonable to think that any one assessment tool or procedure will measure all of these goals.

3. Good assessment requires adequate sampling. The more extensive the sample, the more valid the evaluation. This means that assessment should be something that is performed frequently. Making a judgment about a student based on one observation, one project, or one test is likely to be seriously flawed or even invalid.

4. Good assessment requires multiple measures. This principle is related to the previous one. Not only should there be frequent assessments, but the assessment procedures should also vary. Student learning is best determined using multiple measures. For example, a student might be able to identify the characteristics of a good paragraph on a multiple-choice test. However, this does not mean the student can write a paragraph. A complete picture of what a student knows and is able to do is best constructed using evidence gathered from a variety of assessment types.

5. Good assessment and evaluation should be ethical and fair. The purpose of valid assessment is to distinguish between those who know or have learned and those who have not. Assessment that results in evidence tainted by extraneous variables such as gender, ethnicity, socioeconomic status, disability, linguistic background, learning style, and/or test-taking ability is unfair, unjust, and a barrier to educational improvement.

6. Assessment is an important component of teaching and learning. Teachers have a professional obligation to know the impact of their teaching and to use the results of assessment to assist students in achieving success. Good assessment should inform teachers about the strengths and weaknesses of the students they are teaching, the level of instruction that is appropriate for a given group, the activities and assignments that are most useful, and when it is appropriate to move on (Rudner & Schafer, 2002).

One method that can assist you in applying these principles of assessment is that of developing an assessment plan or a table of specifications to help guide your assessment and evaluation decisions. Box 6-1 is an example of a table of specifications.

Box 6-1   Example of a Table of Specifications for Assessment

Unit Title: Weather and Climate

Objective	Assessment Strategy	Assessment Type
Defines basic terms and vocabulary	Teacher-made test	Multiple-choice and matching Items
Illustrates influence of wind currents	Assessment of student-created map	Develop checklist to use when evaluating accuracy of wind current map
Discusses importance of air pressure	Teacher-made test	Short-answer items
Interprets symbols on weather maps	Portfolio entry	Weather maps will be provided and the student will identify symbols and fronts, low-pressure zones, high-pressure zones, and precipitation types.
Makes weather predictions	Video project	Student will be recorded making a weather prediction based on a map provided. Each student will be given 20 minutes to prepare the presentation and will be given 3 minutes to make the presentation. Develop a rubric to evaluate the presentation.

Assessment Purposes

Why do we need to perform assessments? Much current emphasis is placed on the assessment of learning. This data is then used for making high-stakes decisions such as evaluating schools, evaluating teachers, and comparing students across school districts and states. A number of teachers view this practice with skepticism and as a waste of instructional time.

However, there are at least three other major applications of assessment. Those purposes include diagnosing student knowledge, identifying student progress, and determining student achievement. These three basic functions of assessment are often called diagnostic assessment, formative assessment, and summative assessment.

Diagnostic Assessment

Diagnostic assessment is sometimes called placement assessment. The purpose of diagnostic assessment is to determine the entry level of the students in order to make decisions that will provide them with the best opportunity for success. Diagnosing students' entry levels and their knowledge of prerequisites is important in helping teachers plan so that their lessons are at an appropriate level of difficulty. Few things are more frustrating to teachers than to plan a lesson and have it fail because students simply were not ready for the content.

Diagnostic assessment tends to be overlooked by many secondary teachers. Too many current teachers are faced with pressure to cover the content of their subject and to follow pacing guides. These pacing guides are intended to make sure that students are exposed to content that might be covered on standardized assessments later in the year. However, blindly following pacing guides when students are not ready is a waste of time that will frustrate both students and teachers.

Two important questions are addressed by diagnostic assessment: (1) Do the students have the necessary prerequisite knowledge and skill? and (2) Have the students already achieved all or some of the intended outcomes?

Diagnostic assessment is best performed near the beginning of an instruction sequence or learning progression. If the students do not possess the necessary prerequisite knowledge before beginning the learning progression, failure is the likely outcome, as are loss of student interest and motivation and increased discipline problems. Stop and reflect. How would you react if you were forced each day to spent time on a task where you had no possibility of success? I'm sure your reactions would not be very different from those of some secondary students that have emotionally dropped out. Time spent at the beginning of instruction to identify the entry-level knowledge and, if necessary, providing readiness is time well spent.

Knowing how much the students already know about a topic is important in planning for a learning progression. If students already possess considerable knowledge and skill about a topic, they are likely to become bored. Boredom is a major enemy of teachers!

Diagnostic assessment does not need to be difficult or time consuming. It can often be done relatively quickly and without a lot of extra effort. Diagnostic assessment can be as simple as observing students engaged in an activity or task related to the learning objectives. For example, one physical education teacher began a unit on volleyball with a group of freshmen by having them engage in a game the first day. He then used an observation checklist to identify the knowledge and the skill of the students. This provided him with useful information about where to begin and who might need to have more specialized attention. Similarly, a review of a few math problems or asking the students to write a couple of paragraphs might be all that math and English teachers might need to make a tentative evaluation of what the students know and can do.

Other assessment options that are appropriate for diagnostic assessment include student interviews or a few true/false or multiple-choice items. Remember, the purpose is not to compare students or to give grades. The purpose is to get some information that will be useful in planning and teaching. If done properly, so that the items focus on important concepts students are going to learn and the assessment is performed with little threat or anxiety, diagnostic assessment serves as an advance organizer to help inform students about the content they will be learning.

Formative Assessment

Formative assessment is one of the most important types of assessment for teachers. It is a key component in assessment "for" learning and has been emphasized as an important component of teaching and learning. For example, Popham (2008) reports that research on formative assessment indicates that it is one of the most powerful educational interventions.

Formative assessment is defined as a planned process in which assessment-elicited evidence is used by teachers to adjust their teaching approach and students to evaluate their learning approach (Popham, 2008, p. 6). This definition indicates that formative assessment is a process, not just a test. It is a planned process where the teacher focuses on gathering data about important learning outcomes at key points in the learning progression. This planned process may include a number of activities and may use formal as well as informal assessment tools.

Popham (2008) notes that a number of testing companies market tests that they label as formative assessments. These tests are used periodically to indicate student progress toward large-scale summative assessments. While this practice has some merit, it does not meet the definition of formative assessment as a process that helps teachers make instructional decisions and that helps students make decisions about their learning tactics. Formative assessment provides data that can be used immediately. It informs our decision-making process at a point in time where it can make a difference.

Formative assessment emphasizes the importance of sharing the data with students. In formative assessment, the data is not used to label students or to evaluate them; it is used to inform them. When students have information about their progress toward objectives, they can then make decisions about their learning tactics. This information can reinforce their efforts and help them maintain their motivation. If they are not achieving at an appropriate level, it gives them an opportunity to consider other alternatives.

It has been our experience that, if given the choice, all students want to be successful. One problem is that they don't have information about their progress and are therefore unprepared when the summative assessment is administered. They don't understand why they were unsuccessful, and they may give up because they don't know what to do. If students are given clear information and assistance in identifying what they can do to improve, their estimates of the probability of success increases and their motivation and effort increase.

Formative assessment is more intrusive and systematic than diagnostic assessment. Formative assessment needs to occur at the conclusion of significant steps in the learning sequence, and the data gathered through the process needs to be accepted by the students as important and useful. Some of the typical approaches to formative assessment include quizzes, student work samples, teacher observations, and teacher-student interviews.

Summative Assessment

Summative assessment is assessment that is performed at the conclusion of a learning sequence or unit. The purpose of this assessment is to determine if students have achieved the intended outcomes. Data gathered during classroom summative assessment is typically used for important purposes such as determining the success of a particular student, making decisions about continuing to the next unit of instruction, evaluating students, and assigning grades.

Large-scale standardized assessments are usually summative assessments. They are used to identify the students' knowledge at a given point in time, for example, at the conclusion of the 10th grade. This assessment is often used to assess knowledge of several subjects such as math, English, science, and social studies. Large-scale assessments might be used annually to identify the amount of student learning over the past year.

Large-scale standardized assessments are not generally used to assign grades or to make decisions relating to promotion. However, teachers may encounter situations where school administrators will compare the grades assigned by teachers with student performance as measured by a large-scale standardized assessment.

While many policy makers look to the data derived from large-scale assessments as a central element in data-driven decisions, their use for this purpose is limited. Summative assessments occur at the end of a learning sequence and may provide some data that can be used the next time the material is taught. For example, large-scale assessments are usually administered only once a year, usually during spring. This makes sense because it is near the end of the year and is a better indicator of student progress during the year. However, the results are usually not returned to the school or the teacher for several weeks or even months. The particular students have already moved to other teachers and different content. Therefore, the data are not useful in making meaningful changes that benefit a particular group of students because they have moved on to another teacher.

In addition, the population of students taking the test changes each year, so scores may fluctuate on a year-to-year basis depending on the characteristics of the particular group of students taking the test. Changes in scores from one year to the next might be more a function of student variability that program emphasis. Making changes based on a one-year fluctuation of student scores runs a risk of making the wrong decision.

Data gathered from large-scale assessment can be useful in identifying trends over time or might help a school make decisions about changing a particular part of the curriculum that might need more emphasis. The data is often reported back in terms of norms or percentiles. Therefore, it might help a school to compare the performance of their students with similar students across the state and nation. This might be a stimulus for curricular change.

Because of the important consequences of summative assessment, classroom summative assessment needs to be performed carefully and good assessment practices need to be utilized. Summative assessment influences evaluations and grades that will be recorded and viewed by others. The evaluation will be communicated to parents and other interested parties, such as higher education institutions that will view them as part of the admissions process. Therefore, teachers have a moral obligation to make sure that the data gathered for summative assessment is sound and that the evaluations are fair and ethical.

Summative assessment requires assessment procedures that are generally more complex and demanding than formative or diagnostic assessment. The types of assessment procedures that are most appropriate are those that require higher-level thinking ability, such as applying, analyzing, synthesizing, and creating.

Assessment Options

A variety of assessment options can be used in the classroom. They typically include two general types of assessment: (a) traditional assessment and (b) performance assessment.

Traditional Assessment

Traditional assessment refers to assessment tools that have long been part of teaching. Generally they include techniques such as multiple-choice, essay, true/false, matching, and completion items. These types of assessment tools are frequently used in both classroom assessment and large-scale standardized assessment.

In classroom assessments, teachers construct their own assessments that focus specifically on the content of the lessons and units they are teaching. Teachers write test items, construct the test, and score the test. At this point, our focus will be on traditional assessment items that can be used in classroom assessment.

Using Traditional Assessment in the Classroom   Teacher-constructed assessment is the most common form of classroom assessment. It has a potential advantage of increased content validity because it usually measures what has been taught. However, this advantage is often lost because of poorly constructed tests items. When items are poorly constructed, they are confusing to students and increase the probability of chance and guessing. When this happens, the results may not accurately discriminate between those who know the content and those who do not. In the following sections, we will discuss several guidelines that can help you write tests and test items that increase the quality and the validity of your tests.

Basically, the items used on teacher tests are of two types: selected-response items and constructed-response items. Selected-response items are those that ask the student to choose the correct answer from those provided. Examples of selected-response items include multiple choice, true/false, and matching. Constructed-response items are those that require the student to construct or develop an answer. Examples of constructed-response items are essay, short answer, and completion. Tanner (2001) points out that the difference is in how students respond. Constructed-response items require students to produce what they know, while selected-response items require that students recognize the best response among alternatives.

Both types of items have advantages and disadvantages. Being aware of the advantages and disadvantages will help you develop better and more valid classroom tests.

Essay Items   One of the most common types of test items used in teacher-constructed tests in secondary schools is the essay question. Essay items are powerful because they can be used to assess complex and higher-level objectives. They are best directed to objectives that call on students to apply, analyze, synthesize, or evaluate. Essay items require the student to produce something. These items can be used to probe learning more deeply than other types of items, and they help eliminate guessing. Thus, well-constructed essay items can be useful in discriminating between those who know and those who do not. Another potential advantage of essay items is that they are relatively easy to construct.

However, there are some potential disadvantages to essay items. The advantage of ease of construction is countered by the difficulty in scoring. First, each response takes considerable time to read. Second, scoring essay items can be difficult, and the subjective bias of the reader can influence the scoring. Yet another disadvantage is that variables such as handwriting and writing style can influence the scoring. This can be especially troublesome when assessing the learning of students whose first language is not English.

Essay items also require more time for students to respond; therefore, only a few items can be included on a test. This means that only a limited number of objectives can be assessed. Thus, students' success might be based on their knowledge of a limited range of content. In addition, poorly written items can mislead students and lead to erroneous judgments regarding who has learned and who has not.

Although guessing is reduced on essay items, bluffing is increased. Skilled writers often know how to bluff, often receiving good grades for responses that do not answer the central question.

Although the disadvantages of essay items are serious ones, you can overcome most of them by following a few guidelines. First, use essay items to assess higher-level objectives and main ideas. Tanner (2001) points out that some essay items are little more than elaborate recall items. If the intent is to assess specific bits of information, other types of items would be more appropriate.

Another suggestion is to include several shorter, more specific questions rather than a few general ones (Ward & Murray-Ward, 1999). This allows you to select a broader range of content and helps sort those students who have learned from those who have not.

Third, take care in structuring essay questions. This means that the directions regarding what should be included in a response need to be as precise as possible. Notice the difference in the following two sets of instructions:

A. Write an essay in which you discuss the chromosome hypothesis and the gene theory.

B. Write an essay, about five pages in length, in which you compare and contrast the chromosome hypothesis and gene theory. In your answer, provide specific references to (1) essentials of each position, (2) modifications that have been made to each position since it was initially adopted, and (3) strengths and weaknesses that have been attributed to each view by leading experts.

Students receiving instructions similar to those in instruction set A are not provided many clues as to what is expected. They may be inclined to ramble or to try and bluff. Further, there are no references to the length of the response. One student may write one paragraph and another several pages. In light of this imprecise item, the problem of scoring is compounded and confidence in knowing who has accomplished the objective is diminished. Instruction set B is much better. Students will have a clear indication of what is expected of them. The precision of B also helps eliminate bluffing and provides some clues for what will be included in the scoring.

Finally, try to reduce subjectivity when scoring responses. Begin by establishing a method to score papers anonymously. This helps eliminate a "halo effect," where the scores on a paper are influenced by what the reader knows about the student. You might use student numbers or a code that you later match to students' names.

It is also useful to construct a sample response so that you have a clear understanding of what you expect. Another option is to use a scoring protocol that indicates how many points will be given to different aspects of the response (Tanner, 2001).

Completion Items   Another type of constructed-response item is the completion item. This type of item requires the student to fill in a blank that correctly completes a sentence. Completion items are attractive to teachers because they are easy to construct. In addition, a wide array of content can be sampled because students can respond to a large number of completion items during the time they might spend responding to just one essay item.

However, completion items have some serious limitations. First, they are much less powerful in the kind of thinking that can be assessed. They generally sample only recall learning. However, some teachers tend to prefer these to true/false answers because they eliminate guessing.

There are also some potential scoring problems with completion-type items. One problem is that it is difficult to construct a completion item for which a single answer is the only one that is logically correct. It is especially difficult to decide what to do about student answers that are partially correct. To get some perspective on this issue, look at the following completion-type item:

The person who succeeded George Washington as president of the United States was_____.

Probably, the answer the teacher had in mind was "John Adams." Other plausible answers exist, however. For example students might respond with answers such as "from New England" or "a man." These are technically correct answers, and marking them wrong is certain to cause some serious disagreements with students. The students should not be expected to try and guess what the teacher is thinking.

To avoid these problems, completion items need to be written so that students clearly understand the type of response that is required. For example, the above item could be rewritten to narrow the range of plausible answers. A revised version might be:

The name of the person who succeeded George Washington as president of the United States was _____.

In addition, when constructing completion-type items, it is important to restrict the number of blanks in a given item. Too many blank spaces or poorly placed blanks results in confusion and diminishes the validity of the item. Consider this poor example:

_____ affects_____ independently of _____ except on those occasions when_____ and _____ are inversely related.

This item has too many blanks and does not contain enough information to assist students in choosing an appropriate response. In addition to restricting the number of blanks, it is useful to put the blanks near the end of the sentence. This helps provide the context for the answer and eliminates the need for students to reread the item in order to respond.

Another scoring problem relates to misspelled answers or partial answers. Will you give credit for answers that are misspelled? What will you do if the answer is partially correct? For example, on a completion item asking students to fill in the name of the author of *Alice in Wonderland*, one student wrote "Carroll Lewis." How would you score this answer? To accommodate this concern, you need to establish some rules that will guide your decisions on giving credit for completion items. For example, you might provide students with a list of items that are to be used when responding to the completion items. This helps eliminate spelling errors and partial answers. However, it makes it a modified matching item and introduces the possibility of guessing. Box 6-2 is an example of a completion test with a provided list of terms.

In general, completion items do not represent a particularly good technique for assessing students' proficiencies. In most cases, other types of items can measure the same learning with fewer problems.

Matching Items   Matching items are selected-response items. A selection of responses is provided, and the person taking the test must select the correct or the best one. They are generally used to measure less sophisticated levels of student thinking. They are easy to

---

Box 6-2   An Example of Completion Items

Directions: The following paragraph contains a number of blanks. Below the paragraph, you will find a list of terms. Choose items from this list and print them carefully in the appropriate blanks. Include only terms in the list at the bottom of the page. Terms must be spelled correctly.

In recent years, there has been a trend for people to move away from the core of the city toward surrounding suburbs. Sociologists call this movement _____. Another urban phenomenon involves the movement of people from one social class to a part of the city occupied by people in another social class. This is termed _____. When a new group in society succeeds in taking over a neighborhood, a situation termed _____ results. When minority members of a community are removed by majority members, the situation is called _____. When this causes married couples to move to a locale where neither set of parents is resident, their new family residence is said to be _____. The group an individual interacts with over time on a more or less continuous basis is called a(n) _____.

Terms

recurrent	suburbanization	succession	allotropic	concession
neolocal	separation	expulsion	invasion	
patrilocal	segregation	deviance		

construct, they can be corrected quickly, and there is little subjectivity in the grading. Therefore, there is no danger that one student's test will be graded using a standard that is different from another student's test.

Difficulties associated with the use of matching items usually have to do with item construction. One construction problem relates to the types of items selected for both of the lists to be matched. Students become confused when they are confronted with matching items containing a mixture of unrelated terms and definitions. In addition, this reduces the item difficulty because it allows the good test taker to eliminate a number of the possible choices. Therefore, all terms in a matching item should focus on a single topic or theme. For example, if you decided to prepare a matching test on the Civil War, you might have one column with the names of Confederate generals and another column with a number of exploits associated with them. It would not be wise to mix in other names and events unrelated to the Confederate generals.

As a rule of thumb, the list on the right side (the one providing the choices to be selected as possible answers) should contain approximately 25% more items than the list on the left side. For example, if you want the students to match 10 items, you should provide them with 12 or 13 alternative choices on the right side.

The entire matching item should be on one page. It is unacceptable for any portion of the item to be on another page. When this happens, students often overlook the part of the item on the second page, resulting in mistakes and confusion.

The preferred format is to place a blank before each item to be matched and to provide a letter identifying each possible choice so that the student fills in the blank with the letter of their choice. Drawing lines between the two columns is not recommended because the result can be a confusing tangle of lines that are hard to follow. This will usually result in disputes as students claim that you didn't follow the correct line. Box 6-3 is an example of a properly formatted matching test.

Box 6-3 Example of a Properly Formatted Matching Test

MATCHING TEST: TENNIS TERMINOLOGY
Directions: Find the term in the right-hand column that is defined by the definition in the left-hand column. Place the letter identifying this term in the blank space provided before its definition. Only one term is correct for each definition. Do not draw lines connecting the terms and the definitions.

____ 1. The point that, if won, wins the match for a player

____ 2. The area between the net and the service line

____ 3. Hitting the ball before it bounces

____ 4. Stroke made after the ball has bounced, either forehand or backhand

____ 5. The line that is perpendicular to the net and divides the two service courts

____ 6. The initial part of any swing; the act of bringing the racket back to prepare for the forward swing

____ 7. A ball hit high enough in the air to pass over the head of the net player

____ 8. A ball that is served so well that the opponent fails to touch it with his or her racquet

____ 9. A shot that bounces near the baseline

____10. Start of play for a given point

a. ace
b. backswing
c. center service line
d. deep shot
e. forecourt
f. set point
g. lob
h. match point
i. serve
j. volley
k. dink
l. ground stroke

Multiple-Choice Items   Multiple-choice items are also selected-response items. Evaluation experts have long shown a preference for multiple-choice items (Hatlie, Jaeger, & Bond, 1999) because multiple-choice items are very flexible. They can measure a variety of subjects and have the capacity of testing not only knowledge, but also higher-level thinking abilities. They can be scored easily and quickly, and subjectivity in scoring is very low. Because a person can respond to a number of multiple-choice items in the time it takes to respond to a single essay or short-answer question, content coverage is another advantage of multiple-choice items.

A disadvantage of multiple-choice items is that writing good multiple-choice items can be difficult. It takes a good deal of skill and thought to write items that measure worthwhile outcomes. In fact, the negative reaction that some individuals have to multiple-choice items is related to the hurried and careless construction of items.

Another possible problem with multiple-choice items is that they do allow for a certain measure of guessing. If four choices are provided, a student has a 25% probability of getting the item right simply by guessing. You can overcome these construction problems by following a few basic guidelines.

First, do not wait until the night before a test to write the items. Construct an item bank of possible test items as you are teaching the unit. These can be keyed to the content and the particular objective they are intended to measure. Then when the time comes to construct a test, these items can be reviewed and the test constructed.

Actual item construction poses other challenges that need to be addressed. Poorly constructed items either give away the correct response or confuse students so they do not know what is being asked. In either case, the evidence gathered through the test becomes suspect and an evaluation about what a student knows or does not know is invalid.

In terms of format, multiple-choice items consist of two parts: (1) a stem and (2) some alternative choices. Among the choices are the correct answer and some distracters. Good distracters should be plausible choices that would be chosen by individuals who do not know the correct answer. The difficulty of the item depends on the level of thinking that is required to distinguish correct answers from the distracters. For example, good distracters might require working out a problem or engaging in some high-level thinking in order to identify the correct answer.

You will find it challenging to prepare multiple-choice items where the distracters all appear to be plausible answers. Carelessly written distracters tend to give away the correct answer, even to students who do not know the content. Good items take time to develop; hence, high-quality multiple-choice items cannot be prepared in haste.

When you construct multiple-choice items, make sure that the stem is clear and that you write all distracters in a way that ensures grammatical consistency with the stem. Consider this example:

Nils Johansen, in his novel of the Canadian prairies, **West from Winnipeg,** *called trapping an*

a. science   *b. art*   *c. duty*   *d. nuisance*

A student unfamiliar with this novel who read the question carefully would identify "b" as the correct answer simply because it is the only choice grammatically consistent with the article "an" at the end of the stem. To correct this problem, the writer of the item might have concluded the stem in this way ". . . called trapping a(n)." This revision makes any of the four distracters plausible.

A stem that is too brief fails to cue the students regarding the kind of information they should be looking for in the distracters. Consider the following example:

Roger Williams

  a. sailed on the Mayflower.

  b. established the Thanksgiving tradition.

   c. founded the Rhode Island colony.

   d. developed the New World's first distillery.

Because the stem is so incomplete, students are really faced with four true/false items to ponder rather than with one good multiple-choice item. A better way of writing this question would be as follows:

The founder of the Rhode Island colony was

   a. Sir Walter Raleigh.

   b. John Winthrop.

   c. Roger Williams.

   d. William Bradford.

As noted earlier, multiple-choice items can be designed to test quite sophisticated levels of thinking. Consider the example in Box 6-4. It challenges students to make inferences based on their analysis of the prose. As the example in Box 6-4 illustrates, it is possible to use multiple-choice questions to assess students' abilities to engage in quite challenging levels of thinking. However, you will find that constructing multiple-choice questions such as the one in the box take time. You may decide that essay questions better suit your needs when you want to test your students' abilities to apply, analyze, synthesize, and evaluate.

True/False Items   True/false items, though most frequently used to assess knowledge-level thinking, do have some limited applications when you are interested in assessing your students' abilities to engage in more complex levels of thinking. True/false items can be prepared relatively quickly. They provide a format that ensures consistency of scoring. Finally, true/false items can be scored quickly.

True/false items have some disadvantages. For one thing, they encourage guessing. Because there are only two choices, your students have a 50-50 chance of getting an item correct, even when they have no grasp of the content being tested. True/false items require you to prepare statements that are absolutely true or absolutely false. Much course content tends toward gray areas. For this reason, you may feel constrained by the true/false format,

---

Box 6-4   Multiple-Choice Item Focusing on Higher-Level Thinking Abilities

Directions: Read the passage and circle the letter of the answer you select.

Ellison has the flair of genius, but he was not a genius. Though pedestrian in his approaches, he was a phenomenon. His was a talent of concentration, not of innovation. No other man of his time rivaled his ability to shunt aside irrelevancies to focus on a problem's essentials. For him, noncritical considerations were a trifling bit of detritus to be swept away in a moment. His resolute attack on the nuggety essence of an unresolved issue obviated even the serious possibility of egregious error. Contemporaries described his reasoning as "glistening." Only an audacious few ventured public challenges to his positions. It is not too much to say that he lived out his days surrounded by a nervously approving silence. Later generations have seen his conclusions as less than revolutionary. But in his own time, Ellison's ability to "will" an impeccable solution to a complex issue made others seem small figures destined ever to walk lightly in the dark shadows of a giant.

One assumption revealed in the preceding paragraph is

   a. Ellison was truly competent, but he had a flair for impressing people with the logical structure he built to support his solutions.

   b. Ellison really was a genius whose "glistening" logic resulted in novel solutions to problems.

   c. Today, people tend to be more impressed with Ellison than they were in his own day.

   d. Ellison's form probably was more a significant contributor to his reputation than was the substance of his thought.

Box 6-5 Example of a True/False Test

Directions: Use the data provided in the chart below to respond to the following true/false items. If the statement is true, circle the word *True*. If the statement is false, circle the word *False*.

Number of Individuals Employed As Teachers (in Thousands)*

Year	Elementary	Secondary
1998	1,866	1,243
1999	1,885	1,260
2000	1,903	1,276
2001	1,920	1,291
2002	1,935	1,306
2003	1,943	1,325
2004	1,949	1,347

True False 1. There will be an increase in the numbers of both elementary and secondary teachers in each year from 1998 through 2004.

True False 2. The number of additional elementary teachers added each year from 1998 through 2004 will be larger in the years at the beginning of this time period than in the years toward the end.

True False 3. From this information, we can infer that the numbers of secondary students will increase at a slower rate than will the numbers of elementary pupils in the years 1998 through 2004.

True False 4. There will be a larger total increase in the the number of secondary teachers than the number of elementary teaches over the entire time period from 1998 through 2004.

True False 5. The smallest annual increase in the number of elementary teachers will occur between the same two years as the largest annual increase in the number of secondary teachers.

*Data are from D. E. Gerald and W. J. Husser (1993). Projections of education statistics to 2009 (p. 72). Washington, DC: Department of Education, Office of Educational Research and Improvement, National Center for Education Statistics.

which may require you to stay away from the main focus of your instruction to find the odd example that is absolutely true or absolutely false.

One way to eliminate potential scoring disputes is to include the words *True* and *False* before each item and instruct the students to circle the correct response. An example of a properly formatted true/false test that asks questions about expected changes in the numbers of employed teachers, as projected by the National Center for Educational Statistics (Gerald & Hussar, 1999), is provided in Box 6-5.

Performance Assessment

With the increased emphasis on data-driven decisions and accountability, some experts began questioning the value of data gathered using traditional testing practices. They pointed out that most traditional testing situations involved contrived and artificial situations. They also questioned what was being measured by traditional assessments. They noted that assessment should focus on important intellectual skills and developing "habits of mind," such as critical thinking, problem-solving, making effective presentations based on data, applying knowledge to new situations and working with others (Schmoker, 2009). These are not skills that are often measured using traditional assessment methods.

They claimed that rather than gathering evidence in artificial situations, it would be better to base evaluations on evidence gained from students engaged in authentic, or real, tasks. For example, rather than giving a paper-and-pencil test relating to an important objective such as problem-solving, they advocated assessing students as they address a real or authentic problem.

This is not a new concept. Some important life tasks have involved authentic tasks. For example, when you seek a driver's license, not only must you complete a traditional assessment of your knowledge of the rules of the road, you must also perform the actual task of driving the car while being evaluated by a trained observer. Wiggins (1989) argues that authentic assessments should replicate the challenges and involve standards of performance that typically confront people such as writers, businesspeople, scientists, community leaders, designers, and historians.

This concern about making sure that what is assessed is directly related to important outcomes of instruction has led to an increased emphasis on performance assessment. Performance assessments refers to evaluating the performance of students as they are engaged in complex, authentic tasks requiring them to prepare a product, a response, or a performance (McTighe & Wiggins, 2004).

One of the first steps in performance assessment is to identify authentic tasks that are realistic, ask the students to demonstrate their knowledge and ability, simulate what is required of adults in the workplace or the community, and require the students to use a variety of skills and knowledge. These tasks are developed into a scenario that is presented to the students. The scenario requires the students to assume a specific role and to develop a product that is directed to the accomplishment of a clear goal and addresses a specific audience. It is important to make sure that the performance task is clearly related to important unit outcomes and should be as similar as possible to real-life tasks.

Once the performance task has been identified, you then need to define how you will assess the performance. This can be done using tools such as checklists, rating scales, or rubrics. Therefore, performance assessment requires considerable thought and planning. You can justify the time commitment because what students experience during authentic assessment activities is really an extension of your basic instruction. Performance tasks become a teaching tool as well as an assessment tool.

Using Rubrics   One of the most common methods for assessing performance tasks is the use of a rubric. A rubric is actually a behaviorally anchored rating scale. This means that the points on a rating scale are defined by specific behaviors or indicators related to each point. For example, the definition of each step of the scale goes beyond vague terms such as *excellent, above average, average, or inadequate.* The behaviorally anchored scale or rubric defines specific behaviors or indicators that define what is excellent or average. The content of the rubric defines what to look for in a student's performance or product to determine its quality. It is important that the rubric cover the essential qualities and leave out the trivial (Arter & McTighe, 2001). A good test of a rubric would be the extent to which different observers would view the same performance or product and assign the same assessment.

Rubrics are usually of two types. One type is a holistic rubric that gives a single score or rating for an entire performance or product. The second type is an analytical rubric that divides the performance into essential dimensions so that each dimension can be rated separately. Holistic rubrics are generally best when evaluating a relatively simple product that may have only one important dimension. They are useful for giving a general view of the overall quality. However, they do not give a detailed analysis of the strengths and weaknesses of a performance or product and therefore are of limited use to students in knowing what is required for improvement (Arter & McTighe, 2001).

Analytical rubrics are best for complex performances with several important dimensions. They also provide more specific feedback to students and parents and are more useful in helping you pinpoint areas that might need more instruction (Arter & McTighe, 2001).

One of the drawbacks with rubrics is that good ones are difficult to construct. You need to have a very clear understanding of your objectives and what is expected of students. You then need to be able to identify, in detail, different performance levels.

While there is no one way to construct rubrics, we have a few suggestions. One technique we have found useful is to start by defining acceptable minimal performance. The next step is to identify what would be considered as outstanding performance and what would be unacceptable. This results in a three-point rubric. If more points on the scale are desired, then additional levels can be added between the acceptable level and the two extremes to make a five-point rubric. When you have the beginnings of a rubric, share it with others who know the subject and get their input.

If you have samples of student performances from previous assignments, you can use another useful approach. Take these examples of student work and sort them into three or more piles based on the quality of the example. Then describe the elements that make them different. This will help you identify the elements that might be included for each of the dimensions of the rubric (Arter & McTighe, 2001).

Once you have a rubric, it is useful to test it with other professionals to see if they agree on how they would rate specific examples of student performances. This step can be very valuable in making sure that your rubric is clear and has some validity. Box 6-6 is an example of a holistic rubric that can be used to evaluate an oral presentation. Review it and think about how you might alter it to fit your definition of a good oral performance.

Evaluative Checklists   Another useful tool for assessing performance tasks or products is the evaluative checklist. Checklists are often used when there is a yes or no decision

---

Box 6-6   Example of a Rubric for an Oral Presentation

5   A clear statement of the topic or question
A persuasive argument is presented for the importance of the topic
Facts and information gathered from research are smoothly integrated
Eye contact is maintained throughout
Correct grammar used
Student refers to notes, but does not read
Presentation has a smooth and logical flow

4   A clear statement of the topic or question
Importance of the topic or question adequately stated
Knowledge and data drawn from research is incorporated
Few grammatical errors
Speech is clear
There is a generally smooth flow and logical organization with minimal digressions
Eye contact is made with some lapses
Use of notes is prominent

3   The question or topic is stated
There are occasional errors in grammar, sentence structure

Knowledge and data drawn from research is superficially included
Speech and diction is adequate
There is evidence of organization
Considerable reading of the material
Occasional eye contact

2   The question or topic is not clear
Few facts or information from research is included
There is a lack of enthusiasm in the presentation
Little eye contact
Most of the presentation is read
Significant grammatical and sentence structure errors
Logic of the presentation is unclear

1   The question or topic is not stated
No attempt to justify importance of topic
The presentation is fragmented with no logical flow
Major grammatical and structural errors
Little evidence of research
Presentation is read
Minimal eye contact

and degrees of performance variability are unimportant. For example, a checklist would be an appropriate tool for assessing the ability to drive a car. Drivers either know how to start the car or they do not; they can shift into gear or they cannot. There are few degrees of performance variability. Therefore, spending time constructing a rubric is unnecessary. Arranging items on a checklist in the order they occur makes the checklist easier to use.

If there are certain items on the checklist that are more important than others, they may be given more weight or more points. For example, in the driving example cited above, while it is important to know how to insert the key and start the car, it is probably not as important as signaling and making a safe lane change. Thus, items such as changing lanes safely and stopping at traffic signals would be given more weight and more points in the assessment of the performance.

Portfolios   In recent years portfolios have become a popular assessment tool. A portfolio is a collection of artifacts relating to important learning outcomes. Portfolios have long been used in areas such as art. The artist compiles a portfolio that includes samples of her or his work. These work samples are selected in order to demonstrate the knowledge and skill of the artist. Similarly, the portfolio provides students with an opportunity to select the best samples of their work and present them as evidence of what they know and have learned. The task of the students is to select those items that will best reflect their knowledge and ability.

A potential advantage of a portfolio is that it allows for student choice and therefore prompts student self-evaluation. Self-evaluation is an important type of evaluation that leads to student improvement. In addition, a portfolio is not an event but a process. Portfolios can include a variety of items, ranging from everyday artifacts to samples of performances over time and in multiple settings. The fact that it is a process has the potential of increasing the validity of the data.

Just gathering material together in a portfolio does not automatically mean, however, that portfolios are more valid assessment techniques. Care must be taken in selecting items to be included; they must relate to important outcomes. And a clear set of criteria (such as a rubric) must be used in the assessment.

Components of portfolios vary depending on the subject being taught and the preferences of teachers and students. Some examples of the items that might be contained in a portfolio include the following:

- Completed assignments
- Journal entries (reflections by the students about content that has been learned)
- Answers to prompt questions supplied by the teacher
- Photos, sketches, and other visuals
- Special projects
- Summary statements made at different points regarding what has been learned
- Self-assessment statements regarding areas of strength and areas needing additional work

The artifacts collected in a portfolio have the advantage of providing an opportunity for one-on-one discussions during the evaluation process. With a portfolio, tangible evidence can be discussed that leads to a grading decision. This helps remove some of mystery involved in the grading process. Rather than looking upon a grade as "something the teacher gave me," it can help the student see it as "something I earned."

Identifying material for inclusion in a portfolio is only the first step. Portfolios must be evaluated. Because the content and the complexity of a portfolio can vary widely, the approach to evaluating them can also vary widely. As with other performance assessments, rubrics are the most common method for evaluating portfolios.

More from the Web

Several websites provide help to teachers who are concerned about evaluation and assessment. The following are just a few examples that can provide assistance as you consider the needs of your students and of yourself in your classroom.

RUBISTAR FOR TEACHERS

http://rubistar.4teachers.org

This website provides assistance to those teachers who want to create rubrics for their students' projects. They provide a variety of formats and allow you to modify them and add your own descriptors if you prefer. Your rubrics can be saved and accessed whenever you need to modify them.

THE NATIONAL CENTER FOR FAIR AND OPEN TESTING

www.fairtest.org

This mission of this website is to end the misuses and flaws of standardized testing and ensure fair evaluation of teachers, students, and schools. Excellent links provide access to a number of worthwhile books and articles that stimulate thoughtful consideration of this topic.

Evaluation and Grading

Assessment is the process of gathering data about student learning. Evaluation is the process of interpreting and judging the data. Grading is the process of communicating the judgment to interested parties, including the student. The quality of a particular grading system is the degree to which it communicates valuable information to those interested parties. For example, what does the evaluation or grading system communicate to those who use the data? What does a grade of B actually communicate? What inferences might be made by someone viewing the grade? Does it mean that the student mastered the required objectives? Does it mean that the student is above average? What is "above average"? Does it communicate the work habits and effort that the student put forth?

The fact is that the traditional grading system does not do a very good job of communicating important information to interested parties. This has led to concerns about so-called grade inflation and a movement toward requiring competency tests for graduation rather than relying on a grade point average.

Grading is one dimension of teaching that many teachers dislike. One reason is that it places teachers in a position of being a judge that interferes with their primary role of helping students learn. This conflict is not as apparent when using formative assessments and assessment for learning. Such a conflict arises, however, in summative assessment or assessment of learning.

A second aspect that makes grading difficult is that it places the teacher in a position where she or he often has to make difficult decisions. Teachers develop personal relationships with students and want them to be successful. It is then difficult to be an objective judge basing a grade solely on data. There is always an element of subjectivity in evaluation. Just identifying the criteria for evaluation is somewhat subjective. This subjectivity is what makes grading difficult for most teachers. Teachers ask themselves, Will this grade encourage or discourage students? Is it a fair estimate of my professional judgment? Will the grade affect the future prospects of the student? Will it unfairly label them?

For the most part, teachers get their ideas about how to grade from their own experience. Over the years, you have had numerous teachers and have seen various grading systems. You will favor those that you thought were most fair. Grading will also be based on your personal philosophy of teaching and learning. Those individuals who see their role as one of identifying and rewarding talent will generally approach grading differently than those who view the role of teacher as one of fostering the personal growth of all students (Guskey & Bailey, 2001).

Another consideration in establishing a grading system is school district or department policies. For example, one of us once taught in a district where the policy was that if a student was working at grade level, he or she was to get a C. If he or she was a year above grade level, they were to get a B. While this appeared to be an objective system, defining grade level and what constituted evidence of above or below grade level was subjective. In addition, it did not address the situation where a student might be considerably above grade level and put forth little effort. One the other hand, it did not reward the student who might be below grade level but had made considerable improvement.

One study found that about two-thirds of the school districts have grading policies. However, many teachers reported that these were vague and ambiguous (Guskey & Bailey, 2001). Even though there is a high probability that you will teach in a school district with a grading policy, ultimately, you will have to rely on your knowledge, educational philosophy, and professional judgment to determine your grading system.

Types of Grading Criteria

An important aspect of grading is to make sure there is a clear set of criteria for awarding grades. Basically, two types of criteria can be used in performing an evaluation of student performance: norm-referenced criteria and criterion-referenced criteria.

Norm-Referenced Evaluation

Norm-Referenced Evaluation   In a norm-referenced system, the performance of an individual is evaluated based on the performance of a reference group. The score of an individual is compared to a frequency distribution, often the normal distribution or the bell-shaped curve. The distribution is based on the assumption that given traits will be distributed throughout the population on a normal distribution, with few cases at each of the extremes and most cases in the middle.

In classrooms, teachers use norm-referenced evaluation when they compare the performance of each student to the performance of the rest of the class. This is what is generally called grading on the curve. The grades are plotted on a distribution and cut-off points are determined for different grades.

This practice has several limitations. First, the grade of an individual is based on the quality of work of other class members. A student in a class that contains a large percentage of high-performing students might receive a low grade yet have outperformed students who received higher grades in another class because the class had a group of students that did not score as well. In essence, understanding a grade based on norm-referenced evaluation standards requires knowledge of the characteristics of the reference group. For example, in a university graduate class where the professor graded strictly on a curve, students receiving a grade of F were still getting over 90% of the answers correct. Therefore, the grade doesn't indicate what a student has learned or is able to do. It only identifies the relative standing of the student in a given group.

For this reason some assessment experts criticize the use of norm-referenced standards as a grading system in a given classroom. The normal distribution is best applied to chance and random activities, not to purposeful activities that do not include a random sample of the general population (Guskey & Bailey, 2001).

Second, the norm-referenced system introduces what can be unhealthy competition between students. It is to an individual's advantage that others do poorly. This reduces cooperation between students. For example, one study group of students purposefully gave wrong answers to others or "played dumb" because they did not want to help others get good scores. These practices are counter to the conditions that foster a positive learning environment.

Finally, it is important to remember that competition motivates individuals who believe they have a chance to win. Therefore, students who find themselves in a class of talented students may not be motivated because they do not believe they have a chance to obtain a good grade.

Many large-scale standardized assessments report scores based on a norm-referenced system. In the test development phase, they administer the test to a sample of students and use their responses to establish a normal distribution against which all individuals taking the test are compared. If this is done carefully, then the norm-referenced evaluations that they supply can help a school in a particular district make comparisons between their students and what might be termed a normal distribution of students.

Criterion-Referenced Evaluation A criterion-referenced system compares the performance of an individual to specific criteria. The performance of others in the group is not considered when performing the evaluation. In a secondary classroom, the criteria might be a rubric that indicates the requirements for a given grade. This rubric or other criteria should be based on important objectives that were emphasized during a particular evaluation period.

Generally, a grade that is based on a criterion-referenced system should indicate the extent to which each student has mastered the objectives. Teachers who use this system often define at the beginning of the course exactly what must be done to receive a particular grade. This has the effect of changing responsibility for the grade from the teacher to the students. They know the expectations and can choose to work toward a particular grade.

Criterion-referenced systems are most compatible with mastery learning environments. Mastery learning is based on the premise that nearly all students can achieve success if they are given sufficient time and if they are allowed to redo assignments that do not meet the standard. The intent of mastery learning is to assist all students in achieving success.

Implementing a criterion system is considerably more difficult that implementing a norm-referenced system. Developing a criterion-referenced system requires clear specification of learning goals, defining a criterion level for each level of performance, and deciding what type of evidence will be used to validate student performance. Basically you need to establish criteria for each objective. You need to make sure the criteria for the highest performance levels really are indicative of high-quality performance. However, you don't want the criterion level to be so high that no one can attain it, thus discouraging students. Establishing criterion levels that are fair and appropriate for the students you are teaching requires careful attention and experience.

Once you have decided on an evaluation system, you then need to consider how you will award grades. As indicated above, you may have to follow school policies. However, most school policies are vague enough to allow you considerable discretion in how you are to award grades.

Establishing a Grading Plan

The traditional grading and reporting system that has widespread use is the five-point letter grade system. Each of the letter grades generally has a descriptor that indicates the meaning of the particular grade. For example, it is quite common that the descriptor for the grade of A is outstanding, B is above average, C is average, D is below average, and F is failing. Note that these descriptors are clearly norm-referenced terms because they refer to an average. A criterion-referenced set of descriptors might be A is excellent, B is good, C is satisfactory, D is poor, and F is unacceptable.

As all of us know, these descriptors have value-laden implications that stigmatize students. Who wants to be known as below average, poor, or even average? In recent years, some schools have rejected these value-laden terms in favor of more descriptive categories, and in some instances, they have rejected letter grades altogether (Guskey & Bailey, 2001). For example, Nebraska established a four-category reporting system that is clearly more criterion-referenced and uses terms that are more encouraging. The terms used to define the levels of performance are *beginning, progressing, proficient, and advanced.*

Another common system bases grades on a percentage or a point system. In some instances, the points that are accumulated over a grading period are reported. For example, the grade might indicate that this particular student achieved 90% of the points or achieved 90% of the objectives. This allows for maximum discrimination between students because the difference between a score of 90% and 99% indicates a difference in performance level, even though both would qualify for a grade of A in a letter grade system.

Because many consumers of summative evaluations are familiar with letter grades, some grading systems translate the points or percentages to a letter grade. Those who get between 90% and 100% of the available points receive an A; between 80% and 89%, a B; between 70% and 79% a C; and so forth.

In any of these systems, you will generally have a great deal of responsibility in recording student grades or points on various assignments and assessment activities, and condensing your evaluation into a single grade. This requires that you keep good student records. This will assist you greatly in providing the basis for grades when the grading period arrives. Several sources of evidence that can be included in your grading plan are homework assignments, major projects, test scores, laboratory projects, student portfolios, and oral presentations. Some grading systems also include a score for classroom participation and attendance. Those advocating this practice note that it is important for consumers of the grades to have an indication of important traits such as work habits, classroom behavior, effort, and persistence. However, they contend that these should be recorded separately, or the validity of the grade as an indicator of learning is compromised (Tanner, 2001).

Once you have identified the sources of evidence that you will use in arriving at a grade, you should then decide how much weight you are going to give each one. For example, how much weight you will you give homework scores? Will they count as 25% of the grade? How much will the tests and the major projects count? You will want to take into account the importance of each source of data and how it relates to important course objectives.

FOR YOUR PORTFOLIO

Given the fact that assessment and evaluation have become so important in education, it would be important to include evidence of your understanding of assessment and evaluation in your portfolio. Interstate New Teacher Assessment and Support Consortium (INTASC) Standard 8 focuses on evaluation. Keep in mind that you want to present evidence that you have a solid understanding of the issues and processes of assessment and evaluation. Review what you have learned from this chapter and the assignments you may have completed for your class. You may also choose to do some of the learning extension activities. From these, choose up to three items to include in your portfolio. For each of the items included, write a brief statement indicating why you chose this particular entry and what it indicates about your knowledge of assessment and evaluation.

You might also review the material to determine if your entries relate to any of the other standards. Identify which INTASC standards these entries address using the chart below.

INTASC Standards

Item Number	S-1	S-2	S-3	S-4	S-5	S-5	S-6	S-7	S-8	S-9	S-10
1											
2											
3											

Although a grading and reporting system can be complicated and elaborate, you can develop systems for deciding how to weight various scores and determine a final grade. We suggest you keep it simple. Begin with something that keeps a focus on important objectives, is consistent with your philosophy, takes into account school or district policies, and is fair to the students.

Develop a good recordkeeping system and keep the data that you will include in calculating a final grade to a reasonable amount. It is probably not important that you keep every score. Some of the data you gather might be used for formative evaluation rather than summative evaluation. Focus on the important assignments, performance tasks, and tests. This will keep you from being overwhelmed during grading period.

Key Ideas in Summary

- Assessment refers to the process of gathering evidence about student learning. Evaluation is the process of making judgments about the evidence. Grading is communicating the judgment to other interested parties.

- Assessment should gather data about important and worthwhile goals, should include a variety of procedures, should include adequate sampling of student learning, and be ethical and fair to the students.

- There should be a clear connection between assessment and instruction. If done properly, assessment and instruction are complimentary components of good teaching and learning.

- Developing a table of specifications at the same time that unit planning takes places helps insure that important objectives are measured.

- Teacher-made tests are a common assessment tool. Their value as an assessment tool relates to the quality of the test items that are included. There are two basic types: constructed responses and selected response. Both types have strengths and weaknesses. Constructed response items include essay and completion types. Selected response items include matching, multiple choice and true-false types.

- Authentic, natural assessment refers to the idea that assessment should be a natural part of the teaching process and that evaluation should be based on real or authentic tasks rather than the data gathered though artificial and controlled methods generally associated with traditional tests.

- Individuals interested in authentic assessment often use portfolios. A portfolio is a systematically organized collection of a student's work that covers specific objectives and a specific period of time. They allow for the inclusion of multiple sources of evidence concerning student learning.

- Assessment rubrics are tools that are often used to evaluate the quality of student products or performances that are commonly associated with authentic, natural assessment. They are basically behaviorally anchored rating scales that have clear indicators for each performance level.

- Evaluative checklists are useful tools when a yes or no decision is appropriate or where degrees of performance are unimportant. The checklist should identify all the important components of a required performance. If the items on the checklist can be arranged in the order they generally appear, scoring will be easier.

- Standardized assessment has become an important component in the educational landscape. They are increasingly used for high stakes purposes such as determining student promotion, teacher evaluations, and school accreditation. Standardized assessment is an assessment where there are controlled standards for administrating, scoring and reporting results. They often include well written items. However, because they are developed by for profit corporations who seek to use sell them across the nation, they focus on broad outcomes and may not match the objectives of a given school district.

■ Grading is one dimension of teaching that many teachers dislike. This is due to several factors: (a) grading is time consuming; and (2) grading places teachers in the role of a judge a position that is counter to the role of student advocate.

■ Norm referenced evaluation and grading compares the performance of an individual to the performance of a group. Criterion referenced evaluation and grading compares the performance of an individual to a standard or a set of criteria. In recent years, there has been a movement away from norm referenced grading in favor of more criterion referenced grading.

■ Letter grading is still the most common form of grading. However, some places have moved away from the definition of grades as a norm referenced in favor of a more of a standards approach. Another common form of grading bases grades on percentages.

■ The role of the teacher is defining the sources of data for gathering evidence, weighing the evidence, keeping accurate records and deciding how to summarize the data into a final grade. It can be a very time consuming process so it is important to try and develop a simple yet fair grading system.

Learning Extensions

1. There has been much debate concerning the role of standardized testing in education. Do some additional research and identify a list of the advantages and disadvantages of standardized assessment.

2. Design an assessment plan for a unit in your subject area. Identify at least five objectives, and state the assessment technique you will use and how you will specifically implement it.

3. Construct a sample test that you might use for assessing student learning in your subject area. Construct at least two essay items, several completion items, a matching item, at least five multiple-choice items, and at least five true/false items.

4. Develop a sample rubric that you could use to evaluate a student performance for an objective in your content area.

5. Define some authentic, natural assessment tasks that you could use in your classroom.

6. Identify your philosophy of teaching and learning and how it will influence how you grade students. Will you use norm-referenced or criterion-referenced grading? How will your grading system work?

References

Arter, J., & McTighe, J. (2001). *Scoring rubrics in the classroom*. Thousand Oaks, CA: Corwin Press.

Gerald, D. E., & Hussar, W. J. (1999). *Projections of educational statistics to 2009*. Washington, DC: U.S. Department of Education, Office of Educational Research and Improvement, National Center for Educational Statistics.

Guskey, T. R., & Bailey, J. M. (2001). *Developing grading and reporting systems for student learning*. Thousand Oaks, CA: Corwin Press.

McTighe, J., & Wiggins, G. (2004). *The understanding by design handbook*. Alexandria, VA: Association for Supervision and Curriculum Development.

Popham, W. J. (2001). *The truth about testing: An educator's call to action*. Alexandria, VA: Association for Supervision and Curriculum Development.

Popham, W. J. (2008). *Transformative assessment.* Alexandria, VA: Association for Supervision and Curriculum Development.

Popham, W. J. (2009). Anchoring down the data. In *Educational Leadership,* 66(4), 85–86.

Powell, R., McLaughlin, H., Savage, T. and Zehm, S. (2001). *Classroom management: Perspectives on the social curriculum.* Upper Saddle River, NJ: Merrill.

Rudner, L., & Schafer, W. (2002). *What teachers need to know about assessment.* Washington D.C.: National Education Association.

Schmoker, M. (2009). "Measuring what matters." In *Educational Leadership,* 66(4), 70–73.

Stiggins, R. J. (1997). *Student-centered classroom assessment,* 2nd ed. Upper Saddle River, NJ: Merrill.

Stiggins, R. J., Arter, J. A., Chappuis, J., & Chappuis, S. (2004). *Classroom assessment for learning; Doing it right—using it well.* Portland, OR: Assessment Training Institute.

Tanner, D. E. (2001). *Assessing academic achievement.* Needham Heights, MA: Allyn and Bacon.

Ward, A. W., & Murray-Ward, M. (1999). *Assessment in the classroom.* Belmont, CA: Wadsworth.

Wiggins, G. (1989). A true test: Toward more authentic and equitable measurement. *Phi Delta Kappan, 70*(8), 703–713.

Wiggins, G., & McTighe, J. (2005). *Understanding by design.* Alexandria, VA: Association for Supervision and Curriculum Development.

Planning Units and Lessons

Objectives

This chapter will help you

- identify the three types of instructional planning
- describe the importance of unit and lesson planning
- define the three steps in the backward planning model
- explain the components of unit and lesson plans

- describe the components of several models for planning lessons
- point out some basic issues that need to be addressed in preparing a lesson plan
- help you develop a useable format for preparing unit and lesson plans

Bob Daemmrich Photography

Graphic Organizer: Chapter 7

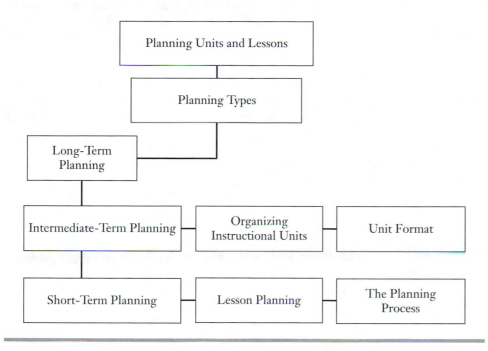

Introduction

One of the most important time investments for a secondary teacher involves planning. While many novice teachers are anxious to get in front of the classroom, good teachers understand that the difference between successful and unsuccessful lessons resides in thoughtful planning. For example, one beginning student teacher, after a particularly difficult lesson, remarked, "But it looks so easy!" Indeed good teachers, like other skilled professionals, make teaching appear easy. To a great extent, this is accomplished through good planning.

Researchers have found that effective teachers spend considerable time planning their lessons. One study found that outstanding teachers devote 10 to 20 hours a week outside the classroom to instructional planning (Clark & Yinger, 1979). Although this represents a considerable investment in time, the payoff is significant. Thorough and thoughtful planning provides teachers with an increased sense of confidence, helps keep lessons moving forward in a logical flow, helps teachers respond to unanticipated occurrences, and helps keep students on task. The importance of planning is often overlooked because the casual observer does not see the time and the decisions that a teacher invests before entering the classroom.

Planning Types

Instructional planning can be divided into three basic types. We label these types as follows:

- Long term
- Intermediate
- Short term

Long-Term Planning

When you are employed as a teacher, you will probably be given a specific assignment. That assignment might be defined as something like "ninth-grade world history," or "senior English." But those titles don't tell us much. There is an enormous amount of content included in world history and several options that could be included in senior English. You need to know what specific aspects of that topic you will be teaching in the approximately 180 days of instruction that make up the academic year. Where do you begin? Where should you end? How rapidly do you need to proceed? What aspects of world history need to be emphasized? How do you make choices about what to emphasize? These are questions you must consider in long-term planning.

You need an overview of the entire academic year so that you can understand the sequence of topics, avoid needless repetition, and begin gathering and ordering materials and supplies. If possible, you should begin your long-term planning as soon as you know your teaching assignment for the academic year. Many experienced teachers spend time during the summer planning for the coming year. So how do you begin?

Generally, the school and the school district will provide you with some guidance. The department in the school, for example, the English department, might have a master plan for the subject that outlines the major topics and the sequences for the academic year. Experienced teachers in the department can be a valuable source for providing information about the unfolding of the academic year.

One of the first steps in the long-term planning process should be to review state standards. Because the state has legal responsibility for the curriculum in the state, state standards are very important. They basically define what you are required to teach. Some states have defined the content that should be used in a given course. These are often found in state documents such as state curriculum frameworks.

In some instances, however, the state may leave the specific content to be taught to the local school district. Therefore, the next step in the long-term planning process would be to identify any district curriculum guidelines that define the content to be taught in the subject you have been hired to teach. These curriculum documents can be quite helpful for a novice teacher. They provide a framework that can be followed and often offer good suggestions for teaching. This is also a good time to meet with the department chair as well as other teachers who teach in your assigned subject area.

Another step in the long-term planning process would be to survey the textbook that is assigned for the subject. Skimming the textbook, especially the teacher's edition, can provide some valuable guidance for identifying an overview of the subject and some suggested unit breakdowns. It is important to remember, however, that the organization of the textbook might not be the best organization for your students and your school. Good teachers view textbooks as a resource, not the definitive curriculum.

The academic calendar for the school year is another important document to consult when engaging in long-term planning. The academic calendar identifies important events during the school year such as holidays, grading periods, and testing schedules. The calendar of each district is unique because the calendar is established by the local school board. Therefore, the calendar should be reviewed each year.

One of the most important of these events is the testing schedule. With an increased emphasis on accountability as measured by large-scale assessments, schools are concerned about making sure that students are prepared for these high-stakes assessments. They want to make sure that content likely to be covered on the tests has been taught prior to the testing. In fact, some school districts that are concerned about test scores have developed pacing guides that define how fast the content should be taught. If the school where you teach is using pacing guides, review these as you plan for the academic year.

In addition to pacing guides, school districts review past student performance on these high-stakes assessments. They identify what appear to be strengths and weaknesses in the curriculum emphasis for the school district. This analysis might have led to administrative mandates about certain dimensions of your subject that need to be emphasized. If you are in a district that is concerned about standardized test scores, you will need to be aware of these mandates.

Breaks in the academic calendar are important to note. You do not want to have a long school break in the middle of an instructional unit. This will require considerable review when students return from an extended break and will waste valuable time. It is best to end units of instruction before major school holidays or breaks.

Knowing the grading periods is critical. You need to know when grades are to be submitted. You must make sure that you have gathered sufficient assessment data to support your grading decisions. Keeping grading periods in mind can help you prevent many long, anxiety-filled nights!

In general, long-term plans help you identify long-range goals and provide a context for the academic year or the academic term. Generally, therefore, they do not include a lot of detailed information about specific lessons. Long-range planning may involve little more than preparing an academic calendar and listing major topics, important academic standards, and major school events. This overall view of the year assists you in planning for any special events such as field trips, guest speakers, or the ordering of educational materials and supplies so that they are on hand when they are needed.

Intermediate-Term Planning

Intermediate-term planning introduces more specificity into the planning process. Intermediate planning focuses on the major academic divisions of the year and involves planning for each division in depth.

Intermediate planning usually results in instructional segments called units. Units are related blocks of instruction that organize the content to be taught over an extended period of time. These units should focus on major divisions of the subject and should be organized into a logical sequence. Some topics, such as mathematics, may have a logical sequence inherent in the subject. Some units must be taught before other units are introduced. Other subjects, such as English, have more flexibility. For example, a novel or work of literature might not require a particular sequence. Where it is placed on your school calendar might depend on the availability of materials and resources. Therefore, coordination with other teachers in the department might be required.

Organizing Instructional Units   Organizing instruction into well-planned units has several advantages. When you group lessons together and systematically sequence them in an instructional unit, you make sure that students acquire knowledge in a manner that maximizes their chances of success. Interrelated lessons can help promote the ability to see relationships and to draw conclusions from analyses based on large quantities of information.

The process of unit planning alerts you to the need for gathering learning resources. For example, as you plan a unit, you may determine that you need certain videotapes or maps that must be ordered from a centralized media facility several weeks in advance. Because you should be planning units some time before you teach them, you will have enough time to obtain the learning materials needed to support your instruction.

Unit plans give you a sense of direction and security as you deliver instruction. They eliminate uncertainty about the question, What should I do tomorrow? They help establish a sense of order and routine that conveys to students that you know what you are doing.

In previous chapters, we have mentioned the backward planning process outlined by Wiggins and McTighe (2005). This process applies to the intermediate planning process and planning instructional units. The backward planning process has three basic steps. The first step is identifying the desired outcomes of the unit. This means that, after reviewing the academic year or the semester and the standards that you will be emphasizing, you should identify the big ideas or generalizations that students should understand and organize them into a sequence. These key understandings will be the focus for your units.

Identifying enduring understandings, generalizations, big ideas   The first phase involves identifying what Wiggins and McTighe (2005) call enduring understandings. These enduring understandings are big ideas, generalizations, principles, or laws that define the core understandings of any subject. They have wide application to a variety of settings and "endure" across time and space.

The terms might be different according to the subject. For example, in science we have the laws of physics. They are conclusions derived from research that almost always lead to predictable outcomes so that they might be called laws. In mathematics, processes are based on well-established rules of logic and are often called principles. On the other hand, areas like the social sciences and the humanities study highly unpredictable human beings. Because the conclusions drawn from these areas of study often have exceptions, they are usually called generalizations. Perhaps the term *big ideas* best captures the nature of these statements.

When planning a unit of instruction, the focus should be on these big ideas rather than on a collection of facts. The importance of the role of these big ideas was discussed in Chapter 5, in the discussion on the structure of knowledge.

The focus of a block of instruction or a unit should be on a limited number of these big ideas. A typical problem is that many teachers and students do not understand the structure of knowledge and tend to focus on facts rather than big ideas. The focus remains on facts so that when a block of instruction is completed, the students are tested and graded on their understanding of the facts and they miss the big ideas. They soon forget a large percentage of the facts, and teachers are puzzled when students do not seem to understand the subject. We know we taught them!

Unfortunately, few lists exist of big ideas for a given subject. However, there are resources that you can use in identifying the big ideas in your subject. One source is your knowledge of the subject. Review the classes you have taken in your teaching subject. What were the big ideas that were the focus of your professors and your own reading and study? What big ideas contributed to your understanding of the subject and have more than a narrow application? While the specific facts you studied in a college class may not be transferable to a secondary classroom, the big ideas, principles, and generalizations are transferable.

Another source for these big ideas is your textbook. Most textbooks are written to explain big ideas or themes related to a given body of content. Skimming through a textbook and identifying the main themes or big ideas can be very useful. Read through a section of a textbook and jot down what you think are the main ideas. Begin with these main ideas and turn them into generalizations or principles that can serve as desired outcomes for your unit.

State and national standards are another source of information. The intent of the standards is to focus on more than just narrow facts. Many of these standards are based on big ideas or principles that have been identified as central to what the state thinks students need to learn. Although the standards may not have been developed by content experts and may need some rewriting, they are a useful resource for identifying desired outcomes.

Let's suppose that, as a result of your survey of the textbook and the state standards, you learn that one of the topics you will be expected to teach is Checks and Balances in American Government. You need to ask yourself, Why are checks and balances important in a governmental system? What are the principles or values that led to the creation of this type of a system? Answering these questions will lead you in the direction of principles or generalizations.

The desired outcomes that you develop as a result of this process should be big ideas or enduring understandings that will inform student understanding of the subject long after students have completed the unit. We want students to develop understandings that can be applied outside the classroom as they evaluate and act on political proposals related to the division of powers in government.

Once you have identified these big ideas and selected what will be the focus of your unit of instruction, you will have a clearer understanding of specific concepts and the specific information that will need to be taught so that students arrive at an understanding of these enduring understandings. In other words, starting with a focus on enduring understandings provides a framework for making decisions about what should be included and what can be omitted.

Broad questions and skills   Some other components need to be considered in this first phase of unit design. Wiggins and McTighe (2005) include the identification of essential questions and important skills.

Every subject has a set of skills or processes central to success in the subject. In fact, student failure can often be traced to a skill deficit. For example, science students are not likely to be successful if they cannot apply the scientific process and conduct an experiment. English students will not succeed if they cannot read for understanding or compose a coherent paragraph. Math students cannot comprehend some of the important equations if they do not understand basic math skills and processes. These skills and processes need to be systematically taught, and they are best taught when students have a need for them. Therefore, as you are organizing your instructional unit, you need to identify the skills and processes that you will expect students to be able to perform by the conclusion of the unit.

After defining the big ideas or generalizations, an important step in building the unit is to identify key questions. These questions should be broad and should make the content of the unit more coherent and meaningful. In fact, one of our professors used to state that the importance of teachers knowing the content of a subject was not that they could then stand and deliver their pearls of wisdom to students. Rather, the importance of knowing the content is found in knowing what questions to ask.

Applying this perspective, McTighe and Wiggins (2004) suggest that it is a mistake to attempt to focus on fact-based statements of standards and big ideas. They indicate that students need to be involved in inquiry and discovery. Therefore, in the first phase of unit planning, broad, provocative questions related to the enduring understandings need to be developed.

You can use several approaches to develop questions that stimulate student interest in the content. McTighe and Wiggins (2004) suggest two types of questions that are useful in organizing units of study. The first type they suggest are overarching questions. These questions focus directly on generalizations and big ideas. They are questions that go beyond a narrow content example. The second type of question is what they call topical questions. The questions focus on a specific selection of content. However, both types of questions should be thought-provoking and open-ended, with no one correct answer.

For example, suppose that you are teaching a history unit on the American Revolution. An enduring idea or generalization that you are using for a focus is, "People revolt when legitimate government is insensitive to their needs and desires." An overarching question that can be developed from this generalization is, Why are some people willing to risk their lives in attempting to overthrow their government? Some topical questions might be, How did the attitude of King George III toward the colonists push them toward rebellion? Why did the stamp acts generate so much anger in the colonies? And do you see the possibility of revolution in our future?

Note that the generalization and the related overarching question focus on revolutions or rebellions in general. They can be applied to understanding revolutions at different times and places in the world. The topical questions, while related to the generalization and the overarching question, focus specifically on the American Revolution. One of the topical questions prompts students to apply what they have learned to our own time. Note that all of the questions are broad and provocative. They can be used to organize and make the information that they might encounter in the unit meaningful.

In this first phase of planning, it is useful to brainstorm possible overarching and topical questions that would be useful in the development of your unit. These questions will prompt you to consider the specific facts or information that you would then need to include in the unit. However, because the facts and the specific information are related to answering questions, it makes them more meaningful to the students.

In summary, the first step in intermediate planning is the identification of desired results. This first step includes identifying enduring understandings or generalizations, noting essential skills that should be learned, and converting the generalization or enduring understanding into overarching and topical questions. When this is completed, it is time to move to phase two of unit planning.

Defining acceptable evidence   The second phase in the backward planning process is the identification of acceptable evidence. The basic question you need to ask yourself is, What evidence would I accept that indicates the students have achieved the desired results?

In Chapter 6, we discussed various methods of assessment. The task now is to identify how you are going to assess student understanding and at what points in the unit you are going to do so. It is useful to consider some form of diagnostic assessment to determine what the students already know and then to identify several points in the unit where you will want to gather formative assessment data so that you can make in course corrections if needed. Finally, you will need to have summative data that you can use in your evaluation and grading.

One possible way of organizing your decision-making about assessment is to match assessment tools to different types of learning objectives that will be included in your unit. For example, performance tasks and rubrics could be used to assess student learning of the enduring understandings and the critical skills. This would be an effective way to assess application and higher-level learning tasks. Other measurement options such as essay or multiple-choice items could be used to assess student learning of important concepts and more specific information. Checklists could be used to assess student work samples, cooperative learning activities, and work habits. This gives you a comprehensive plan that uses multiple assessments and is likely to provide you with a more comprehensive and valid assessment of student learning.

Selecting and sequencing teaching approaches   The third phase of unit design is the selection of teaching approaches and learning activities. There is a temptation for some teachers to place this phase as the first one in the planning process. Once some teachers identify the topic sequence as a result of their long-term planning, they immediately start thinking of interesting or fun lessons that they can develop. Teachers may have observed an interesting lesson, read about an idea on the Web, or attended a workshop where other teachers shared ideas. They are anxious to get back to their classroom and try them. However, beginning with lesson ideas can result in a lack of coherence and a perception on the part of the students that the subject is little more than a series of unrelated lessons and activities. There is nothing wrong with making lessons interesting or fun, or being enthusiastic about designing new lessons. However, they should be developed and applied because they contribute to students' progress toward achieving important outcomes. The lesson activities in a unit should be designed to follow a logical progress to take the students from what they already know and understand to the final phase of having an understanding of the main concepts and the big ideas that were identified in phase one.

There is a progression of experiences in a unit that needs to be considered when selecting and designing lessons. The first part is that of capturing the attention of the students. The first activities in a unit should be those that engage the students and stimulate their curiosity. These activities should help them understand what they are going to learn and why it is important. This beginning stage should also be used to provide the teacher with some diagnostic information about what the students already know and what interests them. The opening stage of a unit might only take a day or two to complete.

The middle stage of a unit is the most extensive part of the unit. This stage of the progression provides the students with the information and the knowledge they will need to successfully accomplish the intended learning outcomes. This stage needs to progress in a logical sequence and contain opportunities for formative assessment so that changes can be made if learning is not going as anticipated.

One way to begin organizing this stage is to review the topical questions that you developed in the first phase of unit planning. Organize these topical questions into what appears to be a logical sequence and then consider specific learning activities that will engage the students in seeking information related to the topical question. A formative assessment activity can then focus on that topical question to help you determine if the students are ready to move on.

The next stage of the unit is what is normally called the culminating stage. This is the stage where the parts of the unit are pulled together and the learning of the enduring understandings is reinforced and applied. This stage also contains activities for gathering summative assessment data.

This third phase is addressed in chapters 9,10,11,12 where alternative instructional approaches are discussed. Different approaches are useful for accomplishing different instructional goals. Understanding different instructional approaches will assist you in choosing instructional approaches for the different stages of your unit.

We recommend a fourth stage, unit evaluation. This stage is for you to reflect on the success of the unit. When the unit is over, take some time with your favorite food or beverage to sit down and review what happened. What went well? Were there any glitches? Was the sequence appropriate? What would you do differently next time? What resource material would have been useful? Jot down your thoughts and ideas, and place them with your unit plan and the unit-specific materials that you used. File them away so that they can be retrieved easily when you next teach the unit. This helps you continually improve your unit and helps you identify changes that you might make when you have the time.

Unit Format   There are numerous ways to format your unit, and there is no right way. The best format is the one that is most useful to you! Criteria you consider should be something that is organized so that other interested observers can see the logic and the plan for achieving desired outcomes. The format should provide you with guidance so that every day, you do not face the question, What am I going to do today? There should be enough detail so that other teachers can understand the overall design and apply it to their classrooms. Keep in mind that the unit is not just a collection of lesson plans. The unit is a road map or an outline for a significant block of time. When well done, a unit plan provides guidance in the development of lesson plans yet is flexible enough to be adapted to match your knowledge abilities as well as the needs and interests of the students. Therefore, a unit might be used by more than one teacher, with each teacher developing different individual lesson plans while following the same outline that focuses on the same desired outcomes.

The basic parts of a unit include the following:

- Unit title
- Rationale
- Audience for whom it is intended
- Overarching and topical questions
- Instructional objectives
- A tentative timeline
- An instructional strategy for each objective
- A list of resources
- Assessment procedures

Unit title   Your unit title should communicate the essence of the content you propose to teach. Unit titles ordinarily are short. Sometimes even one word suffices. Example titles include: The Halogens (chemistry), The Lake Poets (English), Factoring (mathematics), and The Progressives (history).

Audience   It is useful to identify the students who will be taught in this unit. This is useful when units are shared between teachers. By looking at the intended audience, a teacher can determine if this unit is something that might be useful. Identifying the audience can be as simple as stating, "The unit was developed for ninth-grade English students." However, a bit more detail can be helpful. You might want to identify if the students are English language learners, struggling students, accelerated students, or students with special needs.

For example, several years ago one of us developed a number of units for deaf students. Identifying that this was the intended audience helped those who reviewed the units understand that certain activities and approaches we used might not be applicable to another group of students.

Rationale   A *unit rationale* is a statement designed to identify why this unit is important. This rationale will help you focus on the purpose of the unit and how it fits with your long-range plans. The rationale is also useful in explaining to other interested parties (such as students, parents, and administrators) why what you are teaching is important. Remember that these interested individuals are probably not as well grounded in the subject and may not understand the relevance. This is particularly valuable as you anticipate student questions such as, Why do we need to know this stuff?

In recent years, teachers have included state standards to be met during the unit as part of the rationale. This provides additional justification for the unit and can be important in demonstrating to others that you are teaching all required content. For example, one of our local secondary schools requires that each teacher post the state standard that is the focus for the lesson in the front of the classroom each day. Identifying these standards in the rationale makes it easy to identify the standard quickly and then get on with preparing for the day.

Intended outcomes in the form of enduring understandings or generalizations
Stating the intended outcomes helps keep your focus on what is important. They are extremely useful in sequencing the unit and selecting specific instructional strategies. For example, one of our student teachers reports debating between a couple of different instructional approaches she was thinking of using. When she shared her uncertainty with a classmate, she was asked, "What is your intended outcome?" When she focused on the intended outcome, the choice became clear.

Overarching and topical questions   Once you have clearly stated your intended outcomes in the form of enduring understandings and generalizations, brainstorm some overarching and topical questions. This is very useful in selecting teaching approaches. You will want teaching approaches that will help get the students engaged in seeking information relative to the questions. In addition, the identification of topical questions often indicates what might be an appropriate sequence for the unit.

Objectives and suggested timelines   In Chapter 5, we discussed the importance of objectives. You need to develop specific objectives for each day of your unit. What will you expect students to be able to do as a result of their activity that day? Objectives describe what you want students to be able to do as a result of instruction. As you write your objectives, again by keeping the intended outcomes of the unit in mind and sequencing them in a logical progression, you will begin to get an idea of the length of your unit.

Any timeline you develop will be tentative. You will discover that there are some objectives that might be accomplished more quickly than you anticipated. Others may take more time. You might need to reteach some lessons. If you discover that it will take more time than you have available to teach your unit, you may need to reconsider your intended outcomes and the sequence of topics. You may need to omit some activities and parts of the unit to complete the unit in a reasonable time.

The time you allocate for achieving each instructional objective varies according to its sophistication. If the objective asks your students to demonstrate only low-level knowledge and comprehension levels of thinking, you will need to schedule relatively short periods of instructional time. On the other hand, if one of your objectives proposes to have students engage in sophisticated analyses of complex information, you will have to commit considerable instructional time preparing students to succeed at this challenging task.

Instructional strategies   An instructional strategy consists of systematically organized instructional techniques that are directed toward helping students master an objective. You need to identify an instructional strategy for each objective included in your unit. Because some objectives require more sophisticated student thinking than others, some of your instructional strategies will be more complex than others. The worth of any instructional strategy is determined in terms of its ability to help students master the objective to which it relates.

Typically, instructional strategies are not described in great detail in instructional unit plans. A sentence or two describing the general instructional approach to be taken for each objective will suffice. You will describe your instructional strategies in much greater detail in your lesson plans. Lesson plans provide guidance for what you intend to do in the classroom on a given day, and it is appropriate that you include detailed information about instructional strategies you plan to use in these important documents.

Suppose you were teaching a high school physics course. When referring to an objective focusing on student comprehension of the coefficient of the expansion principle, you might write the following information about an intended learning strategy in a unit plan outline:

Conduct an inquiry lesson on the unequal rate of expansion in response to heat of different metals using the bimetallic knife.

You would develop this strategy into a series of clearly defined steps in a related daily lesson plan.

Plans for the beginning and ending   Your unit plans will often feature detailed descriptions of how you intend to introduce the unit to students. The introduction is critically important to the success of the unit. If your initial activity captures your students' interest, it will be easier for you to sustain their enthusiasm as you introduce the new body of content.

Good unit introductions accomplish several purposes. They stimulate initial student interest and give students a general overview of unit content. They also provide students with a clear idea about what you expect them to do.

Conclusions or suggested culminating activities often are written into instructional unit plans. Their purpose is to help students pull together the key ideas that have been introduced. These activities will often require your students to engage in application activities that involve the use of some of the information they have learned. A good culminating activity can build students' confidence by providing them with opportunities to verify for themselves that they have mastered challenging new material.

Assessment procedures   It is necessary to include information about your approaches to evaluating student progress in your instructional unit plan. You need to think about evaluation procedures not just for the culminating assessment at the conclusion but also for interim assessments that you will make from time to time as you teach the material.

Selected evaluation procedures must be consistent with the unit's objectives. For example, if the language of your objective implies that students should be able to engage in analysis-level thinking, you must select an evaluation procedure that has the capacity to assess this kind of thinking.

List of needed learning resources   Well-designed units are supported by a variety of learning resources. You need to identify these resources as you plan your units. You may wish to reference such items as supplemental readings, software, CD recordings, World Wide Web addresses, compact disks, maps, laboratory equipment, and speakers who may be invited to the class. You may also want to list learning materials you have designed yourself that will supplement the text and other basic instructional resources.

Today, budgets, rather than materials' availability, place more limits on the kinds of learning resources you can obtain. Catalogs containing an incredible variety of support materials regularly arrive at school district offices, at individual buildings, and in faculty mailboxes. These catalogs, taken together with district- and building-level library, media, and instructional resource centers, will help you develop a feel for the range of available materials. If you are fortunate enough to be employed in a well-funded school district, you may be allowed to purchase substantial quantities of instructional-support materials for units you develop. If you work in a less affluent setting, it is probable that budgetary limitations will severely restrict your purchases of these materials.

Box 7-1 introduces an example of an instructional unit that includes all of these basic components.

Short-Term Planning

Short-term planning focuses on short periods of instructional time such as one or two days. The most common written expression of short-term planning is the *lesson plan*. One useful way to think about lesson plans is to think of them as plot lines. The plot line outlines the sequence of events and the role of various players during one lesson. While the plot line includes considerable detail, it is not a full script that includes the word-by-word interaction. The plot-line concept provides teachers with a clear sense of direction while providing flexibility.

Lesson Plans   Instructional unit plans describe the general flow of instructional development over a period of several weeks. Shorter-range instructional decisions are expressed in lesson plans. Lesson plans include more detailed information than unit plans. In addition to instructional objectives (discussed in detail in Chapter 5), they often provide details regarding the instructional techniques used, how transitions are to be handled, specific learning materials used, and ideas for monitoring and assessing students. Lesson plans are context-specific. Hence, they are best prepared by you personally.

Typically, you are likely to put more detail into your lesson plans earlier in your career than you will after you have taught for some time. This is sometimes not understood by beginning teachers. They do not observe the detail in the lesson plans of experienced teachers and therefore do not think they need to be very specific. Teachers who have taught a specific lesson several times have learned what to expect and are generally comfortable with the material they have and with the flow of the lesson. An analogy might be a physician who has performed a medical procedure for some time. This physician will generally not be required to spend time reviewing the procedure ahead of time. However, a beginning physician would want to review the procedure in some detail before beginning, perhaps practicing several times in a lab setting.

Once you gain experience, you will develop skills that will allow you to achieve success with less detail in your lesson plans. As a result, you probably will need only a few written prompts to manage the flow of the activities.

There are no precise rules governing how much detail a "good" lesson plan should contain. The detail should be based on how comfortable you are with the lesson and how much difficulty you have managing the time and the class. As a general rule of thumb, we recommend that beginning teachers should have enough detail in a lesson plan so that it could be picked up and taught by a substitute teacher.

Box 7-1   The Struggle for Independence

RATIONALE

The American Revolution was a key event in American history. An understanding of the Revolution helps explain the nature of Americans' basic beliefs and values. The goals of this unit are to help students understand the forces that led the American colonists to band together, and to help students appreciate American values, beliefs, and institutions that, in large measure, are traceable to the American Revolution.

State standards require that this topic be taught at this grade level. The standards specify that students should understand the causes of the war for American independence, identify basic values that led to the conflict, and state the impact of the conflict on the development of the nation.

AUDIENCE

This unit was designed for an 11th-grade American history course. It is designed to be implemented as part of the course required for all students. This course, coming near the completion of the secondary school experience, is designed to explore the topic in some depth.

INTENDED OUTCOMES (ENDURING UNDERSTANDINGS, BIG IDEAS)

A. Revolutions often occur when people believe that legitimate authority is insensitive and unresponsive to their needs.

B. People believe that they possess certain inalienable rights. If those rights are violated by the legitimate government, it gives the people a right to rebel.

C. Revolutions challenge people to rethink their assumptions about the nature of the proper relationship between citizens and their government.

RELATED CONCEPTS THAT STUDENTS WILL NEED TO UNDERSTAND

The following concepts are imbedded in the enduring understandings.

- Revolution
- Legitimate authority
- Wants and needs

- Government rights and responsibilities
- Citizenship rights and responsibilities
- Individual rights
- Role of government
- Loyalty
- Values
- Beliefs
- Continuity and change over time

OVERARCHING QUESTIONS

A. What drives people to risk losing all they have, including their lives, in an attempt to overthrow legitimate government?

B. Are there circumstances when it is right for people to rise up against the legal government?

C. Does military strength and power prevent revolutions?

D. What should be the relationship between government and the governed?

TOPICAL QUESTIONS

A. How did the British crown view the relationship between government and the governed?

B. How did the rebellious colonists view the role of government?

C. Why did the various acts such as the stamp acts cause so much anger?

D. Did the colonists have legitimate reasons for rebelling against England, or were they just trying to serve their narrow, personal interests?

E. In what ways do you think the American Revolution changed ways people thought about the role of government and acted in response to that role?

F. What could lead to revolution today? Do you see events and attitudes in the United States that might contribute to revolution?

STATE STANDARDS ADDRESSED IN THIS UNIT

Here you will add standards from your state document.

(continued)

Box 7-1 Continued

Objectives and Suggested Timeline (Approximately Four Weeks)

Objectives and Time Allocations	Strategy	Assessment
Unit Beginning: *Time Allocation:* One Day *Objective:* At least 50% of students will participate in discussion and will identify at least two reasons why people revolt. *Overarching Question:* **A**	Present accounts of an ethnic or civil conflict occurring somewhere in the world. Ask students questions such as these: What pushes people to attempt to overthrow a government? What happens to the people in a nation when this kind of conflict occurs?	Identify main ideas that the students express regarding revolutions, why they occur, and the consequences on individuals. Address this information in future lessons.
Time Allocation: One Day *Objective:* At least 50% of students will make a contribution to the list. The class as a whole will group items into at least three categories and provide a label to each category. *Overarching Question:* **B**	Perform a diagnostic assessment using a concept formation/diagnosis strategy. Ask the students, What comes to mind when you hear the words *American Revolution*? List, group, and label the responses. Use students' responses to diagnosis what they already know about the American Revolution and what misconceptions they might have.	Use the concept grouping and labeling to identify student knowledge and understanding of the causes and events of the American Revolution. Make sure that misconceptions are identified so they can be addressed in the unit.
Unit Development *Time Allocation:* Three Days *Objective:* Each student will define the view of the British government and King George III toward the needs of the colonists.	Topical Questions A and B Show parts of the CD *The American Revolution.* State that the purpose is to identify how the views of the British crown and the colonists differed in relationship to the needs of each group and the role of government.	Formative assessment: Have students do an independent practice activity in the form of a letter from the king stating what they should do about the rebels and why.
Time Allocation: Three Days *Objective:* Each student will define the specific needs and values of each side of the conflict.	Topical Question C Instructional Strategy: Cooperative learning focusing on the question: Did the colonists have legitimate reasons for rebelling against England, or were they just trying to serve their narrow, personal interests? Divide the class into several groups. Ask each group to conduct research and to report on how each of the following events contributed to the eventual outbreak of the Revolutionary War: • Proclamation of 1763 • Sugar Act of 1764 • Stamp Act of 1765 • Declaratory Act of 1766 • Townshend Acts	Have the group members complete an assessment of their contribution to the group and their view of the contribution of others to the group. Assign a group grade to the group product.

(continued)

Objectives and Time Allocations	Strategy	Assessment
Time Allocation: Three Days *Objective:* Each student will define the conflicting roles of citizens that were held by different groups of colonists.	Continuation of Topical Question D Show the film *Prelude to Revolution*. As a result of viewing the film, students will: • List British advantages and disadvantages for engaging in a conflict. • List American advantages and disadvantages for engaging in a conflict. • List possible British arguments in support of and against going to war. • List possible American arguments in support of and against going to war. Each group will share its list with the whole class. Have students work with the computer-based lesson titled Revolutionary War: Choosing Sides.	Formative Assessment: Give a quiz to the students that focuses on the different events that led to the American Revolution. Make sure to assess the enduring understanding that revolutions occur when people think their needs and rights are being violated.
Time Allocation: Four Days *Objective:* Each student will identify key military developments of the Revolutionary War and explain how the colonists were able to survive in the face of superior military force. *Overarching Question:* **C**	• Assign groups of two or three students to conduct research on key events of the Revolutionary War. • Ask students to view the parts of the CD *The American Revolution* that highlight significant events of the conflict. • Discuss key events of the war.	Formative Assessment: Have the students develop a timeline of important events. They are to place each event at its proper place on a timeline and to write a description explaining what occurred and why the event was important.
Time Allocation Two Days *Objective:* Students will identify core American values and beliefs that can be traced to the American Revolution	Topical Question E • Students working in groups will identify core values and beliefs that arose during the American Revolution. They will describe a contemporary application of that value or belief. Provide students with information about the Treaty of Paris of 1783. Divide class members into four teams. Ask each team to gather information about one of these questions: • What were the issues of interest to France, and how did the treaty affect France? • What were the issues of interest to Spain, and how did the treaty affect Spain? • What were the issues of interest to Americans, and how did the treaty affect the former colonies? • What were the issues of interest to the British, and how did the treaty affect Britain? • How did the war change the attitudes of the major participants?	Perform an assessment of the group work and individual students' contributions to their group.

(continued)

Box 7-1 Continued

Objectives and Time Allocations	Strategy	Assessment
Unit Culmination	Topical Question F	*Assign Performance Assessment Task:* Each student is to take the role of an adviser to King George III. Their task is to prepare a report to the king. The report should present their suggestions on what the king should do about the rebellious colonists and state an opinion on whether the king should go to war with the colonists.
Time Allocation: Two Days	Present the class with the following question: Could there be another revolution in the United States?	
Objective: Students will state an enduring understanding to make predictions about the possibility of a revolution in the United States.	*Instructional Strategy:* Organize a debate on the topic of current feelings and attitudes that might lead to a revolution. The purpose of this activity is to have the students apply what they learned in the unit to the contemporary scene.	
Overarching Question: **D**	Begin by having the students state the big ideas they learned from the unit. Identify some contemporary issues that are causing dissention within the United States. Have students take a position on whether this dissention could lead to a future revolution. They will need to describe what might contribute to a revolution and what could be done to prevent a revolution.	

MY EVALUATION OF THE UNIT: SUGGESTED LEARNING RESOURCES

General Reference Books

Bliss, G. A. (1980). *The American Revolution: How revolutionary was it?* New York: Harper & Row.

Ellis, J. J. (2000). *Founding brothers: The revolutionary generation.* New York: Alfred A Knopf.

Ellis, J. J. (2007). *American creation. Triumphs and tragedies at the founding of the republic.* New York: Vintage Books.

Fritz, J. (1981). *Traitor: The case of Benedict Arnold.* New York: Putnam's.

Gephard, R. E. (Ed.). (1984). *Revolutionary America.* Washington, DC: U.S. Government Printing Office.

Kelly, C. B. (1999). *Best little stories from the American Revolution.* Nashville: Cumberland House.

McCullough, D, (2005). *1776.* New York: Simon and Shuster.

Meltzer, M. (1986). *George Washington and the birth of our nation.* New York: Watts.

Meltzer, M. (1987). *The American revolutionaries: A history in their own words.* New York: Harper & Row Junior Books.

Meltzer, M. (1988). *Benjamin Franklin: The new American.* New York: Watts.

Miller, J. (1959). *Origins of the American Revolution.* Stanford, CA: Stanford University Press.

Student Texts

Bragdon, H. W., McCutcheon, S. P., & Ritchie, D. A. (1996). *History of a free people.* New York: Glencoe/McGraw Hill.

Paine, T. (1776, 1975). *Thomas Paine's Common Sense: The call to independence.* Woodbury, NY: Barron's Educational Series.

Ritchie, D. A., & Broussard, A. (1997). *American history: The early years to 1877.* New York: Glencoe/McGraw Hill.

Ward, H. M. (1991). *The American Revolution: Nationhood achieved, 1763–1788.* New York: St. Martin's Press.

The World Wide Web

American Revolution: Resources at the New York public library. (1995). http://nypl.org/research/chss/subguides/milhist/rev.html

Cole, R. (1995). The role of African Americans in the American Revolution. http://www.ilt.columbia.edu/k12/history/blacks/blacks.html

(continued)

Hispanics in the American Revolution. (1995, 1996). http://www.clark.net/pub/jgbustam/galvez/galvez/html

Medvedev, S. M. (1995). American Revolution: A revolution? http://grid.let.rug.nl/~welling/usa/revo1.htm

Olson, K. W. (1995). An outline of American history. http://grid.let.rug.nl/~welling/usa/

Fiction

Collier, J. L., & Collier, C. (1976). *The bloody country*. New York: Scholastic.

Forbes, E. (1943). *Johnny Tremaine: A story of the Boston revolt*. Boston: Houghton Mifflin.

Snow, R. (1976). *Freeland Starbird*. Boston: Houghton Mifflin.

Film

Prelude to revolution. 13-minute film available from Encyclopedia Britannica Educational Corporation, 425 N. Michigan Ave., Chicago, IL 60611

Video

The American Revolution. Available from Guidance Associates, Communications Park, Box 3000, Mt. Kisko, NY 10549

CD-ROM

The American Revolution: Available from Social Studies School Service, P.O. Box 802, Culver City, CA 90232-0802

The American Revolution for Students: A set of five CDs. They include a mix of live action with photos, documents, and maps. They are developed for grades 5 to 9. Available from Social Studies School Service, P.O. Box 802, Culver City, CA 90232-0802

Posters

"American patriot posters." A set of ten color posters of Revolutionary-era patriots available from Social Studies School Service, P.O. Box 802, Culver City, CA 90232-0802

The Planning Process   As is true for unit planning, there is no correct format for lesson plans. There are several acceptable formats. In general, you should first focus on the objectives or what you want to accomplish in a given lesson. Then you should begin brainstorming how best to achieve those objectives. Some teachers begin by focusing on learning activities and then plan their lesson around a specific activity. However, the difficulty with this approach is that, while the activity might be a good one, it might not contribute to the achievement of objectives and the accomplishment of intended learning outcomes. Some key questions that can guide your lesson planning are the following:

- *What is the lesson objective?* The answer to this question is important. For one thing, it requires you to weigh the importance of what you are contemplating and to determine that the purpose is a worthy one. Thinking about the objective sometimes also prompts ideas about possible teaching approaches.

- *What is a good entry point for instruction?* To answer this question, you must have good information about the students to whom you intend to teach the lesson. What you want to do at the beginning of each lesson is to capture the attention of the students. If an initial interest can be established, your students are more likely to stay with you for the duration of the lesson. They need to understand the importance of the lesson and gain some understanding of why it is important for them to learn the content.

- *What state standards will I address?* If you teach in a state that has mandated standards, you must identify the standards you will include in each lesson. Some administrators require that teachers highlight these standards on each lesson plan and, in some instances, write them on the board each day.

- *What is the best way to sequence lesson content and activities?* This question is difficult because there is no answer that is right for all situations. In some cases, the logic of the subject matter dictates the sequence. For example, in a mathematics lesson, less complex content must precede more complex content. In other subjects, however, the sequencing decision is much more a matter of your personal professional judgment.

■ *How will students become actively involved in the lesson, and what should they do to demonstrate they have learned?* Lessons requiring students to actively manipulate the new content tend to be more successful than those that require them only to read or listen passively. Also, learning theorists say that new information is better remembered when people have had an opportunity to use it in some way. For this reason, it is important to include application activities in lesson plans whenever possible (Good & Brophy, 2007).

■ *How should students be grouped during the lesson?* You need to decide whether your students will be taught as members of one large group or as members of a number of small groups. If the decision is to have them divided into groups, specific thought must be given to deciding how group members will be selected and how students will move smoothly (quickly and quietly) from the large group into the small groups. If it is important for groups to have leaders, you must decide how they are to be selected and how they will report to you. You must also plan ways to distribute materials quickly and efficiently to all group members.

■ *How can the needs of students at different ability levels be met, and what should be done to monitor the progress of individual students?* Because all classes have individuals with vastly different levels of ability and interest, your plans must assume that some students will need different learning materials than others and that some will finish more quickly than others. You also should devise a system for keeping track of how an individual student is performing.

■ *What kind of activities will engage the students in exploring the topical questions and the big ideas?* It is important to think carefully and to prepare in advance activities that allow the students to explore the subject and relate what they are learning to previous knowledge. Good lessons call on students to apply what they have learned.

■ *How will the students demonstrate their understanding of the lesson content?* It is important to have data that indicates which students have learned the content and which might need additional assistance. A lesson plan should provide some time for students to exhibit or practice what they have learned. Students doing this with you available to assist them is called guided practice. When they do it on their own, it is called independent practice.

■ *How should the lesson be concluded?* It is as important to plan a sound lesson conclusion as well as a highly motivating lesson beginning. The conclusion of the lesson should draw together the major points that have been introduced and build a bridge to the next lesson. Taking just a couple of minutes to review the lesson briefly is an important component of lesson planning.

■ *What materials are needed?* Some lessons fail because teachers have not thought about needed materials. Books, handouts, paper and pencils, and other needed items are not available for students to use. You should consider preparing a checklist for needed materials. When you have such a list, you can check off the availability of individual items as you prepare to teach the lesson. This ensures that problems will not arise because of the unavailability of materials.

■ *What rules and management guidelines should be adopted for this lesson?* It may not always be necessary to spend much time on management issues. If something out of the ordinary is taking place, however, some behavioral guidelines can prevent problems.

■ *How much time should be allocated to each part of the lesson?* Time is a scarce commodity in the classroom. This resource needs to be expended wisely to ensure the maximum possible learning benefit for students. Some parts of lessons clearly deserve more attention than others. Careful planners make sure that students have enough time to learn the content.

More from the Web

Units and Lessons

A tremendous number of websites include information about instructional units and lesson plans. You will find instructions about different formatting approaches as well as numerous examples of completed units and lessons. You should have little difficulty in finding material related to the subject(s) you will be teaching. Here are some websites that are representative of what the Web has to offer if you are looking for information related to units and lessons.

LESSON AND UNIT IDEAS

1. www.thegateway.org

This site, sponsored by the U.S. Department of Education, provides a searchable database of literally thousands of lesson and unit ideas.

2. www.readwritethink.org

This website is sponsored by the International Reading Association and the National Council of Teachers of English. It provides excellent lesson ideas primarily for language arts teachers.

3. http://www.geneseo.edu/~stuteach/lesplan.html

There are many existing lesson plan formats. You will find one example later in this chapter. This website includes another.

■ *Providing for the Needs of Special Groups of Students.* Students in today's classrooms reflect more diversity than ever before. You need to prepare lessons that will meet the needs of exceptionally bright students as well as students with any one of a number of special conditions ranging from emotional problems to physical challenges of various kinds, to mild and moderate mental retardation. Today, federal and accompanying state laws require all students to spend as much of the school day as possible in regular classrooms rather than in isolated classrooms where they have little contact with "typical students." This means that your lesson plans must make provisions to meet the special needs of a variety of students. A single approach to teaching a class of 20 to 30 students will not do. Chapter 7 will provide additional information to help you plan lessons for *all* the students who are in your classrooms.

Choosing a Lesson Format   There are many acceptable ways to format a lesson plan. What is important is that you give serious thought to the organizational scheme and to prepare your plan carefully once you decide on an arrangement. Your district may provide you with the required format, or you may have the opportunity to choose your own. Numerous websites provide lesson plan templates that allow you to design and edit your lessons. One such site can be found at www.lessonplanbuilder.org, a site sponsored by the California Department of Education. Here, you can create a lesson, have it peer-reviewed, and subsequently edit it as often as necessary. No matter which scheme you adopt, the format should allow you to refer quickly to the completed plan to keep on track and to ensure that no planned parts of the lesson are omitted inadvertently. Because of the need to use lesson plans while instruction is being delivered, you do not want them to be too long. In addition, you want to avoid formats that make individual items difficult to find. Box 7-2 presents a generic example of a lesson plan format. This format can be modified to suit your individual instructional needs. In addition, you might want to compare it to the online format at the lesson plan builder site mentioned above.

Box 7-2   Generic Lesson Plan Model

Lesson Title _____

Unit Title _____

Objective(s) _____

Standards Addressed _____

_____

Needed Prerequisite Knowledge or Skill

_____

_____

New Terms and Key Ideas _____

_____

Procedures for Accommodating Students with Special Needs _____

Time _____

LESSON SEQUENCE

1. Gaining attention/informing students of objective
2. Presenting new material
3. Checking understanding/monitoring
4. Eliciting behavior/practice/feedback
5. Providing for independent practice/application/extension
6. Providing for closure

   Assessment Plan _____

   Materials Needed _____

   Teacher Evaluation of Lesson Effectiveness

   _____

FOR YOUR PORTFOLIO

1. Interstate New Teacher Assessment and Support Consortium (INTASC) Standard 7 focuses on instructional planning. What materials and ideas you learned in this chapter related to instructional units and lesson plans will you include as "evidence" in your portfolio? Select up to three items of information to be included. Number them 1, 2, and 3. To which other INTASC standards might these materials also relate?

2. Think about why you selected these materials for your portfolio. Consider issues such as the following in your response:

   - The specific purposes to which this information can be put when you plan, deliver, and assess the impact of your instruction
   - The compatibility of the information with your own priorities and values
   - The contributions this information can make to your personal development as a teacher
   - The factors that led you to include this material as opposed to some alternatives you considered

3. Prepare a written reflection in which you analyze the decision-making process you followed. Also, mention the INTASC standard(s) to which your selected material relates. (First complete the chart below.)

MATERIALS YOU SELECTED AND THE INTASC STANDARDS

Put a check under those INTASC standards numbers to which the evidence you have selected applies. (Refer to Chapter 1 for more detailed information about INTASC.)

INTASC Standards

Item of Evidence Number	S-1	S-2	S-3	S-4	S-5	S-6	S-7	S-8	S-9	S-10
1										
2										
3										

Key Ideas in Summary

- Because of the unique characteristics of individual teaching settings, you need to do much of your own instructional planning. Researchers have determined that effective teachers devote a great deal of time to planning.

- As you prepare for instruction, you will engage in long-term, intermediate-term, and short-term planning. Long-term planning embraces a time period of a semester or a full academic year. Intermediate-term planning focuses on time periods ranging from about two to six weeks in length. Instructional unit plans represent the written expression of intermediate planning. Short-term planning focuses on what goes on during one (and sometimes two or three) class periods. Short-term planning decisions are written in the form of lesson plans.

- There are different ways to format instructional units. Many of them contain these key content categories: (1) unit title; (2) rationale and major goals; (3) intended learning outcomes stated as enduring understandings or generalizations; (4) overarching and topical questions; (5) instructional objectives and an indication of the time to be devoted to instruction related to each; (6) instructional strategies for each objective; (7) plans for beginning, developing, and ending the unit; (8) assessment procedures; and (9) a list of needed learning resources.

- Lesson plans include details regarding instructional decisions that will guide teaching for a relatively short period of time. They might be thought of as scripts that teachers follow during a given period, sometimes a time as short as a single class period. Many different lesson plan formats have been developed.

Reflections

1. As a teacher, why do you have to do so much instructional planning of your own when so much excellent information is available in curriculum guides, textbooks, and other learning materials?

2. What are some characteristics of long-term planning?

3. What are some similarities and differences between intermediate-term and short-term planning?

4. How do the components of instructional units relate to success in teaching and learning?

5. Why is it probable that you will include more details in your lesson plans early in your teaching career than during your later years in the profession?

6. How much detail do you think you need in your lesson plans?

Learning Extensions

1. Review some district- or state-level curriculum guides. How many parts of the instructional unit format introduced in this chapter are included in the guides? What would need to be added to this material to make an instructional unit complete?

2. Interview a teacher about the process he or she follows in preparing an instructional unit. How does this person start this task? What goes into his or her decisions about sequencing content? Where does he or she find information about available materials? What kind of format does he or she use?

3. Visit two or more schools and compare how teachers in both approach a common subject. What differences are attributable to teacher variables and student variables? What differences seem to be caused by differences in the teaching context?

4. Get together with several others who are preparing to teach the same secondary school subject. Develop an instructional unit following the format introduced in this chapter. Share your unit with your instructor and request a critique. Be prepared to participate in a class discussion focusing on special difficulties you encountered and how you overcame them.

5. Write a lesson plan focusing on a topic you would like to teach. Be prepared to share answers to the following questions with others in the class: How long did it take you to prepare the lesson? Do you think you would be able to accomplish this task more quickly if you were to prepare another lesson? How comfortable would you feel in teaching this content?

References

Clark, C., & Yinger, R. (1979). *Three studies of teacher planning* (Research Series No. 55). East Lansing: Michigan State University, Institute for Research on Teaching.

Good, T. L., & Brophy, J. E. (2007). *Looking in classrooms* (10th ed.). New York: Longman.

McTighe, J., & Wiggins, G. (2004). *The understanding by design handbook*. Alexandria, VA: Association for Supervision and Curriculum Development.

Wiggins, G., & McTighe, J. (2005). *Understanding by design*. Alexandria, VA: Association for Supervision and Curriculum Development.

One Size Does Not Fit All: Differentiated Instruction

Objectives

This chapter will help you:

- describe some alternative views of differentiated instruction

- identify variables that can be altered to accommodate individual differences

- explain some assumptions made by proponents of the mastery-learning approach, and describe features of the Personalized System of Instruction

- point out some arguments for and against attempting to individualize instruction in ways that accommodate individual learning styles

- describe typical features of a learning contract

- explain components in an activity package

- identify types and purposes of learning centers

- describe features of learning stations

- describe the process for using book circles

- suggest ways in which computers can be used to support differentiated instruction programs

- distinguish between the two major types of peer-tutoring programs

- identify specific techniques for differentiating instruction for English learners

Liz Moore/Merrill

Graphic Organizer: Chapter 8

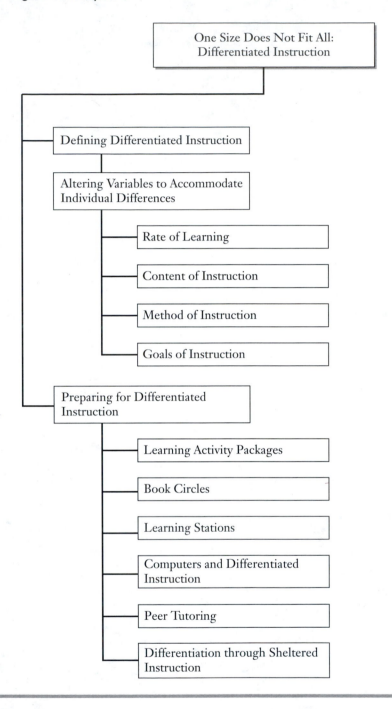

Introduction

As you engage in your lesson planning, one of the variables that you need to consider is the diversity of students in your classroom. A major component of your planning is your attitude. Some view diversity as a burden. They panic when they face the prospect of making changes to their planning in order to accommodate diverse students. Teachers with this attitude often respond negatively to differentiated instruction.

Rather than viewing diversity as a burden, however, we recommend that you view it as an opportunity to make teaching and learning more interesting and exciting. The rich variety of young people in your classes provides a context that allows you to make your classroom an interesting and exciting learning environment.

To exploit the opportunities presented by the rich diversity in your classroom, it is helpful to understand differentiated instruction. *Differentiation instruction* is based on the idea of adapting the curriculum to the needs and interests of the students rather than requiring the students to adapt to the curriculum. There are some misunderstandings regarding differentiated instruction. While differentiation does take into account the needs of individuals when planning, it is not the "individualized instruction" that was common in the 1960s and 1970s, when individual students were isolated in individual carrels and progressed through boring, programmed learning workbooks. Neither is differentiated instruction the preparation of different lessons for every student in your class.

Instead, differentiated instruction requires teachers who are in touch with the students they teach and are willing to "attend to both student similarities and student differences" in an effective and engaging manner. Differentiated instruction is not a teaching strategy; it is not a set of activities. It is a philosophy based on a set of beliefs, namely, that each student is unique with different learning styles, interests, and experiences (Tomlinson & Imbeau, 2010). Differentiation may include adapting the curriculum to include, small groups, individual learning contracts, computers, charts, a variety of books, CDs and DVDs, projects, and flexible pacing.

Students are not viewed as a homogenous and uniform group that will predictably respond to given stimuli. In fact, this is what is so fascinating and so maddening about teaching! Every student is unique, each class is unique, and each year is different. School is not an assembly line, and what worked with one student or one group might not work with another. In essence, one size does not fit all students!

Instructional specialists for years have promoted the use of differentiated instruction (Good & Brophy, 2004). In practice, teachers in elementary schools have been quicker to adopt various differentiated instruction approaches than teachers in secondary schools. It is quite common to find differentiated teaching approaches such as learning centers, project-based learning, and cooperative learning in elementary schools. These approaches are less common in secondary schools.

Why have relatively few secondary school teachers committed to differentiated instruction? One underlying reason is that, while elementary teachers usually have the same students all day and can therefore have a better understanding of specific students and have more flexibility of time, secondary teachers have more students and their day is divided into periods so they have less flexibility in organizing alternative learning activities for different students. For many, there are concerns connected to special features of their school and students. Often we hear "I don't have enough time," "I don't have enough materials," or "I must teach to the standards." Indeed, in some places, group-paced instruction and even scripted lessons have been required of teachers.

Another barrier is that some secondary school teachers have been presented with views of differentiation that make it appear to be an extremely time-consuming and difficult task. After all, no one has enough time to prepare 150 individual lessons every day! Sometimes, too, enthusiasts have provided overblown descriptions of the alleged benefits of differentiated instruction, thus raising doubts among experienced teachers who are appropriately wary when panacea-like qualities are claimed for any instructional methodology.

These are certainly valid perspectives for any secondary school teacher. However, they should not preclude you from designing instruction that is based on the needs of each student whom you teach. Differentiated instruction can begin small, by altering a few aspects of the learning environment to accommodate some students' interests or needs. You do not need to feel compelled to differentiate everything for every student each day. Instead, based on both formal and informal assessment, choose places and times in your instructional sequence where differentiation can be easily applied (Tomlinson & Imbeau, 2010).

Defining Differentiated Instruction

Differentiated instruction is defined as an approach to teaching and learning for students of differing interests and abilities in the same classroom. The purpose of differentiating instruction is to maximize success potential for all students in the classroom. It is based on the premise that instruction needs to be modified to accommodate students rather than students modifying themselves in order to accommodate the curriculum (Huebner, 2009). This type of differentiation is also called personalized education. In personalized education, students are more engaged in deciding what they will learn. Schools offer a variety of educational opportunities matched to student diversity. Teachers serve more as advisers who help students, tutor them, and help them manage their time (Wolk, 2010).

There is some research support for differentiated instruction. A Canadian research group found that differentiated instruction consistently had positive effects across a wide range of ability groups (Rock, Gregg, Ellis, & Gable, 2008). One study found that differentiated instruction kept high-ability students challenged (Tieso, 2005), and another found that differentiated instruction that utilized small groups was effective for students with learning disabilities (McQuarrie, McRae, & Stack-Cutler, 2008).

As you plan lessons in a diverse classroom, remember that the key is good teaching. If efforts are made to account for individual differences but the quality of teaching is poor, the results will be discouraging. Therefore, consideration of the principles of good teaching should be a major consideration in planning for differentiation.

Some of the guiding principles for differentiated instruction include the following:

- Focus on the big ideas and essential understandings as desired outcomes, as discussed in the previous chapter. It is very helpful to begin the process by asking, What big ideas or understanding should the students acquire? Then brainstorm alternative approaches that could be useful in helping different students achieve those outcomes in ways that would be most interesting and efficient for them. Remember that numerous approaches can be used to teach big ideas or enduring understandings.

- Consider student differences and interests. For example, if you know that Suzie likes music or Juan enjoys drawing, can you provide different activities that they could engage in that would stimulate their interest and enhance their success? If Bill has difficulty reading and English is a second language for Maria, how can you use that information to help the students overcome those learning barriers and achieve success?

- Group students according to interests and topics. Groups should be flexible and fluid. Students with different abilities can be grouped together to work on topics of interest to them. This variety of abilities can result in group projects that far exceed what an individual could do.

- Differentiated should be based on diagnostic and formative assessment. Being aware of student entry levels, student interests, and student progress is an essential ingredient in differentiated instruction. In other words, you need to know your students and you need to be aware of their progress.

For some, differentiation suggests a program where all students work independently on the same assignment. In this type of situation, every person does the same activity; only the rate of progress varies. This view of individualization is sometimes labeled continuous progress learning. Continuous progress implies that the rate of academic development of one student will not be held up because others in the class may learn at a slower rate. Individuals proceed along a continuum of instructional objectives at their own pace. Students who finish early are not held back to wait for others, and those who need more time to be successful are allowed that additional time.

Others see differentiation as focusing not on the rate of learning but on the content of instruction. In this view, differentiated programs are those where individual students achieve the same objectives, and they do so by studying different topics, with the teacher acting as an overall learning manager. For example, in a history course, students who have an interest in music could be allowed to learn the content of the topic through music of the era, students who have an interest in art could investigate works of art, and those interested in technology could investigate discoveries and changes that took place. When all of this is brought together, the entire class is transformed and becomes more interesting for all students.

Another conception of differentiation focuses on identifying learning modes of students and allowing students different methods for learning the same content. For example, there is considerable interest in multiple intelligences (Gardner, 1999). Individuals who subscribe to this theory contend that different individuals have varying forms of intelligence based on their learning modality (e.g., visual-spatial, bodily-kinesthetic, logical-mathematical, musical-rhythmic). As a teacher, you are more likely to succeed if you provide particular students with instruction framed in a way that capitalizes on the types of intelligence where they have particular strengths.

These perspectives highlight the folly of assuming any single learning activity will be universally appropriate for all students. For example, some of your students need to engage the material in more visual or kinesthetic ways, while others will learn more efficiently if they work with others and are confronted with probing questions. Still others need time to think and reflect on the material. Some students must see the whole first in order to discern patterns. Others can begin with the parts and build the patterns. Yet others can do quite well by reading about a topic, while others respond more positively to a concrete, hands-on approach.

If you would like to learn more about approaches related to the multiple intelligences theory, you might enjoy reading one of Howard Gardner's books, *Intelligence Reframed: Multiple Intelligences for the 21st Century* (1999). A couple of other books with a similar theme are Robert Sternberg's *Successful Intelligence: How Practical and Creative Intelligence Determine Success in Life* and Daniel Goleman's *Emotional Intelligence: Why It Can Matter More Than IQ*.

Approaches to differentiation based on multiple intelligences and on other theoretical underpinnings reflect a general orientation to teaching, not a specific set of procedures. When you say that you are interested in differentiating instruction, what you are committing to is placing value on "personalizing" learning. In practice, this requires you to design your lessons in ways that fit the special needs of students and seek to avoid forcing students to endure instructional approaches that are ill-suited to their personal learning styles and interests.

Altering Variables to Accommodate Individual Differences

What does a commitment to differentiating instruction mean in practice? Among other things, it requires you to give serious thought to variables that can be altered to accommodate student differences. As you plan instruction, you will be in a position to make changes associated with the following:

- Rate of learning
- Content of learning
- Method of learning
- Goals of learning

Rate of Learning

The term *rate of learning* refers to the pace at which your instruction occurs. When you expose all students in a class to exactly the same instructional program, you assume that everyone is capable of learning at the same rate. This assumption rarely stands up to close inspection. When your instruction fails to respond to differences in rate of learning, students who generally learn faster often get good grades and those who learn more slowly get poor grades or fail.

Time to learn, or what some have called opportunity to learn, has been defined as one of the most important variables in improving student achievement (Gabrieli, 2010). Individuals with this perspective argue that students who fail often do not do so because of lack of aptitude for the subject; rather, they fail because they are given insufficient time. One study of charter schools in New York City found that one feature of these schools that was most positively correlated with academic success was increased learning time (Hoxby, Murarka, & Kang, 2009).

Gabrieli (2010) notes that searching for expanded learning time has been a concern for quite some time. In 1994, a report titled "Prisoners of Time" identified typical school schedules as a "design flaw" (Gabrieli, 2010).

Some of the charter schools and other school improvement efforts (such as Knowledge Is Power Program [KIPP]) have focused on expanding learning time. While most of these efforts have looked at ways of expanding the school day, most secondary school teachers do not have that option. They have a set amount of time and a set number of days that they can utilize. This means that time available to them needs to be used wisely. One dimension they can consider is that different students learn at different rates. Some may learn content more quickly; others might take more time. In addition, a student who might need more time on one topic often needs less time when learning another topic. Therefore, altering the time variable focuses on how to differentiate learning in the classroom based on the time that individual students might need to learn.

When you differentiate instruction by manipulating the learning-rate or pacing variable, the content and the basic requirements remain the same for all students. What you alter is the time allowed for individual students to complete assigned tasks. You make arrangements that allow students who learn at a faster rate to move quickly through the material. Students who need additional time are given that extra time.

Altering the learning rate does pose some problems for teachers teaching in a traditional secondary school. The school year is usually about 180 days in length and the day is usually divided into specific time periods. This places limits on how much the rate of learning can be altered.

Altering the learning rate makes the most sense in situations where you believe it is essential for all of your students to master a given body of content. This form of differentiation is reflected in a number of formal instructional approaches; an example is *mastery learning*. Mastery learning presumes that differences in students' levels of achievement result not from differences in student intelligence or aptitudes but rather from variations in time required by individuals to learn assigned content (Bloom, 1976, 1980).

The Personalized System of Instruction (PSI) represents an example of an application of the mastery-learning idea (Guskey, 1985). Similar to other mastery-learning programs, it features the following:

- Clearly specified learning intentions

- Diagnosis of students' entry-level capabilities

- Numerous and frequent assessment measures

- Specification of mastery levels to be attained

- A structured sequence of facts, principles, and skills to be learned

- Frequent feedback to learners about their progress

- Provision of additional time that allows students who fail to achieve mastery to spend more time mastering the content

Essentially the PSI approach requires that blocks of instruction be broken down into small steps, with support materials and an assessment provided for each step. The students take as much time as they need to master each small step; they do not move forward until they have done so. Students make the choice to take the mastery quiz whenever they feel they are ready. Each quiz has a cut-off point (usually 80 to 90% correct) that is used to indicate mastery. If a student does not pass the quiz, he or she spends more time studying the content with other students until the quiz is passed. When students are successful, they move on to the next small unit. At the end of the course, a summative assessment is administered that covers all of the material. Students who pass the quizzes the first time spend less time on the material than do those who have to recycle (Slavin, 2009). These students move through the content of the course more quickly and may be allowed to move on to another subject or to explore topics in more depth.

Mastery-learning approaches such as PSI have positive as well as negative effects. On the positive side, researchers who have studied the impact of PSI at the college level have found the approach to be quite effective. In general, they have discovered that the mastery approach increases achievement (especially among less able students), results in less variation of achievement, and seems to have a positive impact on student attitudes toward school (Lefrancois, 1994).

PSI also has its critics. They point out that mastery learning does not work in all settings. Some students don't like the format and are not motivated to continue recycling thorough the same material several times. Students often complain about the lack of opportunities to interact and work with others. This may explain the finding that students in mastery-learning approaches were observed to have lower completion rates in college courses than students who were enrolled in non-PSI versions of the same class (Lefrancois, 1994).

Part of the debate about altering the rate of learning focuses on whether the additional time required for recycling might be better spent covering more material. The argument is that, while some additional time might be spent in areas where learners are having some difficulty, recycling them through learning sequences until they reach a high level of mastery might be counterproductive. They point out that some research indicates that the amount of content covered is positively related to increases in achievement (Slavin, 2009). In essence, what is being debated is a tradeoff. Because the amount of time available in secondary schools is relatively fixed, students who do not reach the "mastery" level for a particular objective may spend considerable time in limited areas that focus on their inadequacies rather than moving on to other content where they might have an opportunity to learn new material. Therefore, they do better if they cover more content in a given year at a lower level of mastery.

Mastery-learning programs often divide large tasks into small pieces; if you adopt this approach, you will find yourself confronted with the need to complete a great deal of paperwork. This feature, along with the frequent testing, often creates work for teachers that goes beyond what they face in more traditional instructional programs (Good & Brophy, 2004). This potential for greatly increased recordkeeping responsibilities, usually not a favorite activity of teachers, discourages some secondary school teachers from using mastery-learning approaches. For example, a couple of us taught a summer program for teachers a number of years ago where we applied the mastery-learning model. Most of our day was spent giving assessments, grading them, and providing immediate feedback to the participants in the program. We found little time to engage in small-group teaching, one of our favorite activities!

In summary, mastery-learning programs work best when they focus on a relatively narrow band of content that is required of all students. It is best used when the content can be divided easily into numerous smaller pieces that can be organized into sequential steps. Under these circumstances, mastery-learning programs can be very useful for students who have not learned content well enough to continue and achieve at least some level of success. Those who have experienced chronic failure and who do not believe they can achieve success can be motivated by being successful on the small steps and in having frequent feedback.

Success in altering the rate of learning will depend on your ability to monitor students carefully to assess levels of progress and encourage them to stay on task. It is particularly important that those students who experience limited success receive encouragement and develop confidence in their abilities to succeed. They should also be allowed to move on when they become bored and when there is a good probability that they can achieve success studying other content.

Content of Learning

Instead of focusing on the issue of pacing, you might want to individualize your instruction by altering the content of learning. When you do this, you do not change the learning goals. Rather, your focus is on student interests and content that would motivate them and help them learn the big ideas or enduring understanding that are the desired outcomes of your instruction. A focus on enduring understandings, as opposed to learning specific facts, allows for the use of different content at different levels of concreteness. Therefore, the content might be different for some students, but the desired outcomes are the same.

One example of altering the content of learning is an approach called orbital studies (Tomlinson, 1999). Orbital studies are based on the image of related studies "orbiting," or surrounding, a subject or generalization. To implement orbital studies, you assign students to follow different paths, based on their individual interests and differences, that are related to a common generalization or enduring understanding. For example, if you are teaching a mathematical concept, students interested in mathematics would apply the concept in mathematics, those interested in science would use science as the content of study, and those interested in economics or business would apply the concept to business. All students would be learning the same concept, but they would be learning the concept through content that interests them.

The basic principle for altering the content is that students are more motivated when they see the relevance of the topics they are studying. Some individuals point to the lack of achievement of secondary school students and claim that the traditional pattern of all students learning the same content misses important motivational opportunities and leads students to the conclusion that school has little relationship to their interests and their lives.

Allowing students a choice of topics to study can result in impressive learning outcomes. The quality and the depth of work that students produce when they pursue something of interest to them is often surprising. In addition, altering the content can benefit the whole class because all students observe different applications of the main ideas they are studying.

Differentiating by altering the content of learning does present certain difficulties. For example, it can be a challenge to find learning materials or learning opportunities that are well suited to the diverse interests of your students. However, Coughlin (2010) points out that there is a wealth of free learning resources available to students that many schools and teachers have overlooked. Online courses, podcasts, and video libraries are being created and expanded daily. Teachers can use these resources to allow students to pursue their interests. What is necessary, however, is for teachers to make sure that students have the technology background and skills, such as critical thinking and problem-solving, that will enable them utilize the information that is available.

It may take you some time to develop a degree of comfort with an approach to teaching that alters the content of learning. Our suggestion is that you start small and apply the approach to a limited number of units during the school year. As your comfort grows and you become familiar with the approach, you can expand it. After a couple of years, you may discover that you have differentiated instruction by altering the content for a large part of your curriculum. Use the exercise in Box 8-1 to practice planning teaching scenarios that alter what students study.

Standardized testing is one force that often causes teachers to pause when they consider altering the content of learning. They are concerned that specific facts might be on the test but that students will miss learning them. This is a valid concern. Part of the concern is related to the quality and the validity of the tests that are administered. Some tests do focus on specific bits of information. However, the validity of these tests can be questioned. Good tests focus on big ideas or generalizations rather just recall of facts.

In general, you need to seek a balance between your need to present content to students in ways they will find personally meaningful and your need to introduce it in a

---

Box 8-1

One variable you can manipulate in a differentiated program is the content of learning. When you do this, all of your students seek to master a common set of objectives, but you provide them with the means of doing so that take advantage of their individual strengths and interests. The idea is for you to provide options that are well matched to individual student interests.

As an exercise, identify a specific objective for a subject you would like to teach. Identify three separate interests that might be represented among students in your class. Suggest

different learning options that might help students with each of these interests to master the material.

Objective: _____

Interest A: _____

Suggested Learning Experiences: _____

Interest B: _____

Suggested Learning Experiences: _____

Interest C: _____

Suggested Learning Experiences: _____

---

context that will not be startlingly different from what they will confront when they have to take standardized tests. Keep in mind that when students learn something they find meaningful, they are more likely to retain that content over a longer time. Therefore, helping students learn content in a way that is interesting to them may well result in higher test scores on those once-a-year standardized tests.

Method of Learning

Altering the method of learning is based on principles related to individual learning styles. As stated earlier, some data indicates that individuals vary in their preferred modes of learning and that there are different attributes of intelligence. This is what is called attribute-treatment interaction. The basic premise is that learning is more effective and efficient when instructional methods are matched to the particular learning styles and the particular type of intelligence of individuals.

One approach to altering methods of learning focuses on the modalities of learning. Modalities refer to the sensory channels through which individuals receive and give information. These modalities include visual, auditory, kinesthetic, and tactile. Some people learn more efficiently when they are presented with visual material, others when they hear it, others when they touch or feel objects, and others when they are physically involved in doing something.

Another dimension of learning style that should be considered is something called field dependency versus field independency. Field-dependent individuals see patterns as a whole and have difficulty separating out specific aspects or parts of what they encounter. However, field-independent people tend to focus on the parts that make up the whole. For field-dependent students, presenting them with an overview or a large schema into which they fit the pieces would be helpful. Field-independent individuals might be better served if they obtain the pieces and are challenged to discover the overall schema or pattern.

Several other dimensions are often included in defining learning styles. A number of learning style inventories are available for use in your classroom. You might want to locate one via a Web search and administer it to your students. However, remember that simply because an individual has strength or a preference in a particular learning style does not mean that they cannot learn using other modalities.

When you attempt to individualize by altering the methods of learning, the learning intentions and content of learning remain the same for all students. Your task is to devise ways for students to process new information in ways that are compatible with their individual learning styles. To make this happen, you may decide to provide students with several options for learning new material. For example, some of your students might choose to read information from a textbook, others might choose to view a sound clip from a CD, while others will find it beneficial to listen to a speaker with information about the same topic.

Altering the method of learning based on learning style poses several problems. For one thing, a staggering variety of options are at least theoretically available to you as you attempt to accommodate different learning styles. Just diagnosing the learning styles of the number of secondary school students taught in a normal day can be a formidable task. Current measures of learning style include many dimensions and are often lengthy and difficult to administer. There is no standard test you can give that will reliably identify the preferred learning style of each of your students.

Some critics of this approach challenge the assumption that if you simply allow your students to choose a method of learning that seems right for them, they will choose one that is appropriate for their individual needs. For example, some research indicates that lower-ability students tend to perform better when they are in highly structured classroom environments with few choices. However, higher-ability students tend to perform better in more loosely structured classroom environments with more choices. However, when students are asked for their preferences, many lower-ability students express a preference for permissive, unstructured classes and high-ability students express a preference for highly structured classrooms. These decisions run counter to what research suggests would be the "wise" choice for each group.

The difference might be that higher-achieving students are more interested in grades and simply want to know what they must do to get a good grade. Lower-achieving students have had less success in getting good grades and are therefore more interested in doing something interesting to them rather than what they need to know to get a good grade.

As a practical matter, it is probably impossible for a teacher to try and accommodate all of the learning styles that might be present in a secondary school. However, recognizing that not everyone learns the same way and attempting to accommodate more than one learning style in the classroom can be productive. The bottom line is that you need to reflect on the nature of your students, the nature of your own background, and the nature of your particular instructional context as you decide how you can alter the methods of learning.

Goals of Learning

In differentiated instructional programs that feature altering the goals of learning, the goals are varied to accommodate characteristics of individual students. Programs that alter the goals of learning are relatively rare. This form of differentiation is based on the principle that students have different needs and talents, and when they are involved in determining what they want to learn, learning is more efficient. In an age of accountability, altering the goals of learning is not a popular approach. If students choose different goals, how can they be tested and how can common standards be applied? You will find some charter and alternative schools not bound by state standards and required standardized testing altering the learning goals with individual students.

Wolk (2010) cites the example of The Metropolitan Regional Career and Technical Center in Rhode Island. This school has no curriculum and no rigid schedule of classes, teachers are called advisers, and each student designs his or her personal curriculum in consultation with an advisor, a parent, and a mentor. Students develop special projects, conduct research, and spend two days a week in an internship. Wolk (2010) states that over 90% of the graduates attend college.

Another example is the New Country School in Henderson, Minnesota (Wolk, 2010). This school is a public charter school for Grades 6–12. The school has no curriculum other than a math block, a reading hour, and a painting class. The students spend most of their time on interdisciplinary projects that they design. The students identify what they want to learn and must justify the project as a legitimate learning experience when they submit it to the faculty for approval. They keep a log of their time and evaluate themselves using a rubric. They also work with experts in the community who also evaluate their performance.

It is obvious that the role of the teacher in this type of differentiation is quite different. The role of a teacher is that of a facilitator, adviser, and evaluator. Very little time is spent in large-group instruction and very little time is spent on planning lessons or units. A major requirement of teachers is to know the students. They need to spend time listening to them, questioning them, challenging them, and helping them clarify their personal goals and how they might achieve those goals.

It is obvious that this approach to differentiation runs counter to current trends. Rather than giving students and teachers more choice, the current trend is to give them less choice. State standards and even common standards that cross state boundaries are specifying more of what students should learn. Policy makers are more likely to take the stance that their job is to identify what is to be taught and the role of the teacher is to determine how to teach it. Therefore, it is likely that allowing student to participate in goal-setting and choosing what they will learn will not be a common feature of mainline schools. However, it is likely that, within limits, some altering of the goals of learning will take place within a classroom.

One common approach that has been used to alter the goals of learning (and is a form of the differentiation approach) is the learning contract. This is an agreement negotiated between the teacher and an individual student. Typically, learning contracts list a specific agenda of personalized tasks that a student must complete in a specified period of time and how she or he will demonstrate her or his learning (Tomlinson, 1999). The teacher retains the final word about what the contract will include. The following items are often found in learning contracts:

- A description of what steps the student will take to accomplish the learning intention
- A list of learning resources that will be used
- A description of any product(s) the student will be required to produce
- An explanation of criteria that will be used in evaluating the student's work
- A list of dates when different tasks are to be completed and submitted to the teacher for review

When you use a contract approach, both you and the student sign the agreement. Its provisions become the student's differentiated curriculum. When its terms are satisfied,

CRITICAL INCIDENT

SUCCESS IS KILLING ME!

LaShandra Diaz is a middle school teacher who recently developed a learning contract for one of her students, Cody Wong, who was having difficulty in her classroom. This student had done nothing for her, so she was willing to try anything to get him involved in the learning process. He responded well. His work improved, as did his test scores. Now, Cody's parents are so pleased that they have shared their son's success with other parents whose children are in LaShandra's classroom. Many of them now want her to design learning contracts for their kids.

Even though Ms. Diaz is thrilled with the positive public relations, she just can't figure out how to design 28 learning contracts, given the time it takes to lay out the objectives, find appropriate materials, and prepare individual assessment instruments. The parents are coming to see her on Thursday and she doesn't know what to do.

■ ■ ■

What should Ms. Diaz say when she meets with the parents? Are there others from whom she should seek advice before they arrive? Would it be possible to develop learning contracts for these students without placing an impossibly heavy burden of work on Ms. Diaz? How might school administrators feel about all this?

you and the student move on by developing a new contract or agenda. Completed contracts document what the student has done and learned.

Learning contracts can be especially useful for students who are failing or having difficulty. If they are not engaged in the curriculum, are not motivated, and are simply present in the classroom, taking time to find out what interests them and establishing a learning contract that helps them set realistic goals can have some positive results. For example, one secondary school English teacher had a girl in the class who simply would not write anything. The teacher asked her what she would write and they agreed that each day she would write a few autobiographical sentences. The student was successful in fulfilling the first contracts, so the minimum requirements for subsequent contracts were increased. The result was that, by the end of the term, the student was writing several pages each day. When the term was up, she asked the teacher, "Do I have to stop writing?"

As a prerequisite to initiating a learning-contract approach, you need to have a broad base of content knowledge so that you are aware of alternatives and you can guide the students in the development of meaningful learning opportunities. You also need to know your individual students well enough to recommend inclusion of learning experiences in any contracts where they will have a chance of success. The first contracts should be relatively short and should have a high probability of success.

Preparing for Differentiated Learning

There are approaches that you can use to move gradually toward more differentiated learning in your classroom. The following section discusses a few approaches that secondary school teachers have used.

Learning Activity Packages (LAPs)

One approach you might take in differentiating your instruction involves preparation of learning activity packages. A learning activity package is a highly structured, self-contained guide that breaks content into a series of small steps. It contains a sequence of learning activities that a student completes at his or her own pace. An assessment at the completion of each step or activity must be successfully completed before the student can move on. There is generally a summative assessment that takes place at the conclusion of the LAP.

LAPs are an especially flexible format for delivering differentiated instruction. You can construct packages to address possible needs to (a) vary the rate of learning, (b) vary the content of learning, (c) vary the method of learning, and (d) vary the goals of learning. Your decisions regarding an appropriate focus will be based on your own analyses of the needs of students in your classes. A LAP might be developed for the entire class, groups of students in the class, or for individuals in the class. Regardless of what you decide to emphasize, your LAP might include the following components:

- Title
- General description and rationale
- Objectives
- Diagnostic assessment
- Learning program
- Performance task or summative assessment

Title   Titles play both a motivational and a descriptive function. Because you want to spark student interest in the content of the activity package, you need to think creatively about the title you select. For example, suppose you are teaching music and want to prepare a short activity package exposing students to some basic music theory principles. Simply titling the activity package "Music Theory" is unlikely to prompt much student excitement. You might decide on something a bit more evocative, such as "Beethoven to Heavy Metal: Explorations in Music Theory."

General Description and Rationale   This section of your activity package lets your students know what they must do to complete the work. Often, you will provide some indication of the approximate time required to do this. Also, you will often briefly describe some important new terminology that students will encounter as they work with the material, and you will provide an explanation about why students should attach some importance to learning the new content.

Objectives   In this part of the activity package, you will make clear to students exactly what it is they are expected to learn. You will include information that tells them what they will have to do to assure you that they have grasped the new material. The idea here is to give them some learning targets and to remove any misconceptions they might have regarding your expectations.

Diagnostic Assessment   Typically, you will want students to take a pretest or engage in some other kind of exercise to provide you with information about what they know about the topic before they begin working with the material in the LAP. The diagnosis can inform you about prerequisite student knowledge necessary to succeed. In addition, this information can help you spot students who may already have mastered some of the material in the package. When this situation develops, you can direct these students to skip sections introducing material they have already mastered.

The Learning Program   The heart of your activity package is the learning program. The learning program defines the activities that the students must complete. The program can identify books to be read, films or CDs to be viewed, cooperative learning activities students need to participate in, projects to be completed, and even a large-group session they must attend.

Summative Assessment   The summative assessment is given to a student when the student believes he or she has completed the LAP. Note that it is usually the student's decision to take the summative assessment. If students need a push, however, a deadline can be established. This summative assessment can also be a performance task that is evaluated using a rubric.

Book Circles

Book circles have become a very popular approach to differentiate instruction in content classrooms. Book circles are modeled after the popular book discussion groups that are hosted by local bookstores and celebrity television show hosts. The book circle approach allows you to differentiate by allowing students to choose one of several books related to the objectives and the desired outcomes of the class. The books might be selected because they offer different reading levels for your students, because they appeal to students with different interests, or because they address different dimension of the topic.

The key ingredient for book circle success is structure. Most teachers use a structure suggested by Harvey Daniels (2001): a structure that assigns roles (e.g., discussion leader, artist, word watcher, narrator) to each student. Therefore, the book circle not only differentiates instruction by allowing students to choose what they read, it also allows differentiation by allowing them to perform a role that is of interest to them. Because they know ahead of time what is expected, they can be prepared for each session. Some teachers rotate roles so that each student has an opportunity to experience a variety of roles.

Once all of the book circles in a class have completed their books and the small-group discussions, they come together for whole-class activities. They might explore common themes, complete additional reading assignments, or write essays that demonstrate higher thought processes.

If you are interested in learning more about book circles in the secondary school classroom, you might want to read Harvey Daniels's book, *Literature Circles: Voice and Choice in Book Clubs & Reading Groups* (2001) or one of any number of books now available on this topic. A Web search will generate a list of ten or more. These books will assist you with topics such as teaching your students the process, procedures for selecting books, project ideas, and assessment techniques.

Learning Stations

Learning stations are centers where all the materials related to a given topic or activity are gathered. For example, in a science classroom, students could be required to complete several different lab activities related to the objectives of a lesson. A history class could be divided into learning stations, with each station including different information and interpretations of a historical event. Students would progress through several different learning stations before arriving at their interpretation of the event. In essence, they would be acting as historians, except that they would not have to discover the relevant material.

In some instances, the students would be required to complete the activities in all learning stations; in others, they would have a choice of activities. The students may be allowed to self-pace themselves and take as long as they need to complete each learning station.

In terms of their basic organizational features, individual learning stations typically include general information, directions for completing the station, learning alternatives, needed materials, and details about performance tasks or summative assessments. Because this approach always requires you to develop several interrelated stations, a considerable amount of time might be needed to develop the learning stations. However, you will not have to spend as much time developing lessons plans. During class time, your role will be one of answering questions and monitoring activities in each learning station.

When planning a series of learning stations, it is important to keep in mind the generalizations or enduring understandings that the students should learn. Then you can break the generalization or the enduring understanding into logical blocks or topics. Each of these blocks or topics could then become the focus of a learning station. For example, in an English classroom where particular literary themes are being explored, each station could have information and work by a single author so that students could compare and contrast how different authors approached the same theme.

The material for a learning station might be gathered in a specific location, and a set of instructions and topical questions could be placed at the station to help the students complete each station. Each station could include a number of different activities so that students could choose for themselves the activities that interest them.

Like all forms of teaching, learning stations require that certain management issues are addressed. You need to determine how many students can work at a given station at a time, how students will progress through each station, and how much time individuals can spend at a given station.

It might be useful to have a whole-class discussion when all students have had an opportunity to work through the learning stations. They can share their conclusions and what they have learned with the rest of the class. This might stimulate additional questions and issues that the students want to explore. An occasional use of learning stations can provide an exciting change of pace for the classroom. It helps students move toward becoming more independent learners and can allow students to pursue individual differences while maintaining the focus on an enduring understanding or generalization.

Box 8-2 shows an example of instructions for students using learning stations.

Box 8-2 English: Period 3

In this unit, you will be required to do assigned reading, take two vocabulary tests, identify literary elements, and apply them in some creative writing. To accomplish these tasks, you will be assigned to work through five learning stations. The order of completion for the stations is unimportant. Individuals have been assigned a particular learning station to begin. Go directly to the station to which you are assigned and you will find instructions telling you what to do. (*Do not go to any other station until directed to do so by the teacher.*)

When you complete each assignment at a station, place it in your notebook and use the card signal to inform me that you are done. I will perform a quick check of your material and give you permission to move to the next station. When you have completed the work for all assigned stations, submit your notebook to me.

As you work through the stations, keep track of your progress by completing the following form.

Stations	Date Completed	Score
Station 1: Read different historical accounts and define what is meant by the statement "History is a story well told."		

Station 2: Read the material defining imagery, and identify examples where the historians used imagery in at least two of the accounts.

Station 3: Take one of the original source documents and write an account of the event using imagery.

Station 4: Read the material and the examples on personification. Define personification.

Station 5: Find at least three examples of personification in the historical accounts provided at the station.

Performance Task: Take one of the historical events that we have been studying and write your own account of the event using imagery and personification.

Computers and Differentiated Instruction

The prevalence of computers in schools provides great opportunities for differentiating instruction. By the secondary school level, most students are very familiar with computers and can use them easily. Great resources are available and allow students to pursue topics of interest in great depth. The real task of a teacher is to move students beyond the social networking possibilities of the computer to using it as a productive learning tool.

It should be commonplace for teachers to explore the Internet when they are planning a unit of instruction. You can identify different websites and opportunities for students to explore the subject that you are teaching. Wise use of the computer in the classroom can provide enormous possibilities for differentiating learning. Students can find images, films, and discussions as well as print resources on the Internet. If provided with the opportunity, they can find material that best fits their learning modality. Web-based options can be included in learning activity packages as well as learning stations. The uses of the computer are limited only by our imagination.

In addition to the Web, there is an abundance of specialized software that can be obtained for use on the computer. Educational supply houses sell programs that run the gamut from loosely organized general information about large topics to highly structured programs of study focusing on narrow issues. Some of the better software packages allow you to alter most of the important variables associated with differentiated instruction. For example, you can modify some programs to allow students to work at their own pace. Others allow for variations in how new content is introduced. Many of them provide alternative ways for your students to review content.

Some software features intelligent tutor programs, which are designed to determine what a student already knows in relation to a particular learning outcome. Once this is determined, the program exposes the student to learning experiences that are designed to teach information he or she has not yet mastered. The intelligent tutor program assesses what students already know by prompting them to respond to questions asked by the computer. Their responses are then compared to a database built into the computer. As a result of the comparison, the computer program develops a unique student profile and then establishes a special sequence of learning experiences for the student. Once this step has been completed, the student begins moving through the planned instructional sequence. The program provides correctives as needed and other kinds of feedback related to the adequacy of the learner's performance.

One advantage of intelligent tutor and other computer-based differentiated programs is that the computer has infinite patience. For example, a computer allows students to recycle through difficult material as many times as they need to to master the content. When your students use such programs, they are involved with an instructional process that truly allows them to progress at their own rate. In addition, many computer programs provide a useful record of student progress when they complete a learning session. This allows you to monitor this information at your own convenience. In addition, the information is often stored and used when a student returns for additional work. Based on what students have done previously, the computer provides an appropriate entry point when they return to work again with the computer-based material.

Peer Tutoring

Another approach that can be effective in differentiating instruction is peer tutoring. Peer tutoring involves having students who have mastered new material tutor others who need help. There are two basic types of peer tutoring: same-age peer tutoring and cross-age peer tutoring. As the name suggests, *same-age peer tutoring* features tutors who are about the same age and who are in the same grade as those being tutored. On the other hand, *cross-age peer tutoring* features older, more advanced students working with younger, less advanced students.

Researchers have found that both the person doing the tutoring as well as the person being tutored experience increased levels of learning. In fact, the person doing the tutoring usually gains as much as, if not more than, the person being tutored. Therefore, it is not necessary to require that those performing the tutoring be "experts" or academic stars. It is often best to have those students who are just somewhat ahead of those they are tutoring. This often helps the tutor develop a better grasp of the content. For example, some high school students identified as being at risk of dropping out of school have been assigned to work as tutors in elementary schools. Their involvement gives the high school students an opportunity to revisit information they may not have learned well when they first encountered it. In addition, this arrangement often gives the older students a sense of responsibility that can lead to more positive attitudes toward school. The result is that the achievement of many of these secondary school students improves rather dramatically.

Regardless of the type of tutoring program you decide to implement, your tutors need training (Slavin, 2009). They have to learn how to provide assistance without doing the work for the person they are helping. In addition, you have to monitor tutors' work carefully. If you fail to do so, tutoring sessions can easily turn into opportunities for social conversation having little, if any, connection to academics. Tutors also are more confident about their tasks when they know you are readily available to help them if they run into any difficulties.

Differentiation Through Sheltered Instruction

In Chapter 3, we discussed the changing population in today's classrooms. You will most likely encounter the need to teach English language learners. These students require some special considerations as you design effective lessons. Although some English learners will

More from the Web

Differentiating Your Teaching

In this chapter, you have been introduced to several ways to meet the needs of individual students. The following websites contain information that you may find useful in applying the ideas in this chapter. Some of them contain lesson plans that you can adapt to your classroom. Others provide rich resources that you can use in designing differentiated learning instruction. Still others provide opportunities to learn from other teachers who have developed differentiated programs.

EDUCATOR'S TOOL KIT

http://www.eagle.ca/-~matink/

This website has many valuable resources to help you design differentiated lessons. There are links to lessons plans, a whole section on students with special needs, and ideas on how to teach various subjects.

DESIGNING WEB-BASED LEARNING STATIONS

http://www.essdack.org/stations/sld001.htm

Tammy Worcester has made available at this website information that describes approaches you can use to develop learning stations that feature content from the World Wide Web. The information is introduced in the form of a 17-slide presentation, which includes helpful details for developing a differentiated instruction program featuring learning stations and Web content.

PLANS FOR DIFFERENTIATED INSTRUCTION

http://www.coe.uh.edu/courses/cuin6373/idhistory/individualized_instruction.html

If you are interested in historical developments related to differentiated instruction, you will want to visit this website. Among other topics, you will find information about the Winnetka Plan and the Dalton Plan. Both were forerunners of some individualized approaches that teachers use today to differentiate instruction.

SOCRATES—STYLE AND METHODS

http://www.san.beck.org/SOCRATES3-How.html

At this website, you will find an extensive discussion of Socrates' approaches to teaching. One section, titled Individualized Instruction, explains how Socrates discovered and responded to the special needs of his students.

PEER TUTORING

http://www.nwrel.org

The Northwest Regional Educational Laboratory has posted information at this website. It features an extensive discussion of peer tutoring. In addition to descriptions of the approach, you will find excellent references to research studies that have been conducted to determine its effectiveness.

EXAMPLE OF DIFFERENTIATED INSTRUCTION IN A HIGH SCHOOL CLASS

http://www.ascd.org/pdi/demo/diffinstr/l1hsex.html

If you are interested in seeing differentiated instruction in action in a high school classroom, check out this website. You may also want to explore differentiated instruction in more depth on the website of the Association for Supervision and Curriculum Development (ASCD), which is the group that provides this example.

be mainstreamed into regular classrooms, some will be grouped into special classes classified as *sheltered* or *Specially Designed Academic Instruction in English (SDAIE)*. No matter which configuration you are assigned, the techniques discussed below will help you differentiate instruction for these learners.

Sheltered instruction is defined as grade-level content in English for non-native speakers. It is a means of making content coursework (social studies, math, science, etc.) more accessible for English learners (Echevarria & Graves, 2003). In sheltered classrooms, teachers teach academic skills while assisting development of the student's new language. Ideally, students assigned to sheltered classes should have developed both proficiency and literacy in their first language.

The tips discussed in the following subsections are provided by a number of experts. The tips are helpful in assisting your English language learners (Echevarria & Graves, 2003; Garcia, 2002; Krashen, 1981; Lessow-Hurley, 2002).

Use Simplified English Conversations   Because these students are still learning English, it is imperative that you speak more slowly and enunciate clearly. Consider exaggerating key words and phrases to emphasize their importance. Emphasize vocabulary, preteaching words that you think will be challenging for the students.

Use Cooperative Groups   The socialization process involved in cooperative group structures provides a vehicle for students to improve their academic language. The interaction between students gives English learners opportunities to practice their new language in meaningful ways.

Use a Variety of Visual Aids   English learners need to see as well as hear the concepts being taught. Consider using realia, a variety of primary sources, photos, maps, globes, diagrams, technology, and audiovisual tools.

Don't Constantly Correct Students' Departure from Standard English
Encourage students to talk. Once they do, you can paraphrase their responses to model Standard English.

Increase Your Wait Time   Give English learners more time to respond to your questions than you would give proficient English speakers. They need the extra time to adequately process their thoughts in English.

Adapt Content to Meet Students' Language and Learning Needs   You may be required to use textbooks that are too difficult for English learners. Locate additional resources that can supplement the required text. Consider rewriting some parts into text that is more comprehensible or make available easier editions of the text. And assign real-life activities that are meaningful for students (e.g., letter writing, simulations).

Record Some of Your Lessons   It is relatively easy to record yourself. If English language learners are having difficulty in your class, you might want to record particularly important lessons and allow the students to listen to the lesson several times. This will enhance their understanding and remove some of the anxiety they may experience when trying to keep up when you are teaching.

Reinforce Language Learning While Teaching Content   Model the pronunciation of difficult words and the intonation of the English language used in content material. Emphasize basic grammatical structure to assist students in comprehending content.

Relate the Academic Content to the Students' Experiences   Design lessons that draw on the backgrounds of the students in your classroom. Consider allowing them opportunities to share these experiences and suggest topics of interest.

FOR YOUR PORTFOLIO

1. Standard 3 of the Interstate New Teacher Assessment and Support Consortium (INTASC) standards relates to understanding differences. What materials and ideas you learned in this chapter related to differentiating for learning will you include as evidence that you understand difference? Select up to three items of information to be included in your portfolio. Number them 1, 2, and 3.

2. Think about why you selected these materials for your portfolio. Consider issues such as the following in your response:

   - The specific purposes to which this information can be put when you plan, deliver, and assess the impact of your instruction

   - The compatibility of the information with your own priorities and values

   - The contributions this information can make to your personal development as a teacher

   - The factors that led you to include this material as opposed to some alternatives you considered

3. Prepare a written reflection in which you analyze the decision-making process you followed. Also, mention the INTASC Standard(s) to which your selected material relates (first complete the chart below).

SELECTED MATERIALS AND THE INTASC STANDARDS

There are other INTASC Standards that you might address. Put a check under the numbers of those INTASC standards to which the evidence you have selected applies. (Refer to Chapter 1 for more detailed information about INTASC.)

INTASC Standards

Item of Evidence Number	S-1	S-2	S-3	S-4	S-5	S-6	S-7	S-8	S-9	S-10
1										
2										
3										

Emphasize Literacy Activities   Use interactive journals, silent reading followed by whole-group or small-group discussions, book circles, and mathematics logs. See Chapter 12 for additional ideas.

You may be thinking that many of these tips are just good teaching strategies for any classroom. And you would be right. These suggestions are not exclusive to English language learners. Many of these approaches are useful for any student in the classroom who might be having learning difficulties. Remember that with English language learners, your task is now twofold: You need to inspire students to learn the content as well as improve their English.

In summary, a differentiated classroom is not an option; it is a necessity if you are to provide students with opportunities to learn. As you face increasingly more diverse classrooms—classrooms with gifted students, English language learners, and mainstreamed special education students—we encourage you to heed the words of Howard Gardner. He suggests that the biggest mistake in teaching has been to treat all students as if they were variants of the same individual, and thus to feel warranted in teaching them the same subjects in the same way (Siegel & Shaughnessy, 1994, cited in Tomlinson, 1999). Today's students deserve teachers who are willing to abandon the one-size-fits-all delivery system in favor of a system that responds to the needs of the individual learner.

Key Ideas in Summary

- The diversity of students in classrooms today means that teachers have learners with highly varied interests and aptitudes. This context is particularly appropriate for differentiated instructional approaches that seek to take advantage of the unique characteristics of individual students.

■ One approach to differentiating involves altering the rate of learning. When this is done, all students are exposed to the same basic instructional program, but the speed at which individual students progress through the program varies. Mastery learning is an example of altering the rate of learning to differentiate instruction. Mastery learning presumes that observed differences in students' levels of achievement have little to do with differences in their levels of intelligence or in their aptitudes. Rather, differences occur because individuals vary in terms of how much time they need to do the required work.

■ Another approach to differentiating involves altering the content of learning. Goals pursued by all students may be the same, but the teacher seeks to identify areas in which students are particularly interested and to provide relevant instruction within the context of these interests. This approach assumes that students' levels of motivation increase when learning materials are closely matched to their interests.

■ Differentiated programs that attend to learning style differences of students often involve teachers in altering the method of learning. Objectives and content remain the same for all students, but individuals are allowed to pursue different paths as they seek to learn the material. For example, some students may read about it, others may work with appropriate CDs, and still others may interview people and take notes.

■ Perhaps the variable that is altered the least in differentiating learning is that of the goals of learning. In this approach, great latitude is given to students to select the goals of instruction and to make other important decisions about what they wish to learn. Current trends are toward providing less freedom concerning what students should learn rather than more freedom.

■ One approach to differentiating involves the use of learning activity packages. These packages are highly structured and self-contained guides that break learning content into a series of small steps. Students must successfully complete one step before going on to another. Learning activity packages represent a flexible format. They can be designed to respond to a variety of individual student needs.

■ Learning station approaches subdivide large topics into important subtopics. Each station focuses on one subtopic. Organizationally, each learning station contains the material and instructions for the students to follow when using the learning station.

■ Book circles are an increasingly popular approach to differentiation. Teachers select four or five books that are tied to the learning objectives in a given unit. Students then are grouped with others reading the same book. Structure is imperative if book circles are to work effectively.

■ Electronic technologies, particularly computers, provide tremendous options for teachers who wish to differentiate their instruction. There are good opportunities to find content and applications of interest to the students on the Internet. In addition, software is available that can be used to generate instructional options suited to the needs of individual students.

■ Peer tutoring approaches feature students who have mastered new material working with other students who need additional help. Same-age peer tutoring involves tutors who are about the same age and in the same grade as the students they are helping. Cross-age peer tutoring features tutors who usually are older and more advanced than the students they have been asked to assist.

■ Sheltered classrooms require techniques specially designed to provide comprehensible content for English language learners. Some of these techniques include (1) using simplified English conversations, (2) using cooperative groups, (3) using a variety of visual aids, (4) not constantly correcting students' departure from Standard English, (5) increasing your wait time, (6) adapting content to meet students' language and learning needs, (7) recording some of your lessons, (8) reinforcing language learning while teaching content, (9) relating academic content to the students' experiences, and (10) emphasizing literacy activities.

Reflections

1. What is your definition of differentiated instruction? Which variables associated with differentiation do you think you would be most comfortable altering? Why?

2. What concerns do you have about altering each of the variables for differentiating instruction?

3. Some individuals see a conflict between recent state-level efforts to mandate specific tests that all students must complete and the need to meet the needs of diverse students. What is your response to this issue?

4. Which approaches to differentiated instruction do you see as most consistent with recent trends in education?

5. Which of the specific approaches to differentiated instruction do you think would fit best with your beliefs and skills? Why?

6. Several approaches to differentiating instruction were introduced in the chapter. How would you rate your interest in each? Which do you think would be most difficult for you to implement, and why?

7. Some people suggest that the Internet offers an exceptionally rich resource for the teacher who wants to individualize. However, others argue that to use this resource requires considerable teacher control to prevent abuses. What is your opinion?

8. Suppose you decided to use peer tutors in one of your classes to assist students having difficulty mastering some new content you have introduced. How would you specifically prepare your tutors for their responsibilities?

9. Some critics of differentiated instruction suggest that it is an impractical sham. They allege that the approach sounds good but that, in reality, teachers simply lack sufficient time to plan programs uniquely suited to the needs of each student. What do you see as strengths and weaknesses of this argument?

10. As you reflect on your professional knowledge, what additional information do you think you need to acquire to better meet the needs of diverse students?

Learning Extensions

1. Observe in a secondary school. Look for ways that teachers differentiate and adapt their instruction to meet the needs of diverse students. Using what you have learned in the chapter, identify places where these teachers have altered one of the four differentiated instruction variables introduced. Share your observations with others in your class.

2. Identify a specific topic you would cover in one of the courses you would like to teach. Develop a plan for using learning stations to explore this topic.

3. Identify a topic you wish your students to learn. Suppose you wanted some students to gather as much information as possible about this topic using resources only available on the Internet. Develop a master list of the URLs of websites with information that might help your students. Share this material with members of your class, and describe how you might use this information to individualize your instruction.

4. Reread the material in the chapter that deals with learning activity packages. Choose a topic from your own field and prepare a learning activity package for students. Include alternate ways for students to do the work. Share your work with others in your class, and be prepared to discuss any special challenges you faced in assembling this material.

5. Identify some content that you will teach. Find five or six books that you might use in a book circle approach in your classroom. Prepare material for a book talk on each book, and set up the group roles in a format ready to distribute to students. Design some end-of-reading projects that will provide students with alternatives for demonstrating their understanding of the reading.

6. Work with a group of classmates who plan to teach the same subject. Use a content textbook to design a sheltered lesson using the ideas presented in this chapter.

References

Bloom, B. S. (1976). *Human characteristics and school learning.* New York: McGraw-Hill.

Bloom, B. S. (1980). *All our children learning.* New York: McGraw-Hill.

Coughlin, E. (2010). High school at a crossroads. *Educational Leadership, 67*(7), 48–53.

Daniels, H. (2001). *Literature circles: Voice and choice in book clubs & reading groups.* Portland, ME: Stenhouse.

Echevarria, J., & Graves, A. (2003). *Sheltered content instruction: Teaching English-language learners with diverse abilities* (2nd ed.). Boston: Allyn & Bacon.

Gabrieli, C. (2010). More time, more learning. *Educational Leadership , 67*(7), 38–44.

Garcia, E. (2002). *Student cultural diversity: Understanding and meeting the challenge* (3rd ed.). Boston: Houghton Mifflin.

Gardner, H. (1999). *Intelligence reframed: Multiple intelligences for the 21st century.* New York: Basic Books.

Good, T., & Brophy, J. (2004). *Looking in classrooms* (9th ed.). New York: Longman.

Guskey, T. (1985). *Implementing mastery learning.* Belmont, CA: Wadsworth.

Hoxby, C. M., Murarka, S., & Kang, J. (2009). *How New York City's charter schools affect achievement.* Cambridge, MA: New York City Charter Schools Evaluation Project.

Huebner, T. A. (2009). What research says about differentiated instruction. *Educational leadership, 67*(5), 79–81.

Krashen, S. (1981). *Second language acquisition and second language learning.* London: Pergamon Press.

Lefrancois, C. (1994). *Psychology for teaching* (8th ed.). Belmont, CA: Wadsworth.

Lessow-Hurley, J. (2002, Fall). Acquiring English: Schools seek ways to strengthen language learning, *Curriculum Update.* Alexandria, VA: Association for Supervision and Curriculum Development.

McQuarrie, L. McRae, P., & Stack-Cutler, H. (2008). *Differentiated instruction provincial research review.* Edmonton: Alberta Initiative for School Improvement.

Rock, M., Gregg, M., Ellis, E., & Grable, R.A. (2008). REACH: A framework for differentiating classroom instruction. *Preventing School Failure, 52*(2), 31–47.

Siegel, J., & Shaughnessy, M. (1994). Educating for understanding: A conversation with Howard Gardner. *Phi Delta Kappan, 75*(7), 564, cited in Tomlinson, C. (1999). *The differentiated classroom: Responding to the needs of all learners.* Alexandria, VA: Association for Supervision and Curriculum Development.

Slavin, R. (2009). *Educational psychology* (9th ed.). Boston: Allyn & Bacon.

Tieso, C. (2005). The effects of grouping practices and curricular adjustments on achievement. *Journal for the Education of the Gifted, 29*(1), 60–89).

Tomlinson, C. (1999). *The differentiated classroom: Responding to the needs of all learners.* Alexandria, VA: Association for Supervision and Curriculum Development.

Tomlinson, C., & Imbeau, M. (2010). *Leading and managing a differentiated classroom.* Alexandria, VA: Association for Supervision and Curriculum Development.

Wolk, R. (2010). Education: The case for making it personal. *Educational Leadership, 67*(7), 16–21.

The Instructional Act

Tom Watson/Merrill

Models of Direct Instruction

Objectives

This chapter will help you

- describe components of several direct-instruction models

- point out features of direct instruction that explain the popularity of this approach among teachers, school leaders, and parents

- identify learning intentions for which direct instruction is appropriate

- describe situations for which direct instruction has been found to be a useful instructional approach

- apply the direct-instruction model to specific instructional situations

Bob Daemmrich Photography

Graphic Organizer: Chapter 9

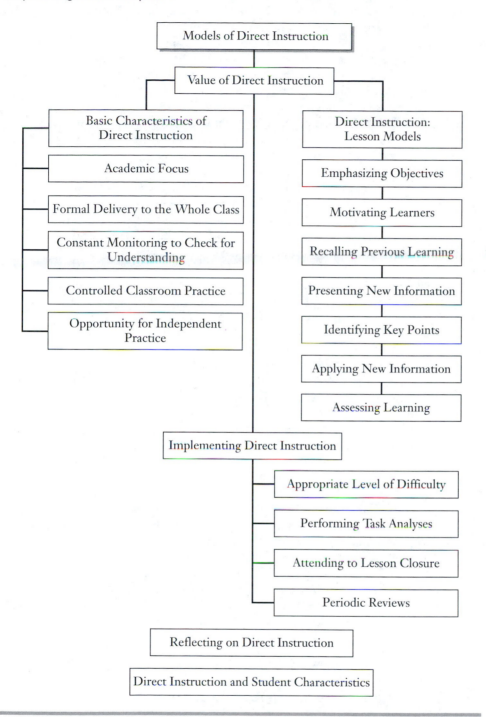

Introduction

What teaching approaches were most common when you were a student? Chances are that what you recall as typical teaching falls into a category called direct instruction. Direct instruction is teacher-controlled instruction that focuses on students learning specific objectives and predetermined content. The role of the teacher is to present information, monitor student understanding, engage students in practice activities, and assess their progress. The teacher decides the content, controls the interaction, and determines the pace of the lesson. Although direct instruction is probably the most often used model of instruction, it is also one of the least understood and most misused instructional models (Lasley, Matczynski, & Rowley, 2002). For many teachers, direct instruction means teacher lecture. They see the steps in the model as talking and presenting information for most of a class period, engaging the students in seatwork to practice what they have presented, and then giving a homework assignment. While this is a general outline of the direct-instruction model, it violates some of the basic principles of direct instruction. Some of the basic principles of direct instruction to which teachers must adhere include the following: (1) They must teach to clear and specific learning objectives; (2) they must present information in a systematic, step-by-step fashion; (3) they must provide frequent opportunities for students to be engaged during their questioning and checking for understanding; and (4) they must provide careful guidance and monitoring during guided practice. The approach typically features whole-class or large-group instruction rather than individualized or small-group learning.

Even though the teacher is in charge of the lesson, good direct instruction includes significant student participation. The teacher must make explicit instructional decisions during the lesson and must thoughtfully assess whether students have learned (Lasley, Matczynski, & Rowley, 2002).

This approach has several different labels, including explicit teaching, systematic teaching, target teaching, active teaching, clinical teaching, and mastery teaching. Some variants of this approach have been used in classrooms for decades. Madeline Hunter popularized this model a couple of decades ago, and it became the basis of the "expected" teaching approach for many school districts and the basis for teacher evaluations that still exist (Lasley, Matczynski, & Rowley, 2002). Other educators such as Bereiter and Engelmann (1966), Gagne (1977), and Rosenshine (1983) also developed variants of direct instruction that added to the popularity of the model across the nation.

This approach has been so widely received for several reasons. First, it does not ask teachers to do anything in the classroom that radically departs from traditional teaching. Therefore, it is familiar to most teachers. Basically, the model provides a systematic approach to teaching that made teacher decisions much clearer. In addition, procedures for implementing direct instruction are easy to learn, and it was found to be effective in reaching some objectives. For example, it has been found to be especially effective in teaching students the kinds of basic information often evaluated on standardized tests. This makes it attractive to teachers and administrators who are concerned about standardized test scores. Finally, most parents remember this kind of teaching from their own school days and are comfortable when teachers use it in the classroom.

In this chapter, we make suggestions about appropriate and inappropriate uses of direct instruction. We also introduce basic components of a direct-instruction model in our presentation of this chapter's contents. After you finish reading this material, you may wish to revisit various sections to see how parts of our direct-instruction model have been incorporated.

Determining the Instructional "Value" of Direct Instruction

You will encounter numerous claims about direct instruction. Some new teachers will find administrators who insist that they use a direct-instruction approach for all lessons. Some experienced teachers will contend that direct instruction is the answer to every teacher's worries and that its use in the classroom will motivate and provide success for all students. On the other hand, it is not difficult to find teachers and experts who attack direct instruction as inappropriate for teaching important 21st-century skills. They claim that direct instruction is just the same narrow and boring approach that is sure to turn off many students.

Why is there such a difference of opinion regarding the value of direct instruction? No doubt, many factors contribute to this situation. One factor is that teachers work within large and generally conservative bureaucracies. It is difficult to win support for new instructional approaches unless there is compelling evidence of a need for change. Parents simply are wary of approaches that they see as untried or experimental. For example, there was much opposition to the introduction of technology, such as calculators in math classes, for fear that their use would obstruct the learning of basic math skills. In some areas, computers were very slow to be introduced to schools. Another factor is that some feel pressured to "oversell" the benefits of a particular instructional approach. They also often feel compelled to engage in open attacks on alternative approaches as a way of attracting support for what they are espousing.

One of the realities that new teachers frequently overlook is that most changes in education are not the result of research findings. Rather, most educational practice is the result of political compromise and tradeoffs. Teachers should be aware of research findings, however, so they can make the best choices and can be advocates of what is best for students.

There are some research-based findings related to the effectiveness of direct instruction. The largest study was Project Follow Through. This study, completed in the 1970s, involved 79,000 students in 80 communities. The results indicate that "direct instruction dramatically improved cognitive skills" (http://www.jefflindsay.com/EducData.shtml). Unfortunately, most of the research on direct instruction was conducted at the elementary level. This does not suggest that direct instruction is inappropriate at the secondary school level; however, it does "indicate the limited scope of research to determine the power of the technique with different populations" (Lasley, Matczynski, & Rowley, 2002, p. 273).

In general, studies have found this approach to be particularly good for purposes such as teaching basic facts, concepts, procedures, and basic skills (Borich, 1992). Research on direct instruction and other instructional approaches typically points out that individual approaches have varying degrees of value for achieving specific purposes with certain students.

Perhaps the most significant thread running through research on instructional techniques can be summed up as follows: No single approach is most appropriate for all situations. Your obligation as a professional is to vary what you do depending on the content to be taught, the nature of your students, the specific learning intentions you have established, your personal comfort and familiarity with a particular instructional approach, and the availability of needed instructional support materials.

Basic Characteristics of Direct Instruction

When some teachers hear the term *direct instruction,* they immediately think of the lecture method. It is true that lecturing features many elements of direct instruction, but there is much more to this approach than simply telling. In a typical lecture, teachers stand in front of the class and deliver information the students are supposed to remember. The role of the students is to try and capture and remember as much of the information as possible. A good lecturer can enhance students' learning by delivering the information with clarity and by using humor and good verbal and nonverbal communication skills. The communication is generally one way, from the teacher to the students; occasionally students may interrupt the flow with questions or requests for clarity.

However, the direct-instruction model involves much more than simply delivering a good lecture. It generally includes more student involvement and involves highly organized sets of interactions under the control of the teacher. The focus changes from the quality of the delivery, although that is important, to that of a focus on student learning.

An elaboration of some of the basic characteristics of direct instruction indicates how direct instruction differs from a typical lecture. In fact, some direct-instruction lessons do not resemble a lecture at all. Instead, the lesson can involve demonstrations, peer interaction, media, or computer-assisted instruction. The key element of direct instruction is the presentation of new information with clarity, the monitoring of student learning, reteaching content when necessary, and having students practice what they have learned. As with a lecture, the teacher does maintain control of the new information to be presented as well as the pace. In general, a complete direct-instruction lesson includes these basic characteristics:

- Academic focus
- Formal delivery to the whole class
- Constant monitoring to check for understanding
- Controlled classroom practice

Academic Focus

Academic focus refers to a lesson that concentrates on teaching academic content or skills. In other words, individuals using direct instruction have an objective or a purpose for teaching a lesson and that focus is maintained throughout the lesson. Explicit instructional objectives guide the planning and teaching. Decisions made during the lesson should focus on the objectives and in keeping the lesson on target so that students master the objectives. Digressions from the content focus should be avoided and, when they occur, action should be taken quickly to refocus student attention back to the content associated with the lesson purpose. Independent seatwork activities that follow the presentation of information should be related to the objectives of the lesson and should provide an opportunity to check student accomplishment of the objectives.

Formal Delivery to the Whole Class

Direct instruction features systematic and formal presentation of information to the whole class. Instruction should be developed in a logical, step-by-step fashion. Typically students are asked to demonstrate their understanding of each step before new information is presented. The teacher determines when to move on and the rate at which content is introduced. Under optimal conditions, the pace is as brisk as possible and is consistent with students' ability to grasp what is presented. It is important to note that this implies some student involvement. There must be opportunities for students to respond in order for a teacher to make a decision to continue to the next step. When direct instruction is implemented effectively, there is considerable interaction between the teacher and the students.

Constant Monitoring to Check for Understanding

Direct-instruction lessons feature many teacher-to-student questions, which is called checking for understanding. Many of the questions tend to be recall questions that merely ask the students to respond to what they have heard. When instruction is effective, students are able to respond to a high percentage of them (Rosenshine & Stevens, 1986). Questions often focus either on a request for specific answers or a request for an explanation of how a student arrived at an answer (Rosenshine, 1987).

The large number of questions asked during a direct-instruction lesson provides many opportunities to interact with students. Many teachers devise procedures for randomly calling on students rather than calling only on volunteers. This helps prevent teacher bias and helps make sure all students have an opportunity to be involved. Because students never know when they might be called on, they tend to stay alert and actively involved.

Students' responses provide cues you can use to adjust the pace of the lesson and to spend more time dealing with content that students are finding difficult. Their responses might indicate a need to reteach some parts of the lesson to ensure student success.

Controlled Classroom Practice

Effective direct instruction features substantial opportunities for students to engage in controlled practice. The key word here is *controlled*. Before students are allowed to engage in application activities requiring the use of presented information, you need to ensure that they have the necessary understanding to be successful. If students are not provided an opportunity to practice under guidance so that their mistakes and misconceptions are corrected, they may practice incorrect responses when they engage in independent practice. Then as a teacher, you have the difficult task of trying to get them to unlearn incorrect responses before they can learn the correct ones (Trautwein & Koller, 2003).

Opportunity for Independent Practice

Practice is an important component of learning. Some repetition is necessary for learning to occur. We seldom learn something through a single encounter. In secondary schools, the independent practice is often called homework.

Homework has a long-standing tradition in secondary schools. In an age of accountability, everyone seems to expect that students will have lots of homework. Individuals seem to equate good schools with lots of homework (Vatterott, 2009). However, the relationship between homework and student achievement is not that clear. Much homework is little more than busywork that has no educational value (Jackson, 2009).

In addition, home and family differences can create disadvantages for some students. Many students may not have parents at home who can assist them with homework. When they are given homework assignments before they understand the material, they are placed at a disadvantage compared to students who do have resources at home to assist them. Therefore, the achievement gap between students widens rather than narrows.

The findings of research on homework are mixed, and you can find research to support just about any position. However, an overall review of research suggests a curvilinear relationship between learning and the amount of homework assigned. Some homework appears to be good for learning, but too much homework can actually interfere with learning (Cooper, 2007).

A commonsense conclusion is that the learning that takes place is important rather than the amount of time required to complete the homework. Vatterott (2009) suggests that homework is just one part of the learning equation; what *is* important is that it is connected to what happens in the classroom.

Direct instruction does emphasize the importance of independent practice, practice where students work with minimal supervision. However, independent practice needs to be related to the objectives of the lesson and should be done only when the student has demonstrated a minimum level of proficiency through controlled or guided practice. Remember, practice doesn't make perfect. Perfect practice makes perfect.

Independent practice is best when it requires students to apply what they have learned in new contexts or in a variety of situations. In other words, good independent practice does not just require a student to repeat the same responses again and again.

■ ■ ■

Take a minute to review what you have just read to this point. What accounts for the popularity of direct instruction? How is direct instruction similar to and different from a lecture? What would you need to do to change a traditional lecture format to make it more consistent with characteristics of effective direct instruction? What questions do you have about direct instruction? Summarize the basic characteristics of direct instruction. Discuss the role that homework plays in the direct-instruction model. How does this compare to what you see in schools where you teach and/or observe?

■ ■ ■

Underlying Principles

Rosenshine and Stevens (1986) identify the basic principles underlying the direct-instruction model. They based these principles on their interpretations of research and theory related to how individuals process information. Generally, these principles can be applied to other approaches in teaching. However, they are specifically addressed in direct instruction.

One principle emphasizes that individuals can process only a limited amount of new information at one time. If too much information is presented at once, students' abilities to process it are hindered. When this happens, students become confused, make faulty associations, and fail to attend to key points. In frustration, students may turn off the processing altogether.

To prevent these kinds of problems, you have to avoid overwhelming students with too much information at once. New material should be presented in the form of small steps. However, the trick is not to break the new information down into so many steps that the students do not see the whole and the relationships among the steps.

Another principle underlying direct instruction relates to the importance of prior knowledge. What people already know establishes a framework for helping them process new information. This means that you need to take time to find out what your learners already understand about a topic that you want to introduce. When you are armed with this kind of information, you can take appropriate action to help your students establish a learning set, or framework, which will help them process the new information correctly. To ensure that students have a good understanding of important prerequisite information, it makes sense for you to review with them what they have already learned and to point out how it connects to the material you are about to introduce.

Another basic principle addresses the transfer of sensory perceptions from short-term memory to long-term memory. Short-term memory is the memory storage system where bits of information received by our sensory perceptors are stored for a brief time—maybe up to about 30 seconds (Slavin, 2009). Unless something is done with the information, it will quickly fade. Students need to be taught in ways that helps them move new learning into long-term memory.

Movement of information into long-term memory requires the brain to review, practice, summarize, and elaborate on the new information. In other words, something has to be done with the information. Relating new information to what students already know, giving it a structure, relating it to personal interests and needs, engaging in active practice, responding to questions, and summarizing information in their own words are actions that assist in the transfer of new knowledge to long-term memory.

The interest in moving information into long-term memory provides a rationale for the need for practice. Information is most readily recalled when it has been acquired through processes involving what sometimes is referred to as overlearning. Overlearning occurs when students practice using the new information to the point that little effort is required to give a correct response. When students can readily recall overlearned prior information, their information-processing systems are free to devote full attention to the task of comprehending the new information presented to them. Because new learning builds on old, it makes sense for you to give students opportunities to overlearn by providing them numerous opportunities to rehearse and repeat what they have learned. However, there is a possible downside to overlearning. It can be done to the extent that students become bored, and boredom is an enemy to learning.

■ ■ ■

This section has reviewed the basic principles that form a foundation for direct instruction. Stop your reading at this point. How do these principles fit with the way you think people learn and remember? Briefly write each principle in your own words. Give an example of short-term memory and long-term memory. Compare your responses with those of another person who is reading this chapter.

■ ■ ■

Direct Instruction: Lesson Models

Several variations of direct instruction have been developed based on the principles discussed in the preceding section (Hunter & Russell, 1977; Denton, Armstrong, & Savage, 1980; Slavin, 1994). As indicated in Box 9-1, great similarities exist among components of these models. (Though each of the three models illustrated in Box 9-1 features seven phases, this is simply a coincidence. It is quite possible for direct-instruction models to have either smaller or larger numbers of components.)

Note that parts of the model are labeled components, not steps. The term *steps* would suggest that users of direct instruction should follow a rigid, mechanistic sequence while delivering lessons. This kind of by-the-numbers teaching is not what proponents of direct instruction espouse. Rather, the models seek to provide you with information about instructional responsibilities that need to be considered as you engage students in new material. The way you decide to accommodate each of the responsibilities should be based on the following:

■ The type of content you are teaching

■ What you expect your students to be able to do

■ Specific modifications you decide to make based on your professional reactions to how students are performing as you engage them with the new content

Box 9-1

Hunter and Russell Model (1977)	Denton, Armstrong, and Savage Model (1980)	Slavin Model (1994)
1. Anticipatory set	1. Emphasizing objectives	1. Stating learning objectives and orienting students to the lesson
2. Teaching to an objective	2. Motivating learning	2. Reviewing prerequisites
3. Presentation of new material or academic input	3. Recalling previous learning	3. Presenting new material
4. Modeling	4. Presenting new information	4. Conducting learning probes
5. Checking for understanding	5. Recognizing key points	5. Providing independent practice
6. Guided practice	6. Applying new information	6. Assessing performance and providing feedback
7. Independent practice	7. Assessing new learning	7. Providing distributed practice and review

Suppose you reviewed various models and decided to work with the one developed by Denton, Armstrong, and Savage (1980). In using the model, you need to make decisions about what you would do in these seven areas:

1. *Emphasizing objectives.* Students need to have a clear answer to the question, What am I supposed to be learning? This component of the model emphasizes informing the student in very clear language what they should be able to do as a result of the lesson.

2. *Motivating learning.* This component of the model highlights your response to "build interest" in what you will be teaching. How are you going to "hook" the students or create a need for them to know what you want them to learn? However, you also need to consider how you will keep them interested throughout the learning process.

3. *Recalling previous learning.* This component is designed to help students see the relationship between what they already know and what they will be learning.

4. *Presenting new information.* Your responsibility in this area is to decide how best to present new information to your students in a logical, connected, comprehensible, and interesting manner.

5. *Recognizing key points.* When students are presented with new information, the volume of what has been presented may overwhelm them. At various points during the lesson, internal summaries are needed to emphasize key points that they will need to know to achieve success.

6. *Applying new information.* If students are expected to master new information, they must have opportunities to use it. You need to identify how you will engage them in both controlled and independent practice.

7. *Assessing New Learning.* This area is related to both formative and summative assessment. You need to determine how you are going to conduct quick formative assessments during the lesson so you can make appropriate decisions about continuing or reteaching, and you need to consider how you will assess what the students have learned at the conclusion of the lesson.

Each of these components of the model is a decision point for a teacher. The information in the following sections will assist you in making those decisions.

Emphasizing Objectives

Instructional purposes expressed as specific objectives establish an academic focus for lessons. They provide you with targets you can use in planning instruction and adjusting what you do as you teach. They also can help you keep on track and avoid temptations to dwell too long on unimportant or minor details.

One decision that you can make at this step is simply to give the objective to the students. This can provide an advance organizer for the information that is to follow and establishes a framework for what they are learning. You do not have to do this using the somewhat stilted language you might employ in a formal lesson plan. It is perfectly acceptable to provide students with a simple statement that lets them know what you want them to learn.

When students know what is expected of them, they often make better choices and become more self-directed. The majority of students want to succeed. Many of them simply do not know what they need to do to succeed. Emphasizing objectives can assist them in identifying what they need to do.

CRITICAL INCIDENT

THIS IS THE WAY WE TEACH

Rosa Garcia has just finished her teacher preparation program. She had an extremely positive student teaching experience with a very creative master teacher. Overall, she feels pleased with her preparation and is anxious to begin her teaching career. She has been hired to teach in a school district near her hometown. She knows little about the district other than that students there typically score below state averages on standardized achievement tests.

Rosa was somewhat surprised by what she learned at the district's three-day orientation session for new teachers. During the first morning of the orientation session, the superintendent mentioned the lower-than-average scores of the students in the district. She noted that the scores are published in the newspapers across the state, tarnishing the reputation of the school district and leading to enormous pressure by the local community to correct this situation. Therefore, the school district has implemented a series of workshops covering a teaching approach that all teachers are expected to use. The superintendent pointed out that this approach has been found to be the most effective approach to teaching. It includes seven steps that must be included in every lesson that is taught, regardless of the subject or the grade level.

A districtwide lesson plan format including these seven steps has been developed, and all teachers are expected to use this lesson plan model and to turn in lesson plans on Friday for the following week. The school district has revised the teacher evaluation forms for the district. The evaluation form focuses on these seven steps and includes a rating for how well a teacher performs each of them. Continued employment in the district will be based on teacher performance on this evaluation form.

Finally, the superintendent stated that, because many new teachers were prepared in teacher-education programs that did not stress this model, the remainder of the three-day new-teacher orientation would be spent teaching them how to implement the seven-step lesson model. This training would prepare them for success in the district.

Rosa was shocked to hear these words. It was as if the superintendent were telling everyone that their preparation was worthless. She began to wonder how the interesting approaches she had learned in her student teaching could be applied. She sensed that the superintendent's final comments seemed to be an uncanny answer to what she was thinking.

"I know that there are some teachers who believe that this approach limits their creativity," the superintendent said. "Well, we believe there is plenty of room for teacher creativity within this approach. If your lesson is so creative that it doesn't fit within this model, then it is probably inappropriate for our students. Education is a serious business here. We expect to see student learning take place, and we won't tolerate cute lessons that don't result in observable student learning."

■ ■ ■

How would you react to this superintendent's approach to teaching? What are some positive aspects of this approach to improving education? What do you see as problems with this approach to school improvement? When you hear that an approach has been found to be the most effective method of teaching, what should you ask?

What are the superintendent's priorities? How are these priorities reflected in the policy requiring all teachers to adopt a common approach to planning and delivering instruction? How might Rosa's views (or those of other teachers) differ? What might their priorities suggest about their values? What do you think you would do if you were Rosa? Would you feel comfortable in this situation? Because this is an approach that is mandated by the school district and is the focus for evaluation, what course of action should Rosa pursue? From what you know about this approach, do you think that there is room for her to use some of the other approaches she has learned?

What could Rosa have done to avoid finding herself in this situation? What implications does this have concerning your future job search?

Motivating Learners

Perhaps one of the most common complaints we hear from secondary school teachers is that students are unmotivated. Indeed, many things vie for the attention of the typical secondary school student, and learning your subject may not be high on the list! Students enter your classroom with many different agendas. They have recently left another classroom, have been engaging in social conversation with peers, are concerned about their own identity, and may be anticipating future events. In addition, they have been away from the class for a day (sometimes more), and many other events have occurred since you last saw them. To respond to these realities, you need to think through ways of capturing and maintaining student interest in what you want them to learn.

Ideally, you should do something that communicates information to students about the importance of what is to be learned and why it may be of special interest to them. Motivational ideas must initially capture their interest, hold their interest during the lesson, and provide reinforcement for their learning at the completion of the lesson.

In planning your motivational strategies, you might find it useful to consider how to respond to questions students might ask themselves. Here are some examples of these questions:

- What personal use will I make of information in this lesson?
- Do people I respect other than the teacher have any interest in this material?
- How does this material relate to the world outside the classroom?
- Can this new information help me reach my goals in life?
- Will I have the necessary background to master this new content?

Recalling Previous Learning

Daily reviews are common in direct-instruction lessons. The idea is for you to provide students with opportunities to quickly review previously learned information that will help them achieve success. Information you gather from students when you engage them in recall of previous learning can provide you with insights regarding some mistaken information or ideas they might have that could interfere with their learning of the new material.

Rosenshine and Stevens (1986) recommend some of the following ideas for making recall of previous learning effective:

- Administer a short quiz on previously introduced material.
- Ask students to summarize the main points of content introduced during the previous lesson.
- Assign students to prepare questions for each other based on previously introduced content.
- Require students to review content of the previous lesson in small groups.

Presenting New Information

Presenting new information (also called input) is central to all teaching. Engaging new information, ideas, values, and skills is necessary if learning is to occur. The goal of a teacher is to present new material to students in ways that are engaging, thought provoking, challenging, and coherent. This is one place where the skill and the knowledge of the teacher are central. To present new material successfully, you have to know your students, your subject, yourself, and the dimensions of the instructional setting. Both artistry and technical skills are required as you develop presentation techniques that are well-suited to your unique instructional circumstances.

Planning for the presentation of new information begins with a careful analysis of the content you want to teach. Is there a logical sequence? Can the content be broken into understandable and comprehensible chunks? For example, if your students are easily distracted and do not have a history of school success, then you need to present content in small steps and allow time to make frequent checks of understanding. If they have a history of school success and they have an interest in the subject, then it makes better sense for you to give them larger chunks of content at a time and move at a faster pace.

If good instructional resources are available, consider how they will be used to present new information. For example, you might choose to present some information using a computer or a CD. However, you may need to develop a structured guide that will focus students' attention on important dimensions of the material. You still need to check for understanding and plan practice activities. In other words, alternative presentation modes still require attention to the basic principles of direct instruction.

In deciding how to introduce material clearly and logically, think about what you will do in three important areas:

- Providing an overview or structure
- Establishing a step-by-step progression
- Modeling what students should do

Providing an Overview or Structure   A lesson structure or overview helps students see relationships among various parts of a lesson. You can present this kind of information in several ways. For example, you might project an outline on an overhead transparency, list main topic headings of the lesson on the chalkboard, or provide students with an incomplete lesson outline to fill out as new information is provided to them.

The outline or structure of the lesson can be presented as the lesson develops. You can write key words on the board or use simple diagrams that show interrelationships among isolated pieces of information. This can be an especially important aspect of direct instruction because of the focus on step-by-step progression. When you emphasize the importance of students' mastering each part of the lesson before moving forward, some individuals in your class may focus on the parts and miss the big picture. Diagrams and outlines can help them see how the pieces go together.

Establishing a Step-by-Step Progression   Good direct-instruction lessons proceed one step at a time. These steps should be presented at a pace sufficiently rapid to maintain student interest, but not so rapid that students fail to keep up. You must monitor individual student progress at key points and alter your pace as needed to maintain levels of motivation and to maximize learning.

You can start this process by identifying individual steps of your lesson before instruction begins. This requires you to think about all the tasks the students must be able to do to master the new material. Once you have identified this information, arrange content into a sequence that is logically consistent and compatible with students' characteristics. This process is sometimes referred to as task analysis.

Modeling What Students Should Do   Many students fail, not because of lack of effort but because they fail to understand what is expected of them. Similarly, if students see examples of what you want them to produce or do, the probability of their mastering the material increases. Good modeling features frequent use of concrete examples, illustrations, or demonstrations.

Providing models or examples can take several forms. For instance, you might simply show an example of a finished product. However, you need to be careful that the students do not get the idea that they are merely to duplicate the model. Sometimes you might be interested in helping students master a process of some kind. Talking aloud as you work through a difficult or complex decision is one way to model thinking. This kind of demonstration reassures students that they will be approaching your assignment in a manner that is consistent with your expectations.

■ ■ ■

What should you consider when you are planning to present new information to a group of students? How would you apply the direct-instruction approach when using media to present new material to a class? How does teacher creativity enter into planning?

■ ■ ■

Identifying Key Points

Remember that the students with whom you work will not always be experienced and sophisticated learners. They generally have not developed the skill of being able to distinguish between trivia and key points. In fact, in a short research study we conducted a number of years ago, we discovered that college freshmen were rarely able to identify key points in a lecture. To help students learn this important skill, you should focus specifically on helping students identify key points in your lesson.

Techniques that you can use include internal summaries and marker expressions. When using internal summaries, stop at a point in the lesson where a key concept has been taught and take a quick moment to summarize what was just introduced. A series of internal summaries in a lesson can help the students keep track of what they are learning and how key concepts relate to each other.

Most of us have found that when reading new material, it helps if we highlight key points. Marker expressions are one method for helping students highlight verbal input. Marker expressions are phrases you use to draw attention to key points. Some examples of marker expressions include the following:

- Write this down.
- This is a key idea.
- You will need this information.
- Pay attention to this point. It's important.
- I want you to remember this.

Applying New Information

Learning is enhanced when students have opportunities to use what they have learned. Individuals need sufficient experience using what they have learned in order to increase retention. Applying new information is often done during the latter parts of lessons in controlled practice.

To gain the maximum benefit from providing students with opportunities to work with new information, you have to monitor them during this phase of instruction. It is important to move through the room to ensure that your students are engaging in lesson content. You need to be accessible to the students. You want students to feel free to ask you any questions they have about the new information with which they are working. Applying new information facilitates learning only when your students have a good grasp of the information they will be asked to use. If they do not, the practice activity can reinforce mistaken impressions and can be a barrier to subsequent learning.

Your students need to experience a high degree of success as they apply new information. Researchers have found that students should respond to questions and perform other guided practice activities with about 80% accuracy before teachers introduce additional new information (Rosenshine & Stevens, 1986).

■ ■ ■

What are the purposes of actions you might take during the applying-new-information phase of a lesson? Why is a high rate of student success during this part of a lesson considered important? What are some things you might do to maximize students' learning when they are applying content you have just introduced?

■ ■ ■

Assessing Learning

Assessment during a lesson need not be a lengthy or complicated matter. What is needed is something quick that will not interrupt the flow of the lesson but will give you some important information about student learning. One simple approach to formative assessment during the lesson is to ask questions about the content and randomly ask students to respond. By sampling a broad range of students, you can then generalize about the progress of the whole class.

One of your obligations during this phase of a lesson is to provide feedback to students and correct their mistakes. This is what is termed inferential diagnosis, which means that you make diagnostic inferences based on your students' responses. As you work with individual members of your class, you need to ask yourself, What does this response tell me about what this student understands and is thinking? The inferences you make in response to this question inform instructional decisions you will make about what kind of feedback you should provide or what you need to do to correct a student's mistakes.

Your feedback and corrective options are varied; what you do should be in response to the kinds of answers you get from your students. Rosenshine and Stevens (1986) have identified the following categories of student responses:

- A correct and quick student response
- A correct but hesitant student response
- An incorrect student response due to carelessness
- An incorrect student response due to lack of knowledge or skill

A Correct and Quick Student Response   If you get this kind of student response, you should take it as a signal that students have properly understood the material. Your reaction should be aimed at keeping the lesson moving along at a brisk pace. Ordinarily, a brief comment to students affirming the appropriateness of their answers will suffice. What you do should take place quickly so your actions do not interrupt the momentum of the lesson.

A Correct but Hesitant Student Response   In some situations, you will get a student response that is correct but that comes so slowly and hesitantly that you will suspect the person has doubts about the accuracy of what he or she is saying. Your response should be directed at removing the student's uncertainty. For example, you might affirm the accuracy of the student's answer and briefly review why the response is correct. All of this must be accomplished relatively quickly so you can maintain the basic flow and pace of the lesson.

An Incorrect Student Response Due to Carelessness   Over time you will develop a feel for when a student's mistake is simply a careless slip and not evidence of misunderstanding. Asking a student to explain his or her answer will often reveal whether the mistake resulted from a lack of understanding or from carelessness. A quick comment or two from you before formal instruction resumes ordinarily will be enough to help the student who has made this kind of error.

An Incorrect Student Response Due to Lack of Knowledge or Skill   When a student mistake clearly reflects a lack of understanding, you need to do some reteaching. If only a few students are having difficulty, you may be able to continue with the rest of the lesson content, make assignments to the entire group, and then call together the students who are having difficulty and reteach them the aspects of the content they are finding difficult to understand. Sometimes you may want to put students who have mastered the content to work as peer tutors to work with those individuals who are having difficulty grasping it. Peer tutoring works well as long as you and class members have confidence in the abilities of the students selected to work as tutors. Use of student tutors allows you to monitor the work of others in the class while the tutors provide assistance to students who need some additional help mastering basic information that most class members have already learned.

■ ■ ■

What purposes are served by actions you take during the assessing-new-learning phase of the instructional process? What is the relationship between the assessment process and instructional actions you take once you have gathered and thought about information related to students' understanding of material you have introduced? What are some approaches to assessing new learning that you might use in teaching your own subject?

■ ■ ■

Implementing Direct Instruction

In addition to the specific components of direct instruction, other dimensions of teaching need to be considered in order to have a successful lesson. Some of these additional dimensions include the following:

- Teaching at the appropriate level of difficulty
- Conducting appropriate task analyses
- Attending to lesson closure
- Conducting periodic reviews

Teaching at the Appropriate Level of Difficulty

Obviously, to make your teaching effective, it must be at a level that is neither too easy nor too difficult for the students. Something that is too difficult will go over their heads. Material that is too easy will bore them.

The issue of teaching at an appropriate level of difficulty has grown in importance with the increased diversity of students in classrooms. Many students in secondary schools come from homes where the primary language is not English. In addition, student mobility means that students in your classroom might have attended a variety of schools before they reach your class. You cannot assume that all students come to your classroom with the same academic preparation. In addition, full inclusion of students in regular classrooms who, in the past, would have spent their school years in special education classrooms further increases the need to teach at the appropriate level of difficulty.

Teaching at the appropriate level of difficulty requires constant diagnostic assessment of students. This means that careful analysis of students' present levels of knowledge and general interests should be an integral part of your instructional planning. As you consider what you want students to learn, you need information about what individuals in your class may already know or be able to do. This information enables you to begin the instructional sequence at an appropriate entry point. It also helps you decide what approaches to take in introducing material and in involving students in meaningful applications of the new content.

Analyses you perform as part of your planning process may be formal, informal, or both. Sometimes you may wish to administer formal pretests to determine students' entry-level understanding. On other occasions, you may find that a review of students' previous work is sufficient. Of course, after you have worked with a class for a while, you will be able to make inferences about what individuals know and do not know simply by observing their daily performance in class.

Teaching at the appropriate level of difficulty requires you to look at student work not just as a means of assigning a grade but as a source of useful diagnostic data. This information can help you decide what to teach next and how you might introduce new material. A diagnostic mind-set will lead you to regard performance of students that is below your level of expectations as an opportunity for analysis and reflection. The result of this kind of thinking can help you design new instructional approaches with the potential to respond more effectively to students' needs.

Conducting Appropriate Task Analyses

Teaching to the correct level of difficulty and performing sound diagnosis is facilitated by task analysis. Task analysis is the breaking down of complex learning into smaller components and then sequencing those components in a logical manner. In simple terms, it is the analysis of the act of learning specific content.

To illustrate how you might use task analysis, consider this example. Suppose you are teaching English and you want your students to learn how to write a three-paragraph essay. The purpose of your task analysis is to define each step of the task. For example, the students would have to know how to define a paragraph, how to write a topic sentence, how to punctuate and format a paragraph, and how to sequence three paragraphs.

If you determine that students are deficient in any of these areas, you would want to spend time teaching whatever might be needed to fill in any knowledge gaps. Sequencing the tasks in a logical manner would help you decide on your lesson sequence. The task analysis will also help you to identify places where it would be wise to pause and check for understanding once you began teaching the new material.

Attending to Lesson Closure

Another important support for the direct-instruction model is something called lesson closure. Lesson closures refers to a lesson's culminating activity or conclusion. It requires you to do more than simply inform your students that it is time to stop or that the lesson is over.

During lesson closure, you help students draw together the pieces of what they have learned so that they can make sense out of what they have been doing. Actions you take at this time help students organize what they have learned. These actions also allow you to reemphasize the major points of the lesson. The thinking students do during lesson closure enhances their levels of comprehension and helps ensure that they process new information so it can be moved into long-term memory.

Conducting Periodic Reviews

It is important for you to provide periodic reviews when you teach direct-instruction lessons. These reviews allow you to help students recall critical aspects of new content that you have introduced. You should schedule regular times for periodic review. For example, you might choose to set aside the first few minutes of class periods on Mondays to review what was learned the previous week. Such periodic reviews reinforce learning and help students maintain levels of expertise. They also help your students see that they are making progress. This kind of evidence enhances their self-images by allowing them time to reflect on their academic accomplishments.

■ ■ ■

Review what you have read about some important instructional actions that you can take to make your direct-instruction lessons more effective. What are the purposes of these actions? Think about a particular lesson you might teach. Specifically, what might you do to make sure you will be teaching the appropriate level of difficulty? What kinds of task analyses might you perform? How would you provide for lesson closure? How would you provide periodic reviews?

■ ■ ■

Reflecting on Direct Instruction

Direct instruction has several advantages. Because lessons are presented to the class as a whole, planning is simplified. One lesson plan suffices for the entire group; hence, planning time is less than when you must develop alternative plans for individuals or small groups. Of course, this single lesson plan can have several tracks or options that allow you to differentiate what you do to meet the needs of inclusion students, students who are non-native speakers of English, and other students with special learning requirements. Direct instruction puts you in control.

The focus of direct instruction on transmitting important elements of teacher-selected content allows you to prepare students well for tests. This is viewed as a particular advantage in schools and districts that face pressures for students to achieve high scores on standardized achievement tests. (For more information about standardized tests in the schools, see Chapter 7.) Researchers have found that students score well on achievement tests when they have been exposed to direct instruction in their classrooms. Direct instruction seems to increase the amount of student engagement with the kind of content that is featured on tests (Good & Brophy, 2007; Rosenshine & Stevens, 1986).

In a more general sense, direct instruction has been found to be effective when students are asked to master a well-defined body of content or a skill that can be broken down into parts and taught one step at a time (Rosenshine & Stevens, 1986). Basic skills instruction of all kinds is facilitated by direct instruction (Savage, 1989). These studies suggest that direct instruction makes sense when teachers are interested in providing basic information

What Do *You* Think?

Appropriate Uses of Direct Instruction

No single instructional approach is best for promoting the wide range of learning outcomes expected in the schools. The direct-instruction model is more appropriate for some students than it is for others. It is more appropriate for content that can readily be divided into parts, teaching basic skills, teaching students with an external locus of control, introductory material, and a prescribed body of content. It is less appropriate for content with constituent parts that are difficult to define, teaching higher-level thinking, teaching students with an internal locus of control, affective outcomes, and learning that requires creative thinking.

Questions

1. Why do you think direct instruction is less appropriate for some students and some outcomes?

2. What are some specific outcomes in your teaching areas for which direct instruction would be most appropriate?

3. What parts of the direct-instruction model (and supplements to it introduced in this chapter) do you think will be easiest for you to master? Which do think are most difficult? What might you do to prepare yourself better to do a good job with those components that, at this point, seem most troublesome to you?

that students will need as a prerequisite to engaging in complex higher-level thinking and problem-solving activities.

Direct instruction does have some drawbacks. For example, it tends to work best when your intent is to transmit specific content items to students, so direct instruction may be less effective when you seek to develop students' abilities to reflect on complex problems and develop solutions of their own. Successful direct instruction also requires you to have excellent presentation skills. You must be well organized; able to identify an appropriate pace; and be quick to gauge levels of student interest and adapt instruction, as needed, to maintain students' attention.

So much content can be disseminated in a relatively short period of time during a direct-instruction lesson that you may overwhelm students with too much information if you fail to pay attention to their reactions. This can lead to high levels of frustration and undermine students' confidence. When this happens, both their motivation and achievement levels may decline.

■ ■ ■

At this point, stop and take a minute to write your own brief definition of direct instruction. Compare your version with that of another person in your class who is also reading this chapter. How are the definitions alike? How are they different? What questions do you have about implementing direct instruction?

■ ■ ■

Direct Instruction and Student Characteristics

Direct instruction has been found to be particularly effective with younger students, students who are having academic difficulty, and students who are in the introductory phases of learning a specific body of content (Rosenshine & Stevens, 1986). Direct instruction works well with students from lower socioeconomic backgrounds and with those who have an external locus of control (Savage, 1989). (Students with an external locus of control tend to attribute their successes and failures in school to chance factors or to factors they perceive as being beyond their personal ability to control.)

Approaches other than direct instruction seem to be more effective with high-achieving, task-oriented students who have an internal locus of control. (Students with an internal locus of control perceive school failures and successes to be directly connected to their own, controllable behaviors.) These students seem to benefit from instructional approaches that give them more choices in the classroom and that feature an instructional pace that is less subject to direct teacher control.

■ ■ ■

In summary, what questions do you have about general characteristics of direct instruction? Write down your questions and share them with several others. Present a master list of questions from your group to your instructor, and ask your instructor to react to them.

■ ■ ■

This Chapter as an Example of Direct Instruction

We attempted to use elements of direct instruction in organizing content in this chapter. The direct-instruction approach calls on instructors to provide students with information about learning intentions or objectives as well as with an overview and structure for the new learning. We began this chapter with a list of chapter objectives, followed by a formal introduction to the content. (This same approach is followed throughout the text.)

Direct-instruction lessons break content into small pieces or steps. Content in this chapter was broken down into major sections as well as subordinate subsections. At the end

FOR YOUR PORTFOLIO

1. What ideas have you learned in this chapter related to direct instruction will you include as evidence in your portfolio? Select up to three items to be included. Number them 1, 2, and 3.

2. Think about why you selected these materials for your portfolio. Consider issues such as the following in your response:

   ■ The specific purposes to which this information can be put when you plan, deliver, and assess the impact of your instruction

   ■ The compatibility of the information with your own priorities and values

   ■ The contributions this information can make to your personal development as a teacher

   ■ The factors that led you to include this material as opposed to some alternatives you considered

3. Prepare a written reflection in which you analyze the decision-making process you followed. Also, mention the Interstate New Teacher Assessment and Support Consortium (INTASC) standard(s) to which your selected material relates. Complete the chart below first.

MATERIALS YOU SELECTED AND THE INTASC STANDARDS

Put a check under those INTASC standards numbers to which the evidence you have selected applies. (Refer to Chapter 1 for more detailed information about INTASC.)

INTASC Standards

Item of Evidence Number	S-1	S-2	S-3	S-4	S-5	S-6	S-7	S-8	S-9	S-10
1										
2										
3										

of many of these chapter divisions, we checked for understanding when we asked you to reflect on what you had read by responding to questions, summarizing the content, checking your reactions with someone else, or generating questions of your own.

Direct-instruction lessons often feature examples, illustrations, or models. Illustrations are provided at various points throughout this chapter, and the general layout of the chapter is consistent with a direct-instruction format.

Authors of a text are not really in a position to see that guided practice takes place; we are not with you in the classroom, nor can we listen to you, watch what you do, or react to your comments in person. However, we hope that some of the practice activities scattered throughout the chapter as well as those at the end will allow your instructor to monitor your progress as you engage in various guided-practice activities.

Some of the end-of-the chapter activities are designed to provide opportunities for independent practice. They call on you to apply what you have learned and to extend your understandings of the material. Ideally, an independent-practice experience related to direct instruction would be for you to prepare a direct-instruction lesson and deliver it to a group of students. If you are currently in a classroom, perhaps you could plan a lesson to teach to one of your classes. If you are not, you might teach a lesson to a small group of your peers in your university classroom.

To summarize, we hope the way we have introduced direct instruction in this chapter has helped you to grow in your understanding of this approach. Its success is something you will have to evaluate for yourself. If you feel more comfortable about your knowledge of the essentials of a direct-instruction lesson and have confidence in your ability to design and deliver this kind of instruction, we will have met our own aims. We hope you think we have succeeded.

Key Ideas in Summary

- There is no one best method for teaching. Various approaches are appropriate for helping students master different kinds of objectives. For some purposes, direct instruction has proved to be a desirable way to organize and deliver instruction.

- Direct instruction is a teacher-centered approach in which the teacher controls selection and delivery of content, mode of presentation of the content, pace of lesson development, and patterns of classroom interaction. Continuous monitoring throughout the lesson ensures student understanding. The focus is on transmission of academic content. Instruction is provided to the class as a whole, not to individual groups of students. Complex content is broken down into parts, and each part is introduced sequentially, one step at a time. The teacher takes pains to ensure that students grasp information associated with one step before going on to the next.

- The underlying principles that support the direct-instruction model are taken from information-processing theory and research. Among these principles are as follows: (1) An individual can process only a limited amount of information at one time, (2) prior knowledge influences how a person processes new information, (3) information must be transferred from short-term to long-term memory for retention to occur, and (4) overlearning through rehearsal or practice is necessary to facilitate comprehension of future information.

- A number of direct-instruction models are available, including those developed by Hunter and Russell (1977); Denton, Armstrong, and Savage (1980); and Slavin (1994). These models present components that should be included in complete direct-instruction lessons.

- In addition to accommodating components enumerated in formal direct-instruction models, teachers have other options for increasing the probability that their students will learn. They can also take actions related to (1) teaching to an appropriate level of difficulty, (2) task analysis, (3) lesson closure, and (4) periodic reviews of newly presented information.

■ Direct instruction has advantages. Because the teacher works with the whole class, planning is somewhat simplified. Planning assumes that all students will be exposed to basically the same instruction. The teacher is very much in a central position of control during direct-instruction lessons. Direct instruction allows for a clear focus on specific academic content. Some people feel the approach functions well as a means of preparing students for standardized tests.

■ Some criticisms of direct instruction have been identified. Although the approach has merit as a way to help students recall specific information, it is less effective in helping students develop higher-level thinking skills that require them to reflect on complex issues and generate solutions of their own. Also, some teachers lack the ability to diagnose the needs of their students and student reactions as instruction is being delivered. This is a particular problem when direct instruction is being used. Because it is so teacher-centered, an unaware teacher can overwhelm students with content and undermine their interest in what is being taught.

■ Direct instruction is more appropriate for meeting some kinds of instructional objectives than others. It works best when the content to be covered lends itself to being broken down into small parts that can be presented in sequential steps. Researchers have found that direct instruction works particularly well when the intent has been to teach skills. It has been found to be less appropriate, however, when lesson objectives call on students to engage in higher-level thinking and problem-solving activities. Also, it is not a favored approach when instructional plans are guided by affective objectives.

■ Some students seem to profit more from direct instruction than do others. It has been found especially effective with younger students, students who are having academic difficulty, and students who are just beginning to work with a new content area. Studies have found that direct-instruction lessons are often effective in working with students who have an external locus of control.

Reflections

1. What are some reasons for the popularity of direct instruction?
2. What are some basic characteristics of direct instruction?
3. What advantages and disadvantages have been claimed for direct instruction?
4. What is meant by the statement, Direct-instruction lessons feature a strong academic focus?
5. How would you explain the phrase *controlled classroom practice*?
6. For what kinds of learning outcomes does direct instruction seem most appropriate?
7. What elements would you expect to see in a complete direct-instruction lesson?
8. Some people argue that direct instruction is rigid and cold and likely to create negative student attitudes. How do you react to this contention?
9. How would you feel if an administrator told you that he or she expected you to use a direct-instruction approach every day?
10. What problems, if any, do you envision as you think about implementing direct instruction in your own teaching?

Learning Extensions

1. Review your content field. Identify three or four topics that might be delivered appropriately using a direct-instruction approach. For each topic, identify a series of parts or steps you would use in presenting information to students. Share your ideas with your instructor, and ask for a critique of your work.

2. Look over parts of one of the direct-instruction models introduced in this chapter. Observe a teacher in a secondary school who is using a direct-instruction approach to introduce information. To what extent did you find each of the elements of a formal direct-instruction model being used? Write your findings in the form of a brief report and submit it to your instructor.

3. Organize a debate on this topic: Resolved that too much direct instruction occurs in today's secondary schools. Hold the debate during a regular class session. When it is over, engage the entire class in a discussion of this issue.

4. With assistance from your instructor, identify some summaries of what researchers have found about the effectiveness of direct instruction. Prepare a short oral report for class members in which you summarize what researchers have found.

5. For a topic in your own subject area, prepare a complete lesson plan based on direct instruction. Share it with others in your class, and ask them to suggest places where your plan might be improved. You might also solicit reactions from your instructor.

References

Bereiter, C., & Engelmann, S. (1966). *Teaching disadvantaged children in the preschool.* Englewood Cliffs, NJ: Prentice Hall.

Borich, G. (1992). *Effective teaching methods* (2nd ed). Upper Saddle River, NJ: Merrill/Prentice Hall.

Cooper, H. (2007). *The battle over homework: Common ground for administrators, teachers and parents* (3rd ed.). Thousand Oaks, CA: Corwin.

Denton, J. J., Armstrong, D. G., & Savage, T. V. (1980). Matching events of instruction to objectives. *Theory into Practice, 19*(1), 10–14.

Gagne, R. M. (1977). *The conditions of learning* (3rd ed.) New York: Holt, Rinehart and Winston.

Good, T., & Brophy, J. (2007). *Looking in classrooms* (9th ed.). New York: Longman.

Hunter, M., & Russell, D. (1977). How can I plan more effective teaching lessons? *Instructor, 87*(2), 74–75, 88.

Jackson, R. R. (2009). *Never work harder than your students and other principles of good teaching.* Alexandria, VA: Association for Supervision and Curriculum Development.

Lasley, T. J., II, Matczynski, T. J., & Rowley, J. B. (2002). *Instructional models: Strategies for teaching in a diverse society* (2nd ed.). Belmont, CA: Wadsworth.

Rosenshine, B. (1983). Teaching functions in instructional programs. *Elementary School Journal, 83*(4), 335–352.

Rosenshine, B. (1987). Direct instruction. In M. Dunkin (Ed.), *The international encyclopedia of teaching and teacher education* (pp. 257–262). New York: Pergamon.

Rosenshine, B., & Stevens, R. (1986). Teaching functions. In M. Wittrock (Ed.), *Handbook of research on teaching* (3rd ed.), (pp. 376–391). New York: Macmillan.

Savage, M. K. (1989). The impact of different instructional models on teacher performance scores as measured by the Texas teacher appraisal system (Unpublished doctoral dissertation). Texas A&M University. College Station, TX.

Slavin, R. (1994). *Educational psychology: Theory and practice* (4th ed.). Boston: Allyn & Bacon.

Slavin, R. (2009). *Educational psychology: Theory and practice* (9th ed). Boston: Allyn & Bacon.

Trautwein, U., & Koller, O. (2003). The relationship between homework and achievement—still much of a mystery. *Educational psychology Review, 12*(2), 115–145.

Vatterott, C. (2009). *Rethinking homework: Best practices that support diverse needs.* Alexandria, VA: Association for Supervision and Curriculum Development.

10 Teaching for Higher-Level Outcomes

Objectives

This chapter will help you

- define higher-level thinking skills

- explain the constructivist learning theory

- state how metacognitive techniques help students learn to direct their thought processes to higher levels

- define discovery learning

- describe the process of inquiry teaching

- suggest how comparing, contrasting, and generalizing might be used in the classroom

- explain how simulations can be used

- describe implementation procedures for and differentiate among purposes of creative thinking, critical thinking, problem-solving, and decision-making

David Mager/Pearson

Graphic Organizer: Chapter 10

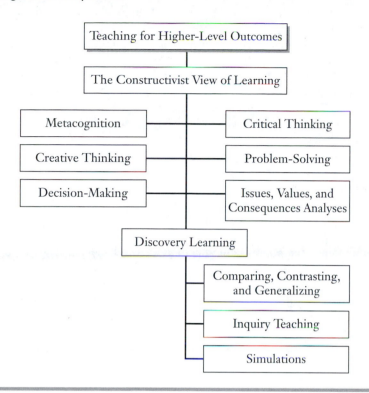

Introduction

What do you see as the purpose of education? What should students learn? These are important questions that shape what you teach and how you teach. For example, if you view the purpose of education as providing students with a common core of knowledge that everyone should possess and that helps them score well on standardized tests, then your teaching approaches should focus on how to get that knowledge into the students. However, if you think that education ought to equip students with skills and processes that will allow them to solve problems, make decisions, and learn how to adapt to a rapidly changing world, then you need to teach in ways that will help develop sophisticated thinking skills such as problem-solving, decision-making, and critical thinking. Currently some educational experts share this view and contend that schools are not doing a good job of preparing students with the skills they will need in the 21st century, such as comparing, contrasting, criticizing, creating, interpreting, generalizing, identifying assumptions, and making valid inferences. These skills are generally grouped under the label higher-level thinking. Learning higher-level skills does require different models of teaching than the acquisition of information.

The Constructivist View of Learning

Teaching higher-level thinking processes relates to the constructivist view of learning. This orientation assumes that knowledge cannot simply be given to students. The brain is not like a camera that just stores a snapshot of information that is retrieved in whole when needed. The brain actively engages in constructing knowledge and establishing the meaning of the information based on previous knowledge and current interactions with the environment. When new information is encountered, the brain attempts to fit it into an existing schema or organization. Therefore, different individuals may encounter the same bit of information and interpret it differently.

The implication for teaching is that the methods used in the classroom should be those that (1) encourage students to experiment, discover, and apply ideas on their own; (2) help students develop and become aware of their own schema; and (3) teach students to consciously monitor their own learning and the strategies they use to learn (Slavin, 2009). Because students are constructing their own meaning out of their experiences and interactions, teaching should mirror reality as much as possible. By mirroring reality, the material learned is more likely to be organized in a way that facilitates retrieval when it is needed. This does not imply that certain basic skills are not important and should be ignored. Rather, basic skills are taught as needed and are embedded in lessons that emphasize the resolution of complex, authentic problems. This kind of instruction focuses simultaneously on development of basic skills and higher-level thinking abilities. Some research indicates that this type of instruction is invaluable for students who have experienced academic difficulties (Woolfolk, 2009).

A constructivist approach requires you to adopt a role that differs from what you might do in implementing more traditional models such as direct instruction. More emphasis is placed on students taking more responsibility and control of their learning. In addition, you have to be prepared for the possibility that at least some students will arrive at conclusions different from your own. You also have to accept that it is more difficult to evaluate what students have learned from lessons focusing on higher-level thinking than those that focus on the acquisition of new information. Simple paper-and-pencil tests featuring objective items will not always result in valid data. You must rely more on performance tasks and assessment techniques that produce evidence of learning and that require considerable time to develop and to evaluate.

A special atmosphere permeates classrooms that feature an emphasis on developing higher-level thinking abilities. For example, you will need a wide repertoire of instructional techniques, a tolerance for considerable ambiguity, and a general sense of personal and professional security for these kinds of lessons. You have to be comfortable with turning a great deal of responsibility for learning over to students. You must know how to model higher-level thinking processes in ways that connect with students. In essence, you must be willing to act as a learning manager. Your role is to present students with the task to be accomplished, provide the basic information they will need to use as they work toward a solution, nurture their thinking processes as they engage in the assigned problem, and challenge them to test their conclusions.

Interest in promoting higher levels of thinking has led many educators to advocate the direct teaching of specific thinking skills to students. They contend that learning how to think is at least as important as instruction in the information that is learned. However, this position does not imply an either-or dichotomy; it is necessary to teach both academic content and thinking skills (Joyce & Weil, 1996). Sound thinking skills help students achieve maximum benefit from the learning of academic subjects and prepares them to cope with challenges they will face throughout their adult lives. What is important for you to remember is that you still plan strategies based on your objectives. The difference is that you need to make sure that the objectives are focused on higher-level thinking skill.

This chapter introduces several strategies designed to promote higher-level thinking skills:

- Metacognition
- Discovery learning
- Creative thinking
- Critical thinking
- Problem-solving
- Decision-making

Metacognition

Metacognition refers to knowledge about one's own learning or knowing how to learn (Slavin, 2009). It involves bringing to a conscious level the kinds of procedures people follow as they think. Metacognitive processes serve an important monitoring function. When people are aware of the steps they are taking as they think, they make more conscious choices about whether approaches they have selected for a given task are appropriate. The basic idea is to help develop conscious control over the process of learning. This is important because the student must be actively engaged if learning is to take place.

You can provide instructional experiences that help students learn strategies for monitoring and modifying their patterns of thinking. Several approaches will help you achieve these purposes. Two that have been used by a number of teachers are teacher modeling and visualizing thinking strategies.

Teacher Modeling

Modeling has long been known to be a powerful instructional tool. As applied to metacognition, modeling seeks to help students recognize that people who think successfully about challenging topics carefully monitor their own thinking processes. They engage in a type of silent personal dialogue as they confront pertinent issues. They may speculate about alternatives, consider numerous responses, evaluate available evidence, weigh the relevance of competing views, and get deeply involved in other considerations related to the issue at hand. One useful approach for helping students understand how such thinking processes operate is thinking aloud. Thinking aloud means that you talk through the mental processes as you and members of your class attack an issue together. The idea is to prompt your students to use thinking patterns that are appropriate for accomplishing a similar task. As students observe you, they will note general approaches to the issue that have proven to be productive. They will see the importance of thinking carefully about their own approaches to the task. If you have done a good job in thinking aloud with them, you will find that your students often perform better on an assigned task than if you simply assume that they already know how the task should be approached.

Suppose you are a teacher in an English class and you are about to introduce a unit on descriptive writing. You might ask each student to write a two- to three-page paper on the tourist attractions of a selected location. Your intention might be for students to prepare an initial draft, think about it, and then prepare a revised version. If your directions to students go no further than a statement such as "Prepare a draft, think about it, and then rewrite it," you will not cue students to the kinds of thought processes that should be used as they approach the task of revision. A more productive way to get them started on the revision task would be for you to model what they should do. For example, you might prepare an overhead transparency from a first draft of the same assignment prepared by a student from a previous semester. Then, you could think aloud with students in this way:

> All right, look at this draft of a paper on Easter Island. Now, if this were my paper and I were about to revise it, these are some of the changes I would want to make.
>
> First of all, people will be reading literature about many different places. They will be turned off by anything that has been written hastily without careful attention to spelling and grammar. The first thing I'll want to look for is spelling errors. Then, I'll want to be sure that verb tenses are correct and consistent throughout.
>
> I will want to hold the attention of my reader. I don't want to lose anyone with long, complicated sentences. As a quick check on this, I'll read the paper aloud. Anytime I run out of breath before I finish a sentence, I am going to mark that sentence. Later, I will go back and cut these long sentences into shorter ones. Also, as I read, I will try to spot any places where I am using the same word too frequently. If I find any excessive repetition, I will make a note to correct this situation in a revision.

As I read through the material, I will mark every sentence that has as its main verb some part of the verb *to be*. This tends to be a very weak, dull verb for the reader. As I rewrite the material, I will try to replace these verbs with more action-oriented words.

Look at this sentence: "The giant statues are visited by many tourists." There are two serious problems here. First of all, the verb is in passive voice, a weak, uninteresting construction. Second, the reference to the statues simply being visited is not particularly exciting. I would rewrite the sentence to eliminate the passive voice and to add some color. One possibility might be a sentence like this: "The giant statues of Easter Island challenge tourists' views of so-called primitive peoples."

As students listen to you thinking aloud about the thought processes involved in revising the sample paper, they acquire a model of verbal prompts that they can follow. Modeling can also plant the idea that thinking about what the task requires is an essential prerequisite to beginning to address the task. This perspective is one that you want students to adopt as a result of your thinking-aloud demonstrations.

Visualizing Thinking

Visualizing thinking refers to the process of consciously organizing information so that relationships between parts of the information are identified. This act of organizing information into some sort of visual representation encourages students to monitor their own learning schema and their thinking processes. This visualization can take the form of a chart, a spider graph, a Venn diagram, or any other visual representation that helps the students organize the information and identify relationships. The graphic organizer at the beginning of each chapter of this book is one form of visual representation of the content.

Let us take a simple example to show how a diagram or a visual representation of information influences what individuals learn. Suppose that you decided to have class members read the following material from a text:

Early Spanish Explorers of the Caribbean

In the year 1492, the Spanish explorer Christopher Columbus landed on San Salvador Island, a rather small island in the West Indies. San Salvador is in the group of islands that we know today as the Bahamas. Columbus later explored many other Caribbean islands. He set up a fort on one of the largest islands in the region, Hispaniola. Today the countries of Haiti and the Dominican Republic occupy Hispaniola.

Another well-known early Spanish explorer was Nicolas de Ovando. In the year 1502, he was sent out from Spain to become governor of Hispaniola. He brought a large number of colonists with him. These colonists sought to make their fortunes in two ways. Some of them attempted to strike it rich in gold mining. Others started large plantations. A common problem all of these early Spanish colonists faced was a lack of a large supply of local workers.

In response to this situation, the colonists initially tried to make slaves of the local Indians. This was not successful. The Indians did not take to slavery and many of them died. Once the local supply of Indians on Hispaniola had been exhausted, the Spanish for a time tried bringing in Indians from other Caribbean islands. They, too, died. Later, slaves from Africa were brought to the island. Though many of these slaves survived, Hispaniola continued to have a need for more workers than could he supplied.

As a result of this labor shortage, many Spanish colonists began moving from Hispaniola to other islands in the region. One of the other large islands that attracted a number of Spanish settlers was Puerto Rico. The first settlers arrived there in 1508 under the leadership of Ponce de Leon. The Spanish moved into Jamaica in 1509 when Juan de Esquivel led a group of settlers there. Spanish settlers reached Cuba, the largest island in the region, in 1514. In time, it became the most prosperous of Spain's Caribbean territories.

Box 10-1   Leaders and Islands

Leaders   Islands

_____   _____

_____   _____

_____   _____

_____   _____

_____   _____

Because of differences in the ability levels of students, you might wish some students to focus on different aspects of this material than others. For example, you might want some of your students to read with this learning task in mind:

Task: Who were the four famous Spanish explorers who made discoveries in the Caribbean between 1492 and 1514, and what large islands did Spain occupy during this period?

To help students focus on this task as they read the material and take notes, you might prepare a visual-thinking diagram like the one in Box 10-1.

You might want others in the class to read for the purpose of accomplishing a somewhat different task:

Task: What actions were taken by the early Spanish settlers of Hispaniola to solve the labor shortage, and what happened as a result?

To help students focus on this task as they read the material and take notes, teachers might prepare a visual-thinking diagram or schema like the one in Box 10-2.

Note that, although the students were assigned the same material to read, the thinking task assigned to some students differed from the thinking task assigned to others. These differences are reflected in the visual-thinking diagrams in both boxes. What a

---

Box 10-2   Why Were Laborers Needed?

_____

_____

What Was Tried First?   What Was Tried Second?

_____   _____

What Were the Results?   What Were the Results?

_____   _____

Final Outcome

_____

_____

given student learns is influenced by the schema or learning diagram that he or she uses. When students are left on their own, they may lack a good schema for organizing the information and may miss the important information altogether. Therefore, a teacher may supply a learning diagram to assist students until they develop a conceptual understanding of a subject and begin developing their own visual representations. Students who develop an understanding of the visualized thinking process often develop very creative visual diagrams that really help them make sense of the material they are encountering.

Use of the diagrams helps students to monitor and adjust their own thinking processes as they work with assigned materials. As a result, their work is likely to be more productive and their levels of achievement and self-satisfaction higher. A variety of additional reading-thinking tools are included in Chapter 12.

Discovery Learning

Discovery learning refers to learning that requires students to identify key ideas and principles themselves rather than memorizing information taught directly by teachers. Discovery learning was given considerable impetus several decades ago by Jerome Bruner (1960). Bruner emphasized the importance of students' understanding the structure of a subject, that is, the basic concepts and principles that form its foundation.

If a student is to grasp the structure of a subject, Bruner indicated that he or she must be actively engaged in the learning process. This kind of activity requires students to identify the concepts, the principles, and their relationships for themselves (Woolfolk, 2009). Good discovery learning lessons require careful teacher planning. In part, to emphasize this point, some proponents of the approach use the term *guided discovery*. Guided discovery means that the teacher provides prompts and structures the learning environment in order to facilitate discovery rather than expecting students to discover ideas or principles on their own. The important guidance function is to create conditions that help students discover meaningful concepts and principles.

One of the primary tasks in a guided discovery lesson is to identify and present activities or examples that will stimulate and facilitate students' search for information. For example, if you are teaching a social studies class, you might give students a blank map of a country and ask them to mark places where they think cities might be located. Once they have done this, they are asked to compare their guesses with a printed map. As they seek to explain the reasons for their correct as well as incorrect guesses, students are moving toward the identification of key concepts and principles related to urban location and growth. Students might be further prompted to seek relationships though the skillful use of questions that require them to think of new variables or to evaluate their responses. In a science class, students can be asked to explain why they think some phenomena occur; then the teacher designs and has them conduct an experiment that challenges their explanations.

Discovery teaching presents several challenges. As indicated in Chapter 5, a solid academic background in the subject is important in order to identify its basic concepts and principles. You also need to have available good examples or situations that will stimulate student discovery of the basic concepts and principles. In addition, discovery learning can be unpredictable. You never know where it might lead. Therefore, your subject-matter background is important in knowing how to respond to student inquiries, in asking good questions, and in providing additional information.

Today's electronic technologies make it easier to implement discovery approaches. A major condition for the effective use of discovery learning is the availability of information and data. The ready availability of data on the World Wide Web makes it possible for students to access tremendous quantities of information. No longer are they limited to what is available in a textbook or in the school library. Once students have learned how to ask the right questions and how to connect to the available sources, discovery-learning activities can be taken to levels that were unimaginable only a few years ago.

Discovery learning is based on the inductive reasoning process. This process proceeds from the specific to the general. A simple example will illustrate the general procedure. Suppose you want to teach a group of learners the concept *fish*. You might begin by providing them with photographs of different fish. Through a series of questions, you would encourage students to identify common features of the images in the individual photographs. To conclude the exercise, you would urge students to develop their own description of the concept *fish* and ask them to describe its necessary defining characteristics.

In summary, discovery learning can take many forms. The following are some variations of discovery approaches:

- Comparing, contrasting, and generalizing
- Inquiry teaching
- Simulations

Comparing, Contrasting, and Generalizing

One effective way of helping students discover basic concepts and principles is by presenting pieces of information in ways that allow them to be easily compared and contrasted. By using questions that prompt students to identify specifics in the data, they can note patterns and subsequently form generalizations or principles.

A data retrieval chart is one approach to organizing data for learning activities that require students to compare, contrast, and generalize. This chart is basically a matrix that includes concept categories under which relevant information can be listed. Students can then be prompted to find relationships between the concepts and then form generalizations.

A lesson using a retrieval chart might develop along these lines. Suppose you were teaching English and decided to have your students read a novel called *Mines and Dreamers*. This novel features many interactions among the five major characters: Joe Carmody, Luella McPhee, Tony Marino, Gordon Duffy, and Selma Steele. In planning lessons designed to promote students' abilities to compare, contrast, and generalize, you might develop a chart that students could use to organize basic information from the novel. The chart might call for information about each character under these major headings:

- Family background
- Education
- Occupation
- Basic motives

Students are asked to gather information individually or they can identify information for each category as part of a group discussion focusing on the novel. In either case, the result would be a completed data chart. This chart would be displayed for all students to see or individual charts could be distributed to all students. An example of such a chart with data filled in might look something like the one in Box 10-3.

The completed chart becomes the basis for a discussion designed to prompt students to compare, contrast, and generalize. The activity begins by asking students to look carefully at the information on the chart and to respond to this sequence of questions:

1. What similarities do you see among these characters? Possible responses:

   - Joe Carmody, Luella McPhee, and Gordon Duffy were reared in one-parent homes.
   - Joe Carmody and Luella McPhee have less than a high school education.

Box 10-3

	Family Background	Education	Occupation	Basic Motives
Joe Carmody	Divorced parents; reared by mother	Grade 8	Union organizer; former coal miner	Improving lives of the working poor
Luella McPhee	Divorced parents; reared by mother	Grade 10	Owner of successful real estate firm	Personal social advancement; wants to hide nature of her family background
Tony Marino	Upper middle class; reared by both parents	College graduate	Attorney	Betterment of the condition of the working poor
Gordon Duffy	Upper middle class; divorced parents; reared by father	College graduate	Attorney	Promotion of his own economic self-interest; insensitive to needs of others
Selma Steele	Upper class; reared by both parents	College graduate	Business manager	Believes that what is good for business is, in the long run, good for everyone

- Tony Marino and Gordon Duffy are attorneys.
- Joe Carmody and Tony Marino are both interested in improving the conditions of the working poor.

These are examples. Students may identify additional similarities among the novel's characters.

2. What are some differences you see among these characters? Possible responses:

- Their educational levels are different.
- They come from a variety of home backgrounds.
- Some of them are basically out for their own interests.
- Some of them are interested in improving the conditions of others.

3. From looking at this information, what general statements can you make about what the author might believe to be true about how individuals develop and grow? Possible responses:

- There is not necessarily a connection between a person's occupation and his or her sensitivity to the needs of others.
- The kind of home a person grows up in as a child does not necessarily predict the kinds of attitudes toward others he or she will have as an adult.

The generalizations that students develop in this exercise result from consideration of a very limited amount of information. You would need to remind them that these conclusions should be regarded as only tentatively true. As you involve your students in the study of additional material, you can have them test the accuracy of these generalizations as they acquire new information.

Inquiry Teaching

Inquiry teaching is a specific form of discovery learning that emphasizes use of the scientific method. When using an inquiry approach, students become engaged in hypothesizing, gathering data, and verifying or modifying their conclusions. Inquiry thinking involves students in the process of knowledge creation. This does not mean that they are creating new knowledge for the world; rather, they are creating their own new knowledge. They are doing this as they arrive at their own conclusions after considering and organizing pieces of data.

Knowledge generation can be very motivating. It is exciting to develop new ideas and see new relationships. In addition to its high potential to motivate students, inquiry teaching helps young people develop the kinds of rational thinking abilities they will be called on to exercise throughout their adult lives. In life, they will not be able to ask what the "right" answer is to questions such as these: What vocation should I pursue? Where should I go to college? What home should I purchase? In short, supporters of inquiry thinking place more emphasis on helping students learn how to learn rather than on the specific information that is acquired. Lasley, Matczynski, and Rowley (2002) remind us that "[i]nquiry requires many more intellectual skills of a student than merely knowing content; the student must also be able to understand the dynamics that ground that academic content" (p. 147).

Basic Steps in Inquiry Teaching   Inquiry teaching in U.S. schools traces back to a famous book published by the eminent U.S. educational philosopher, John Dewey. In *How We Think,* originally published in 1910, Dewey suggested basic steps for sequencing inquiry instruction. The following steps, derived from Dewey's work with some variation, form the backbone of inquiry lessons:

- Identify a focus and describe the essential dimensions of a problem or situation.
- Suggest possible solutions to the problem or explanations of the problem or situation (hypothesizing).
- Gather evidence related to these solutions or explanations.
- Evaluate possible solutions or explanations of the problem in light of evidence (verifying hypotheses).
- Develop a conclusion that is best supported by the evidence (generalizing).

The first step is the establishment of a focus for the inquiry. Your role at this step is to present a puzzling situation (sometimes called a discrepant event) to students. This discrepant event is something that challenges their present conceptions. For example, in science you might conduct a science demonstration where something unexpected or surprising occurs. A social studies focus might be on the following question: Why do cities grow up in some places but not in others? Students might comment that many cities seem to grow up near a river, large lake, or ocean. When this idea surfaces, the teacher presents them with the example of Mexico City, which is located in the south central highlands of Mexico, a considerable distance from large and important bodies of water. The discrepancy presented by the inland location of one of the world's largest cities from factors they suggested accounted for the rise of large cities becomes a point of departure for further development of the lesson.

The second step in the inquiry process requires students to develop hypotheses or possible explanations for the puzzling event. This can be done in a large- or small-group setting, and students are asked to generate as many explanations as possible. When working with students during this phase of an inquiry lesson, your role is to help them clarify their hypotheses and encourage them to state these ideas clearly so that others understand the relationships they are establishing.

The third step in the process requires students to gather specific information related to the guesses or the hypotheses they made. During this part of the lesson, your task as a teacher is to challenge students to think about the type of information or evidence that they would need to help them determine whether their guesses or hypotheses are correct.

At this point, you have some choices about how to proceed. One option is for you to function as a data source. If you do this, the role of the students is to identify and phrase questions they ask you that get them the information they want. This information is what they use to verify or reject their hypotheses. This approach turns typical teaching on its head. Rather than the teacher asking questions, the students ask questions. Part of what students are learning is how to ask good questions. The teacher often has to help the students rephrase the questions. With experience, students can learn how to phrase good questions.

Another alternative at this point in the lesson is for you to direct your students to seek information about their tentative hypotheses from a variety of sources. If you decide to proceed in this manner, you will need to help students identify appropriate questions and direct them toward the type of information they need to gather. Then you'll need to make arrangements for them to access appropriate information sources, for example, the World Wide Web, documents, books, and videos, and perhaps questioning experts in the area. After students have gathered data, your role is that of helping them review and evaluate their hypotheses in light of this information. This process relates to their accepting, rejecting, or modifying their original hypotheses. At this point, it is sometimes useful to remind students that just because they failed to verify their hypothesis does not mean they have failed. Finding out that a particular hypothesis is not valid is sometimes just as important as verifying one.

An inquiry lesson is brought to a close by summarizing student hypotheses and conclusions and the evidence used to verify, reject, or modify them. Students should also be challenged about the steps they followed in the process. Remember that the process is also an important lesson objective.

An Example of an Inquiry Lesson   Let's see how an inquiry lesson might develop. Suppose you wanted students in a high school humanities class to probe the relationship between urbanization and the life expectancies of U.S. women. An inquiry lesson with this focus might develop along the following lines.

Step 1

Present Focus: Begin by writing the statistics shown in Box 10-4 on the board.

Teacher: Look at this information. What trends do you see? Notice that women seem to be living longer in each of the three years. Notice, too, that more people seem to be living in cities. Now, I want you to think about two questions. First, what might be the connection between longer lives for women and the trend toward living in cities? Second, are there other possible explanations for women living longer in the more recent years?

Step 2

Students provide answers to each of the following questions.

Question 1: What might be the connection between longer lives for women and the trend toward living in cities?

A Sample of Possible Student Responses

- People in cities might have earned more. Women may have eaten better and stayed healthier in the cities.
- Women in cities may have had better access to newspapers. They may have read more about good health standards.
- There may have been better access to doctors in the cities. Thus, women may have begun to live longer because they were more likely to get treated when they were sick in cities than when they were sick in rural areas.

Box 10-4

Percentages of Females in Three Age Groups*

Year	Under 30	30 to 50	51 or Older
1850	71	20	9
1910	61	25	14
1970	50	23	27

Median Age of U.S. Females in 1850, 1910, and 1970

Year	Median Age (in Years)
1850	18.8
1910	23.9
1970	27.6

Percentages of U.S. Urban and Rural Population in 1850, 1910, and 1970

Year	Rural	Urban
1850	84.7	15.3
1910	54.3	45.7
1970	26.5	73.5

*Data are adapted from U.S. Bureau of the Census. (1975). *Historical statistics of the United States, Colonial Times to 1970, Bicentennial Edition, Part I* (pp. 11–12, 16, 19). Washington, DC: U.S. Bureau of the Census.

- Cities tended to bring more medical scholars and researchers together. This resulted in an explosion of new information about health and medicine. This new information increased the life spans of all people in the later years.

Question 2: Other than the move from rural areas to the cities, what other factors might have led to higher percentages of women in older age groups in the later years?

A Sample of Possible Student Responses

- Women could have started having fewer children. If this happened, fewer would have died in childbirth, and more would have lived to an older age.

- In the earlier years, a high percentage of women could have been immigrants. Immigrants tend to be younger. This would account for higher percentages of younger women in the earlier years.

- There could have been some fatal diseases that killed women in their twenties and thirties for which cures became available in later years.

- In earlier years, society may not have cared as much for older women as it did in later years. There could have been a deliberate failure to care for older women in the earlier years.

Step 3

During this phase of the lesson, you direct students to gather evidence supporting or refuting each of the possible explanations they generated in response to the two questions in Step 2. You will want to direct them to additional resource materials containing information. Students then gather as much relevant information as possible.

It is important to have specific sources of information readily available for student use. Directions to students to "go to the library and find it" are a sure prescription for failure. Many will give up. Frustrations in finding information can undermine the motivational potential of a good inquiry lesson for students who have not had as much experience with inquiry. Classroom computers are especially useful for this step. Students can access numerous databases and websites on the World Wide Web.

Step 4

During this phase, the responses to the focus questions are reexamined in light of the additional information that has been gathered. The nature and reliability of the evidence is discussed. Once all information related to a given explanation has been considered, the class decides whether to accept, reject, or revise the explanation. You conclude this phase of the activity by writing on the board those explanations for which students found the most evidential support.

Step 5

Ask students to review hypotheses for which they have found good support. You might ask questions such as the following:

- Given all the evidence you have seen supporting these explanations, what do you think is the single best explanation for more women living longer in 1910 than in 1850, and in 1970 than in 1910?

- Why do you make this choice?

- How confident are you that it is correct?

When the students make a final choice, review the supporting evidence and remind class members that this conclusion should not be regarded as final. They might revise it if additional information becomes available.

This description of an inquiry lesson has been compressed for purposes of illustration. Good inquiry lessons may require considerable time if the issues addressed are complex. On the other hand, issues that are familiar, issues that have an abundance of data, and issues about which students have previous knowledge might be completed rather quickly. One of us remembers a demonstration science inquiry lesson where the students arrived at a valid hypothesis within about 15 minutes! This suggests that, as a teacher, you must be prepared with additional lesson material.

It often takes time for students to master skills associated with logical thinking. If time is at a premium and the primary objective is content coverage rather than teaching the inquiry process, an inquiry approach may not be the best choice. Once again, your objectives should guide your choice of strategy.

Simulations

Another powerful form of discovery learning uses simulations, often called simulation games because they include a goal that is to be achieved by the player and some rules that must be followed in order to achieve the goal. The term *game* also captures the playlike environment created when students are engaged in a simulation activity. Simulations are actually complex and sophisticated forms of role-playing.

Simulations are simplified slices of reality that place the participants in a situation where they must make choices and face the consequences of those choices. Thus, the consequences of choices and hypotheses can be tested. An analysis of their choices and the consequences assist students in discovering principles and higher-level thinking processes. In addition, simulations can help them apply learning to real problems. Simulations are often motivating to students because they are a different way of learning, have a gamelike dimension, tend to mirror reality setting, and usually involve social interactions.

The increased availability of technology and computers in the classrooms has greatly increased the use of simulations. Excellent educational simulations are available online, and some interesting software is available from educational materials supply houses. In some cases, students can experience working alongside experts such as scientists and archaeologists online. Computer-based simulations make it possible for students to experience the results of their actions immediately. This feature allows them to try multiple approaches as they test the adequacy of their initial solutions to problems.

An important step in all simulations is debriefing. When using a simulation with students, some of the most important learning occurs during the discussion at the end of the exercise. This gives students an opportunity to analyze their actions and begin to develop concepts and principles based on what they experienced. This debriefing also provides an opportunity for students to learn from others.

The basic steps in using a simulation in the classroom are the following:

- Assign roles to the students.

- Explain the objective for each role.

- Explain the rules and the operating procedure.

- Conduct a demonstration.

- Conduct the simulation activity.

- Debrief the activity: discuss what happened; identify principles; and, if needed, repeat the activity.

It is difficult to give an example of a simulation because many of them are so lengthy. However, many students have been involved in online simulations. A couple of popular ones are "Oregon Trail" and "Sim City." You might want to become involved in one of these simulations and analyze the strengths and weaknesses of the teaching strategy.

Using simulations sometimes requires considerable time. When considering the use of a simulation, you should decide whether the time investment in a particular simulation is worth the learning payoff.

Creative Thinking

The world has a never-ending supply of serious problems. Throughout history, solutions to problems have often come from people who respond to them in unusual, creative ways. Problems would not be problems if conventional solutions could be easily applied. It takes someone who has the curiosity, insight, and emotional security to try a novel approach to a problem. As the common phrase indicates, creative thinking usually involves "thinking outside the box."

Often, creative solutions result when people make unusual associations between different things. For example, Ruggiero (1988) points out that the inventor of the forklift truck got the idea from watching mechanical fingers lift donuts out of an oven. He notes that Gutenberg's invention of the printing press resulted, in part, from his observation of a wine press. Velcro was created through an observation of how burrs cling to clothes.

The ability to generate creative solutions is not widespread among students. By secondary school, many students have learned that education pays off when they give the right answer. They have not been encouraged to be or rewarded by being creative. To remedy this situation, specific instructional techniques have been developed to enhance students' creative thinking. Creativity in the classroom is enhanced when students think their ideas have value, when unusual questions and ideas are encouraged, and when the threat of evaluation is reduced. Creativity is inhibited if students feel pressure to conform, they are ridiculed for unusual ideas, and there is an overemphasis on grades.

While there tends to be an absence of student creativity in most classrooms, there also tends to be an absence of instructional approaches that foster creativity. One approach that is widely used is brainstorming. Brainstorming is designed to stimulate original solutions to problems. It seeks to unleash mental power by encouraging students to move away from relying on ordinary and conventional responses. The goal of brainstorming is the generation of large numbers of responses rather than just a few "correct" ones.

Brainstorming developed in the business world. Concerned leaders noticed that junior-level managers shied away from proposing novel solutions to problems. Often, they simply parroted positions of senior executives. As a result, insights of these younger executives rarely got a hearing. The brainstorming technique was developed to encourage a broad sharing of innovative ideas. The technique ensures that all ideas will be heard and considered.

Rules for conducting a brainstorming exercise are simple:

- Provide students with a problem to consider. ("Suppose all books were printed with an ink that would disappear after six months. What would happen if that were true?")

- Invite students to share as many ideas as they can generate. A student is free to speak whenever an opening of silence occurs. The idea is to generate a rapid outpouring of ideas. Students are free to say whatever comes to their minds as long as it is relevant to the problem.

- Caution students not to comment positively or negatively on ideas suggested by others. All ideas are accepted. This rule helps break down students' fear of "saying something stupid."

- Record all ideas. The recorder should not be concerned about neatness. He or she needs to be someone who can write fast. Student ideas can come at a very rapid rate.

- Stop the exercise when there is a noticeable decline in the rate of presentation of new ideas.

- Conclude the exercise with a general discussion of the ideas.

Brainstorming can then be used as stimulus for students to engage in the development of an idea or in suggesting creative solutions to problems. This process of following up on brainstorming often leads to cooperative learning because students compromise and share their perspectives with each other. Many creative products begin with the process of brainstorming.

Many content areas in the secondary school are places where brainstorming can be applied. It does not require a lot of preparation time, and it can be used to give a creative start to many instructional units.

Critical Thinking

Whereas the primary function of creative thinking is to generate ideas, the primary function of critical thinking is to evaluate ideas. Paul and Elder (2009) define critical thinking as the ability to analyze and evaluate thinking with a view to improving it. Critical thinking always involves judgment that is based on rigorous standards. Critical thinking conclusions are based on more than uninformed opinion. Critical thinking requires that judgments be made in terms of defensible criteria. Here are some of the important critical thinking skills:

- Distinguishing between factual claims and value claims

- Distinguishing relevant from irrelevant facts, claims and arguments

- Determining credibility of a source

- Identifying unstated assumptions

- Detecting bias
- Identifying logical fallacies
- Recognizing logical inconsistencies

Sometimes you will be able to link activities that ask your students to engage in both creative thinking and critical thinking. When you do this, the creative thinking activity takes place first. During this phase of the lesson, give your students directions that encourage them to produce ideas. During the second phase, direct class members to use critical thinking approaches to evaluate these ideas.

We introduced a basic procedure for brainstorming in the earlier section on creative thinking. A critical thinking application (based on an approach originally developed by Dunn & Dunn, 1972) to the initial results of the brainstorming activity can be as follows:

- Begin by taking the results of the brainstorming lesson. For example, given the recent disaster involving the oil spill in the Gulf of Mexico, a brainstorming activity could ask for responses to the question, What is the best thing that could be done to prevent pollution of Gulf Coast beaches and marshes?

- When proposed solutions are listed and the critical thinking phase begins, ask students why these solutions have not already been applied. "What is getting in the way of implementing these 'best solutions?' " (Students engage in another form of brainstorming in listing as many barriers as they can.)

- The next step focuses on how to overcome the obstacles. "What can be done to remove the obstacles?" Again, students identify possible actions.

- Now, ask students to gather data related to their proposals. To do that, they need to address the following questions: What assumptions were we making? What really are the facts about pollution in the Gulf Coast? What is the credibility of the sources making statements about pollution? Are there logical inconsistencies in the data?

- Once students have gathered data, they return to their original proposals and analyze them based on the data they have gathered. This can be followed with the question, Considering all the data we have gathered and the potential solutions we have identified, what should be the first steps toward a solution?

In general, critical thinking involves approaches to making evaluative judgments that are based on logical consideration of evidence and application of appropriate criteria. Critical thinking skills can be applied across the curriculum. For example, identifying logical inconsistencies and propaganda can be addressed when evaluating advertisements and reading novels in English classes, and finding logical inconsistencies is important in mathematics. Identifying bias certainly needs to be addressed in evaluating historical accounts or in reviewing data regarding scientific controversies such as global warming.

Controversial issues often function well as stimuli for critical thinking lessons. Unfortunately, some teachers hesitate to bring such issues into the classroom. This is often due to fear of parent or community protests. Not wanting to stir up unnecessary resistance to school programs, these teachers steer the safe course and avoid discussing issues involving strong disagreement. We disagree. Students need to know that there are responsible ways of dealing with controversial issues. In addition, the introduction of real-life disputes often motivates them. Students appreciate the importance of these issues, and they often commit enthusiastically to lessons featuring content that is relevant to the world they live in outside the school.

Lessons that feature controversial issues need not generate negative parental and community concern. In teaching this kind of content, you have to recognize that it is not your role to force students to arrive at a given conclusion. Rather, your purpose is to help students apply critical thinking to the process so that each person in the class can arrive at an intelligent and thoughtful position.

Problem-Solving

Problem-solving approaches are used when students are asked to think about problems for which there is likely to be a best or correct solution. This does not necessarily mean that these solutions will not be challenged in the future. However, they are considered best, correct, right, or appropriate given the evidence that is available at the time the problem is considered. Here are examples of issues that you might ask students to address when using a problem-solving approach:

- What is causing the leaves on my houseplants to turn yellow and fall off?
- Why is it colder in the winter months in Minneapolis than in Juneau, even though Juneau is much farther north?
- Why do people in Maine and Alabama speak with different accents?
- Why don't armadillos live in California?
- What has caused 20th-century English to differ more from 17th-century English than 20th-century French differs from 17th-century French?

When introducing students to problem-solving, the following steps are useful.

- Step 1: Identify the problem.
- Step 2: Consider possible approaches to its solution.
- Step 3: Select and apply approaches.
- Step 4: Evaluate the adequacy of the conclusion.

Suppose you were teaching a high school algebra class and wished to apply this model. This is how your lesson might unfold.

Step 1

TEACHER:	All right, class, I want each of you to solve this equation. (On the board, the teacher writes this equation: $2x - 46 = 116$.) In this problem, what are we trying to find? (Student raises a hand.) Ruby?
RUBY:	You want us to solve for x, right?
TEACHER:	Right.

Step 2

TEACHER:	Now, before you start, I want someone to tell me how you're going to go about it. John, how about you?
JOHN:	Well, we're going to have to get this thing down to a simpler form. The first thing I would do is get rid of the $2x$ by dividing both sides by 2.
TEACHER:	Okay. That makes sense. What would need to be done next? Gabriella?
GABRIELLA:	I think we'll need to arrange it so we'll have the x on one side and all of the numbers on the other.
TEACHER:	Fine. Now what do we need to remember about the sign of a number when we move it from one side of an equation to the other? I mean, if I had the equation $x - 3 = 4$, what would happen if I moved the minus three to the other side? Kim?
KIM:	The minus three would become a plus three. So you would end up with $x = 4 + 3$, or 7.
TEACHER:	Excellent. Remember the sign changes when we move from one side to the other. Now, once you moved all the numbers to one side, what would you have to do to solve for x? Jean?

JEAN: You would need to add all of the numbers together and then take the square root of the total.

Step 3

TEACHER: We seem to have the basic procedures well in mind. Now I want each of you to solve the problem. If you get stuck, raise your hand, and I will try to help you. [Students individually begin working on the problem.]

Step 4

TEACHER: I see that everybody has come up with an answer. Now let's check our work to see whether the answers are correct. Jennifer, tell me how we might do that.

JENNIFER: I'm not sure.

TEACHER: Anyone have an idea? Raoul?

RAOUL: We could substitute our answer for x in the original equation to see if it works.

TEACHER: Good idea. Let's try that. Raoul, what did you get as your answer?

RAOUL: Nine.

TEACHER: Fine, now let's substitute 9 for x in our original equation. [The teacher writes the following sequence of substitutions on the board]

$$2x - 46 = 116$$
$$2(9 \times 9) - 46 = 116$$
$$2(81) - 46 = 116$$
$$162 - 46 = 116$$
$$116 = 116$$

Your answer seems to be correct. Does everybody see what I have done here? [The teacher goes on to answer questions and to emphasize the importance of checking the accuracy of answers to problems.]

The case study approach is another way to involve students in problem-solving. For decades, the case study approach has been used in law schools and many graduate schools of business. In recent years, case study instruction has been applied to subjects commonly taught in the secondary school. For example, if you were teaching a lesson involving geometry, you might try to liven up your instruction by presenting brief cases involving flight problems that pilots face in which they have to apply principles of geometry. Cases have also been used in social studies classes that focus on landmark Supreme Court cases.

When you use the case study method, you present the class with a fairly complete account of a situation that raises important questions. Students then identify the key issues and gather information that will help them try to resolve them. Case studies are especially useful promoters of active student involvement. They help students understand that problems do not always come with clear answers.

Cases you select as a focus for this kind of instruction can be real or contrived. Actual cases bring an air of reality to the classroom but may have the disadvantage that some students will know the resolution and therefore will fail to take the problem-solving process seriously. Good cases focus on issues that the students see as important and for which there is not a simple right or wrong answer.

Decision-Making

Not all problems have answers that are clearly right, correct, or appropriate. Some questions do not have simple or correct answers. In this situation, people must often make choices from among a variety of acceptable alternatives. This process involves a thinking skill known as decision-making (Beyer, 1988). Because it involves choosing from among a number of competing appropriate responses, decision-making involves consideration of personal values and relevant evidence.

The thinking model for decision-making varies from that used in problem-solving. The major reason for this difference is that value judgments play a much more important role in decision-making than they do in problem-solving. The following seven-step model is an example of an approach used in decision-making lessons:

1. Describe the basic issue or problem.

2. Point out alternative responses.

3. Identify evidence supporting each alternative.

4. Identify values reflected in each alternative.

5. Point out possible consequences of each alternative.

6. Make a choice from among available alternatives.

7. Identify evidence and values considered in making this choice.

CRITICAL INCIDENT

WHY DON'T MS. LEVIN'S "GOOD" STUDENTS LIKE DECISION-MAKING?

Naomi Levin teaches 11th-grade American history in a high school in a medium-size city in the Rocky Mountains. She is midway through her fourth year of teaching. Last summer, she attended a special institute on higher-level thinking skills, and she came back determined to use some of the techniques she learned in her own classes. She decided to emphasize decision-making skills in a unit on the Great Depression and selected these focus questions:

- What should the government have done (that it didn't do) to prevent the Great Depression?
- What should the government have done to end the Great Depression sooner?

To help students gather information about these questions and likely alternative responses, Naomi worked closely with the school librarian. A special shelf of resource materials was organized for members of Naomi's class to use. After she gave students a general orientation to the decision-making approach, students dug into the materials.

After students had a chance to think about the questions, some possible responses, and some more-or-less final conclusions that made sense to them, Naomi led the class in a general discussion centered on the focus questions. She said that the intensity of student interest and the level of involvement were outstanding. She thought everything had gone very well. This view changed when some of her A students dropped by to talk after school.

These students reported that they had really enjoyed what was going on in class, but that they had some concerns. Most of them indicated that they were going on to college and that the class had spent a lot of time just on one topic. They indicated that they were worried about not covering other topics that they might need to know about to do well in college.

Also, they felt very uneasy about the kind of test they would be facing when "all this discussing and speculating ends." Though they didn't say so in so many words, they seemed to be indicating that they knew how to get A's when content was taught in a more traditional way but that they weren't sure how their performances would stack up when they were evaluated on "this decision-making stuff." Several students strongly hinted that they would prefer to go back to a more familiar way of dealing with course content.

Naomi had always counted on her good students for support. She was disappointed that these class leaders expressed concern about an approach that, in her mind, works well. Now she is in doubt about what she should do.

■ ■ ■

What values were implied by the reaction of some students to Naomi's new approach? Why were they concerned about this change? Did their values conflict with Naomi's? How might values of others (the principal, parents, community leaders, and other teachers) influence their reactions to Naomi's approach? How concerned should Naomi be about this situation? Do you think it is possible that any change from a familiar pattern will result in student concerns of this kind, or is there something attached specifically to the decision-making technique that brought it about in this situation? Is it acceptable to cover less content in more depth, or does such a decision deny students access to important information they should have? What kinds of assessment might be appropriate when the emphasis has been on developing students' decision-making proficiency?

An Example of a Basic Decision-Making Lesson

Step 1 A local school board has taken under consideration a proposal to require every freshman to take four years of mathematics in high school. The issue or problem might be framed like this: Should all students be required to take four years of mathematics?

Step 2 Take a position. This case has just two basic alternatives: Alternative one is to support the requirement and the other is to oppose it.

Step 3 Some of the following evidence might be gathered to support a four-year mathematics requirement:

- SAT scores in mathematics have failed to reach levels achieved by students in the 1960s.
- The nation is facing an impending shortage of engineers and other technical people who must have a sound background in mathematics.
- Students will begin college-level mathematics instruction at higher levels because of better high school backgrounds.
- The requirement will improve the general quality of the high school curriculum by making the whole program more rigorous.

Some of the following evidence might be gathered to oppose a four-year mathematics requirement:

- The requirement will weaken existing math courses. This is true because all high school students do not have the talent for the math courses that they will now be required to take.
- The requirement will result in an unfortunate reduction in the number of available electives.
- Not all high school graduates go to college.
- Not all occupational fields, even for college graduates, demand an extensive background in mathematics.

Step 4 Individuals who support a four-year mathematics requirement might cite the following values, among others:

- Mathematics courses are difficult, and they provide a needed element of rigor to the high school program.

- Too much elective choice in high school is not good.

- Society needs more technically trained people, and it is the school's job to provide them.

The following values might be among those cited by individuals who oppose a four-year mathematics requirement:

- Individual choice is an important part of the high school experience.

- Mathematics is not necessarily more rigorous than other subjects it might displace.

- The society should not go overboard in imposing its priorities on individuals.

Step 5   A supporter of a four-year mathematics requirement might cite the following consequences of implementing such a policy:

- Quantitative SAT scores may be expected to rise.

- High school graduates will be better prepared for college.

- The nation will be better able to compete with technology-oriented nations such as Japan.

An opponent of a four-year mathematics requirement might cite the following consequences of implementing such a policy:

- The dropout rate among high school students will increase as academic frustrations become too much for some students.

- Discipline problems will increase among students who remain because those who are not talented in mathematics will sense that they have been put in a no-win situation.

- Because vocation-oriented electives will decrease in number, some employers will begin to attack the schools for failing to provide relevant instruction.

Step 6   At this point, a decision is made. In this case, because there are only two alternatives, a choice would be made to either (1) support the decision to require four years of mathematics or (2) oppose this decision.

Step 7   A person *supporting* the decision might identify the pieces of information and values relevant to his or her conclusion in this way:

> I was impressed by the data showing the decline in quantitative SAT scores since the early 1960s. The growing shortage of engineers and technicians also impressed me. Thinking back on my own high school experience, I concluded that high school students lack the maturity to choose electives wisely. In the long run, they would be better served by a more prescriptive curriculum. Finally, I think the schools do have a responsibility to require students to take courses in areas where we have a critical national shortage.

A person *opposing* the decision might identify the pieces of information and values relevant to his or her conclusion in this way:

> It is clear to me that requiring four years of mathematics will reduce the number of electives available to students. Many vocational electives in the high school program do a fine job of responding to the needs of students who will go to work once they graduate. We need to preserve these programs. Finally, I don't think we should allow needs identified by bureaucratic federal agencies to force content on students in the schools. Local control and freedom of choice are a cherished part of our educational heritage.

Issues, Values, and Consequences Analysis

Decision-making applies to the affective or the values area of the curriculum as well as to the cognitive domain. One application of decision-making to the values area is that of issues, values, and consequences analysis. The general steps are basically those usually used

Figure 10-1

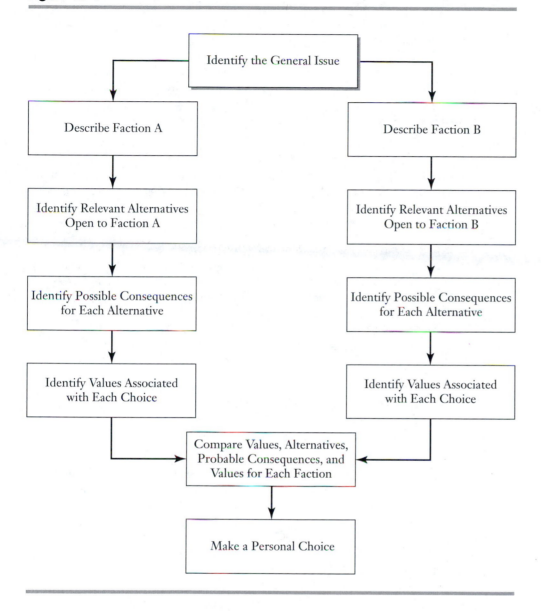

for decision-making, with the additional requirement that students consider values related to the focus issue(s) as they move toward making a decision. Listed below are the steps that you would typically follow in implementing this approach (see Figure 10-1):

- Identify the general issue.
- Describe faction A, including basic beliefs and values.
- Identify relevant alternatives open to faction A.
- Identify possible consequences for each alternative.
- Identify what would be valued in choosing each alternative.
- Repeat the above steps for faction B (and any other remaining groups).
- Compare the values, alternatives, and consequences of all factions.
- Make a choice about the best alternative in terms of what you consider to be the most important values.

Step 1: Identify the General Issue

During this step, you work with the entire class to ensure that all students understand the issue. You may do this by introducing the students to a problem. For example, during the 1950s, China was not a member of the United Nations. Some people thought it was strange that the world's most populous nation was not a member. Others feared that admitting China would give additional voting power to nations with communist governments. There was much debate over whether China should be admitted to the UN. What was the basic issue involved here? What was the basic disagreement? What are the two different groups that were involved?)

Step 2: Describe Each Faction

Decision-making is needed in lessons such as this because there are two or more positions that are in conflict. Different groups have different opinions about what should be done. During this phase, your intent is to have the students, working in groups, gain as much information about each one of the supporting positions. Who are they? What are their goals? What are their beliefs? What things are most important to them?

Step 3: Identify Relevant Alternatives Open to Each Faction

During this phase of the lesson, you ask students to work in groups to identify alternative courses of action open to members of the faction they are considering. Sometimes you will encourage students to brainstorm alternative answers to questions. For example, you might ask them to think about different answers to questions such as the following: What did the opposition do to prevent China's admission into the UN? What are some things supporters could have done to gain China's admission? Were there options other than full admission or full denial?

More from the Web

Higher-Level Thinking

Much information related to teaching higher-level thinking skills is available today on the Web. The volume of information attests to the high level of interest that both professional educators and the general public have in approaches to teaching that will prepare students to deal intelligently with the complex challenges they will face as adults. Here are some websites that you may wish to visit.

INTRODUCTION TO CREATIVE THINKING
http://www.virtualsalt.com/crebookl.htm
This material, produced by Robert Harris, includes an excellent overview of creative thinking. Among the topics addressed are (1) creative methods, (2) negative attitudes that block creativity, (3) distinctions between creative thinking and critical thinking, and (4) mental blocks to creative thinking.

CRITICAL THINKING: PRIMARY AND SECONDARY INFORMATION
http://www.criticalthinking.org/K12/default.html
This website includes numerous resources that you can use in lessons that integrate critical thinking into your instructional program. This site is maintained by a number of organizations that are interested in promoting the development of critical thinking.

PROBLEM-SOLVING
http://mailer.fsu.edu/~jflake/probSol.html
At this website you will find excellent links to sources where you can obtain useful sample problem-solving strategies.

Step 4: Identify Possible Consequences for Each Alternative

Different courses of action may produce different results or consequences. During this step, encourage students to look at each alternative course of action and to consider the possible consequences of that action. Here are some example questions for considering the admission of China to the UN: What might have been the consequences of a massive information campaign to discredit China? What might have been the consequences of some sort of conditional admission?

Step 5: Identify Values Associated with Each Choice

Once the alternatives and their possible consequences have been identified, the students should now identify what would be valued by choosing each alternative. For the admission of China to the UN, students can consider the following questions: What was most important for those who opposed China's admission? What was most important for those who favored admission? What would those who advocated a smear campaign have valued most highly? What would those who advocated partial admission have valued?

Step 6: Compare the Values, Alternatives, and Consequences of All Factions

At this point, the information gathered by the different groups investigating different factions can be brought together and compared. Your purpose at this point is to help students understand that many decisions involve a conflict of values and value priorities. For example, some people may have seen that their value of preserving democracy as a justification for opposing China's admission to the UN would have been in conflict with their value of honesty—particularly if smear tactics involving the use of false information had been used by some opponents of China's admission.

FOR YOUR PORTFOLIO

1. Standard 4 of the Interstate New Teacher Assessment and Support Consortium (INTASC) standards focuses on the use of a variety of strategies that encourage higher-level thinking. What materials, ideas you learned in this chapter, will you include in your portfolio as evidence of your learning? Select up to three items to include. Number them 1, 2, and 3.

2. Think about why you selected these materials for your portfolio. Consider issues such as the following in your response:

   - The specific purposes to which this information can be put when you plan, deliver, and assess the impact of your instruction

   - The compatibility of the information with your own priorities and values

   - The contributions this information can make to your personal development as a teacher.

   - The factors that led you to include this material as opposed to some alternatives you also considered

3. Prepare a written reflection in which you analyze the decision-making process you followed. Also, mention the INTASC standard(s) to which your selected material relates. Some of your material might relate to several standards. First complete the chart below.

MATERIALS YOU SELECTED AND THE INTASC STANDARDS

Put a check under those INTASC Standards numbers to which the evidence you have selected applies. (Refer to Chapter 1 for more detailed information about INTASC.)

INTASC Standards

Item of Evidence Number	S-1	S-2	S-3	S-4	S-5	S-6	S-7	S-8	S-9	S-10
1										
2										
3										

Step 7: Make a Choice

At this point, challenge students to make a personal decision about the issue that has been considered. Encourage them to think about which values they consider to be most important and then to reflect on which decision would be most consistent with their own values.

In summary, issues, values, and consequences analysis is designed to help students appreciate that decisions are not made just by dispassionate consideration of evidence. Individual values play a role. In addition, decisions frequently involve a conflict between two or more values. When people make decisions, they have to think about and weigh the importance of both their own values and those of others.

Key Ideas in Summary

- There is much less centralized teacher control in techniques designed to develop students' higher-level thinking skills than in direct-instruction lessons. The teacher functions as a manager who presents students with a problem and assists them, as needed, as they work toward a conclusion.

- *Metacognition* refers to thought about the process of thinking. Metacognitive instructional approaches seek to help students become conscious of their own thought processes and to select those that are relevant for solving particular problems and tasks with which they are confronted. Examples of these metacognitive approaches include teacher modeling and visualizing thinking.

- *Discovery learning* involves getting students to learn how to identify basic concepts and principles, or the structure of a subject, rather than having them taught directly by the teacher. Learning how to discover is at least as important as what is discovered. This develops thinking skills that will be useful in a variety of life situations. Contrary to some popular notions, effective discovery teaching requires teachers to spend more time planning than is true when some other instructional techniques are selected.

- *Inquiry teaching* is based on inductive learning, a learning process that proceeds from the specific to the general. This means that students first are presented with specific examples that they are asked to study. From this study, they derive general explanatory conclusions or principles. Inquiry teaching involves students in the creation of new knowledge. Approaches typically follow a logical, step-by-step sequence that is thought to develop students' rational thinking powers.

- *Simulation* is a powerful approach to helping students discover important processes and values as well as higher-level thinking skills. Simulations involve placing the students in situations that allow them to experience the consequences of their actions. An analysis of actions taken and the resulting consequences help students discover important principles and processes.

- Creative thinking frees people to develop unusual or novel solutions to problems. It involves unique insight. Creative thinking is thought to be stimulated when people are able to defer final judgment until many alternatives have been considered and when they do not fear failure. Brainstorming is an example of a classroom technique that is designed to elicit creative thinking.

- *Critical thinking* focuses on the evaluation of ideas. It aids students in making judgments based on consideration of evidence. Brainstorming approaches are just one example of a classroom technique designed to encourage the development of critical thinking abilities.

- *Problem-solving approaches* are designed to help students consider problems for which a single best answer is thought to exist. This does not mean that this best answer will be right every time. It simply implies that it is best given presently available evidence. The following steps are included in many problem-solving approaches: (1) identifying the problem, (2) considering alternative approaches to solving it, (3) selecting and applying one or more approaches, and (4) making a final judgment regarding the best approach (or solution).

- Decision-making refers to thinking sequences that are relevant when the problems that students confront have no generally agreed-on correct or right answers. A number of appropriate answers may be identified. The alternative selected reflects both a consideration of evidence and of values.

Reflections

1. Some scholars argue that teaching students how to engage in sophisticated thinking should be the primary mission of the school. Why might they take this position? Do you agree? Explain your response.

2. Teachers today feel obligated to cover much academic content in the courses they teach. Given this reality, should they devote class time to instruction designed to help students develop appropriate metacognitive processes? Why or why not?

3. Why are relatively few people creative thinkers, and what might you do in the classroom to prompt more creative thinking from students?

4. What are some key features of approaches designed to elicit critical thinking?

5. Under what conditions would a problem-solving approach be an appropriate instructional choice?

6. Why do different people arrive at quite different conclusions when a decision-making approach is used to consider an issue?

7. In what ways do problem-solving and decision-making differ? Is it worthwhile for teachers to teach both approaches to students? Why or why not?

8. What are basic steps followed in issues, values, and consequences analysis? Is it proper for school lessons to deal with issues involving values? Why or why not?

Learning Extensions

1. Secondary school teachers are pressed for time. Some people argue that time devoted to teaching students learning processes and thinking skills (e.g., metacognitive approaches, creative thinking skills, problem-solving skills, critical thinking skills, decision-making skills, and so forth) takes valuable time away from content instruction. Find another student in your class to work with you on a project to prepare arguments related to the following question: Is taking class time to teach thinking skills to students responsible? Make an oral presentation to the class in which one of you presents evidence supporting a yes answer and one of you presents evidence supporting a no answer.

2. Select a topic from a subject you are preparing to teach. Describe how you might incorporate one of the following into a lesson related to this topic:

- Inquiry teaching
- Problem-solving
- Creative thinking
- Decision-making
- Critical thinking

Present this information to your instructor in a short paper.

3. Interview teachers who have incorporated inquiry teaching into their instructional programs. Ask them to describe pluses and minuses of this approach. Share your findings with others in the class as part of a general discussion of inquiry in the secondary school classroom.

4. Prepare a collection of articles from professional journals or from Web sources that describe practical classroom applications of inquiry and creative thinking approaches. You may wish to use the *Education index* to locate article titles and journals. A search engine will help you find items posted on the Web. Try to include at least ten articles. Present them to your instructor for review. Keep these materials as a resource to use when you begin teaching.

5. Invite several department heads from a local secondary school to visit your class. If this is not possible, try to get a director of secondary education, a director of secondary curriculum, or another central school-district office administrator to come. Ask about the relative emphasis on inquiry instruction and on teaching thinking skills to students. Specifically ask whether teachers are encouraged to use these approaches and whether any effort is made to provide in-service training to help teachers become more proficient in implementing them.

References

Beyer, B. K. (1988). *Developing a thinking skills program*. Boston: Allyn & Bacon.

Bruner, J. (1960). *The process of education*. Cambridge, MA: Harvard University Press.

Dewey, J. (1910). *How we think*. Boston: D. C. Heath.

Dunn, R., & Dunn, K. (1972). *Practical approaches to individualizing instruction: Contracts and other effective teaching strategies*. New York: Parker.

Joyce, B., & Weil, M. (1996). *Models of teaching* (5th ed.). Boston: Allyn & Bacon.

Lasley, T. J., II, Matczynski, T. J., & Rowley, J. B. (2002). *Instructional models: Strategies for teaching in a diverse society* (2nd ed.). Belmont, CA: Wadsworth.

Paul, R., & Elder, L. (2009). *The miniature guide to critical thinking: Concepts and tools*. Dillon Beach, CA: Foundation for Critical Thinking.

Ruggiero, V. H. (1988). *Teaching thinking across the curriculum*. New York: Harper & Row.

Slavin, R. E. (2009). *Educational psychology* (9th ed.). Boston: Allyn & Bacon.

Woolfolk, A. E. (2009). *Educational psychology* (11th ed.). Boston: Allyn & Bacon.

Small-Group and Cooperative Learning

Objectives

This chapter will help you

- describe a rationale for using small-group learning

- identify conditions that facilitate small-group learning

- define competitive, individualistic, and cooperative goal structures

- describe some techniques you can use to prepare students for small-group learning

- point out some examples of popular small-group learning techniques

- identify features that distinguish cooperative learning from other small-group approaches

- explain purposes and procedures associated with several cooperative-learning techniques

Graphic Organizer: Chapter 11

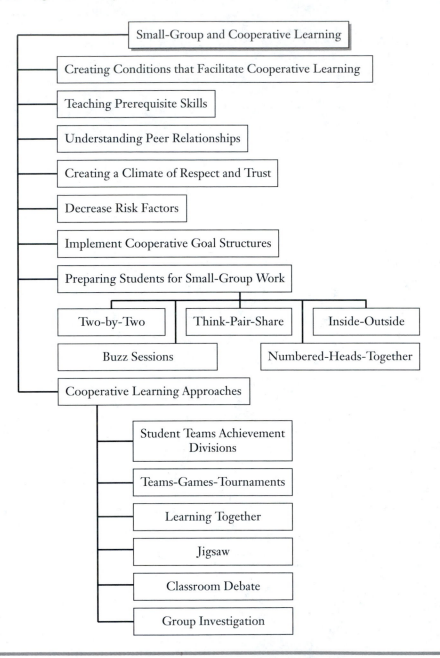

Introduction

Consider these points: (1) students in secondary schools love to socialize and (2) learning is social. What students learn through interactions with others forms the basis for complex thinking and understanding (Frey, Fisher, & Everlove, 2009). It makes sense to take advantage of these principles in planning instruction. If students love to socialize, why not use socialization as a teaching tool? If social interaction is the basis for learning, then classrooms should focus on social interactions to promote thinking and understanding. Group and cooperative learning is an approach where these principles can be applied. This model of instruction promotes learning by providing a context for students to learn as they watch, listen, talk to, and support others. However, many students and teachers are reluctant to implement group work because they do not know how to establish groups where there is genuine collaboration and because they have had negative experiences where group work was ineffective and frustrating (Frey, Fisher & Everlove, 2009).

It is important to remember that just because students are required to work together in groups does not mean that they are engaged in meaningful group and cooperative learning. Cooperative learning is defined as a process involving students working in structured teams with the goal of every student improving (Stahl & VanSickle, 2009). Therefore, success in cooperative learning is not determined by a group completing a project or attaining a goal; it is determined by the learning of each student in the group.

When properly implemented, cooperative learning does have some significant benefits, according to the evidence. Some of the claimed benefits include the following:

- Consistent academic improvement
- Longer retention of academic content
- Improved critical reasoning abilities
- Improved intrinsic motivation
- A reduction of disruptive behaviors
- Improved social relationships in the classroom
- Improved attitudes toward school, teachers, and the subject matter

(Stahl, Van Sickle, & Stahl, 2009)

Why is this so? One explanation is that student motivation increases when students are allowed to work with each other and when there are group (rather than individual) goals and rewards. Another explanation is that, through interaction with others, students are better able to clarify, reflect, reformulate, and elaborate on material than when they work alone. This intensive engagement with new content promotes development of the kinds of cognitive changes that are necessary for learning to occur. In addition, small-group work and cooperative learning provides good conditions for learning through modeling.

Modeling involves learners observing how others take action, seek solutions, or think about a situation. Teachers are in a prime role for providing modeling. For a variety of reasons, however, some students reject teacher modeling. Having the opportunity to observe and interact with peers or significant others in small-group settings provides excellent opportunities for students to learn from modeling.

There is some evidence that small-group learning approaches can help you and your students develop a more positive working relationship. Lessons organized in this way give you and your students opportunities to work together more personally than when you are teaching a more traditional lesson to an entire class of students. Because this kind of instruction keeps you closely involved with individuals, you ordinarily are able to spot and respond quickly to difficulties that particular students might be having. Any assistance you provide to promote students' success adds to their sense of self-confidence and tends to promote favorable feelings toward you and your teaching.

Learning occurs when students become active participants in lessons. In traditional large-group instruction, some individuals in your classes simply do not get very involved. In a group discussion, some students rarely speak up. Perhaps they are shy and lack self-confidence, perhaps they are unprepared or fear failure, or perhaps they aren't feeling well. Small-group learning lessons provide contexts that encourage all students to become actively engaged in lessons. The increased student-to-student and student-to-teacher interactions that these instructional experiences provide help develop students' oral-language proficiencies, increase the probability they will acquire new content, and add to their sense of personal competence.

You may face potential difficulties when you begin using small-group approaches with a new group of students. For example, they may not know how to work together productively in small groups. If this happens, you may find individuals arguing about what they should do or abandoning academically related work in favor of a spirited social chat. You may also find that a few individuals in small groups may be inclined to sit back and let others do the work. Finally, it is possible you will encounter some students who simply do not like small-group work. It may be that these students have always experienced high levels of academic success when they have been involved in classes featuring traditional large-group instruction. It could be, too, that they have had unfortunate experiences on previous occasions when they have been involved in small-group lessons that were poorly structured.

To remedy these problems, you need to know your students well, diagnose what obstacles may be standing in the way of their commitment to small-group learning approaches, and develop a response that seems appropriate for individual members of your class. In general, the best remedy is to plan small-group lessons carefully. If you do, you will greatly increase the probability that students will enjoy their experiences and look forward to occasions when you ask them to work in small groups. In this chapter, you will find information about what you can do to create conditions that facilitate small-group work and some examples of small-group learning techniques that many secondary school teachers have used successfully.

Creating Conditions That Facilitate Small-Group Learning

As is true of all instructional techniques, small-group learning operates within the context of the individual classroom. Some classroom characteristics are more compatible with certain instructional techniques than are others. For example, you are likely to have more initial success with small-group learning if your students have some knowledge about how to work productively in this type of instructional setting.

One of the most important requisite conditions is that your students understand the purposes of the activity and what they are going to learn from it. You want to point out the specific personal benefits that they can derive from their participation in small-group lessons. For example, you might explain that a major reason people are dismissed from jobs is because they cannot work productively with others. You can let students know that, in addition to learning new content in a pleasing way, their involvement in small-group learning will add to their level of comfort while working in close proximity with others who may have personalities and perspectives quite different from their own.

Many teachers who are reluctant to use group and cooperative learning express concerns that some students they put into groups will not work productively in this type of instructional setting (Frey, Fisher, & Everlove, 2009). To be sure, if a group task is poorly structured, the purposes of the activity are unclear, and there is little individual or group accountability, then group learning approaches are likely to be ineffective. Generally, however, most of your students will have no problem working well together if they are provided with an appropriate structure and orientation (Johnson & Johnson, 2009). This implies a need to give them clear guidelines regarding what they are to do and what the expected outcome of the lesson should be. You will find it particularly helpful to require group members to produce some kind of tangible "product of learning" at the end of the lesson. This will provide both you and your students with tangible evidence that something worthwhile has been accomplished.

Teaching Prerequisite Skills

It makes sense for you to provide students with some initial instruction that focuses on specific skills that will help them work together. Examples of these types of skills include active listening, giving clear explanations, resolving conflicts, avoiding put-downs, and asking for clarification (Slavin, 2009). Your students should have little difficulty mastering these competencies. During initial small-group learning lessons, you might give students opportunities to practice these skills by organizing members of the class into groups of two or three students and assigning each group to perform simple tasks. As students become more comfortable with these skills, you can start assigning the students to larger groups of up to about six people.

Understading Peer Relationships

How well your students know one another, the norms of their peer group, the feelings individuals have about how well others in the group accept them, their general levels of interest in your subject, and how students in the group assess their relative chances of succeeding in your class help shape the general character of every student you will teach. As you prepare for a career in secondary education, you might want to see these variables in action. To do so, make arrangements to visit a secondary school classroom and follow a few students as they pass from class to class throughout the school day. Don't be surprised if you observe that students who are uncooperative in one class demonstrate completely different behaviors in another. The special dynamics of the group and the psychological climate created by the teacher often account for these differences.

All of this underscores the importance of taking time to learn something about your students every time you get a new group. What you find will vary somewhat depending on the particular setting of your school. For example, in small, rural secondary schools in areas where there is not much moving in and out of the area, students may know each other very well. However, this does not necessarily guarantee they will all get along well in your classes. If past relationships have not been positive, this interpersonal relationship history may carry forward year after year. Over the years, some of your students may have been labeled in ways that diminish their expectations of success and otherwise introduce tensions into the overall classroom learning environment.

If you find yourself teaching in a large urban school, you may find that only a few students in your classes know each other before the school year begins. Initially, this can inhibit their willingness to participate actively in classroom discussions. You may need to take action to make class members comfortable with one another and more willing to become active participants in classroom activities. In particular, you will want to identify and help students who seem to be generally isolated from others in the class and who are particularly reluctant to become fully engaged in assigned activities that require students to work together.

Creating a Climate of Respect and Trust

Productive group work demands mutual respect and trust. If your students do not respect one another, they will have difficulty accepting the contributions of all members of the class. Under such conditions, your efforts to promote cooperative learning may well fall short of their goal, and students may develop antagonistic attitudes. This is especially likely to happen if some of them feel they are being asked to do more than their share of the work. If you suspect that some students are concerned about this issue, you need to take action to ensure that each student is carrying part of the load.

In addition to distributing the workload equitably, you also need to help students involved in small-group work develop attitudes of mutual respect. This will not happen simply by telling students that this is your expectation. Respect must be earned. What you can do is assign individuals to complete tasks for which they have a particular aptitude. When they complete these tasks successfully, others in the group see clear evidence of their contributions. This, in turn, leads others to respect and appreciate their value as group members.

What Do *You* Think?

"I Don't Need Their Help"

Suppose you are teaching a group of high school sophomores and receive the following reaction from a student after you announce plans to involve class members in a small-group learning exercise that will require them to work closely together and to assist one another to master the new content:

> Why do we have to do this? I don't need help from these people. I work hard and I get good grades. I know that when we start this small-group thing that I'll end up carrying the load for everybody. It just isn't fair.

Questions

1. How legitimate are the concerns of this student?

2. Is the student really distressed about the issue of fairness, or is something else a likely cause of this person's concern?

3. What would you say to this person in response?

4. Given the concerns raised by this student, what special directions might you give to members of the groups about their individual responsibilities?

Decreasing Risk Factors

One of the greatest risk factors that interferes with student involvement is fear of failure. For individuals to cooperate, they must feel that they are in a safe environment. You must take action to lower the risks of participation and active involvement. For small-group learning lessons to be effective, your students must first believe that working together will enhance their opportunities for success. Sometimes, academically talented students fear that working in small groups puts them at risk. They may be convinced that they can do better working alone rather than as members of a small group that has collective responsibility for a task. If you are confronted with this situation, you must assure these students that there will be real benefits for them as a result of their participation in small-group lessons.

Many of your students are also likely to be concerned about the issue of grading. Some students fear any approach that alters the way grades are given. They often feel that a change will put them at a competitive disadvantage. When you introduce small-group learning, you have to take care to explain how students will be assessed and to make a case in support of the idea that the evaluation scheme will not increase the risk that they will receive bad grades.

Implementing Cooperative Goal Structures

The way you structure goals of small-group work can affect students' learning. The term *goal structure* refers to the way individuals relate to each other in accomplishing a particular goal (Woolfolk, 2009). Each of the following three basic types of goal structures requires a different relationship between an individual and the group:

- Competitive goal structure
- Individualistic goal structure
- Cooperative goal structure

Competitive Goal Structure   In a competitive goal structure, students are placed in competition with each other. There has long been an emphasis on competitive goal structures in education because it is believed that competition is motivating. While there is a certain element of truth to this belief, competition is only motivating to those who think they can win. Individuals who do not believe they have a chance to win are not motivated; they are discouraged and tend to drop out. While competitive goals do have some use in education, the task is that of increasing students' perception that they have an opportunity to win.

Competitive goals have traditionally been the most common type of goals in secondary schools. Ranking students according to their scores on tests and grading on the curve are two examples of competitive goal structures. Another difficulty with competitive goals is that the identification of so-called winners and losers tends to be based on a narrow range of abilities measured by paper-and-pencil tests. These tests tend to favor students with specific abilities over students who may have strengths in other areas.

To illustrate this point, suppose that grades are based on a narrow range of ability, such as being among the first five runners to finish a mile run. Some students would see this as possible, and they would be motivated to accomplish this goal. They would practice hard and put forth a great deal of effort. But suppose that other individuals have superior strength rather than endurance. These individuals would despair of their ability to reach this goal. While some practice might improve their running times, the probability of a successful payoff would be limited. To them, practicing for a mile race is simply wasted time. However, they would willingly engage in competitive tests based on strength.

An inappropriate application of competitive goal structures leads some students to commit to the idea that the "cards are stacked" against them. This happens frequently in the classroom when some students refuse to "play the classroom game." In fact, their frustration might be so high that they engage in actions that hinder the ability of others to attain success. For example, in one highly competitive graduate program where grades were based on class norms, graduate students were deliberately giving each other wrong answers in study sessions in an attempt to increase their own opportunity to win!

Individualistic Goal Structure   Individualistic goal structures do not require students to perform at better levels than others. In this arrangement, attaining success is purely an individual endeavor that is unrelated to the efforts of others. An individual performance standard for each student is set. You judge an individual student based on how well he or she does relative to this standard, not relative to the performance of someone else. For example, when we enter an airplane, we are more concerned with how the pilot met all of the standards required for piloting an aircraft rather than how the pilot compared to the rest of the class.

While individualistic goal structures decrease risk factors associated with competition, there are some potentially negative consequences. For example, individualistic goal structures might do little to increase group cohesion or acceptance of others. This is an important consideration because data suggests that a large number of individuals fail at their jobs when they are unable to work with others. Individualistic goals also overlook the fact that your students do not live their lives in isolation; instead, they are part of an interdependent culture. Individualized goal structures also tend to overlook the human need for belonging and socialization.

Cooperative Goal Structure   To achieve success in classes with cooperative goal structures, your students have to know how to work productively together. The cooperative goal structure recognizes that different individuals have unique skills and abilities. When these skills and abilities are joined together, greater accomplishments are possible. For example, the success of an orchestra, a choir, or an athletic team requires individuals with different abilities to work together to achieve a goal. It would not work if everyone in a choir was a soprano, all the members of the band played a tuba, or all the members of the football team were quarterbacks! In life, the success of most organizations requires a variety of individuals with complementary skills and perceptions. Therefore, cooperative settings in the classroom mirror the world outside the classroom.

The potential difficulty with cooperative goals is that some individuals will not "pull their own weight." Some individuals are content to sit back and let others do the bulk of the work. The task required when using cooperative goal structures is to try and make sure that all members of a team use their skills and abilities.

Preparing Students for Small-Group Work

Successful group work takes some preparation. Frey, Fisher, & Everlove (2009) suggest that teachers start small by using two-student conversations so that students have multiple opportunities to interact successfully. They suggest providing students with prompts focusing on activities such as explaining ideas, checking for understanding, responding to the ideas of another person, and handling disagreements as a way to help students learn the skills that will be useful in larger groups. They also suggest that teachers introduce group work systematically by presenting the goals and expectations of group work and by giving students opportunities for guided practice that focus on how individuals interact with lots of short two-person activities. This helps students develop interpersonal and social skills that will be useful later on. The following subsections discuss several approaches that can be used to help introduce group learning.

Two-By-Two

You can use an approach called two-by-two to break the ice with a new group of students. You begin by asking each student to find out something specific about one other person in the class. Once this has been done, ask students to join together to form groups of four. Each of the four students tells what they have learned about the person they interviewed. Tell students in each group that their task is to remember information about all four group members. Give them a little time to do this, and then ask individuals in each group to stop and tell what they can remember about each person in the group. Follow the same general procedure as you go on to organize the groups of four into groups of eight, and then the groups of eight into groups of 16.

You will be amazed at how many students will be able to remember information about nearly every group member, even at the stage where groups feature 16 students each. This activity helps students become more comfortable with each other. When you later organize them into small groups for academic work, they will be comfortable in engaging in the intense person-to-person interaction that small-group lessons feature.

Think-Pair-Share

Think-pair-share is a technique that you can use to introduce small-group learning by beginning with a focus on dialogue between two students. Begin this approach by giving members of your class a question or problem to consider. In the first phase, each student thinks individually about the focus issue you have selected. Next, ask students to work in pairs for the purpose of sharing their responses to the question or the problem. Follow this step by asking each pair of students to share their responses with the entire class.

Think-pair-share helps students learn how to discuss and share their ideas with others and to understand that "two heads are better than one." To enhance the probability that this approach will be effective, you want to select a focus question or problem that will be of interest to a large number of your students. To ensure that no student will feel diminished in any way at the end of the exercise because of a position he or she has taken, the question or problem you select should be one where there is no single "correct" or "right" response. Your intent is to encourage a diversity of answers and respect for a diversity of opinions. Think-pair-share can help students recognize that (1) it is possible to develop many reasonable responses to complex problems; (2) individuals of integrity may take different positions on these issues; and (3) a willingness to think, consider, and sometimes compromise are characteristics that contribute to the successful functioning of small groups.

Inside-Outside

Inside-outside helps students develop skills that assist them in becoming more productive members of small groups. In this approach, you organize members into two circles. People in one circle are located inside a larger, surrounding outside circle. You assign the "outsiders" (members of the outside circle) to observe behaviors of "insiders" (members of the inside circle). Each "outsider" is given one "insider" to watch. At this point, you give the "insiders" a problem to discuss or a task to complete. Members of the "outsiders" observe how the "insiders" conduct their assigned work. Allow this phase of the lesson to continue for 10 or 15 minutes.

Next, ask students to reverse their positions. Members of the former "insider" group now become members of the "outsider" group, and members of the former "outsider" group become members of the "insider" group. Following the same procedure as before, assign each person in the "outside" group to observe one person in the "inside" group. Next, give the new group of "insiders" a task to complete. The "outsiders" observe the "insiders" as members of this group begin doing what you asked them to do.

After 10 or 15 minutes have passed, bring the entire class together again as a group. Ask individuals to share what they observed their "insider" doing. Ask them to comment especially on those contributions that helped the whole group complete the assigned task. You might also conduct a general discussion of some kinds of behaviors of individuals that were not especially helpful to the entire group. It is important for you to discuss the inappropriate behavior and model ways to correct that behavior. This will alleviate any hurt feelings in either group. The purpose of the exercise is to help students recognize and commit to kinds of behaviors that facilitate completion of small-group tasks.

Numbered-Heads-Together

You can use the numbered-heads-together approach to introduce students to the idea of group scoring and individual accountability. Begin by organizing members of the class into groups of about four students each. (You can vary this number slightly if you wish.) Give every student in each group a number ranging from 1 to 4. Next, provide each group with a question or a problem. Explain that the group must develop an answer and share it among group members in ways that will ensure every member of the group knows it. Give groups sufficient time to develop answers. At this point, ask groups to stop. Announce one of the numbers you have assigned (1, 2, 3, or 4). Students in each group with the number you have called out raise their hands. If the person you identify knows the answer, all members in his or her group get a point (Kagan, 1989). (If the answer is incorrect, you can call on another volunteer.) Repeat this process several times. Members of the group with the most points are declared the winners.

Numbered-heads-together allows you to set up conditions that ensure each student in every group will be involved. There is also an incentive for every person in the group who has information relevant to solving the problem or answering the question to share what he or she knows with all group members. In addition, the expectation that every group member will be able to respond correctly when called upon encourages students to listen carefully to what others in the group are saying. In summary, the technique promotes the development of student behaviors that characterize effective, contributing members of small groups.

Buzz Session

Another technique you can use to build effective small-group participation skills is the buzz session. Begin a buzz session by organizing members of your class into small groups.

Each group is given a focus topic. Choose one student to be a recorder. Provide this person with a piece of chart paper with three columns. These headings appear across the top of the first through third columns, respectively: (1) what we already know about the topic, (2) what we would like to know about the topic, and (3) how we might find out what we would like to know. (*Note:* This technique is similar to the K-W-L discussed in Chapter 12.)

The buzz session begins by group members generating as much information as they can related to what they already know about the topic. (The recorder writes information under the appropriate column heading.) Next, the group develops some ideas related to what group members would like to know. (The recorder writes ideas that are generated in the second column.) The group then considers how members might find out what they would like to know. (The recorder adds this information in the third column.)

The buzz-session technique helps students think about how they can start a group task. It also tends to make new tasks somewhat less intimidating because group members learn that some students may already know quite a bit about the assigned topic. Finally, this approach provides opportunities for students to think carefully about how they might find needed information. This kind of preplanning can add an important dimension of efficiency to their work once they actually start responding to the assigned task.

Cooperative Learning Approaches

In recent years, interest in cooperative learning approaches has been growing. It is a technique that emphasizes cooperative goal structures. Cooperative learning approaches follow certain guidelines that distinguish them from just "group work." Johnson and Johnson (2009) identify five characteristics that distinguish cooperative learning from other small-group approaches. The first characteristic is *positive interdependence*. This means that individuals in the group must depend on each other to accomplish a given task. This interdependence might be accomplished through a division of labor, a division of resources, the assignment of different roles to each individual within the group, or the establishment of goals that cannot he reached unless everyone works together.

CRITICAL INCIDENT

COOPERATIVE LEARNING BLUES

I went to this cooperative learning workshop last summer. It was great. There were teachers there who were using cooperative learning in their own classrooms, and they talked us through some of the pitfalls. I left pumped up and ready to try some of the ideas myself.

The speaker was Nora Bennington, a second-year English teacher at J. V. Ortonsen High School. Rene Wu, Nora's former college roommate and herself now also a high school teacher, listened attentively.

"So how has it gone?" Rene asked.

"I got off to a smoother start than I really had expected," Nora responded. "Having those teachers work with us helped a lot. I picked up good tips, and I managed to avoid stupid mistakes I probably would have made otherwise. Also, I decided to start with Learning Together, one of the techniques that isn't a killer when it comes to planning."

Nora continued. "The students were a bit reluctant at first, but now they're really into it. I tend to mix it up a bit. We do Learning Together a while, and then we do a day or two of large-group work. By and large, I think I'd have a revolution on my hands if I went back to using large-group work all the time."

"No real problems, then?" Rene asked.

"Well," replied Nora, "there has been a glitch. I've had one parent on my back constantly since I started using Learning Together. She's come to see me, and she's complained to the principal."

"What's her problem—an unhappy son or daughter, or what?" Rene inquired.

"No, that's not it at all. Her son, Eric, is really bright. He has gotten into the swing of things, and he tells me he likes the small-group work. His mother has a real problem with the grading thing. You know, each student in the group gets the same grade."

"And, I suppose," put in Rene, "that she's convinced that her Eric is doing everybody else's work."

"Yes, that's part of it. But there's a bit more. Every time she calls me I get this lecture about how competitive the world is and that this kind of learning just isn't preparing students for reality. She also makes pointed remarks about how each student has to take the SAT [Scholastic Achievement Test] alone and that his or her personal score is what will be evaluated. She says this small-group work will make our students too dependent on others. She thinks the lazier ones will find somebody bright to carry the load and never really develop their own talents."

"Did they give you any information from the research this summer that you might use as ammunition?" asked Rene.

"As a matter of fact, they did," Nora replied. "And I've shared some of this information with her, but she's not impressed. I think she feels the researchers were people with a vested interested in cooperative learning. Since the results don't square with her biases, she questions the researchers' real motives."

"Rene, I don't mean to ramble on so long about this, but I'm in a quandary. I just don't know how to respond to this person. I hate to abandon a program I believe in and the students like. But I am afraid Eric's mother is going to make my professional life very uncomfortable unless I give up on Learning Together."

■ ■ ■

What does Nora Bennington's commitment to Learning Together tell us about what she thinks is important in teaching and learning? How do her values differ from those of Eric's mother? What should Nora Bennington do next? Can you think of some other arguments that might make sense to Eric's mother? To what extent should other professionals be brought into the picture? What might these people do? Is it fair that one parent's concern might lead Nora to change her instructional program? Or should she change only if a number of parents complain? Do you think the complaints of all parents would be equally weighed by school administrators? If not, which parents would be listened to most? What would you do if you were faced with this situation?

A second characteristic of cooperative learning is its requirement of *face-to-face inter-actions*. In other words, a lesson cannot be properly labeled as an example of cooperative learning if (1) it requires students to be physically separated, (2) each student works completely independently, and (3) the results of this totally independent work is simply a pulling together of these independent efforts into something called a group product. There must be interconnectedness among your students throughout the activity, even though specific individuals may have specialized responsibilities.

The third characteristic is *individual accountability*. This means that each member of the group is held accountable for a particular contribution to the overall effort. The purpose of cooperative learning is to enhance the learning of all of your students, not just a few. Therefore, the term does not apply appropriately to situations when one or two students do all of the work and the rest sit and watch. All class members must he actively involved and appreciate that their contributions are vital to the success of the work of the entire group and that they will be held accountable for them.

The fourth characteristic of cooperative learning is that it requires students to use *social and small-group skills*. Cooperative learning will not work if individuals who lack social skills are placed in a group and asked to cooperate. Students need to have some leadership, decision-making, communication, and conflict management skills in order to have academic success in cooperative learning. While some basic social skill is required, one of the basic purposes of cooperative learning is to teach important social skills.

The fifth characteristic of cooperative learning is *group processing*. Group processing means that members of the group are involved in evaluating the functioning of their group and identifying those behaviors and actions that were helpful and those that were not. They should be involved in formative assessments of their group progress so that all members of the group receive feedback and are assisted in the development of their social and academic skills. Group processing requires that teachers communicate clear objectives about group processing and that time is allocated for the process. This is an important step in helping to maintain a healthy group and in helping students learn and practice collaboration (Johnson & Johnson, 2009).

Researchers have found that cooperative learning lessons result in higher levels of student achievement than do more traditional approaches throughout the grades (Slavin, 2009). The approach has been found to be effective when the learning task involves complex learning and problem-solving, especially for lower-ability students (Woolfolk, 2009). In addition to its value in promoting desirable academic achievement, cooperative learning has also been determined to have a positive impact on social and personal outcomes such as race relations, self-esteem, attitudes toward school, and acceptance of students with disabilities (Slavin, 2009).

The following are some examples of widely used cooperative learning strategies:

- Student Teams–Achievement Divisions
- Teams-Games-Tournaments
- Jigsaw
- Learning Together
- Group investigation

Student Teams–Achievement Divisions

The Johns Hopkins Team Learning Project developed Student Teams–Achievement Divisions (Slavin, 1980). If you are interested in trying a cooperative learning approach, you will find Student Teams–Achievement Divisions to be one of the easiest to implement. It can be used in many different kinds of secondary school classrooms.

General Background   The Student Teams–Achievement Divisions approach involves students in a learning format designed to promote cooperation and active participation by all. The scoring system used gives students a vested personal interest in their own learning *and* in the learning of all group members.

Implementation   Begin by assigning students to learning teams consisting of four or five members. Each team has a mix of high, average, and low achievers. If your class has a diverse ethnic makeup, you want to make an effort to achieve a reasonable ethnic balance among members of each team. You should also try to have a gender mix on each team that closely approximates the percentages of males and females in the whole class.

The first step in the process requires nothing out of the ordinary. New content can be presented to a class using the traditional direct instruction approach. At the conclusion of the presentation of new content, however, each team is provided with task sheets related to the content and that you have prepared. The task sheets provide students with directions regarding what they are to do, and they are designed to help all group member work with each other in completing the sheets. Give students directions that specify the responsibilities of team members and ensure that each student understands the task. Students then work as a team until they are convinced that every member understands and has mastered the content on the task sheet. They notify you that they are ready to take the summative assessment. The students are then tested on the material. During testing, team members may not help one another.

Use a special system of scoring designed to emphasize the importance of cooperation and the active participation of all group members. This system yields test scores for each student; each student's score also plays a role in the process used to develop a score for the entire team. An individual team member, depending on how well he or she does on the test, may add from 0 to 10 points to a team score. To determine how much an individual student's score will add to the team score, that student's performance on the test is compared to an average (or base score) of his or her previous performances. For example, suppose one of the students in the group has a previous average of 50% correct. On this test, the same student had an average of 55%. The difference between 55% and 50% (base score and this summative test score) is 5. Five points are added to the team score as a result of this student's performance. The points for all team members are added together to form a team score. The team that has the most points or the most improvement over their base scores is the winning team.

Using this point structure makes it important that all team members work together to help every team member improve and add to the team score. Note that they inform the teacher when they believe they are ready to take the summative test. This gives them some input and helps them make sure that all team members have a good understanding of the material before taking the test.

Each student may provide a maximum of 10 points to the overall team score. This 10-point maximum can be earned in two ways. Ten points are awarded if the student scores 10 or more points higher on the present test compared with her or his base score. Ten points are also awarded for any perfect score on the test, regardless of the student's average. This is an incentive for those students in the group who enter with an average of over 90%. They cannot ignore their learning while they help others in the group.

Box 11-1 illustrates an array of scores for one group of students in a biology class where a Student Teams–Achievement Divisions approach was used. Notice that Joyce R., who received the lowest grade on the quiz, still contributed the maximum of 10 points to the total group score because her quiz score of 55 was significantly higher than her base score of 40.

Student Teams–Achievement Divisions encourages lower-ability students. These students have an incentive to do as well as they can. Even though their individual scores

---

Box 11-1

Example of a Group's Score in Student Teams–Achievement Divisions

Student	Base Score	Quiz Score	Team Points
Raoul A.	57	64	7
LaShandra C.	63	60	0
Joyce R.	40	55	10
LaRue T.	83	88	5
Samuel W.	75	95	10

Team Total = 32

may not be high, they can make important contributions to the total score of their team. Higher-achieving students are encouraged to help lower-achieving members of their group because all group members benefit when they exceed the expectations reflected in their base scores. Each member of a group has a stake in the learning of every other member. Thus, every student has a reason to want to help all group members to learn, and improvement of all team members becomes the goal as team members strive to increase overall team scores. If you wish, you can arrange for some special recognition for high-scoring teams at the end of a regular grading period.

Debriefing   During the debriefing, focus on the quality of the interactions you observed among individual team members. You can share team scores with the group, making a special point of emphasizing how the contribution of every group member contributed to the group's overall score. The debriefing phase also gives you an opportunity to single out for special recognition those students who did very well themselves and who you observed to be especially helpful in assisting others to master the content.

Teams-Games-Tournaments

The Johns Hopkins Group also developed Teams-Games-Tournaments (Slavin, 1980). The two approaches have some similarities. Both place a major emphasis on both group and individual accountability. They differ, however, in how they approach these two dimensions of cooperative learning. Teams-Games-Tournaments does not require the establishment of a baseline for all students. However, it does require knowledge of the ability level of all students. Teams-Games-Tournaments also approaches the summative evaluation of student learning in a different way and can involve more direct competition between students.

General Background   Teams-Games-Tournaments is basically an extension of Student Teams–Achievement Divisions. Students are organized into heterogeneous groups that contain students at a variety of ability levels. However, the determination of individual contributions to team scores is the result of participation in academic tournaments.

Implementation   Your first task is to assign each student to become a member of a four- to six-member team. To the extent possible, each team should include students representing both males and females and students who vary in their ethnicity and ability levels. Teams-Games-Tournaments can begin much like Student Teams–Achievement Divisions. New material can be presented to the students in a large-group setting. Then the teams spend time studying the material together. Again, their role is to try and make sure that all of the team members have mastered the content. Much like Student Teams–Achievement Divisions, team scores are calculated to determine winning teams. However, the manner in which individuals contribute to their team score is different. In Teams-Games-Tournaments, there is no need for a baseline score. Members of teams contribute to team scores by how well they do in the tournament against others at a similar ability level. Therefore, Teams-Games-Tournaments can be implemented based on a relatively simple diagnosis of student ability levels rather than calculating an average or base score for every student. At the end of the allocated time for learning the new material, a tournament is held and the scores of individuals of similar ability levels are compared. The team that gains the most points from the ability level competitions is the winner.

The academic tournaments can take a couple of forms. One form is that students participate in a public contest much like the *Jeopardy* game show. The other is that they complete a paper-and-pencil summative assessment. The format for the public tournament requires you to reorganize students from the individual teams into tournament groups. Three students of approximately the same ability level, each from a different team, constitute a complete tournament group. Once you have made student assignments to tournament groups, the next step is for each group to sit at its own table. For example, if you have 27 students in your class, you will need nine tables to accommodate each of the groups of three. Because students have been organized into tournament groups according to ability level, this means you will have nine different gradations of ability levels represented in your nine groups, ranging from a group that includes the three highest-ability students to the group including the three lowest-ability students.

Next, questions are asked of students placed in the tournament groups. A practical way of managing the tournament is to ask the question and then publicly direct it to one of the tournament groups. Exercise care to make sure that all tournament groups are called on numerous times. Points are awarded to individuals in the tournament groups when they answer the question correctly. It is not necessary that all groups receive the same number of questions. For example, the group with the highest achieving group might have more questions addressed to their group than is addressed to the lowest achieving group. At the conclusion of the tournament, the student at each table who answered the most questions correctly is awarded three team points, the second highest scoring student is awarded two team points, and the lowest scoring student is awarded one team point. The team that gathers the highest number of points is the winner of the tournament.

An alternative to the public tournament is to present the students in the groups with a test or a summative assessment. The easiest route would be to present the same assessment to all students in all groups. However, that might not provide the range of scores that are desired. For example, an assessment that might help distinguish between the learning of the students in the highest tournament group might be too difficult for the lowest tournament group. Therefore, you might need to prepare a couple of variations of the summative assessment at different levels.

The summative assessment does have the advantage of taking the pressure off some students who are fearful or embarrassed about responding in front of the entire class. However, it requires more teacher time to prepare fair assessments that can be used to distinguish between members in a tournament group.

After a few tournament rounds, it is often wise to reassess student performance and reassign students to different tournament groups based on how they have performed. For example, if a particular student won the tournament round three or more times, that student would be moved up to the next higher group. A student who consistently scored at the bottom of the tournament group would be moved down to the next tournament group. When this is done, it might require a reassignment of teams so that each initial team has only one student in each tournament group.

The Teams-Games-Tournament approach combines cooperative and competitive activities. You will find that this activity develops your students' abilities to work actively in groups because the design of the approach makes it personally advantageous for individual group members to help others to master the assigned content. In addition, the format tends to keep competition among students at approximately the same level, and your students will tend to feel the reward system is fair. Teachers who have used Teams-Games-Tournaments report that even reluctant learners become interested in school when the approach is used (Slavin, 1990).

Debriefing   During the debriefing phase, focus on the processes that the students have followed in their groups to learn content. You need to emphasize the importance of mutually supportive, collaborative behavior. Finally, the debriefing phase gives you an opportunity to respond to students' questions.

Jigsaw

Jigsaw is a cooperative learning method that can be used in many different kinds of secondary school subjects. Because of the structure, it is a favorite among secondary teachers. This approach is appropriate when you want to teach a topic that can be divided conveniently into several major components. It is also helpful if information related to each component can be organized under a common set of headings. For example, if you were teaching a unit on Latin America in a geography course, the components might be the individual countries. Information about each country might be organized under the common headings of (1) physical features, (2) population size and ethnic makeup of the population, (3) major languages, (4) major economic activities, and (5) education and literacy.

Most of us are aware that we learn more about a topic when we have to teach it to someone. Teachers often report how much more they learned and retained information when they had to teach it. Jigsaw takes advantage of that finding by requiring each student to become a teacher.

General Background   Prepare for a jigsaw lesson by identifying a topic and dividing the content into major headings or subtopics. Each heading becomes the focus for a group of students in the classroom.

Implementation   Suppose you are teaching English to a class of 30 students and have decided your focus topic will be the following: A Comparison of the Literary Work of Selected 20th-Century American Writers. You may decide to have students gather information related to these major writers: (1) Theodore Dreiser, (2) Eudora Welty, (3) F. Scott Fitzgerald, (4) Ernest Hemingway (5) Willa Cather, and (6) Joyce Carol Oates. Your next step is to divide students into five *home teams*, each of which has six members. Each home team assigns one student to become an "expert" in information related to one writer. In this situation, each six-person team would include one Theodore Dreiser expert, one Eudora Welty expert, one F. Scott Fitzgerald expert, one Ernest Hemingway expert, one Willa Cather expert, and one Joyce Carol Oates expert.

Once individual experts for each of the home teams have been identified, each of these experts meets with the experts from the other home teams to learn about their topic. For example, all of the Theodore Dreiser experts meet together. (There will be five of these experts, one from each of the five home teams consisting of six members.) Members of each expert group will be provided with resources focusing on one specific writer. The resources could include videos, websites, books, and even teacher presentations. The role is for the members of each expert group to work together and learn as much as possible about their writer. The teacher can facilitate the work by providing worksheets or study guides that assist the students in their learning. Box 11-2 provides an example of how home teams and expert groups can be organized.

When the expert teams have finished their cooperative study on a particular writer, they return to their home teams. The experts then have the task of teaching what they have learned about their writer to the home team. In this way, members of each home team receive information about all six authors. Because students know you will be giving everyone a criterion test at the end of the lesson, all students in the home teams have an incentive to listen carefully to presentations by experts related to each writer and to insist that the experts share all their information.

Some changes in the original Jigsaw has led to what is called Jigsaw II. This approach incorporates the group reward structure of Teams-Games-Tournaments and Student Teams–Achievement Divisions. Individual student improvement on a summative assessment results in points awarded to the home team.

A variation of the Jigsaw described above could be for the class to have only three writers they need to learn about; then two students from each home team could be assigned to become experts on a particular writer. This would require some additional time for the experts to work together, but it could also compensate for the lack of ability on the part of a particular student to become an expert or if a student was absent for some of the expert group time.

Jigsaw requires you to monitor the work of expert teams carefully. Members of each expert group must understand all of the necessary information. Each expert group student must know the information well enough to pass it along successfully to members of his or

Box 11-2　Focus: A Comparison of the Literary Work of Selected American Writers

Home Teams

Team 1
Anna (Dreiser)
Rodney (Welty)
Juan (Fitzgerald)
LaRue (Hemingway)
Spencer (Cather)
Agnes (Oates)

Team 2
Paul (Dreiser)
Sondra (Welty)
Norman (Fitzgerald)
Sally (Hemingway)
Nora (Cather)
Raoul (Oates)

Team 3
Yu (Dreiser)
Monica (Welty)
Lee (Fitzgerald)
Helmut (Hemingway)
Rene (Cather)
Roy (Oates)

Team 4
Sarana (Dreiser)
Ming (Welty)
Kara (Fitzgerald)
Renaldo (Hemingway)
Price (Cather)
Travis (Oates)

Team 5
Tasha (Dreiser)
Karl (Welty)
Courtney (Fitzgerald)
Toshi (Hemingway)
Rocky (Cather)
Cole (Oates)

Expert Groups

Dreiser Group
Anna
Paul
Yu
Sarana
Tasha

Welty Group
Rodney
Sondra
Monica
Ming
Karl

Fitzgerald Group
Juan
Norman
Lee
Kara
Courtney

Hemingway Group
LaRue
Sally
Helmut
Renaldo
Toshi

Cather Group
Spencer
Nora
Rene
Price
Rocky

Oates Group
Agnes
Raoul
Roy
Travis
Cole

her home team. If working in an expert group requires multiple days of group work, one potential problem is the handling of student absences. This could harm the ability of the home team to obtain this important information. If this occurs, you must step in to provide the missing information to the home team that is affected.

Debriefing　Debrief students following their participation in a jigsaw lesson by organizing them into a single whole-class group. In your discussion, review all information that has been introduced. Encourage your students to take notes during the discussion to record any new information that did not come out during their own group meetings. The debriefing session gives your students an opportunity to fill in any remaining information gaps. In addition, the session allows you to engage students in analytical thinking that will help them make interpretations beyond a simple knowledge-level understanding of the new content.

Learning Together

Some cooperative learning approaches include strong incentives for each student to help all others assigned to the same small group. Learning Together places an especially high premium on students helping students (Johnson, Johnson, Holubec, & Roy, 1984).

General Background   Learning Together differs considerably from the previous cooperative learning approaches in how positive interdependence and individual accountability is applied. In the previous approaches, individual accomplishments contributed to group success. In Learning Together, a team-generated product is the outcome. Because a team product is the end product, Learning Together also places greater emphasis on heterogeneous grouping and on team building than do the other approaches (Slavin, Chamberlain, & Hurley, 2009). Students with different skills and abilities are very important so that the group product combines these abilities into a product that is better than could be expected by any one individual. Unlike Jigsaw, Learning Together does not require content that can be easily broken down into a set of parts or subtopics. Rather, it requires a group product that includes skills such as art, music, creative writing, etc.

Implementation   Your first step in implementing a Learning Together lesson is to organize students into teams that include a cross section of ability levels and talents. You give each team a task or project to complete. Individuals on each team assume responsibility for completing part of the overall project that is compatible with their own interests and abilities. The idea is to maximize the strengths of individual students to get a better overall group effort. One basis for grouping might be the different types of intelligence as defined by Gardner (1999). Each group might include a student with high visual intelligence, another with good logical-mathematical intelligence, a third with musical-artistic intelligence, and a fourth with bodily-kinesthetic intelligence. The basic point is that you need to define tasks that require considerable diversity and that the basis for grouping should be the nature of the task. Roles of individuals in Learning Together teams can vary. For example, if the final product is to be a short play, one or more students might assume roles such as (1) coach and production manager, (2) writer, (3) information seeker, (4) group artist, (5) evaluator-critic, and (6) recorder.

Each team is responsible for gathering the information and materials needed to complete its assigned task or project. The final assessment is based on the quality of the team's performance. Each student on a team receives the same grade. This encourages individuals to pool their talents so that each student's work adds the greatest possible contribution to the effort. Individual accountability can be applied by having individuals, group members, and the teacher evaluate the contributions of each individual to the final group product.

Is it appropriate to give each team member the same grade? This issue has been researched. Johnson and Johnson (1985) report that, although students tend to favor competitive grading before they engage in cooperative tasks, after they have completed a cooperative learning project, they commit to the idea that awarding every group member the same grade is a fair approach. Many teachers give students the opportunity to complete a group evaluation form. The evaluation form gives students the opportunity to self-evaluate as well as evaluate each member of their group.

Debriefing   During this stage, work with students to help them focus on the processes they used in their groups to respond to their assigned task. Ask questions that will encourage your students to think about what they learned from their experience and what they might do differently another time to improve the levels of understanding of all group members.

Group Investigation

You can use group investigation when you want to give your students considerable freedom in deciding what they are going to do and how they are going to do it. You do not assign students to specific groups as you do when you are getting students involved in Jigsaw or Learning Together lessons. Instead, encourage them to form groups that include members of their own choosing. Ensure that each group represents the diversity present in the class (Leighton, 1994). You accomplish this by giving students some guidelines in the beginning, such as "I don't want to see an all-girls group or an all-boys group. Try to make your group as diverse as possible."

General Background   The basic ideas incorporated in the group investigation technique can be traced to the philosophical ideas of the eminent American educational philosopher, John Dewey (Joyce & Weil, 1996). However, the specific group investigation model was developed by Thelen and then refined by Sharan (Slavin, Chamberlain, & Hurley, 2009). In this approach a topic or unit is studied by the whole class. Students organize themselves into democratic problem-solving groups and decide on one or two subtopics from the unit that they want to investigate. Some types of group investigation are called group inquiry.

Members of each small group follow the methods of inquiry as they investigate their subtopic of interest. (For more information about inquiry instruction, see Chapter 10.) This approach is designed to help your students learn how to define a task, search for and synthesize information, and present it in an interesting and coherent way to others. Because interaction and trust among group members is critical to the success of group investigation and because each member has to assume considerable responsibility, use this approach with students who have already demonstrated some skill in small-group work and who trust one another (Leighton, 1994).

Implementation   Begin by presenting your students with a broad topic, question, or puzzling event. For example, if you are teaching science, you can pose questions to your students related to how pollution in the local region might be reduced. If you are teaching world history, you can ask students to consider what happened to the Maya civilization of Central America. If you are teaching English, you can ask students a question involving common literary themes. Sometimes, you may decide to leave the choice of a focus topic to the members of your class (Leighton, 1994).

Once a focus has been established, students think about the topic individually, list questions they have, and develop speculative hypotheses that might explain the inquiry question. For example, if you are teaching science, you might ask, What can be done to reduce pollution in our region? If you are teaching social studies, you might inquire, Why did the Mayans seem to just lay down their tools and walk away from the great cities they had created? If you are teaching English, you might ask, Why do you think these themes have been written about by many writers at different times? Are there other themes that you would expect to find in literature?

You organize students into small groups to develop responses to your questions. After they have had adequate time to generate some responses, reassemble the students as a whole class. Ask students in each small group to state the group's conclusions. List important questions, hypotheses, perspectives, and/or issues that arise out of this phase of the lesson on the board or on an overhead transparency. Next, work with the class to organize responses into categories. These categories become the topics for the group investigations that comprise the next phase of the lesson.

At this point, organize learning teams based on students' interests. To do this, ask your students to look at the focus questions and decide which one they want to explore. People with similar interests join together and form a group. If more than one group wants to pursue a single question or topic, you can divide it into several parts, with one group assigned to work on each. Each group meets, and group members begin working on the topic they have selected. As they begin, you need to help them understand the focus of their work, list important questions, and identify some resources they need to complete their investigation. As they begin, members of groups have to decide what each person is going to do and

More from the Web

COOPERATIVE LEARNING IN THE SECONDARY SCHOOL

http://www.ncela.gwu.edu/

As the title suggests, material at this site provides specific information about implementing cooperative learning at the secondary school level. A search of the site will provide excellent articles and ideas related to issues such as (1) working with culturally and linguistically diverse students, (2) promoting students' social development, (3) maximizing content learning, and (4) implementing successful cooperative learning lessons.

JIGSAW

http://www.jigsaw.org

This website features basic descriptive information about the Jigsaw method. You will find an overview, a description of steps, and useful tips. Links to additional sites will give you more information.

GENERAL INFORMATION

Two websites feature information organized by individuals long associated with cooperative learning.

http://www.co-operation.org

This website was created by Johnson and Johnson and is maintained by the Cooperative Learning Center of the University of Minnesota.

http://www.cooperativelearning.com

This website is sponsored by Spencer Kagan and his associates. It provides helpful, free information as well as products that you can purchase.

how group findings will be presented to the rest of the class. In practice, different students end up doing different tasks. Some may seek the data, others may organize it, and still others may organize findings for the group's presentation to the whole class.

Debriefing   When groups have had sufficient time to pursue their inquiry, they present their findings to the entire class. Again, the major evaluation is an evaluation of the team, with a primary focus on team building and the group processes rather than on "right" answers. Individual accountability is determined through self-evaluation, team member evaluation, and teacher evaluation of individual contributions.

Classroom Debate

Classroom debates are organized differently than the familiar high school debating tournament. You can use them when teaching a variety of subjects, and you can adapt them to fit different time periods. Classroom debates feature two teams of students who prepare positions on different sides of an issue. You can structure these in various ways. Here is one format that many secondary teachers have found useful.

Assign as follows:

- Three students to the pro position
- Three students to the con position
- One student to the role of critic

Ask the three students on the pro side to gather as much information as possible that supports a proposal. Direct the students on the con side to gather as much evidence as possible to attack the position. Ask the critic to learn as much as possible about both sides of the issue and to ask questions toward the end of the debate that will highlight weaknesses of both positions. Each member of the team is expected to participate actively.

In preparation for the activity, select an issue that clearly has two sides. For example, if you are teaching English, you might choose an issue related to a selection of literature such as the consistency of actions taken by one or more of the main characters. If you are teaching a social studies class, your focus issue might center on a historic event or on actions of some historic figure. If you are teaching science, you might choose a topic related to a threat to the environment.

Once you have identified a topic, you need to gather as much support material as possible for the students to use as they prepare for the debate. You may need to allow several class periods for them to develop an adequate background on aspects of the topic that will be considered during the actual debate. You need to do considerable monitoring during the preparation phase to ensure that students are doing the necessary work to build the knowledge backgrounds they will need to make a credible case as they participate in the debate.

When the teams are ready, you can use a sequence of steps such as those listed here. This example presumes that the debate is completed during a single, 50-minute class period.

1. Each member of each team speaks for two minutes. Pro and con speakers alternate. Approximate time: 12 minutes.

2. Members of the pro team cross-examine members of the con team for a team total not to exceed six minutes. The members of the con team cross-examine the pro team for a team total of not more than six minutes. Approximate time: 12 minutes.

3. Members of each team make a final statement. The total time for each team is not to exceed three minutes. Approximate time: 6 minutes.

4. The critic questions members of both teams. His or her questions are directed to the team as a whole or to individual team members. The critic's purpose is to ask probing questions that point out the weak spots of the arguments. Approximate time: 8 minutes.

5. The whole class votes to determine a winner. Approximate time: 2 minutes.

6. You debrief the whole class. Your comments should be as supportive as possible and should highlight the important issues. During the debriefing stage, you might ask questions such as the following:

- What were the best arguments you heard?
- What made these arguments effective?
- What other points would you have brought up?
- What are some other questions the critic might have asked?

Classroom debates often generate high levels of student interest. They can help you teach students important skills such as cooperating, speaking in front of a group, mustering evidence to support a position, listening, and learning how to analyze and synthesize information.

Cooperative Learning in Diverse Classrooms

In an age of reform such as we are experiencing, the emphasis on standardized testing has stimulated much debate about the applicability of cooperative learning in today's classrooms. Although some conservative educators (e.g., E. D. Hirsch) have questioned the effectiveness of this model, Izumi and Coburn (2001) believe that it enhances student motivation and learning. Lasley, Matczynski, and Rowley (2002) assert that "cooperative learning is not a fad or a fashionable idea that suits the fancy of the intellectual elite. Cooperative learning is effective because the undergirding tenets of the strategy are good for all students" (p. 323).

FOR YOUR PORTFOLIO

1. What materials, ideas you learned in this chapter related to small-group and cooperative learning, will you include as evidence in your portfolio? Select up to three items of information to be included in your portfolio. Number them 1, 2, and 3.

2. Think about why you selected these materials for your portfolio. Consider issues such as the following in your response:

   ■ The specific purposes to which this information can be put when you plan, deliver, and assess the impact of your instruction

   ■ The compatibility of the information with your own priorities and values

   ■ The contributions this information can make to your personal development as a teacher

   ■ The factors that led you to include this material as opposed to some alternatives you considered

3. Prepare a written reflection in which you analyze the decision-making process you followed. Also, mention the Interstate New Teacher Assessment and Support Consortium (INTASC) standard(s) to which your selected material relates. First complete the chart below.

MATERIALS YOU SELECTED AND THE INTASC STANDARDS

Put a check under those INTASC standard numbers to which the evidence you have selected applies. (Refer to Chapter 1 for more detailed information about INTASC.)

INTASC Standards

Item of Evidence Number	S-1	S-2	S-3	S-4	S-5	S-6	S-7	S-8	S-9	S-10
1										
2										
3										

The challenge for you is to implement cooperative learning in a thoughtful manner and differentiate tasks in an effort to personalize learning for all students. By grouping students heterogeneously, differentiating tasks by complexity and quantity, and varying criteria for success, all students can learn something new and contribute to the identified learning goals (Schniedewind & Davidson, 2000).

The key to success in your classroom is to use a variety of teaching strategies. Select the appropriate cooperative learning approach for the students you teach and combine cooperative learning with other strategies discussed elsewhere in this text. All students will then have a chance to succeed.

Key Ideas in Summary

■ Small-group learning capitalizes on students' interests in working together. It promotes supportive student-to-student interaction and encourages students to learn from one another.

■ Success in small-group work is not automatic. To profit from this kind of instruction, students must be prepared. Conditions that facilitate group work include teaching students necessary skills for group work, understanding the peer group dynamics at work in a particular group, creating a climate so students respect and trust one another, decreasing the fear of failure, and implementing cooperative goal structures.

■ It is useful to introduce small-group work gradually by first involving students in some introductory activities that teach them prerequisite skills and the necessary attitudes of respect and trust.

- *Cooperative learning* is a general term used to describe small-group learning techniques that base each student's evaluation, in part, on the overall level of performance of his or her group. Researchers have found cooperative learning approaches to (1) have positive effects on students' self-esteem, (2) generate peer support for academic achievement, (3) increase the amount of time students spend on academic tasks, (4) improve students' attitudes toward the class where cooperative learning has been used, and (5) help students develop more positive attitudes toward others in their class.

- There are many cooperative learning techniques. Among those that are widely used are (1) Student Teams–Achievement Divisions, (2) Teams-Games-Tournaments, (3) Jigsaw, (4) Learning Together, and (5) group investigation.

- Student Teams–Achievement Divisions and Teams-Games-Tournaments are similar because they feature some competitive elements. However, the competition is between and among teams. There is an attempt to make competitive aspects fair by ensuring that they take place between and among individuals of similar ability levels.

- Jigsaw is best used for content that can be broken into separate but related components. Jigsaw involves expert groups, where students learn about one aspect of the topic, and home teams, where those from the expert group teach the rest of their group about their specialty topic.

- Learning Together is best used when the task requires a diversity of skills. Students are grouped together, and each student is given a specific role in the group that best matches his or her talents. The group then produces a product that is generated through the collective work of all group members.

- In group investigation, students are presented with an opportunity to select a general focus issue, problem, or topic. Individual students join with others to pursue an investigation of a topic of common interest. Findings ultimately are shared with members of the entire class. Two of the purposes of group investigation are (1) developing higher-level thinking skills such as how to learn and (2) synthesizing large quantities of information. Supporters of this approach argue that what students learn about the processes of productive inquiry is just as important as what they learn about the content they study.

Reflections

1. What are some variables that you would consider in deciding whether to use small-group learning in your classroom?

2. What are some conditions you need to create before you can expect small-group or cooperative learning approaches to function well in your classroom?

3. What do you think you need to learn in order to implement small-group techniques successfully in your classroom?

4. What distinguishes an educational simulation from a game?

5. What is the difference between a competitive goal structure and an individualistic goal structure, and why is this distinction important when you are considering using a cooperative learning approach?

6. Some cooperative learning approaches award the same grade to each member of a group. How do you feel about this practice?

7. Can you think of examples from your own experience when a group activity was tried and failed because characteristics of the classroom environment did not support this approach? What could have been done to change these circumstances?

8. What do you see as the strengths of the various cooperative learning approaches?

Learning Extensions

1. Observe a secondary school classroom. What opportunities do you see for implementing small-group or cooperative learning approaches? What might be some challenges that teachers you observed would face in implementing these kinds of lessons?

2. Using content in this chapter as a focus, organize a Jigsaw scheme that members of your class can use to review chapter content. Share your design with your course instructor and, if he or she agrees, implement the technique during one of your class sessions.

3. Identify a topic in your subject area that could be the focus for a group investigation. Break the broad topic into some specific questions or subtopics that might be used as a research focus for different groups.

References

Frey, N., Fisher, D., & Everlove, S. (2009). *Productive group work: How to engage students, build teamwork and promote understanding.* Alexandria, VA: Association for Supervision and Curriculum Development.

Izumi, L. T., & Coburn, K. G. (2001). *Facing the classroom challenge.* San Francisco: Pacific Research Institute for Public Policy.

Johnson, D. W., & Johnson, R. T. (2009). Implementing cooperative learning in social studies classroom: A conceptual framework and alternative approaches. In Stahl, R. J., VanSickle, R. L., & Stahl, N. N. (Eds.), *Cooperative learning in the social studies classroom* (2nd ed., pp. 41–50). Silver Springs, MD: National Council for the Social Studies.

Johnson, D. W., Johnson, R. T., Holubec, F., & Roy, P. (1984). *Circles of learning: Cooperation in the classroom.*

Alexandria, VA: Association for Supervision and Curriculum Development.

Johnson, R. T., & Johnson, D. W. (1985, April). *Structuring conflict in science classrooms.* Paper presented at the annual meeting of the National Association of Research in Science Teaching, French Lick, IN.

Joyce, B., & Weil, M. (1996). *Models of teaching* (5th ed.). Boston: Allyn & Bacon.

Kagan, S. (1989). The structural approach to cooperative learning. *Educational Leadership, 47*(4), 13.

Lasley, T. J., II, Matczynski, T. J., & Rowley, J. B. (2002). *Instructional models: Strategies for teaching in a diverse society.* Belmont, CA: Wadsworth.

Leighton, M. (1994). Cooperative learning. In J. Cooper (Ed.), *Classroom teaching skills* (5th ed., pp. 282–325).

Lexington, MA: D.C. Heath.

Schniedewind, N., & Davidson, E. (2000). Differentiating cooperative learning. *Educational Leadership, 58*(1), 24–27.

Slavin, R. E. (1980). *Using student team learning.* Baltimore: Johns Hopkins Team Learning Project, Center for Social Organization of the Schools, Johns Hopkins University.

Slavin, R. E. (1990). *Cooperative learning: Theory, research, and practice.* Upper Saddle River; NJ: Prentice Hall.

Slavin, R. (2009). *Educational psychology* (9th ed.). Boston: Allyn & Bacon.

Slavin, R. E., Chamberlain, A. M., & Hurley, E. A. (2009). Cooperative learning is a powerful way to balance the social and the studies. In R. J. Stahl, R. L. VanSickle, & N. N. Stahl (Eds.), *Cooperative learning in the social studies classroom* (2nd ed., pp. 59–65). Silver Springs, MD: National Council for the Social Studies.

Stahl, R. J., & VanSickle, R. L. (2009). Using optimal cooperative learning for effective social study in the classroom. In R. J. Stahl, R. L. VanSickle, & N. N. Stahl (Eds.), *Cooperative learning in the social studies classroom* (2nd ed., pp. 9–21). Silver Springs, MD: National Council for the Social Studies.

Stahl, R. J., VanSickle, R. L., & Stahl, N. N. (2009). *Cooperative learning in the social studies classroom* (2nd ed.). Silver Springs, MD: National Council for the Social Studies.

Woolfolk, A. (2009). *Educational psychology* (7th ed.). Boston: Allyn & Bacon.

Reading Across the Curriculum

Objectives

This chapter will help you

- identify procedures that enhance reading development in content classrooms

- identify different reading levels present among students in content classrooms

- define readability

- provide procedures to assess the readability of text material

- identify a framework for content reading instruction

- identify strategies appropriate for the preparation phase, the assistance phase, and the reflection phase of the reading framework

- discuss the importance of vocabulary development in enhancing reading improvement

- discuss the importance of the reading-writing connection

- give you ideas for supplementing textbooks with trade books

Carolyn A. McKeone/Photo Researchers ($$)

Graphic Organizer: Chapter 12

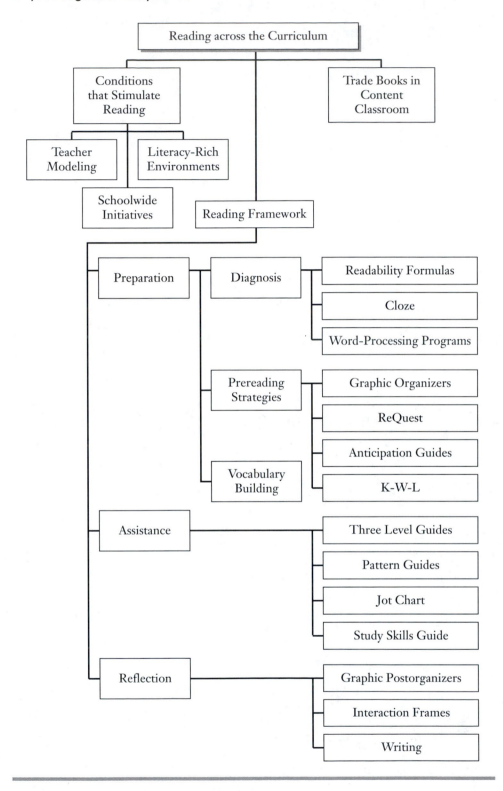

Introduction

Most secondary school teachers view themselves as experts in the subjects they teach. Their enthusiasm for their subjects may lead them to overlook one of the essentials for success in the classroom—students' ability to read and understand the material. If teachers expect students to develop desired levels of competence, they must consider how they learn through reading. Postman (1979) pointed out the important link between reading and competence in school content areas when he said, "Biology is not plants and animals. It is language about plants and animals. History is not events. It is language describing and interpreting events" (p. 165).

Middle school and high school teachers charged with teaching content material often take the reading abilities of their students for granted. They assume that the students have learned the requisite reading skills in the elementary grades. However, this is often not the case. Even the most talented students occasionally have difficulty with some of the text material. Some students find reading so difficult that they do not succeed in many of their school tasks. Although most of them can decode, they need explicit instruction in how to use specific strategies that help them comprehend text in the content classroom (Donahue, 2003).

This chapter will acquaint you with some of the key concepts associated with teaching reading in the content areas. It cannot, however, take the place of a class that concentrates strictly on teaching this content. The references section at the end of this chapter provides information about additional reading to enhance your knowledge about this subject.

Creating Conditions to Stimulate Reading

As a teacher in a content classroom, you have an obligation to help students learn to read and comprehend the material presented in class. Part of this obligation requires that you create conditions that support reading. First, you must model reading. Students should see you reading books, newspapers, and magazines and deriving personal enjoyment from this activity. They should also hear you read aloud on occasion. Literacy expert Janet Allen (2002) recounts sitting in a 10th-grade classroom listening to the teacher reading aloud to her students: "No one was sleeping, no one was whispering or writing notes, no one was applying makeup, and no one interrupted the reading for a bathroom pass" (p. 1). The power of language, and a book that students enjoyed, had them mesmerized.

Second, you must create a literacy-rich environment by providing high-interest reading material in your classroom. Jim Burke (2000) says that when you walk into a classroom that honors reading, it is obvious immediately. The walls, the shelves, the conversations are all literacy-rich.

Where do you start, especially in today's packed classrooms? Perhaps a corner of the classroom or a special table can be set aside for reading material. Consider including all genres of young adult literature, as well as state department of motor vehicles booklets and sports stories. When students have completed assignments or when they have some available time (perhaps before or after school), invite them to read these books. One football coach, for example, stimulated an interest in reading by making copies of the sports section of several major newspapers available on a daily basis. Students, both athletes and nonathletes, were invited to stop by his office in the morning to read the newspapers. This provided a lively forum for discussion for many students who did not normally spend much time reading.

In many communities, newspaper publishers will make newspapers available for a class of students. They might also have materials around which you can build content lessons using newspapers. Many teachers have found these newspapers and related materials beneficial in developing students' interest in reading.

Finally, consider a schoolwide initiative that promotes reading and writing across the curriculum. Many schools have adopted the sustained silent reading (SSR) model that sets aside time each day (or sometimes once a week) for everyone to read. Everyone, including the teacher, the principal, the janitor, and the students stop whatever they are doing and read something of interest to them. Although this has been most common in middle schools, high schools are beginning to adopt the model in an effort to increase literacy rates for their students.

In addition to establishing basic conditions that emphasize reading, you can also use a variety of reading strategies to increase the probability of students' learning through reading. The following sections will introduce some of the approaches that secondary school teachers have found useful.

A Reading Framework

Many literacy experts (e.g., Herber, 1978; Singer & Donlan, 1985; Vaughn & Estes, 1986; Vacca & Vacca, 2002; Richardson, Morgan, & Fleener, 2009) have identified frameworks that can assist in planning content reading instruction. You may see these identified as pre-reading, during-reading, and after-reading phases or as preparation, assistance, and reflection phases. No matter what the label, the framework provides the components of an active and successful reading process in your content classroom. These frameworks are based on three assumptions:

1. The students must be ready to learn. Therefore, you must prepare the students before they read.

2. The students must be guided through the reading process in order to enhance comprehension. As a teacher, you must provide activities that assist them as they read.

3. The students must have an opportunity to review and reflect on what has been read. As a teacher, you must design opportunities for students to help them retain important ideas and concepts (Richardson, Morgan, & Fleener, 2009).

For our purposes in this text, we will use the framework suggested by Richardson, Morgan, and Fleener (2009): preparation, assistance, and reflection.

Preparation Phase

The most important, yet most often overlooked, phase of the reading framework is the preparation phase: the time you spend preparing students for reading text material. This phase actually begins when you assess text material and subsequently the students themselves.

One of the major problems teachers face in all subjects is the match between the material and the skill level of the students. Even when you have a variety of resources available, you usually have one major text that plays a dominant role. The inability of some students to read the text may create serious difficulties for you as you attempt to provide appropriate text material. To address this issue, you must begin by diagnosing the reading proficiency levels of your students and comparing these to the difficulty levels of available course reading materials.

Diagnosing Reading Levels   A variety of activities can assist you in determining the reading levels of your students. One such activity is the cloze. In the cloze, a passage is cut up (words are omitted) so that students can fill it in. Cloze as we use it today was designed by William Taylor in 1953 (Taylor, 1953) to determine the readability of material for diverse readers. The procedure is based on the assumption that, as readers, we rely on our prior knowledge to make sense out of the whole when only parts are available. The following steps will help you construct a cloze test for your classroom.

1. Select a text passage of 250 to 300 words from material that you plan to assign for reading.

2. Leave the first sentence intact, then consistently delete every fifth word throughout the passage until you reach 50 deletions. Make all blanks a uniform length.

3. Leave the last sentence intact.

4. Write precise directions for the students. Inform them that they should work alone. Make sure they understand that this test does not affect their grade. It is important to discuss these directions with the students.

5. Count the number of correct responses for each student and multiply by 2 (unless you have chosen more or less than 50 omissions). Count as correct only exact words. Do not count synonyms. Scoring criteria have already taken this into account.

6. Use the scores to determine whether students are reading at an independent level (above 60%), an instructional level (40 to 60%) or a frustration level (below 40%).

Independent reading level   Students are functioning at the independent reading level when there is a good match between their reading skill and the difficulty of the material being read. They understand what the author is trying to communicate, they are familiar with the vocabulary, and they easily understand concepts without outside assistance. This level is best suited for independent study or homework assignments. If students are unable to read the material at the independent level, the time they spend reading the material will be unproductive. Students with a history of academic difficulty may give up if presented with an assignment that is beyond the independent reading level.

Instructional reading level   Students functioning at the instructional reading level do not have the necessary prior knowledge or reading skill to completely understand the material and concepts contained in the material. However, these individuals are able to comprehend the material when provided with some assistance. Material at this level is appropriate for classroom use when some assistance is available. For example, in-class reading assignments may feature instructional-level materials.

Frustration reading level   Students functioning at the frustration reading level are unable to handle the material unless given considerable assistance. The gap between the reading ability and the prior knowledge of the student is simply too great and cannot be spanned without considerable individual attention. Because the difficulty of the material clearly exceeds the skill of the student, his or her attempts to read this material may well lead to frustration and anger. These negative emotions are destructive to the development of a positive attitude about both the subject being studied and reading in general. Therefore, you should avoid asking individual students to read materials that, for them, are at the frustration level.

The cloze procedure can provide important information regarding students' prior knowledge about a given subject and whether the material is appropriate for your students. Ashby-Davis (1985, cited in Richardson, Morgan & Fleener, 2009) cautions, however, that it should not be the only indicator of a student's general reading skills because it is different from the usual reading activities of students.

Analyzing reading material   The general reading difficulty of a specific piece of prose material can be determined by applying one or more readability formulas. *Readability* refers to the relative difficulty of a given prose selection. Richardson, Morgan, and Fleener (2009) define it as the match between reader and text. The readability of a selection varies with the complexity and the length of the sentences; the number of many-syllable as compared to one- or two-syllable words; and the number of words that, for some reason or another, the students do not know.

Readability formulas are used to identify approximate grade-level readabilities. That is, a given selection might be found to have a grade-level reading difficulty of Grade 8, Grade 9, Grade 10, or some other grade level depending on the results of the application of the readability formula. When you use readability formulas, it is important to recognize that grade levels are described in terms of averages. That is, simply because we find a given book to have a readability level of Grade 11 does not mean that every student in Grade 11 can read the material without difficulty. It means that the average 11th-grader should be able to read the material. The term *average* suggests that, nationally, about half of the Grade 11 students will be able to read material at this level and about half will experience difficulty.

One of the most commonly used readability formulas is the Fry Readability Formula developed by Edward Fry in the 1960s and later revised in 1977 (Fry, 1977). This procedure involves selecting a number of 100-word passages from the text material and performing several simple calculations. Plotting the data on a graph provides an estimate of the reading difficulty of the material. A variety of sources are available to you if you want to use the Fry Readability Formula or any other readability formula. One of the most helpful is the website www.readabilityformulas.com. This site has detailed descriptions of nine different formulas (including the Fry formula and graph), links to software, and enough information about each formula so that you can choose the one that is most appropriate for you and your students. Most secondary reading textbooks (e.g., the Richard, Morgan, and Fleener [2009] text referenced in this chapter) contain detailed information about these formulas and how to use them.

Using your word processor   Most word-processing programs (Word Perfect, Microsoft Word) include statistical analysis of text material. For example, in Microsoft Word you can perform readability statistics on text material by clicking on "Tools," then "Options,", and finally "Show readability statistics." Check your owner's manual to find the appropriate procedure for your word-processing program. Most of these programs utilize the Flesch-Kincaid measure that reports a grade-level score similar to that reported by the Fry measure. Some programs are more sophisticated than others and provide a variety of information to assist in determining readability. Typing or scanning text rather than counting syllables, sentences, and words is a timesaver for today's busy teachers.

Even though readability formulas have provided consistent results over time, experts caution us to be aware of their limitations. Vacca and Vacca (2002), for example, describe them as a "rubber ruler" (p. 104). Many of the formulas fail to take into account student interests and motivation, the relationship between students' prior knowledge and the material, the quality and appropriateness of the visuals that accompany the text, the organizational pattern(s) of the material, and the writing style of the author. All of these factors can influence the suitability of a text for a given group of learners.

Prereading Strategies   Your students' prior experiences play a critical role in their ability to comprehend text material. These prior experiences provide the students with a frame of reference that helps them fit what is read into a meaningful pattern. To test this principle, find a technical manual in an area you know little about and try to read it. Even an excellent reader who lacks the necessary background may not be able to derive much meaning from specialized material dealing with, for example, sophisticated electrical circuits. The organization, vocabulary, and lack of a useful mental picture of what is being described make the reading difficult.

This example illustrates what many secondary school students experience when asked to read in different subject areas. Students with little previous knowledge or background in the topic sometimes feel they are being required to make sense out of a random collection of words. The task they face is extremely difficult, so many of these students simply give up.

You will encounter two major problems as you work with students in this preparation phase of the reading framework. First, secondary school students may not have sufficient previous experience in the area being studied. Second, even when they have had appropriate prior experiences, they may not recognize the relevance of these experiences for the assigned reading task. You must help them to identify the connection between prior learning and present academic work. Students need a frame of reference as they attempt to derive meaning from their reading.

The famous learning theorist, D. W. Ausubel (1963), emphasized the importance of this phase almost half a century ago. He suggested that the use of advance organizers, broad or general ideas that were provided to the student before beginning the study of material, enhanced learning and retention. These general ideas or organizing frames of reference should be drawn from the previous experience of the student.

Graphic organizers Several techniques are available to help you build students' background knowledge and thus provide students with a frame of reference prior to the time they begin reading. One of these is the graphic organizer. These organizers include webs; structured overviews; maps; or any diagrams that visually display relationships among concepts, ideas, and/or terms. You will find an example of a graphic organizer at the beginning of each chapter in this text. If you examine the overview at the beginning of this chapter, you will notice that this is basically a visual outline that displays relationships among the concepts in this chapter. Three major topics are highlighted in bold. Under each main topic, you can find the important concepts discussed in relationship to the main topic. A content-specific example is included in Figure 12.1. As with any reading strategy, you must discuss it with the students the first time you use it, model how to use it, and give students multiple opportunities to practice (Barton & Jordan, 2001).

Figure 12-1

Structured Overview for Westward Movement

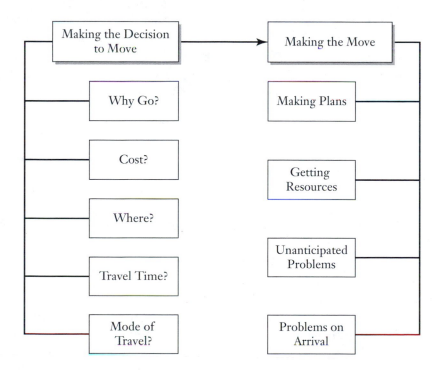

You might be curious how the example in Figure 12-1 can help build background for the westward movement. Although students studying the westward movement in American history obviously could not have had direct personal experience in this historic settlement pattern, many of them will have been involved in a permanent family move. Some of them will have taken an extended trip. Use these experiences as you discuss the organizer so that, when your students begin reading, they are able to connect their experiences with those of the individuals discussed in their text.

ReQuest   Manzo (1969) designed a questioning procedure that is particularly appropriate for struggling readers. If you are teaching classes populated with many English language learners (ELLs), you might find this strategy particularly helpful. It involves short text passages so students do not become as easily frustrated.

ReQuest is an abbreviated term for "reciprocal questioning." It involves both the students and the teacher in asking and answering questions. Student participation in the framing of the questions helps them relate their previous knowledge and their interests to the topic to be studied. A unique and important feature of the ReQuest procedure is that it provides modeling for the students in how to ask and respond to questions. The following steps provide guidance if you choose to use this procedure in your classroom:

1. The teacher and the students read the first sentence of a selection together. (If one sentence fails to provide sufficient information for meaningful questions to be asked, the teacher is free to extend the reading to include several sentences.)

2. The teacher closes his or her book while the students keep theirs open. Students may ask the teacher any question they wish that relates to the first sentence (or to whatever length of material they were asked to read). The teacher answers the questions as accurately as possible. The teacher may choose to make some comments to students about the quality of their questions, including some suggestions for improvement.

3. The students then close their books and the teacher asks questions. The teacher should try to ask questions that will help the students recall any previous information they have about the topic or a similar topic and questions that will provide a model for student questioning during their next turn.

4. This procedure may be repeated for several paragraphs until the students can answer a predictive question such as What do you think you will find out in the rest of this selection? Their answers to this question help them develop a framework for the rest of the reading, as well as learn how to ask questions to guide their own reading.

You can see that this procedure provides much flexibility as you use it with different groups of students. You can extend the reading passages (especially in classrooms with proficient readers), teach students to ask questions at different levels, and help students set purposes for reading.

Anticipation guides   Some prereading techniques are designed primarily to motivate students to read text selections. These guides, also called prediction or reaction guides, require students to respond to a series of statements that are related in some way to content material (Unrau, 2004). Because a variety of possibilities exist for designing the guides, the following steps can assist you as you create and use these guides with your students. A sample guide is included in Box 12-1.

1. Read the text material and determine the important concepts you want students to learn.

2. Write four to six statements based on these concepts. The statements should reflect the students' world yet challenge in some way their prior experiences. Write some statements that will stimulate discussion and are thought-provoking enough to incite argument among your students.

Box 12-1   Anticipation Guide for a Science Lesson: Universe Unit

Prior to reading the text, place a checkmark in the "Agree Now" column for each statement with which you agree. As you read, place a checkmark in the "New Ideas" column if, based on new information, you change your mind about the statement. In the "Where Supported" column, note the page number where this new information is discussed.

Agree Now	New Ideas	Where Supported
_____	_____	_____
_____	_____	_____
_____	_____	_____
_____	_____	_____
_____	_____	_____
_____	_____	_____
_____	_____	_____
_____	_____	_____
_____	_____	_____
_____	_____	_____

Statement

1. The universe in which we live is one of many, and scientists are discovering new ones all of the time.
2. A light year is a unit of time.
3. Gravity holds stars together in space.
4. The Milky Way is the name of our solar system.
5. About 10 billion stars exist in our universe.
6. The big bang theory and the steady state theory are scientific ideas that explain the origins of the universe.
7. The stars in the constellations we see are located together in space.
8. The brightest stars in the night sky are the closest to Earth.
9. All planets have moons.
10. A lunar eclipse occurs when the sun, the earth, and the moon are in a straight line.

Developed by Patricia A. Nelson, Ph.D., high school science teacher.

---

3. Ask the students to respond to the guide. Make sure you give clear directions.
4. Discuss students' responses before they read.
5. Assign the reading.
6. Ask students to reconsider their original responses after reading the text material. Small-group discussion works well for this phase.
7. Review with students what they have learned and clarify misunderstandings.

Although many guides ask students to check either agree or disagree, some, such as the one in Box 12-1, extend this learning by asking them to indicate specific pages where they find information that changes their mind about the concepts. These guides provide opportunities for you and your students to discuss the concepts across all phases of the reading process.

K-W-L   Another prereading guide that many teachers find useful is the K-W-L chart (Ogle, 1986). This guide is designed to help teachers identify the conceptual limitations that their students are bringing to a particular piece of text. Students are given an opportunity to identify first what they already know (the K) about a given topic. Then they list questions they want to answer (the W) as they read about the topic. The third category provides an opportunity for students to identify what they learned (the L) during the reading experience. Teachers enjoy these guides because they are easy to develop, they identify prior knowledge that students bring to the learning experience, and they also serve as a stimulus for reflection after the students have read. To construct a K-W-L chart, simply make three columns and title them in the following order: What I Know (K), What I Want to Know (W), and What I Learned (L). Some teachers add other columns such as What I Still Want to Know or How I Will Find Out What I Still Need to Know. This simple guide not only activates students' prior knowledge, it also provides opportunities for exciting discussions and writing assignments once the reading is complete.

Vocabulary Instruction   No discussion about the preparation phase of the reading framework is complete without some comments about vocabulary. One of the significant problems for secondary school students is understanding the vocabulary they encounter in their texts. Several decades ago, reading specialist Robert C. Aukerman (1972) identified the following categories of words that frustrate many secondary school readers: obsolete words or phrases, colloquial vocabulary, unfamiliar vocabulary, and technical vocabulary.

1. *Obsolete words or phrases*—terms that have either undergone alterations in meaning or have passed out of usage (e.g., nosegay [a small bouquet of flowers]).

2. *Colloquial vocabulary*—words that occur frequently in prose selections that attempt to provide the reader with the flavor of regional speech. These words may be deliberately misspelled to capture the sound of regional speech (e.g., the language in Mark Twain's *The Adventures of Huckleberry Finn*).

3. *Unfamiliar vocabulary*—there are two types of unfamiliar vocabulary: words that students know and may even use but have never seen in print and nontechnical words that are simply not known to students.

4. *Technical vocabulary*—specialized words associated with a particular discipline or area of interest.

More recently, Blachowicz and Fisher (2010) discuss the following guidelines for effective vocabulary instruction in all classrooms:

■ Teachers provide word-rich environments.

■ Teachers help students develop independent strategies.

■ Teachers help students develop academic content and general vocabulary.

■ Teachers use assessment that matches instruction (p. 7).

Vocabulary overview guide   To help students overcome vocabulary problems, consider using a vocabulary overview guide. It outlines steps that students can follow as they work to master unfamiliar vocabulary. Begin by providing the students with a blank form and a set of directions. The directions to the students are as follows:

1. Survey the material to identify the topic.

2. Skim the material and identify unknown vocabulary words. Mark them using sticky notes.

3. Try to figure out the meaning of the word from the sentences around it. Then ask someone or use a dictionary to check the meaning.

4. Write the definitions on paper so that they will be available when you read the text.

5. Read the text.

6. Complete the vocabulary overview guide by including the following:

   a. The title of the passage

   b. Categories for grouping the vocabulary words according to topics the words discuss or describe (give each category a title)

   c. The vocabulary word

   d. The definition underneath the vocabulary word

   e. A clue to help you connect the word to something you already know

Box 12-2   Vocabulary Overview Guide

Chapter Title: The Basics of Economics

Category: Production

> Word: Resources
>
> Definition: Anything used to make a product
>
> Clue: People, factories, natural resources

> Word: Specialization
>
> Definition: Each person doing one thing well
> goods and services
>
> Clue: Plumbers, electricians

Word: _____

Definition: _____

_____

Clue: _____

Category: Consumption

> Word: Market
>
> Definition: A meeting of people to buy and sell
>
> Clue: Wants and demands of people

> Word: Income
>
> Definition: Money a person makes that can be
> spent on goods and services
>
> Clue: Salary, wages, interest

Word: _____

Definition: _____

_____

Clue: _____

An example of a vocabulary overview guide is provided in Box 12-2. A collection of words learned during the semester can help students see how their vocabularies are growing. In fact, many teachers make a word wall a permanent addition to their classroom. (Word walls are simply pieces of paper attached somewhere in the classroom. Teachers record new words as students encounter them in their text material as a permanent reminder of new vocabulary learned throughout the year.) In addition, you might want to review the vocabulary overview guides to help you identify words that should be addressed the next time the material is used with a class.

Assistance Phase: Building Comprehension

Once you have prepared students prior to reading selected text, you will find that it is important to provide assistance as they are reading. Vacca and Vacca (2002) point out that study guides are useful to help "scaffold students' understanding of academic content and the literacy and thinking processes needed to comprehend and learn with texts" (p. 324). When used consistently, these guides can help students become independent readers.

Strategies appropriate for this phase help students gather information productively and efficiently. Useful guides help students identify their purpose for reading, think about the strategy they will use, and assist them in identifying relationships in the passage they are reading. Four guides commonly used by secondary teachers are three-level guides, pattern guides, jot charts and study skills guides.

Three-Level Guides   Three level guides are designed to develop students' higher-level thinking skills. These guides follow a taxonomy similar to that identified by Gray (1960). Herber (1978) labeled the levels as literal, interpretative, and applied. In other words, students first read for literal understanding before reading between the lines and reading beyond the lines (Gray, 1960). Three-level guides are organized around three basic questions, each establishing a focus on a given level of understanding:

1. What did the material say? (This question is designed to help students grasp the literal meaning of what they are reading, e.g., to read the lines.)

Box 12-3 Three-Level Guide for Math Story Problem

Problem: Tan has 145 boxes of cereal that must be placed on shelves in the supermarket. He is able to place 68 of the boxes on the biggest shelf. He must now place the same number of boxes on two remaining shelves. How many will he need to put on each shelf?

Level 1: Read the problem above. Check those statements that contain important information to help you solve the problem.

_____ Tan works in a supermarket.

_____ There are 145 total boxes.

_____ The boxes contain cereal.

_____ He placed 68 boxes on one shelf.

_____ The remaining boxes are to be placed on two additional shelves with an equal number on each shelf.

_____ There are three shelves total.

Level 2: Check the following statements that contain math ideas related to this problem.

_____ Division is putting an amount into equal groups.

_____ When we take an amount away, we subtract to find the amount left.

_____ Adding groups with the same amount is multiplying.

_____ When we put an amount into groups of the same size, we divide the amount by the number of groups.

Level 3: Below are possible ways of getting an answer to the problem. Check those that apply to this problem.

_____ $145 - 68$

_____ $145 + 68$

_____ $(145 - 2) + 68$

_____ $(145 - 68) - 2$

---

2. What does the material mean? (This question encourages students to interpret and make inferences, e.g., to read between the lines.)

3. How can I apply this meaning to something else? (This question prompts students to think about how they might apply what they have learned, e.g., to read beyond the lines.)

These questions are helpful as you prepare three-level guides related to a specific reading assignment. Using question 1 as a point of departure, begin by identifying some literal information contained in the assigned reading. Next, identify inferences that might be drawn from the passage, and finally identify information that might suggest applications of content. This information is organized and presented for students to use as they read the material. A three-level guide is included in Box 12-3.

Pattern Guides As they write, authors usually follow a specific organizational pattern. These patterns vary in terms of their purposes. For example, historical text is often written following a chronological pattern, while scientific text is often organized into large categories. Other common patterns found in secondary school reading materials include the compare-and-contrast pattern, the cause-and-effect pattern, and the simple listing pattern. To enhance students' comprehension of text they read in your classroom, consider designing pattern guides that make them aware of the pattern of organization used in the texts.

Pattern guides can follow several formats depending on the pattern of organization. Some of them are simply skeleton outlines that list some main ideas, with a few missing parts provided for students to fill in as they read. Somewhat more sophisticated pattern guides may list some effects and call on students to fill in information about their causes. Other pattern guides appear as complex webs that display relationships among ideas. In these webs, instruct your students to fill in the missing words using information they derive from their reading.

When constructing a pattern guide, you must first read the material and identify the pattern of organization. One way of doing this is to look for key words. Words such as *first,*

Box 12-4   Topic: Building the Transcontinental Railroad

Generalization: Improved Transportation Facilitates Growth and Trade Between Regions.

CAUSE	EFFECT
1. The first locomotive was built in 1829.	1. _____
2. _____	2. It was very difficult to travel between the East Coast and the West Coast.
3. The government provided incentives to build the railroad by paying for each mile of track.	3. _____
4. _____	4. The cost of shipping goods was greatly reduced.
5. The amount of time required to go between the two coasts was reduced.	5. _____

---

second, third, before, and *after* usually indicate a sequential or chronological pattern. Use of the conjunctions *but* and *and* often indicate comparisons and/or contrasts (Estes & Vaughan, 1985, p. 162).

After the pattern has been identified, decide on a format that will be most appropriate for the organization of the material. When you first introduce pattern guides, you might find it useful to provide students with a considerable amount of information, for example, useful cues to students as they seek the information they will need to complete the guide. As students become more familiar with the procedure, more and more detail can be omitted, which makes completing the guide more difficult. An additional challenge you might try is allowing students to construct their own guides as they approach new material, especially after they have had some experience with guides that you provide. This process reinforces the idea that authors' patterns vary and that, in part, a successful reading strategy involves the ability to recognize the scheme used by the writer(s) of the assigned material. A cause-and-effect pattern guide is included in Box 12-4. As you can see, this guide can be used in a variety of ways. You might choose to use it as displayed, or you can give students all the causes and have them identify the effects. Alternatively, you could give them all the effects and have them identify all the causes.

Jot Charts   A third strategy that you can use to assist comprehension is a jot chart. These charts are data-retrieval charts displayed in the form of a matrix. They allow students to compare and contrast ideas as they read. Typically, teachers design the matrix and students complete it as they read. Other variations are also appropriate. Consider giving students a matrix with some cells already filled in, especially when students are first introduced to the strategy.

As you can see in the example in Box 12-5, jot charts are easy to design and have potential in any content area. This makes them a favorite of secondary school teachers. The first example allows you to add as many countries and characteristics as you prefer; the second example, as many characters and dimensions as you prefer. Many teachers like to design these not only as handouts for the students but also as wall charts that can provide easy discussion starters.

Study Skills Guides   Study skills guides are designed to help students monitor their own reading skills and think about the material they are reading. Often, students read their assignments superficially. They may read the words, but they fail to think about what they have learned or what is important. The study skills guide prompts students to stop at

Box 12-5

Jot Chart 1—Countries of the Ancient World

Country	Location	Form of Government	Religion(s)	Resources
Egypt				
Greece				
Mesopotamia				

Jot Chart 2—Character Analysis: *A Midsummer Night's Dream*

Character	Physical Traits	Personality Traits	Main Conflict	How the Conflict Is Resolved	Quote That Is Important to Understand the Character
Theseus					
Lysander					
Demetrius					
Hippolyta					
Hermia					
Helena					

critical points as they read and respond to questions or engage in an activity. The purpose is to increase their levels of motivation and to help them monitor what they have read. When they find they cannot answer the questions or perform the required activity, they can either reread the material or seek assistance from the teacher. In time, students begin to incorporate key questions of their own as they read. When this happens, their levels of comprehension increase.

Study skills guides are not difficult to construct. As a first step, you must read through the material and identify places for your students to stop reading. Questions are developed for students when they stop. Sometimes, required activities are described. If questions are used, they should prompt students to monitor their own comprehension and reading strategy. The following examples can be included in a study skills guide:

- Summarize the section you read in one sentence.

- What do you think will happen next?

- What information from this section do you think might be on a test your teacher might prepare?

An example of a study skills guide appears in Box 12-6.

Reflection Phase: Questioning, Writing, Discussing

The final phase of the reading process develops critical thinking skills, an area that is often overlooked. Research reports (Parker, 1991; Kirsch & Jungeblut, 1986; Sternberg, 1994) point out that while students are able to read, they have difficulty with reading that requires them to think critically. The Parker report suggests that the teaching of critical thinking skills is often neglected in today's classrooms. Richardson, Morgan, and Fleener (2009)

Box 12-6   **Study Skills Guide**

Directions: As you read the assigned pages, follow the steps listed below. You will be asked to stop your reading at specific places and review what you have read. It is important for you to be aware of how you are thinking about and organizing the material as you read.

Step 1: Start on page 20 and read to the bottom of page 21. What do you think is important for you to know about this section? _____
_____

Step 2: After reading to the third paragraph on page 23, write two or three sentences about what you have learned. If you cannot do this or you do not understand what you are reading, what can you do to get help? _____
_____

Step 3: Before reading the next section, predict what will happen._____
_____

Step 4: Read to the end of page 25. Was your prediction correct? What information in this section is likely to be on

a test? _____
_____

Step 5: Read to the second paragraph on page 27. List in sequence the events that happened. Do you understand the material? Would rereading help? _____
_____

Step 6: The last sentence of paragraph 3 on page 28 states the main point of this chapter. Rewrite this statement into a question. _____
_____

Step 7: After finishing the chapter, what pictures or images of the events come to mind? _____

How is this like something you know about? _____
_____

What was most difficult to understand? _____
_____

Write a short summary of what you have read. _____
_____

---

implore us to develop strategies that teach important reflection skills: critical thinking, problem-solving, decision-making, etc. These strategies will move us toward our goal of developing independent, lifelong learners.

Several reflection strategies are available to assist you as you teach your students to become critical thinkers. Among them are graphic postorganizers, interaction frames, and a variety of writing activities such as RAFT.

Graphic Postorganizers   The graphic postorganizer technique is an extension of the structured-overview approach discussed earlier (Estes & Vaughan, 1985, p. 182). In the structured-overview approach, teachers prepare a framework for students to use while they are reading. Graphic postorganizers are developed by the students themselves. Students reflect on what they have read and construct their own structure. The process of construction helps them relate what they have read to prior levels of understanding. The technique is designed to help students refine and modify previous information by reflecting on new information and insights they have gained from their reading.

Constructing the graphic postorganizer can be done rather simply using index cards of two different colors. Each group of four to six individuals is given a packet of cards. The group's goal is to identify the basic concepts or main ideas that were covered in the passage they just read. Each group member records on the cards of one color what he or she believes were the major concepts or ideas. Each member then presents these to the rest of the group and defends his or her choice. The group then reaches a consensus on the major concepts or ideas.

Individuals then take a card of another color and identify key information or supporting ideas that fit under each of the major concepts or ideas identified on the cards completed during the first part of the exercise. Individual group members once again defend their choices of supporting information. Finally, each group arranges this information under the appropriate concept or idea.

When members of a group have arranged their cards in a manner that is satisfying to them, they design a graph or chart that visually depicts the relationship among the major ideas that have been identified and the important subordinate information associated with each. The graph can be prepared on a large sheet of paper, on a blank overhead transparency, or on the computer. Once all groups have completed this phase, the graphs are displayed. They become a focus for a class discussion and perhaps a written assignment. The teacher as well as classmates can react to the various organizational schemes, leading students to discover that there are several ways to organize what they have read. A discussion of these issues helps students to think about ways of organizing and thinking about what they read.

Interaction Frames   Interaction frames are especially useful in helping students to organize information from reading selections that refer to interactions between or among two or more individuals or groups. These guides are particularly appropriate for text that students read in English and social studies classes. Interaction frames are organized around these four basic questions:

1. What were the goals of the various individuals or groups?
2. What actions did they take to try to accomplish these goals?
3. How did the individuals or groups interact?
4. What were the outcomes of the interactions?

Students are asked first to respond to these questions, then provide a brief summary of their responses. Often teachers assign students to groups to complete this activity. However, it can also be completed individually. The group discussion does have an added benefit of providing students with opportunities to consider the thinking processes of others and to reflect more carefully on what they have read. An example of an interaction frame is provided in Box 12-7.

Writing as Reflection   Teachers often use writing to help students reflect on their reading. Indeed, writing activities can help students clarify what they read. A number of school districts have mandated writing across the curriculum. They sometimes require that all teachers include writing assignments on a regular basis. Many of these decisions were based on the need to improve writing scores on standardized tests. But teachers and administrators acknowledge that students need good writing skills just as much as they need good reading skills. Their future education and employment necessitate that they are able to write clearly and concisely.

Many writing strategies are appropriate for use during the reflection phase. RAFT (Vanderventer, 1979) is one such strategy that many teachers have found useful in assisting students to demonstrate understanding of text material. The technique stimulates students to be much more creative as they respond to assigned text material, and it helps them focus on the appropriate audience. RAFT is an acronym that stands for the following:

- *Role of the writer*—What is the writer's role?
- *Audience*—Who will read the written product?
- *Format*—What is the best way to present the material?
- *Topic*—What (or who) is the subject of the writing?

Although you may assign the RAFT prompt, you will probably find that students prefer making some of the choices themselves. If you choose to design the prompt, the following example might work in an art classroom where students have been studying the quilting process:

> Imagine that you are giving a lecture at a local quilting show. Although most of the attendees are quite knowledgeable about quilting, many are beginners who are there

---

Box 12-7   Interaction Frame

Faction A	**Faction B**
Goals of Faction A	Goals of Faction B
1.	1.
2.	2.
Actions:	Actions:
1.	1.
2.	2.

How these two factions interacted

Conflicts:
1.
2.

Compromises:
1.
2.

Cooperations:
1.
2.

Results for Faction A	**Results for Faction B**
1.	1.
2.	2.

Summary

---

to learn. Describe to these beginners the procedures and processes that they need to know in order to begin quilting.

The matrix in Box 12-8 shows the versatility of the RAFT technique. You can insert any number of RAFT components that are appropriate for the content you are teaching in your classroom. Keep in mind that, although some assignments may contrive audiences and situations, others should provide opportunities for real-world writing such as letters to newspapers, politicians, authors, etc. (Vacca & Vacca, 2002).

Box 12-8

Role	Audience	Format	Topic
Quilt teacher	Beginning quilters	How-to demonstration	Quilting process

Other writing techniques are available online. A quick search of the Web will give a plethora of choices no matter what your subject specialty. The secondary reading texts mentioned throughout this chapter can also provide you with a variety of choices. Whichever ones you choose, we recommend that you keep in mind the following tips:

■ Teach writing as a process.

■ If you are not a good writer yourself, seek help. Remember you are a role model for your students.

■ Use rubrics to communicate to students your expectations for their final product. Then, use the rubric to score the product.

■ Include a variety of types of writing: formal (e.g., essays) and informal (e.g., journals).

In summary, the reflection phase is one of the most important phases of the comprehension process. Not only do the activities help students reflect on their own thinking, they also help students develop more systematic and sophisticated ways of interpreting information they have read.

Using Tradebooks in the Content Classroom

Considering the disconnect between the reading levels of textbooks and the levels at which many students are reading, today's teachers find that trade books offer one way of supplementing textbooks. Richardson, Morgan, and Fleener (2009) define trade books as "books that are considered to be in general use, such as books borrowed from a library or bought at the local bookstore, rather than textbooks bought and studied as a major course resource" (p.171).

In today's diverse classrooms, multiple texts are almost a necessity. Trade books offer teachers the opportunity to provide reading material that appeals to a variety of cultures and student interests. Savage and Savage (1996) point out that a variety of genres are appropriate in the classrooms. Although fiction is most often recommended, nonfiction is an especially important genre to help students develop the capacity to raise critical questions. Stories about real people and real events can help students develop an understanding of the values, perspectives, and frames of reference of individuals from a variety of cultures.

McGowan and Guzzetti (1991) provide four reasons for using trade books in all content classrooms:

■ *Interest*—The engaging format and writing style of most trade books are interesting for today's secondary student.

■ *Variety*—Many books are available for different student reading levels and interests.

■ *Relevance*—Trade books connect students' real-world experiences with the classroom.

■ *Comprehensibility*—Trade books focus on relationships among concepts. For example, science trade books provide background knowledge for scientific concepts discussed in class and help students make connections with events in their everyday lives.

As you choose trade books for you classroom, choose for enjoyment as well as for instruction. For example, Savage and Savage (1992) remind us that we should include books that can help the reader identify with characters from other cultures. *Roll of Thunder, Hear My Cry* by Mildred Taylor is included on many required reading lists. This book provides an opportunity not only to discuss issues related to the Great Depression in rural Mississippi, it also provides an opportunity to discuss prejudice and racism. After reading the book, students might compare their own experiences to those of Cassie, the main character, considering issues such as what they learned that might help them confront racism and prejudice (Savage & Savage, 1992). Lois Lowry's award-winning novel *Number the*

Box 12-9   Selection Guide for Trade Books for Middle School and High School

The Alan Review (Assembly on Literature for Adolescents, National Council of Teachers of English). Urbana, IL: National Council of Teachers of English.

Book Links: Connecting Books, Libraries, and Classrooms. Published by the American Library Association.

Christenbury, L. (Ed.). (1995). *Books for you: A booklist for senior high students* (11th ed.). Urbana, IL: National Council of Teachers of English.

International Reading Association. "Children's Choices." Published every October in *The Reading Teacher.*

Lesesne, T. (2003). *Making the match: The right book for the right reader at the right time.* Portland, ME: Stenhouse.

National Council for the Social Studies, *Carter Woodson Book Award Winners.* Published yearly in the spring

issue of *Social Education.* Also available on their website: www.ncss.org

Norton, D. (2010). *Through the eyes of a child* (8th ed.). Columbus, OH: Prentice Hall.

Notable children's trade books in the field of social studies. National Council for the Social Studies. Published yearly in a spring issue of *Social Education.* Also available on their website: www.ncss.org

Outstanding science trade books for children. Published yearly in a spring issue of *Science and Children.* Also available on their website: www.nsta.org

---

Stars, a fictionalized account of an incident in Nazi-occupied Denmark, "offers opportunities for students to research the Holocaust and identify reasons why Nazis were attempting to annihilate the Jews" (Savage & Savage, 1993, p. 35). Many books provide us with similar scenarios. Make sure that you examine all alternatives available to you when including trade books in your classroom.

Finally, make sure that literacy permeates your classroom. Many students discover the pleasure of reading when they discover books related to topics that are of interest to them. Include a reading center in your room that stocks not only discipline-related books, but books on topics that middle school and high school students enjoy. By doing this, you communicate that reading is important. Box 12-9 lists sources of information to help you select high-quality trade books.

FOR YOUR PORTFOLIO

Because most schools emphasize literacy across the curriculum, you will want to demonstrate that you have a solid understanding of how to design literacy strategies for your students. Choose two strategies that you have designed to include in your portfolio. Include a brief statement that explains why you chose each entry as well as what it indicates about your knowledge of reading across the curriculum.

Review both the material you have decided to include and the Interstate New Teacher Assessment and Support Consortium (INTASC) standards. State which INTASC standards these entries address or complete the chart below.

INTASC Standards

Item Number	S-1	S-2	S-3	S-4	S-5	S-6	S-7	S-8	S-9	S-10
Entry 1										
Entry 2										

Key Ideas in Summary

- All teachers share the responsibility for helping students learn how to comprehend reading material. Part of this responsibility involves the creation of conditions that emphasize the importance of reading. You establish these conditions by modeling good reading habits, providing a variety of reading material, and testing students on material they have been assigned to read.

- Teachers must identify the reading levels of students in their classroom. Readability, or the match between the reading level of students and the difficulty of the material, is a critical variable in creating a successful classroom environment. Material that is so difficult that it places students at the frustration level should not be used.

- Several formulas for identifying the readability of material are available. One of the most popular is the Fry Readability Formula Graph. Using this formula, or one provided in your word-processing program, in combination with a cloze test can help you select material that is appropriate for the reading levels of students in your classroom.

- Students' abilities to learn from a given reading assignment are related in part to their prior knowledge and experience. Several approaches can be used to help students relate this prior knowledge to the material that is to be read. Among useful approaches are structured overviews, ReQuest, and anticipation guides.

- Vocabulary difficulties are a prime source of confusion for students. Several types of vocabulary tend to cause problems for secondary school students, including obsolete words or phrases, technical vocabulary, colloquial vocabulary, and unfamiliar vocabulary. Vocabulary overview guides are useful in helping students become familiar with potentially confusing words.

- Providing guidance during the reading phase prompts students to consider whether they understand what they are reading. Classroom activities during this phase of the reading process seek to help students develop effective techniques for organizing and understanding the material they are reading. Three-level guides, pattern guides, jot charts, and study skills guides are particularly effective for accomplishing this purpose.

- Effective after-reading strategies help students clarify and modify their conceptual frameworks. A good approach to the after-reading phase is to have students work in small groups to reflect on and react to what they have read. In addition, working in small groups provides unsuccessful students an opportunity to observe students who are successful.

- Trade books add an extra dimension to your classroom. They provide one avenue for instruction *and* they create interest in the topic being taught.

Learning Extensions

1. Examine some content reading textbooks to find specific reading and writing activities designed for your content classroom.

2. Examine some of the research on reading across the curriculum. Use this information to write your own philosophy of literacy as it applies to your content classroom.

3. Perform the Fry Readability assessment (or try another readability formula) on the textbook you are using in your content classroom. (*Note:* If you are not currently teaching, select a college textbook or go to your university library and select a book that might be appropriate. The process is what is important for this assignment.) In addition, design a cloze activity and administer it to your students. Based on the

results of these two assessment instruments, discuss how you might need to design reading experiences that would be appropriate for your students.

4. Design a prereading activity, a during-reading activity, and an after-reading activity that would be appropriate for reading selected text material you will use in your classroom.

5. Design a series of writing activities that you might include in a unit of instruction in your classroom. Consult the website of your national organization, secondary reading texts, and the teacher's edition of the textbook used in your classroom.

6. Compile a list of trade books that would be appropriate additions to your classroom.

References

Allen, J. (2002). *On the same page: Shared reading beyond the primary grades.* Portland, ME: Stenhouse.

Ashby-Davis, C. (1985). Cloze and comprehension: A qualitative analysis and critique. *Journal of Reading, 28,* 585–593. Cited in J. S. Richardson, R. F. Morgan, & C. E. Fleener (Eds.), *Reading to learn in the content areas* (7th ed., p. 187). Belmont, CA: Wadsworth.

Aukerman, R. C. (1972). *Reading in the secondary school classroom.* New York: McGraw Hill.

Ausubel, D. W. (1963). *The Ps of meaningful verbal learning.* New York: Grune and Stratton.

Barton, M. L., & Jordan, D. J. (2001). *Teaching reading in science.* Aurora, CO: McREL.

Blachowicz, C., & Fisher, P. J. (2010). *Teaching vocabulary in all classrooms* (4th ed.). San Francisco: Allyn & Bacon.

Burke, J. (2000). *Reading reminders: Tools, tips and techniques.* Portsmouth, NH: Boynton/Cook Heinemann.

Donohue, D. (2003). Reading across the great divide: English and math teachers apprentice one another as readers and disciplinary insiders. *Journal of Adolescent & Adult Literacy, 47*(1), 24–37.

Estes, T. H., & Vaughn, J. L. (1985). *Reading and learning in the content classroom: Diagnostic and instructional strategies* (2nd ed.). Boston: Allyn and Bacon.

Fry, E. (1977). Fry's readability graph: Clarifications, validity, and extensions to Level 17. *Journal of Reading, 21,* 242–252.

Gray, W. (1960). The major aspects of reading. In H. Robinson (Ed.), *Development of reading abilities* (Supplementary Educational Monographs No. 90). Chicago: University of Chicago Press.

Herber, H. L. (1978). *Teaching reading in content areas* (2nd ed.). Upper Saddle River, NJ: Prentice Hall.

Kirsch, I. S., & Jungeblut, A. (1986). *Literacy: Profiles of America's young adults.* Princeton, NJ: National Assessment of Educational Progress.

Manzo, A. V. (1969). "ReQuest Procedure," *Journal of Reading, 11,* 123–126.

McGowan, T., & Guzzetti, B. (1991, January/February). Promoting social studies understanding through literature-based instruction. *Social Studies,* 16–21.

Ogle, D. M. (1986). K-W-L: A teaching model that develops active reading in expository text. *The Reading Teacher, 39*(6), 564– 570.

Parker, W. C. (1991). Achieving thinking and decision-making objectives in social studies. In J. P. Shaver (Ed.), *Handbook of research on social studies teaching and learning.* New York: Macmillan.

Postman, N. (1979). *Teaching as a subversive activity.* New York: Delacorte.

Richardson, J. S., Morgan, R. F., & Fleener, C. E. (2009). *Reading to learn in the content areas,* (7th ed.). Belmont, CA: Wadsworth.

Savage, M. K., & Savage, T. V. (1992). Exploring ethnic diversity through children's literature. *Oregon English Journal, 14*(1), 7–11.

Savage, M. K., & Savage, T. V. (1993). Children's literature in middle school social studies. *The Social Studies, 84*(1), 32–36.

Savage, M. K., & Savage, T. V. (1996). Achieving multicultural goals through children's nonfiction. *The Journal of Educational Issues of Language Minority Students, 17,* 25–37.

Singer, H., & Donlan, D. (1985). *Reading and learning from text.* Hillsdale, NJ: Erlbaum.

Sternberg, R. L. (1994). Answering questions and questioning answers. *Phi Delta Kappan, 76,* 136–138.

Taylor, W. L. (1953). Cloze procedure: A new tool for measuring readability. *Journalism Quarterly, 30,* 415– 433.

Unrau, N. (2004). *Content area reading and writing: Fostering literacies in middle and high school cultures.* Columbus, OH: Pearson, Merrill, Prentice Hall.

Vacca, R. T., & Vacca, J. L. (2002). *Content area reading: Literacy and learning across the curriculum* (7th ed.). Boston: Allyn & Bacon.

Vanderventer, N. (1979, Winter). RAFT: A process to structure prewriting. *Highway One: A Canadian Journal of Language Experience,* 26.

Vaughn, J., & Estes, T. (1986). *Reading and reasoning beyond the primary grades.* Boston: Allyn & Bacon.

Successful Management and Discipline

Objectives

This chapter will help you

- define the terms *management* and *discipline*

- list the key areas that lead to success in management and discipline

- explain how you can go about establishing authority in the classroom

- describe elements of the physical environment that need to be considered when organizing the room for instruction

- explain how to manage time in order to prevent problems

- define principles to be followed when responding to behavior problems

- state the importance of dialogue and negotiation in the classroom

- describe some approaches to conflict resolution in the classroom

- develop a range of responses that can be used when responding to misbehavior

Bob Daemmrich Photography

Graphic Organizer: Chapter 13

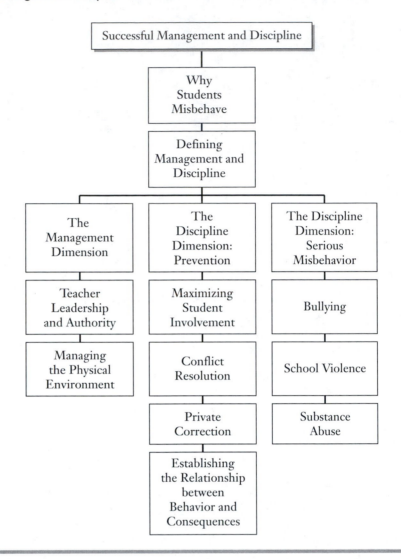

Introduction

Teachers have two major responsibilities: instructing students and managing the classroom. These two responsibilities are interdependent. An analysis of research indicates that classroom management—and discipline—is the single variable with the largest impact on student achievement (Elias & Schwab, 2006). This variable seems to be more important than knowledge of subject matter. The explanation for this link between good teaching and good management is that teachers who create interesting and relevant lessons have fewer discipline problems. Good classroom managers spend more quality time focusing on teaching rather than on control. The result is a more productive classroom.

As you consider the link between good management and good teaching, you should know that the lack of success for beginning teachers is often associated with an inability to manage and control the classroom (Good & Brophy, 2007). This is why the ability to manage the classroom and respond to inappropriate behavior is high on the list of concerns for new and inexperienced teachers. There is a consensus among researchers that the most common source of stress among teachers stems from teacher–student relationships. The most important dimension of teacher–student relationships is management and discipline (Friedman, 2006).

Therefore, learning how to manage classrooms and establish constructive relationships is a key to achieving success as a teacher. Evertson and Weinstein (2006) indicate that the inability to resolve challenges posed by classroom management and discipline is a major cause of teacher dissatisfaction and burnout. Many of the teachers who experience this burnout leave teaching.

Given the importance of this aspect of teaching, one might expect that it would receive considerable attention in teacher preparation programs. However, this is not often the case. The reason for this inattention is that some view discipline and management as primarily related to the personality of the teacher and therefore not something that can be taught. Others contend that learning how to manage a classroom is best left to experience. While we agree that personality and the interpersonal communication style of the teacher is important, this is not the whole story. Principles, skills, and attitudes can be taught to help all individuals achieve success in managing the classroom and keeping control.

Hoping that success can be achieved by experience is simply too costly. Learning on the job results in too many teacher and student failures. For example, studies indicate that a very large percentage of teachers leave teaching within the first three to five years of teaching. Many cite classroom management as a major factor in their decision to leave. We certainly cannot address the serious issue of educational improvement if we are constantly changing the personnel in the teaching force.

The graphic organizer at the beginning of the chapter identifies key dimensions of this domain that will be discussed in this chapter. It indicates that, to be effective in the management and discipline domain, you must first understand why students misbehave. Next, you need to define what management and discipline means. Then the domain can be divided into three basic areas: management, actions to prevent problems, and systematic responses to problems.

Marzano, Marzano, and Pickering (2003), in a review of the research on classroom management, underscore the importance of the management and discipline domain. They indicate that teachers who used effective disciplinary interventions had an average of about 980 disruptions over the course of a year, whereas those who did not had an average of about 1,800 disruptions.

Disruptions not only cause teacher stress, they result in a loss of learning time for all students. The loss of learning time and lower student engagement can be translated into student achievement: Those teachers with effective discipline and management techniques had student achievement scores that were about 20 percentile points higher than those who did not. Therefore, good management is a key area of attention when seeking to improve student achievement.

However, you need to understand that there is no universally applicable set of quick-fix remedies that you can learn and that will readily resolve every potential management difficulty you may face. If there were easy solutions, classroom management would not be such a serious concern among teachers, parents, and students.

The key to developing a program that results in successful and effective classroom control is in knowing something about these four areas:

- Actions you take in the classroom that are designed to prevent control problems
- Actions you take to establish your credibility and authority
- Actions you take to motivate and engage pupils
- Actions you take in response to inappropriate student behaviors

Why Do Students Misbehave?

First, it is important to remember that students are still immature human beings. All humans misbehave at times. Therefore, some misbehavior is to be expected just as a function of being human. At their stage of development, secondary-school-age students are seeking a sense of identity. Belonging to the group and feeling accepted are important goals. Their peer group is extremely important to them, and concerns about being accepted by peers my take priority over all else. Therefore, some behavior can be viewed as attempts to belong and be accepted by peers. Students are also searching for meaning and purpose in life.

Teachers who are insensitive to students' developmental needs run the risk of responding to misbehavior in ways that only worsen the behavior and do not provide the students with opportunities to learn from their mistakes. Good teachers understand that students' needs provide opportunities. If the classroom is viewed as a place that provides opportunities for them to meet their needs, students are less likely to misbehave.

Schools are part of society and reflect what is happening in society. Charles (2005) contends that television violence, dysfunctional families, poverty, unequal educational opportunities, child abuse, domestic violence, drugs, gangs, and poor emotional and cognitive development are all factors that contribute to school violence and behavior problems.

Many students also experience frequent change in their lives. Such changes, particularly in family circumstances, mean that some of your students may come to school without the benefit of ongoing family support and encouragement. Many of these young people lack a strong sense of self-identity and an accompanying sense that they have the ability to succeed at school-related tasks.

Your students do not leave their personal histories at the classroom door. These personal histories influence how they interpret their experiences. In other words, it is not so much what you think you are doing to them; it is what students think you are doing that will influence their interpretations and subsequent actions.

Students do understand the impact of their actions on teachers. They choose to comply or resist rules, support or sabotage teacher actions, and follow or question teacher authority. Students indicate that they often misbehave as a form of resistance. In other words, they are getting even with teachers whom they perceive to be ineffective, mean, or disrespectful (Hoy & Weinstein, 2006).

Students also understand that their behaviors influence teacher feelings and satisfactions. They can often enumerate specific behaviors that are likely to irritate teachers. Speaking out of turn, talking with others, getting out of their seat, and inattention are often listed by students as behaviors that upset teachers. In addition, some students interpret their failure as synonymous with teacher failure. They know that their lack of success is disturbing to the teacher, so they choose to fail as an attempt to "punish" the teacher. While this might seem shortsighted to many of us, to the student, failure might be one of the few options they have for striking back.

This data supports the view that student behavior is purposeful. When students like their teachers and believe that they are effective, caring, supportive, and fair, they are more likely to engage in prosocial behaviors, act responsibly, and adhere to classroom rules and norms (Hoy & Weinstein, 2006).

In summary, there are many reasons for student misbehavior. Some of the possible causes for inappropriate behavior are beyond the control of the teacher. However, teachers who demonstrate personal caring were cited by students as especially important to those who were experiencing outside pressures and problems.

Some inappropriate behavior is simply the result of developmental and social needs. However, a portion of inappropriate behavior is student protest about educational conditions. Therefore, a first step is to try and identify the causes of the misbehavior. Once the causes have been identified, it is easier to define appropriate responses.

Initially, your focus should be on factors that you can control and on creating an environment that will lead to the prevention of inappropriate behaviors. You can begin this process by asking yourself these questions:

- Are you creating educational environments that respect students and value their input?
- Do your students feel a sense of power and control?
- Is the curriculum culturally relevant and worthwhile?
- Does your school provide opportunities for success rather than pose threats of failure?
- Do your students feel they really belong in your classroom?
- Are you establishing personal and academic caring relationships with the students?
- Does the educational experience offered to students by your school offer them opportunities sometimes to simply have fun?

Defining Management and Discipline

Before proceeding any further, you need to have clear definitions in mind of the terms *management* and *discipline*. Both management and discipline are examples of concepts that have been defined in different ways by teachers. Understanding how these terms are defined will provide some common ground for discussion.

Management

Some view management as the right of a person in authority to impose her or his will on others. This is what might be referred to as boss management. In this definition, the person who is in charge is the boss and has the right to expect compliance and unquestioned obedience. Our definition of management is quite different. We define management as creating the conditions that facilitate the success and satisfaction of all students. This is what can be defined as lead management, where the power and authority of the manager is used in service to others to help them achieve their goals rather than the goals of the manager (Glasser, 1990). In teaching, it includes the part of your role that focuses on creating an environment and establishing conditions that facilitate student academic and social success. It involves your exercise of classroom leadership, facilitation of student motivation, arrangement of the physical environment, and management of time and lessons. Some of the tasks associated with lead management are the following:

- Involve students and get their input in discussions of the work to be done and the conditions under which it is to be completed.
- Communicate expectations clearly, model tasks you assign, and continually solicit input from students.
- Ask students to inspect and evaluate their own work for quality and then willingly listen to students and accept that they know a good deal about how to produce high-quality work.
- Function as a facilitator who provides students with the tools they need to learn in an environment that is noncoercive and nonadversarial.

Discipline

Discipline is sometimes defined as punishment for disobedience. The role of the student is to obey the authorities; if the student does not obey, he or she experiences punishment. This definition identifies the role of the teacher as someone who must enforce conformity and obedience and administer punishment.

More from the Web

Several sites on the Web provide information about classroom management and discipline. The following website provides excellent links to a number of topics related to the general theme of classroom management. It provides ideas on topics such as dealing with late arriving students and getting the period started.

http://www.teachnet.com/how-to/manage/index.html

Another useful site is compiled by the Northwest Regional Educational Laboratory's School Improvement Research Series. Author Kathleen Cotton provides excellent information on topics such as defining discipline, research findings related to discipline, discipline practices that have been found to be successful for different types of students, and formal discipline programs that have been adopted around the country.

http://www.nwrel.org/scpd/sirs/5/cu9.html

We reject this conception of discipline as inconsistent with an educational system designed to prepare students to become citizens in a democratic society. This definition also leads to a teacher role that places teachers and students in unproductive adversarial roles.

We define discipline as the process of developing self-control, character, orderliness, and responsibility. Developing these qualities is among the most important purposes of education. Education in a democracy requires the development of good people as well as good students. A society filled with educated individuals yet one where citizens lack self-control is a society destined for difficulty. Unfortunately, contemporary society reflects too many examples of the difficulties created by the lack of self-control involving politicians, business leaders, educators, and even clergy.

This definition of discipline provides clear guidance for teachers as they develop their disciple plan and as they respond to students. When responding to inappropriate behavior,

What Do You Think?

Reflecting on Personal Experience

Your experiences as a secondary school student can serve as a valuable source of information for teaching. However, you need to think seriously about specific experiences you remember. For example, consider how your own teachers handled discipline problems. Think about what they did that worked well and what did not. What do you remember about teachers who seemed to have few discipline problems? What do you remember about those who had difficulty in this area of professional responsibility?

Prepare a list of characteristics of both effective and ineffective managers of student behavior. How were students regarded and generally treated by teachers in each category? What did teachers in each category do when they had to respond to student behavior problems?

Questions

1. What differences do you remember about teachers in each category?

2. What do you think are the most important differences between teachers in each category?

3. What are some principles that you might formulate based on your reflections about teachers in each category?

4. Share your principles with others in your class. How are yours similar and different from those developed by other class members?

5. Develop a master list of principles and compare them to ones outlined later in this chapter.

you should ask yourself, What actions will best help this individual move toward self-control? If there does not appear to be a growth in students' self-control as the school year unfolds, then the teacher needs to evaluate the discipline plan. This perspective also allows you to view incidents of misbehavior as opportunities to teach students important lessons that will yield personal benefits to them throughout their lives. Your responses to inappropriate behavior should promote students' development of patterns of self-control that are important to productive and satisfying adult interpersonal relationships.

In summary, you, as a teacher, have responsibility for both management and discipline. Your responsibilities for management should focus on organization and planning practices that can prevent problems. Your role in the area of discipline should focus on helping students develop responsible patterns of self-control. These patterns, once mastered, will serve students well throughout their adult lives.

The Management Dimension: Preventing Problems

Several dimensions of the classroom need to be addressed in the management category, including the organization and management of time, materials, and space. Attention to these dimensions of the classroom helps create a smooth and productive classroom. Also included in this dimension are specific actions and behaviors of the teacher that establish your classroom leadership.

Well-managed classrooms appear rather effortless to the untrained observer. These classrooms sometimes seem to run themselves. As skilled professionals, expert teachers make management look easy. In fact, these apparently problem-free classrooms are the result of hard work and lots of decisions. They certainly are not chance occurrences that have come about because these teachers have been lucky enough to draw groups of unusually well-behaved students (Evertson, Emmer, & Worsham, 2003).

Teacher Leadership and Authority

One of the most important steps in classroom management is that of establishing teacher leadership. Your philosophy, values, understanding of individual students, beliefs about learning, and leadership style all affect the social environment of the classroom. If you are to be effective, your students have to willingly accept you as a leader. In general, teachers who are viewed as leaders are secure, confident, and optimistic. This requires that you do a self-check regarding your attitudes and sense of efficacy. Do you believe that you can teach students and they can learn? What is your attitude toward the students? Are you afraid that they will take advantage of you if you display kindness?

One of the roots of serious discipline problems at the secondary school level is a sense of hopelessness. As a teacher, you must maintain a sense of optimism and hopefulness even in difficult times. You must maintain a sense of hope for all students if you are to expect them to remain hopeful.

Your beliefs about your students will affect your personal leadership style. For example, if you are a person who believes students are lazy and untrustworthy, you will develop management and control patterns different from those who trust and respect students. Students will quickly sense any negative attitudes you may have about them. If they believe you do not respect or trust them, they become very reluctant to accept you as a leader.

In preparing to work with secondary school students, you need to remember that young people in this age group are striving to establish some sense of personal identity. As part of this effort, it is natural for them to engage in some limited testing of imposed authorities (parents, teachers, and others). Secondary students cannot be expected to defer quietly to every one of your demands, particularly if they sense an element of unfairness or if they feel you are challenging their self-respect.

Over 50 years ago, French and Raven (1959) identified some perspectives of social leadership that are still helpful in developing teacher authority and power. They identified five sources of power or authority that are applicable to classroom environments:

- Legitimate power
- Reward power
- Coercive power
- Expert power
- Referent or attractive power

Legitimate Power   Some roles in U.S. society, including teaching, carry with them a certain amount of power and authority regardless of who fulfills the role. This is termed legitimate power. When you are hired as a teacher, some power and authority goes with the role. In other words, you are not another student or a volunteer. This authority is conferred upon you by the state, the school district, and the school administration. This means that the authority is ascribed or given with the role rather than earned. For this reason, your legitimate authority may have limited impact on the students. In fact, it has been our observation that a place where many new teachers have difficulty is that they expect their legitimate authority to be sufficient for managing the classroom. They are then surprised when certain students challenge their authority and are not moved by commands that they should do something simply because the teachers tells them to! Simply put, legitimate authority is insufficient for establishing leadership in the classroom.

Reward Power   A dimension of legitimate authority is the power to give certain benefits or rewards to students. Rewards available to teachers usually include grades, praise, and privileges. While we all like rewards and most of us seek to avoid environments where there is little possibility of obtaining rewards, reward power has some limitations in the classroom. For example, all students may not value the kinds of rewards you are in a position to give. If students have had a history of school failure and have developed a sense of hopelessness, they may attach little or no importance to getting good grades. In addition, many students value the rewards they get from peers more than they value the rewards they get from the teacher. Therefore, the promise of a higher grade may have little impact on the behavior of certain students.

Coercive Power   Another dimension of legitimate authority is the opposite of reward power, which is coercive power. This is the authority to administer punishments. Like reward power, however, coercive power has some serious limitations in the classroom. Some of the punishments that might be administered are reprimands, loss of privileges, and failing grades. Reprimands from individuals that are not respected by students have little effect, loss of privileges presumes that they have some privileges that can be lost, and failing grades have little impact on those who have given up. In addition, it may well be that the rewards the students get from other students for their actions have much more influence than the punishments administered by teachers.

Placing heavy reliance on punishment as a means of asserting your authority often has the effect of diminishing teacher leadership rather than encouraging it. Punishment encourages your students to view combat as a normal part of their relationship with you. Rather than following your leadership, they may engage in power struggles to show you that they are not intimidated. Harsh punishment has been found to be linked to behavior problems (Emmer & Gerwels, 2006).

Research studies indicate that students define "good" teachers as those who have authority, are firm, set limits, and enforce expectations. However, they do not respect teachers who are "mean," and they do not like being coerced or controlled. They do not respond well to teachers they view as being mean or punitive (Hoy & Weinstein, 2006).

How do we reconcile these dimensions of how students define "good" teachers? Perhaps it can be found in looking at another type of power and authority: earned authority.

Expert Power   Earned authority is earned rather than ascribed by others. One type of earned authority is called expert power. Individuals perceived by a group to have superior knowledge or skill are accorded some authority or power. This type of authority is earned, not ascribed. Positions and titles must be accompanied by the perception that the individual holding the position has the knowledge required.

As a teacher, you need to establish yourself as an "expert." You need to know the subject you are teaching, know how to make it meaningful, and know how to manage the classroom so that it is a safe and productive learning environment. Research consistently indicates that student respect for teachers is a key variable in a productive classroom. This respect must be earned and a good deal of the respect comes from being defined as an "expert" teacher.

Referent or Attractive Power   This is a second type of earned authority. This type of authority refers to individuals who are perceived to be caring, trustworthy, and interested in the well-being of others. For example, we willingly seek advice from and even entrust our prized possessions to those we believe care about us and have our best interests at heart. These individuals have what is termed referent or attractive power.

In the classroom, there are two types of caring: academic caring, where the teacher is interested in the academic success of the students, and personal caring, where the teacher is interested in the personal welfare of the students. Adolescents want to be valued by their teachers. They want teachers who take the time to talk with them and to listen to what they have to say. They respect teachers who are friendly and maintain a sense of humor. They want teachers who provide both academic and social support. They want teachers who know when they are having academic difficulty and provide assistance, and they want teachers who recognize when they are about to get in trouble and can intervene when needed (Emmer & Gerwels, 2006).

How can these dimensions of leadership be implemented in the classroom? One of the most important steps is to realize the importance of the beginning of the year. Generally, disruptions and off-task behavior is quite low during the first week of school (Emmer & Gerwels, 2006). This provides an opportunity for you to influence the classroom climate and to begin developing your leadership. During this time, you need to begin establishing your expert and attractive authority. It is important that you communicate enthusiasm and the importance of the subject during the first days of the school year. If you appear nervous, uncertain, or bored, the first impression that the students receive will be a negative one that will invite challenges from them.

Your expert authority can be enhanced by creating a warm yet businesslike atmosphere. The goal you should seek is to create the image of a "warm demander": a teacher who is friendly and concerned about the students but who is also demanding in making sure that all students will be held accountable for their behavior and their classwork. As you begin your year, establish classroom rules and procedures that provide clear expectations for the students. Spend time orienting the students to the subject and helping them understand what they will be doing in the class. Be careful, however, not to overwhelm the students so that they become discouraged. Establishing the beginnings of your expert authority requires that you be extremely well-prepared and well-organized. The beginning of the school year is the time to be overprepared.

Your referent or attractive authority is enhanced if you quickly learn student names, are respectful toward students, and listen to their questions and concerns. Students want to know if this is a place where they will feel comfortable and whether you are the type of teacher who is interested in them as individuals. They want to know if this will be a psychologically safe and supportive environment. If the first few days help them answer these issues in a positive way, your attractive authority will increase and you will be on the way to preventing problems. For example, one high school teacher was confronted by several upset students when they perceived that his expectations were inconsistent with the expectations of another one of their teachers. He established immediate credibility and attractive authority by going to the other teacher and working out a compromise. The students now believed that he was listening to them and was interested in helping them achieve success.

While the beginning of the year is critical, you need to continue establishing your expert and attractive authority as the year unfolds. Becoming familiar with the students and their interests is helpful. One secondary school English teacher made it a point to go to numerous school activities in which students in her classroom were involved. She would also highlight student accomplishments on a special bulletin board she kept in the classroom. The students in her classroom rarely misbehaved. Allowing student input into decisions and listening to their perspectives and concerns also helps establish a warm and productive learning environment. The classroom needs to be viewed as a place where students belong and where their needs are regularly met.

Creating such an environment can be a difficult task for you as a secondary school teacher because you may teach several different groups of students and see them only once a day for less than an hour. However, it can be done. Many of us can identify secondary school teachers who do this on a regular basis.

The most powerful combination of authority styles involves both expert and referent power. If your students see you as an expert who is interested in their welfare, you will find that your legitimate, reward, and coercive powers increase. Rewards given by highly valued and trusted individuals are especially powerful. By the same token, reprimands or punishments meted out by someone who is valued and trusted are also very powerful. In fact, a simple reprimand by a highly valued teacher is often more powerful that a physical punishment administered by someone who is not trusted or respected.

Teacher Consistency   Another category of your behavior that is a foundation for a smoothly functioning classroom is consistency. Consistency means that you are fair and predictable. The students know what to expect, and they see you acting in ways that are consistent with the way you treat students and apply the classroom rules. Teachers who are very strict one day and very lenient the next are inconsistent. So are teachers who appear to treat some students with anger and hostility and others with acceptance and respect (Savage & Savage, 2010). Student behavior you find unacceptable on one day should generally be considered unacceptable on another. If you fail to be consistent, some of your students may come to class wondering, What can we get away with today? This may lead them to test you to see how far they can go. When you apply your rules consistently across time, you will eliminate students' incentives to challenge the limits you have established.

You must also apply rules and regulations consistently to all students. This means that you cannot simply overlook a situation when a "model" student breaks a rule. Selective enforcement will undermine your referent power and credibility. Student hostility and disrespect is the normal outcome of such inconsistency. Consistency of follow-through is also important. When you make a promise, you need to carry it out. If you make a threat, be prepared to implement it. The idea is not to make any promises or threats you cannot carry out.

Managing the Physical Environment

The physical properties of your classroom affect student behavior. The size, shape, attractiveness, seating arrangements, and lighting create an environment where students will spend a considerable amount of time. Consider these questions as you prepare the physical environment of you classroom:

- Do I want to encourage interactions among students?
- Will students be moving from place to place during the class period?
- Do I want to focus students' attention on a specific part of the room?

As you arrange your classroom, you will need to direct your attention to the following categories of concern:

- Classroom ambiance
- Floor space
- Time management
- Establishing routines
- Providing assistance

Classroom Ambiance The ambiance of a place refers to its general atmosphere or feel. Think about spaces outside the school. What makes a place appear inviting? Why you are more comfortable in some places than you are in others? Are there some places where you feel stimulated and other spaces where you feel bored? These feelings generally relate to the ambiance that has been created. Interior decorators make their living creating ambiance for spaces that meet the needs and the goals of those inhabiting the space.

Classrooms are no different from other spaces. The ambiance of the classroom affects the behavior patterns of both teachers and students (Weinstein, 1979). As the quality of the physical environment declines, teachers make more control statements and are less friendly. Students in such classrooms are less involved in lessons, and feelings of conflict among students increase.

While teachers are not expected to be interior decorators, they do need to understand that the quality of the space where they are teaching exerts an influence on them and on the students. You can improve the quality of a space and create a positive ambiance without much effort.

Some of the variables that can be considered in improving the ambiance of a classroom include lighting, decoration of wall space, orderliness of the classroom, and temperature control. Lighting in a classroom is often difficult to control because the lights are controlled by just one or two switches. Sometimes the type of lighting creates a "harsh" environment. It might be possible to soften the lighting by adding some floor lamps and turning off some of the overhead lights. Sometimes teachers share a classroom with other teachers, so they may be limited in what is put on the walls. However, simply putting up some wall hangings and making sure the walls are free of clutter can improve the ambiance. Some studies have revealed that cluttered and "ugly" environments increase off-task behavior, an increase in feelings of fatigue, and an increase in student conflict (Weinstein, 1979). Therefore, having an orderly and pleasant environment has some concrete benefits. Again, it may be difficult to control the temperature in a classroom. However, if the classroom is not comfortable, students will have difficulty focusing on the task.

Floor Space The arrangement of desks and other classroom furniture can cue students to your expectations. Arrangements need to vary to accommodate different kinds of learning activities. For example, different patterns may be helpful when you want students to listen to you, work individually, study together in small groups, or take part in a large-group discussion.

In determining a specific arrangement, you should begin by thinking about what your students will be required to do. When you plan to present new information, it is important that student desks be arranged so that each student can see you without having to look around visual obstructions. Sometimes you may want to widen the spaces separating individual desks to discourage too much social interaction among students.

If your intent is for students to work individually on assignments, it makes sense to arrange classroom furniture so that you can move quickly to help any individual in the class. Ideally, you should be able to move easily to help anyone experiencing a problem. An arrangement that allows you to go immediately to any place in the classroom also promotes on-task behavior. (Students know you will arrive in a hurry if a disturbance breaks out.)

When you want students to work in small groups, you need to decrease spaces separating individuals in each group. This will allow all group members to see papers and other materials, and it will permit easy conversation among all participants. It is helpful if you can arrange chairs so that all group members can see one another easily. (This is difficult if your students are required to sit in rows.)

Managing Time   Class time in secondary education is limited. Generally, teachers have about 50 minutes per day with a given class. A common complaint of teachers is that they lack the time to do all that is required of them. Proposals for school improvement often target time as an important consideration. This has led to recommendations to increase the school day as well as the school year. It has also led to more schools experimenting with block schedules.

Effective time management can help teachers capture just a few more minutes of instructional time per class. When this time is accumulated over the space of a school year, it can have a significant impact on learning (Good & Brophy, 2007). In addition, good time management will result in fewer behavior problems.

The basic concept we propose is to eliminate "dead air time." Dead air time refers to the time in the classroom where the students are not engaged and are not focused on the objectives of the lesson. We all know that when we encounter "dead air time" in the media, we change to a different station. Consider that when there is dead air time in your classroom, students are "changing the channel." You may hear experienced teachers state that they keep the students so busy that they don't have time to misbehave. There is a fair amount of truth to that approach.

Two aspects of time management that can help you make productive use of classroom time are (1) establishing and using routines and (2) providing assistance to students who need help.

Establishing Routines   Routines are especially important in secondary schools because most secondary teachers have several periods during a given day. Students are coming and going on an hourly basis, and materials have to be distributed and collected efficiently or considerable time can be wasted. For example, it is not uncommon to observe a secondary school classroom where the first 10 minutes is spent taking attendance, collecting homework, distributing materials, and making announcements. A 50-minute period has now become a 40-minute period. In addition, if several students become engaged in other activities, it requires considerable effort to get them to focus on the lesson. Therefore, routines need to be developed for these repeated events so that they can be done quickly and efficiently.

Your goal should be to get students in the room quickly and get them on task. Some teachers accomplish this by having a task identified on the board when the students enter the room. This might be a quick review of the previous lesson. While they are doing this, the routine tasks such as attendance taking can be completed quickly. It is also useful to have student assistants for each class. These assistants perform routine tasks. And students like to do it! At the end of the period, the class needs to be brought to closure and all materials collected. If assignments need to be made, they must be finished with enough time left so that students can ask questions. A common excuse for not doing homework is that the students didn't hear or understand what they were supposed to do.

Providing Assistance   Assisting individual students can consume tremendous quantities of classroom time. Frederic Jones (1987), a researcher who studied this issue, concluded that many teachers spend more time than necessary working one on one with each student in their classrooms. Jones suggests the *praise-prompt-leave* procedure. When a student needs assistance, provide some praise for something the student has done correctly. Then give a prompt or a direct suggestion regarding what the student should do next. Now, leave and move to another student. In a couple of minutes, check back to make sure the student has moved on. If not, repeat the praise-prompt-leave procedure. The value of this procedure is that it prevents some students from depending on the teacher to do the work for them. In addition, it increases the number of students that a teacher can assist in the classroom and allows more time for the teacher to monitor the whole class.

You do not always have to be the one providing the help. One junior high school teacher created "consultant" badges that students earned and wore proudly. The "consultants" were allowed to leave their seats to help other students who requested assistance. The teacher limited the number of consultants, and members of the class worked hard to win the honor of being among the "consultants of the week."

The Discipline Dimension: Solving Discipline Problems

There are no surefire remedies or guaranteed fixes for behavior problems. What is effective in one setting and with one individual may not be effective in another. However, there are some things you can do to increase the probability that your management plan will be work.

CRITICAL INCIDENT

HOW DO YOU ESTABLISH CONTROL?

Hillary Carter remembers dreaming about becoming a teacher when she was in high school. She recalls the thrill of encountering new literature and applying the insights of the great writers to her own life. As an undergraduate student, her enthusiasm for her subject increased. She worked at perfecting the communication and planning skills she knew she would need to inspire high school students. She had great confidence in her ability to be a good teacher. She started her first teaching job this past fall. Things have not worked out quite as she imagined they would.

For one thing, her students are quite different from what she expected. She had wanted to teach advanced secondary students who were capable of appreciating good literature. Instead, she finds herself teaching ninth-graders. The students display little enthusiasm for academic pursuits and seem consumed by social and recreational interests. They view Hillary's classroom as a social gathering place where they can show off and challenge her authority. In addition, several of the students have limited English proficiency and consequently have difficulty reading some of the literature selections she would like to use.

To remedy the situation, Hillary has tried several options, but nothing has worked. She started the year by being friendly with all of the students and hoped her enthusiasm would be contagious. She told the students that she trusted them and was sure that they didn't need a lot of rules. Instead of appreciating this expression of confidence, the students have taken this as an invitation to do whatever pleases them.

In thinking about her classroom situation, Hillary has concluded that the students behave this way because they don't understand why it is important to know something about good literature. Yesterday, she took time to talk to the class about the importance of good literature. The students rejected her logic. One student made this comment: "Look, you may like this stuff, but we think it is really boring. We would much rather see a movie." She has considered using some literature that ties in more clearly to students' interests. But the more she has pondered this approach, the less promising it has seemed. How, she wonders, can I build a responsible literature program around student interests that seem limited to film stars, sports, and sex?

Recently, she's also been thinking about the advice experienced teachers sometimes give newcomers: Don't smile until Christmas. She thinks she may have been demanding too little of her students. For the past several weeks, she has started lowering grades of students who misbehave or fail to do their work. This has only made matters worse. Many students laugh when they get a failing grade. Some actually seem to be competing to see who can get the most F's.

At this point, Hillary is about to give up. She has been telling her friends that "students have really changed since we were in school." She is thinking about looking for a job where she can work with college-bound students. She commented recently, "I would do anything to work with some students who care."

■ ■ ■

What do you think are the key issues in this incident? What do you think about what Hillary has tried? Do you agree that students have changed a great deal in the past few years? What supports your view? What are Hillary's key values? Where did she acquire them? How might her values be different from those of the students? How might these differences affect what Hillary thinks is important and what the students think is important? Is there any way Hillary can bridge these differences, or do you think a move to another school would be the best solution for her? What do you think she needs to change? Where might she go to get help? What should Hillary's next step be?

Teaching Conflict Resolution

Secondary school teachers soon learn that they cannot do it all alone. They must have the cooperation and commitment of the students or their class becomes an unproductive nightmare. Secondary students are at a stage of development where they want to have some power and authority. One useful way of gaining their cooperation and commitment is through teaching them how to handle conflict. Actions you take related to conflict resolution will make life in your classroom better for both you and the young people you serve (Lee, Pulvino, & Perrone, 1998).

Some secondary schools have adopted conflict resolution on a schoolwide scale. In other schools, individual teachers have taken the time to teach conflict resolution in their classroom. While some teachers may argue that they do not have the time to teach conflict resolution, the time and the effort they save over the course of the year makes the time spent worthwhile.

Schools that have adopted formal conflict-avoidance strategies tend to follow one of two basic approaches (Johnson & Johnson, 1995). One of these focuses on training groups of students who serve as peer mediators for the school. The other approach teaches all students in a school or a classroom how to manage conflict constructively. Johnson and Johnson (1995) point out that this involve-all-the-students model has proved the more effective of the two basic approaches in helping young people learn how to negotiate and mediate conflict. Johnson and Johnson (1995) include the following six basic steps in their conflict resolution approach:

- Getting students to describe what each person wants
- Having students describe their feelings
- Explaining the reasons underlying their wants and feelings
- Reversing perspectives in order to view the conflict from both sides
- Inventing options that have mutual benefit
- Reaching a wise agreement

You may find it useful to address conflict resolution by developing specific lessons that focus on the above steps. For example, you might develop lessons that include emphases on issues such as identifying conflicts, identifying different conflict resolution styles, identifying emotions, practicing active listening, identifying problem-solving approaches, and evaluating resolutions. The conflict resolution component of lessons can be embedded within lessons that focus on your regular academic content. For example, if you are teaching English, you might choose to use a particular literary selection as a starting point for a discussion of an issue related to conflict resolution. The field of social studies contains rich content resources that can be used for teaching conflict resolution while also addressing required content.

Content is best taught and learned when students have a need to know. Therefore, the best time to teach conflict resolution is when your students face a real conflict. In addition, you need to remember that a certain amount of repetition is needed for learning. You cannot expect one or two lessons taught at the beginning of the year to have much impact on your students' patterns of behavior.

Emphasizing Private Correction

Students generally report that they respect teachers who have firm control over the classroom. This respect diminished, however, if the teacher used public humiliation or threats. Teachers were considered to be adversaries if they engaged in public acts intended to convey their power and authority. What students want is calm control, where teachers convey respect for the students (Hoy & Weinstein, 2006). Simple interventions work best with the majority of the students (Emmer & Gerwels, 2006). These findings underscore the importance of private correction when dealing with secondary school students. Some of the most common forms of private correction are proximity control, eye contact, and conferences.

Proximity control refers to the act of moving closer to the individual who is demonstrating inappropriate behavior without calling attention to the student. This signals to the students that you are aware of the difficulty and provides an opportunity for them to self-correct. It is hard for even the most difficult students to misbehave when the teacher is standing next to their desk.

Nearly everyone has experienced the teacher who can send a clear message through eye contact. The "cold hard stare" does have an impact on students without publicly "calling them out." Eye contact, combined with proximity control, can be very effective.

If these nonintrusive responses don't achieve the desired result, a conference with the student can be effective. However, these conferences need to be done in private and handled calmly. One possible response might be to try actions such as proximity control; if that doesn't work, transition to a whole-group student activity for a couple of minutes. Then pull the student aside and discuss the situation. It is best to get the student talking. You might ask the student, "What are you doing? What happens when students do that?" It can be effective to send I-messages (Gordon, 1974). An I-message basically identifies the behavior, and states the consequences of the behavior and the impact of the behavior on the feelings of the teacher. For example, a teacher might send the following I-message, "When individuals get out of their seats it attracts my attention and that of the rest of the students. This interferes with our learning and causes us to waste time. This makes me impatient and angry." The I-message does not demand a change but opens the door for discussion. It allows the student an opportunity to talk and helps her or him to understand why the behavior was considered inappropriate.

Private correction shows respect for the students. It helps eliminate the power struggle and the escalation of inappropriate behavior that often accompanies public correction.

Choosing to Misbehave Means Choosing to Expereince Consequences

Emphasizing private correction does not mean that there are no consequences for inappropriate behavior if a student persists. For example, part of the dialogue in a student conference allows you to point out that when people choose to misbehave or violate the law, they also choose the consequences of their actions. Students need to understand that you are not just "picking on them" but that they are choosing to experience undesirable consequences when they choose to misbehave. They need to realize that they will be held accountable for their inappropriate actions. This connection between behavior and consequence is not understood by some secondary school students. They blame others for the consequences they experience. For real progress toward self-control, individuals first must understand and accept that they choose the consequences through their own actions. However, this also implies that as a teacher, you need to spell out clearly both acceptable and unacceptable behavior and the nature of the consequences for each choice.

It is best to discuss the consequences in an individual conference with the student. If this is done privately, students are more likely to be honest with you in discussing the issue of consequences. During such a conference, you might discover underlying emotions and feelings that need to be addressed in order to help the student accept consequences and a sense of responsibility for his or her behavior.

Severe Misbehavior in Secondary Schools   Most new teachers have a tremendous fear of teaching in classrooms where severe misbehavior is the norm. Indeed, media attention on incidents such as gang-related deaths, severe examples of bullying, and attacks in high schools such as the famous one at Columbine have fueled the image of secondary schools as unsafe places filled with serious behavioral problems and out-of-control students.

However, this is not an accurate perception. The most serious forms of violence (robbery, aggravated assault, homicide, rape, sexual assault) rarely occur in schools (Center for Disease Control and Prevention, 2007). Although homicide and suicide are the second and third leading causes of death, respectively, among students between the ages of 15 and 24, less that 1% of the homicides and suicides occur in the schools (Center for Disease Control and Prevention, 2007). In addition, contrary to popular perception, the rate of violence in schools has decreased since 1994. The rate of violent crime was about 13 per 1,000 students in 1994 and about 6 per 1,000 in 2007. This represents about a 50% decrease (U.S. Department of Justice, Bureau of Educational Statistics, 2009). In fact, it is actually safer for students to be in school than it is for them to be in a car!

We do have an expectation that our schools should be safe places. Effective schools are places where teachers can teach and students can learn without feeling unsafe. Keep in mind that teachers have a legal obligation to protect the health and safety of their students. This elevates the importance of teacher decisions. Serious misbehavior simply cannot be ignored; to do so may result in some legal action.

Categories of Serious Misbehavior

Bullying   One of the most serious types of misbehavior, yet one that has often been ignored by teachers and school officials, is bullying. Many adults, teachers, administrators, and parents tend to view bullying as just a phase of growing up and therefore not something that deserves serious attention. For example, one study found that 70% of the teachers surveyed believed that they responded to almost every incident of bullying. However, only 25% of their students agreed with their assessment. Students indicate that they are reluctant to report bullying because they believe they will be ignored and they fear retaliation (Hyman et al., 2006).

There is some troubling data about bullying. Approximately 160,000 students report staying home from school each day for fear of being bullied (Charles, 2005). Somewhere between 15% and 25% of all students report that they are bullied frequently (Hyman et al., 2006). Bullying has been identified as the unacknowledged crime of violence in schools because adults are generally unaware of its prevalence. However, bullying is a serious issue that harms the learning environment. Bullying creates an atmosphere of fear and anxiety that can harm the learning of all students. In addition, bullying is often a precursor to increased violence in the schools (Hardin, 2008). Many educators have failed to grasp this connection. For victims, repeated bullying can lead to their use of extreme measures. A common thread that runs through school shooting is that the shooters felt bullied, harassed, or victimized (Blassone, 2007).

Bullying also has a negative impact on those who bully. Bullying may establish patterns of behavior that lead to more serious problems. Students who bully are more likely to engage in acts of vandalism and fighting (Olewus, 2003), are more likely to drop out of school, and are four times more likely to engage in substance abuse. Children identified by their peers at age 6 as bullies are six times more likely to commit a crime by age 24 and are five times more likely to end up with a serious criminal record (Melissa Institute for Violence Prevention and Treatment, 2007).

In summary, bullying is a serious issue and can no longer be overlooked as merely a phase of growing up. Simplistic advice to victims to just stand up to bullies is neither effective nor wise.

One reason for the low teacher response to bullying is a lack of understanding of the different forms of bullying. In general there are two types of bullying: direct and indirect. Direct bullying is the face-to-face type of bullying that is generally recognized by teachers. It includes physical forms of bullying as well as taunting, name-calling, humiliating, gesturing, and staring.

Indirect bullying is often called social or relational bullying. This type of bullying involves gossiping, spreading rumors, undermining friendships, excluding, and shunning. Many of these indirect types of bullying are common in secondary schools. One particular form of indirect bullying that has become a special concern is that of cyberbullying. Cyberbullying is using electronic devices such as cell phones and computers to demean and/or belittle others. Cyberbullying occurs through e-mails, instant messages, blogs, and websites. One study found that 43% of teens reported that they experienced some form of cyberbullying during the past year (National Crime Prevention Council, 2007). Cyberbullying received considerable national attention when the mother of a girl helped her cyberbully another girl. The result was that the bullied girl committed suicide. Remember that secondary students are seeking a sense of identity and are strongly influenced by peer acceptance. Relational bullying can have a devastating effect on them.

Systematic efforts to address bullying are relatively recent. Some of the early work has been done in European schools, where administrators were prompted to take action to prevent suicides. Recent research indicates that good programs of bullying prevention are effective. Good antibullying programs have reduced the incidents of bullying from 30% to 70% (Hyman et al., 2006)

Schoolwide programs are effective because much bullying takes place outside the classroom. General characteristics of schoolwide programs include a policy statement against bullying, a clear plan for responding to incidents of bullying, informing parents of the seriousness of bullying and the consequences for those who engage in bullying, and schoolwide support for victims. Schoolwide programs do take time to make a change, mainly because they require a time-consuming change in culture.

Classroom-level programs need to be multifaceted. One of the key elements is an emphasis on respect for one another. Teachers might consider the modeling they are providing if they attempt to use their power to coerce and dominate students. Other elements of classroom programs involve helping students with anger management, impulse control, developing prosocial behaviors, and developing empathy. Teachers should also look for opportunities to include bullying prevention in the curriculum. This can be done through activities such as literature selection, role-playing, creative writing, and classroom meetings.

Peer relationships should be the main focus in bullying prevention. Bullying almost always takes place in a group context. Bullies want power and acceptance, and the reactions of the group may be providing them with reinforcement for their actions. Studies indicate that peer intervention is a more effective deterrent than victim aggression or retaliation (Hyman et al., 2006). Therefore, an effective approach to bullying is to create a climate where bullying becomes unacceptable. Bystanders need to be taught to communicate that bullying is unacceptable and will not be supported. When bullies sense that they are not

More from the Web

Several Internet sites provide good information about bullying and bullying prevention programs. These can be very helpful in identifying steps that you can take to prevent bullying. Some of the places where you might start are the following:

Bullying UK: http://www.bullying.co.uk

Keep Schools Safe: http://www.keepschoolssafe.org

National Violence Prevention Resource Center: http://www.safeyouth.org

Stop Bullying Now: http://www.stopbullyingnow.hrsa.gov

TeachSafeSchools: http//www.teachsafeschools.org

being supported and their actions are rejected, they are likely to stop. Removing group support for bullying is effective for indirect bullying, too. Students need to understand that these actions are a form of bullying and will not be tolerated.

Cyberbullying can be confronted by discussing the impact of cyberbullying on others. Again, all students need to know that they are participating in bullying if they are passing on inappropriate messages or photographs about others. Schools can establish policies that include consequences for students participating in cyberbullying on school equipment. Parents should be informed of the negative consequences of cyberbullying and the potential consequences of participating. They need to encourage their children to report incidents of cyberbullying to them. Students need to understand that cyberbullying messages, whether from home or school, that contain threats of violence, extortion, harassment, or pornography are illegal and the police should be notified. In addition, Internet providers have policies regarding the use of language and threats, and participation in cyberbullying may result in the Internet provider taking action. In addition, civil law permits victims of bullies to sue for damages.

In summary, cyberbullying has some serious consequences. Once students understand these consequences, they may not view cyberbullying as a funny prank.

School Violence   Another serious form of misbehavior is school violence. While school violence receives considerable attention in the media, it is listed by teachers as the least prevalent among the challenges that hinder student learning. About 9% of teachers state that violence is a problem that inhibits learning for at least a quarter of their students. In 2008, 93% of the students reported that they felt very or somewhat safe in school (MetLife, 2008).

Violence in the school is not easy to understand nor are there simple profiles of students who resort to violence. Some experts point out that violence is common in our culture given the number of incidents of violence in the media as well as the videogames played by many students. For example, by the time a student reaches seventh grade, that student is likely to have encountered about 8,000 murders and 100,000 acts of violence on television (Constitutional Rights Foundation, 2007). It is somewhat surprising that there is actually not more violence in schools.

Violence and aggression against other students is the most common category of school violence. Students who engage in violence against others often suffer from alienation and stress. They often resort to gang membership as a way of meeting belonging needs and to feel significant. Therefore, teachers must make a concerted effort to make sure the classroom is a place where students feel they belong and where they are connected and engaged.

Violence in the form of fights and acts of aggression sometimes occurs when horseplay and teasing get out of hand. Some students with low self-esteem or high power needs may feel disrespected and feel they must defend their dignity or their "turf." Thus, while some elements of fun are useful in classrooms, teachers should step in quickly if horseplay and pranks move to the stage of demeaning other students.

When situations escalate toward a violent confrontation, one can take several actions, including using humor or a calm voice to bring down the level of anxiety and to communicate a sense of teacher control, using a firm and assertive voice with a clear verbal directive, and giving the onlookers a firm directive to leave and thus remove the audience. Separate students and give them an opportunity to calm down before taking further action.

The acronym DEFUSE can provide guidance when you face tense or violent situations.

D: Depersonalize and don't lose your cool. Do not take the words and the actions of the student personally.

E: Encourage students to vent. Encourage them to talk and try to get them to talk in a respectful voice.

F: Find out the facts. Don't be quick to judge.

U: Understand feelings. Keep in mind that, in threatening situations, emotions hijack the brain and block rational thought. Remember that students might be guided by the fight-or-flight response and they might do or say things they do not mean.

S: Suspend ego. *Ego* is a dangerous word for teachers in these situations. Letting your ego take control may make the situation worse and lead to actions you will regret.

E: End on a positive note. Find something positive or encouraging to say.

(Adapted from The Melissa Institute for Violence Prevention and Treatment, 2007)

Some tactics should be avoided when dealing with a potentially disruptive situation. First, you should be careful not to overreact to the attitude of the student. If students are otherwise complying but demonstrating a bad attitude, keep the focus on the actions. There is a tendency to be offended by attitude, but taking offense usually escalates the situation.

Do not take verbal attacks personally. This takes a secure teacher. None of us wants to be insulted or to be attacked verbally. However, verbal attacks are usually designed to provoke an angry response, which the student then uses to justify her or his actions.

Respect the personal space of the student. "Getting in his or her face" challenges a student's personal space and makes the student feel trapped. This increases anger and thus increases the probability that a student will strike back.

If acts of violence do occur, it is serious and there may be some legal issues involved. School administrators need to be notified immediately, and mandatory actions are often required. To ignore mandated procedures relating to acts of violence is unprofessional and can lead to some negative consequences.

In summary, while there is a lot of attention to violence in the schools, it is not one of the major concerns of teachers or students in most schools. Wise teachers who continue to show respect for students and who can respond calmly are often able to stop actions before they reach the violent stage. If violence does occur, however, mandated actions need to be followed.

Substance Abuse   Substance abuse has received considerable attention for the past couple of decades. It continues to be a serious issue that concerns secondary school teachers. The good news is that the use of illicit drugs has declined in the past decade. For example, since 2001, the annual use of illicit drugs has declined by 32% among eighth-graders, 25% among 10th-graders, and 13% among 12th-graders. However, there has not been a decrease in the nonmedical use of prescription drugs. About 15% of high school seniors report the nonmedical use of at least one prescription drug over the course of a year (National Institute on Drug Abuse, 2008).

Students who are involved in substance abuse tend to be those who have low self-esteem and lack confidence. Peer influence also plays a role in influencing substance abuse. Keep in mind that secondary-level students are at a stage of psychological development where they have the perception that bad things may happen to others, but they will not happen to them. They simply do not believe that they will become addicted. This form of denial leads to risk-taking and diminishes the impact of substance abuse programs that primarily focus on the risks of addiction. Many schools use zero tolerance as a means of addressing substance abuse. While zero tolerance programs have had some success in reducing the availability of drugs in the school, zero tolerance programs do not address critical factors such as depression, anxiety, low self-esteem, and parental substance abuse.

Instead of trying to "scare students straight" with programs focusing on the ravages of addiction, a more effective approach to substance abuse is to stress academic success. This can be accomplished by developing a culture of success and caring, helping students learn how to cope with pressure, assisting students in learning drug refusal skills, and helping them develop self-control.

Prevention should be the goal in substance abuse programs. The programs that appear to be most effective are those that focus on both schools and families. Family-based programs focus on developing better communication skills, helping parents understand the problems of their children, talking to students about drugs, and monitoring their activities. School-based programs focus on enhancing the relationships between students and the school, dropout prevention, and improving social and academic skills, and helping students improve their self-control, coping, and refusal skills.

A word of caution for teachers: It is very hard to treat physical addiction. That is a problem few individual teachers can solve alone. Because attempting to do so may be harmful to the student, others, such as school counselors and family members, should be involved as soon as possible.

On some occasions, parents will express a sense of hopelessness and frustration. Be prepared to share addresses and phone numbers of various social service agencies that the parent can contact for help. You are not a professional psychologist or counselor, and you should not try to be one. If parents are reluctant to follow through, you need to point out that it is really for the welfare of the student.

Involving Other Professionals Because classroom management is seen as such an important aspect of being a successful educator, you may feel hesitant about seeking the advice of others. Seeking advice is not a sign of incompetence; rather, it is a hallmark of a true professional. The fact is that some students in every school have serious problems and are in need of professional help. Your unwillingness to seek help from other professionals could be harmful to the student.

Other professionals can be involved in alternative ways. One is through what might be called a buddy system, a system where teachers are teamed together to help each other in a time of crisis or need. If your school has such an arrangement, your assigned "buddy" probably will be teaching in a classroom close to yours. If either of you experiences a serious problem (perhaps an out of-control student or a fight), the other person can be there in a matter of seconds to provide extra help. Pairs of "buddy" teachers frequently spend some time at the beginning of the school year laying out general plans for how they will react to crisis situations. If your school lacks a formal buddy system, you might want to work out your own arrangement with an experienced teacher you trust.

Some secondary school principals, recognizing the serious consequences of frequent misbehavior and its relation to school violence, have instituted a formal on-call support system. This system designates a member of the staff for each period of the day who will be available to render quick assistance to a teacher who needs it. This person can be an administrator or an experienced faculty member trained in conflict management and mediation.

In extremely serious situations, a group of professionals may need to be consulted to develop a plan of action for a student with a particularly difficult and persistent misbehavior

As might be expected, classroom management is a major concern of those who will be supervising and hiring you. You can certainly expect questions in your interview focusing on your management abilities. This is also recognized in the Interstate New Teacher Assessment and Support Consortium (INTASC) standards. Standard 5 combines motivation and management, and focuses on creating a learning environment that encourages positive social interactions. Therefore, this dimension of your teaching should be clearly represented in your portfolio.

1. Select at least three items related to the content of this chapter that you will include in your portfolio. One suggestion is to include a discipline plan that clearly spells out how you plan to organize the environment and how you plan to respond to incidents of misbehavior.

2. Think about why you selected these materials and consider the following:
   - Does the information communicate your values and priorities?
   - Does this material give the person reviewing them a clear picture of your abilities and understanding of this important dimension of teaching?
   - How does this material relate to your professional growth?

3. Prepare a written reflection on the material you have chosen. Indicate why you chose the three items and what you think they communicate about your ability to manage a classroom.

problem. These professionals might include school administrators, counselors, psychologists, other teachers, and even representatives from youth and community services agencies outside the school. You need to present a well-documented case to the group so members will have a clear picture of the situation. This team can then recommend specific courses of action that might even include removing the student from the classroom or the school.

In summary, keeping issues associated with classroom management and discipline in proper perspective is a challenge for those who are new to the teaching profession. On the one hand, it is important to recognize that the problems of discipline and violence in the school are important and cannot be ignored. On the other hand, you also need to understand that more than 90% of the problems that occur in classrooms are minor ones. We do not want to raise your level of anxiety about the problem of discipline in the schools or to give the impression that students in secondary schools are out of control; that simply is not the case.

In every secondary school across the United States, regardless of the community context, teachers experience few problems. You, too, can be part of this group. However, this will not happen automatically. It requires considerable thought and hard work. The ideas introduced in this chapter are designed to help you become part of the large group of teachers who find teaching a rewarding profession.

Key Ideas in Summary

- Establishing and maintaining discipline in the classroom is one of the key elements of achieving success in teaching. Changing societal attitudes have made this a more difficult task for teachers. Teachers need to attend to four key areas in meeting this challenge: (1) managing the classroom environment, (2) establishing teacher authority and credibility, (3) motivating and engaging the students in learning, and (4) responding appropriately to incidents of misbehavior.

- The major purpose of classroom management and discipline is to help individuals learn self-control and the acceptance of responsibility. Therefore, discipline is connected to one of the central values of education and is critical to the development of effective citizenship.

- You, as a teacher, are the key player in establishing good classroom control. A vital part of the process is how you establish your authority in the classroom. Authority based on students' perception of you as an expert and a trustworthy, dependable individual is the best type of authority. Your consistency will make a major contribution to your effort to establish credible authority with students.

- The physical environment of the classroom has an impact on students. You need to attend to how you organize the floor space and where your desk is located. Having an attractive and inviting classroom also contributes to positive behavior patterns.

- Establishing routines for recurring events and handling student requests for assistance are two ways of using time efficiently.

- Teaching students that conflict is a naturally occurring part of life and helping them learn how to manage and respond to conflict are important tools in helping to defuse potentially disruptive situations in the classroom. This also involves teaching students verbal and nonverbal communication skills as well as specific steps in mediation and conflict resolution.

- When students choose to misbehave, they need to realize that they are also choosing to experience the consequences of their actions.

- Bullying has been identified as a serious problem that must be confronted. Bullies as well as the victims of bullies face serious long-term consequences. Cyberbullying has become a serious concern for both teachers and parents. Good bullying prevention programs have been effective in reducing the instances of bullying. However, they take time to work, and immediate changes should not be anticipated.

- Although violence in the schools receives a great deal of attention, the frequency of violence is actually quite low. However, even one incident of violence is one too many. Teachers do need to be aware of how violence can erupt. They can then help prevent violence by staying calm and using the DEFUSE strategy.

- Substance abuse has been on the decline in recent years. However, abuse of prescription drugs remains high. Teachers need to remain alert to the signs of substance abuse and to remember they that are ill equipped to deal with serious substance abuse. They should not hesitate to involve professionals.

- When serious problems occur, it is important to involve other professionals. Involving others is not a sign of poor teaching but a signal of a good professional attitude. The seriousness of many problems may well go beyond your capacity to solve; hence, it makes good sense to consult professionals.

Reflections

1. What perceptions do you have about the problem of discipline in the classroom? Did they change as a result of reading this chapter? How can you check the accuracy of these perceptions?

2. Why do you think students misbehave?

3. What do you define as the purpose of discipline in the secondary school? What are the implications of this purpose for the way you will respond to classroom incidents?

4. How can a teacher demonstrate respect for the dignity of all students and at the same time communicate that certain behaviors are unacceptable in the classroom?

5. How do you think teachers establish credibility and authority in the classroom? What is your plan for doing this?

6. What do you think are some advantages and disadvantages of a formal buddy system as an approach to dealing with misbehaving students?

Learning Extensions

1. Take a few moments to list some of the concerns you have about classroom management and discipline. What worries you most? Brainstorm possible actions that you could take to address these concerns. Share your concerns and responses with others.

2. Research the seriousness of violence in the secondary school classroom. Read articles in professional journals and then check that information by interviewing several secondary school teachers. How serious is the problem for them? Are their perceptions similar to those found in the literature? What might account for any differences you find?

3. Visit a secondary school and pay attention to the physical arrangement of the classroom. What aspects of the physical environment might contribute to problems? How might the physical environment be altered?

4. Discuss with experienced teachers the routines they have established for recurring classroom events. Begin making your own list of routines and procedures you will implement. Follow this by developing your own range of possible responses to misbehavior. Develop them into a range of responses similar to the examples presented in the chapter.

5. Do some research to see if any secondary schools in your area have implemented conflict resolution programs. Visit the schools and talk with students and teachers about the process. What are the steps that are used, and how are they implemented?

References

Blassone, M. (2007, November 13). Working to stop bullying at school. *Modesto Bee,* pp. A1, A12.

Centers for Disease Control and Prevention. (2007). The effectiveness of universal school-based programs for the prevention of violent and aggressive behavior. *Morbidity and Mortality Weekly Report, 56*(RR07), pp. 1–12.

Charles, C. (2005). *Teaching and learning in middle schools and secondary schools: Student empowerment through learning communities.* Columbus, OH: Merrill Prentice Hall.

Constitutional Rights Foundation. (2007). *Talking points: Causes of school violence.* Retrieved November 12, 2007, from http://www.crf-usa.org/violence/intro.html

Elias, M., & Schwab, Y. (2006). From compliance to responsibility: Social and emotional learning and classroom management. In C. M. Evertson & C. S. Weinstein (Eds.), *Handbook of classroom management: Research, practice, and contemporary issues* (pp. 309–341). Mahwah, NJ: Lawrence Erlbaum.

Emmer, E., & Gerwels, M. (2006). Classroom management in middle and high schools. In C. M. Evertson & C. S Weinstein (Eds.), *Handbook of classroom management: Research, practice and contemporary issues* (pp. 407–437). Mahwah, NJ: Lawrence Erlbaum.

Evertson, C., Emmer, E., & Worsham, M. (2003) *Classroom management for elementary teachers* (6th ed.). Boston: Allyn and Bacon.

Evertson, C. M., & Weinstein, C. S. (2006). Classroom management as a field of inquiry. In C. M. Evertson & C. S Weinstein (Eds.), *Handbook of classroom management: Research, practice and contemporary* issues (pp. 3–16). Mahwah, NJ: Lawrence Erlbaum.

French, J., & Raven, B. (1959). The bases of social power. In D. Cartwright (Ed.), *Studies in social power* (pp. 118–149). Ann Arbor: University of Michigan Press.

Friedman, I. (2006). Classroom management and teacher stress and burnout, In C. M. Evertson & C. S. Weinstein (Eds.), *Handbook of classroom management: Research, practice and contemporary issues* (pp. 925–944). Mahwah, NJ: Lawrence Erlbaum.

Glasser, W. (1990). *The quality school: Managing students without coercion.* New York: Harper & Row.

Good, T., & Brophy, J. (2007). *Looking in classrooms* (10th ed.). Boston: Allyn and Bacon.

Gordon, T. (1974). *Teacher Effectiveness Training.* New York: David McKay.

Hardin, C. (2008). *Effective classroom management: Models and strategies for today's classroom* (2nd ed.). Upper Saddle River, NJ: Merrill Prentice Hall.

Hoy, A. W., and Weinstein, C. S. (2006). *Student and teacher perspectives on classroom management*. In C. M. Evertson & C. S. Weinstein, *Handbook of classroom management: Research, practice and contemporary issues* (pp. 181–219). Mahwah, NJ: Lawrence Erlbaum.

Hyman, I., Kay, B., Taboria, A., Weber, M., Mahon, M., & Cohen, I. (2006). Bullying: Theory, research and intervention. In C. M. Evertson & C. S. Weinstein (Eds.), *Handbook of classroom management: Research, practice and contemporary issues* (pp. 855–884). Mahwah, NJ: Lawrence Erlbaum.

Johnson, D., & Johnson, R. (1995). *Reducing school violence through conflict resolution.* Alexandria, VA: Association for Supervision and Curriculum Development.

Jones, F. (1987). *Positive classroom discipline.* New York: McGraw-Hill.

Lee, J., Pulvino, C., & Perrone, P. (1998). *Restoring harmony: A guide for managing conflicts in schools.* Columbus, OH: Merrill.

Marzano, R., Marzano, J., & Pickering, D. (2003). *Classroom management that works.* Alexandria, VA: Association for Supervision and Curriculum Development.

Melissa Institute for Violence Prevention and Treatment. (2007). *Reducing bullying: Meeting the challenge.* Retrieved November 12, 2007, from http://www.teachsafeschools.org/bullying-prevention.html

MetLife. (2008). *The MetLife survey of the American teacher: Past, present and future.* Retrieved October 12, 2009, from http://www.metlife.com/assets/cao/contributions/citizenship/teacher-survey-25th-anniv-2008.pdf

National Crime Prevention Council. (2007). Teens and cyberbullying. Retrieved March 2, 2008, from http://www.surfsafety.net/Cyberbullying

National Institute on Drug Abuse. (2008). NIDA InfoFacts: High school and youth trends. Retrieved May 23, 2008, from http://www.nida.nih.gov/infofacts/hsyouthtrends.html

Olewus, D. (2003). *Bullying at school: What we know and what we can do.* Cambridge, MA: Blackwell.

Savage, T. V., & Savage, M. K. (2010). *Successful classroom management and discipline: Teaching self-control and responsibility* (3rd ed.). Thousand Oaks, CA: Sage Publications, Inc.

U.S. Department of Justice, Bureau of Educational Statistics. (2009). *National crime victimization survey: Table 2:2 Indicators of school crime and safety.* Washington, DC: Author.

Weinstein, C. (1979). The physical environment of the school: A review of the research. *Review of Educational Research, 49*(4), 577–610.

The Professional Context

Krista Greco/Merrill Education

Legal Issues

Objectives

This chapter will help you

- describe some of the rights and responsibilities of students and teachers

- state conditions under which school officials may limit student rights

- explain basic principles that guide court decisions regarding student and teacher rights

- define limitations that can legally be placed on teachers' out-of-school behavior

- define various forms of teacher negligence

- explain teachers' responsibilities for reporting suspected cases of child abuse

- describe implications of copyright law for teachers

Barbara Schwartz/Merrill Educatio

Graphic Organizer: Chapter 14

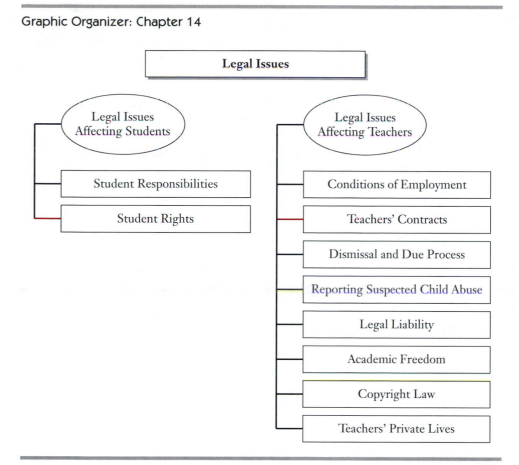

Introduction

Teachers need to be knowledgeable in several areas. They need to have a depth of knowledge about their subject matter. They need to have a good grounding in learning theory and understand how people learn. Teachers need to be literate and skilled in reading and writing. However, individuals often overlook the need for teachers to have legal literacy. They need to understand their rights and responsibilities and those of the students they teach. They need to realize that they function in a complex legal environment, and ignorance of the law is not an acceptable excuse.

Legal issues permeate education. In recent years, legal questions have arisen in diverse areas such as curriculum content, copyright law, dress codes, school assemblies, cyberbullying, harassment, censorship of student publications, student discipline, teacher contracts, tenure and dismissal, school discipline, and copyright issues. Just about every aspect of the work of a teacher is associated with a potential legal issue.

It is not our intention to scare prospective teachers. In fact, most teachers will seldom confront a direct legal challenge. However, ignorance of legal concerns can be costly, and understanding some legal principles can help teachers avoid unnecessary legal entanglements. It is our intention to provide a few basic legal principles that can provide teachers with some peace of mind as they go about their work.

Concern about legal issues that can affect teachers led to the inclusion of a provision in the No Child Left Behind (NCLB) Act of 2001 that was labeled the Teacher Liability Protection Act (Schimmel, 2006). The purpose of this provision was to provide teachers with legal protection when they implemented reasonable actions to establish a safe and appropriate educational environment. This act provided additional support for teachers in controlling their classrooms and provided protection from frivolous lawsuits (Schimmel, 2006).

In this chapter, we will address only a couple of areas where secondary school teachers need some knowledge of legal issues. The graphic organizer at the beginning of this chapter illustrates the chapter content, which will focus on legal issues that affect students and legal issues that affect teachers.

Students have both responsibilities and rights. Their responsibilities include attendance, following school rules, not interfering with the right of the school to provide a safe school environment, and behaving in socially appropriate ways. Their rights include freedom of speech, freedom of conscience, dress and appearance, freedom from unreasonable search and seizure, privacy of records, and the right to due process.

Legal issues that affect teachers include two basic areas. One area encompasses issues related to conditions of employment, such as contracts, dismissal, due process for teachers, academic freedom, copyright law, and teachers' private lives. The second area relates to teacher rights and responsibilities when working with students. This area includes required reporting of suspected child abuse, use of force in discipline, and teacher negligence.

Legal issues are complex, and the purpose of this chapter is not to provide with you legal advice or provide you with unequivocal answers to every situation. That is simply not possible. Each court case is decided on its own merits, and each case is unique. However, legal precedents have been established; by looking at these cases, we can identify some basic principles that will provide you with guidance in this complex area.

Legal Issues Affecting Students

Few issues in secondary schools generate as much discussion as student rights and responsibilities. In recent years, the legal relationship between students and school authorities has been legally altered. Since the 1980s, students in school have enjoyed legal rights that are basically the same as those extended to all adult citizens.

As a beginning point, you need to understand that legal issues are generally the result of a conflict between different sets of rights. For example, legal issues relating to student rights have arisen because of a conflict between the legal rights of students as citizens and the rights and responsibilities of schools to create safe and orderly learning environments. At one time, the rights of the school officials were given precedent and students had few rights. With the changes in society, the rights of students were clarified, and many school rules and practices were challenged. Rules established by school officials had to respect the rights of students and had to be related directly to the establishment of a safe and orderly learning environment.

Contrary to what some believe, legal decisions have not just defined student rights. They have also defined student responsibilities. In fact, in recent years, because of incidents such as the violence at Columbine High School, more attention has been directed to the area of student responsibilities. A few individuals have suggested that student rights need to be severely limited to prevent such tragic occurrence.

Student Responsibilities

The law is not static; it is constantly changing as a result of legal challenges and court decisions. Just as student rights have changed in the past, they will continue to change in the future as decisions are made regarding issues such as the use of cell phones in educational environments and dress codes. The following student rights have been developed over the past few decades and do provide guidelines for student conduct.

School Attendance   An educated and informed citizenry is essential to the health of a democratic society. Therefore, the state has a compelling interest in the education of all students. Students have a legal responsibility to participate in educational experiences. The courts have consistently upheld this principle. In recent years, however, there have been many cases regarding the meaning of the regulations regarding the education of students. These cases have emphasized the rights of the state to require an education for students. They have indicated, however, that this does not necessarily mean that the only place education can occur is in a school.

One of the areas where there has been some focus is on compulsory attendance laws. What exactly is required of students? Does homeschooling meet compulsory attendance laws? What about attendance in private schools?

In general, court decisions have reflected the view that the interest of the state is in promoting a quality education for each person, not in defining the place or the manner of the education. This has raised some legal questions concerning what constitutes a quality education and what is required to satisfy the state interest in an education for all citizens. This legal issue is the result of a conflict between the compelling interest of the state for an educated citizenry and the rights of parents to direct the upbringing of their children. Because most parents lack the breadth and depth of knowledge required to prepare young people for the complex roles they will face as adults in a rapidly changing society, the courts have generally supported the rights of the state to insist that their students either attend a state-supported school or an acceptable alternative.

What constitutes an acceptable alternative varies from state to state. In a typical situation, an acceptable alternative must be equivalent to what is provided in the public school curriculum. These alternatives might be either private schools or home schools. Some states require that a qualified individual teach students who enroll in acceptable alternatives to the regular public schools. In some places, this means that the person teaching the students must possess a teaching credential. In other places, other evidence of expertise is acceptable. Some school districts require that students not attending the public school be given examinations at regular intervals to make sure they are learning the required content.

A few challenges to compulsory attendance have been made on the grounds that school conditions can place the students in physical or emotional danger. Court decisions relating to these challenges have followed a consistent pattern. The judges have usually placed a heavy burden of proof on the parents to prove their contention that the school environment is unsafe (Valente, 1994).

Another challenge to compulsory attendance has been based on the claim that school attendance can have a negative impact on religious beliefs. Most challenges of this sort have not been successful. An interesting exception was a ruling made in response to a challenge brought by Amish parents in Wisconsin (*Wisconsin v. Yoder*, 1972). These parents refused to send their children to school beyond the eighth grade. They contended that the general emphasis in the secondary schools was contrary to the basic tenets of their religion and way of life. The Supreme Court ruled in their favor, holding that the Amish way of life constituted an acceptable alternative to formal secondary education. However, the Court was careful to note that this did not set a precedent for other groups who wished to challenge compulsory attendance laws (Fischer, Schimmel, & Steelman, 2007).

Following Reasonable School Rules   Because schools have the right to establish a safe and orderly educational environment, school officials have the right to establish reasonable school rules. Students have the responsibility to obey them and to submit to the authority of the teachers. For example, the California School Code states that every teacher in a public school has an obligation to hold each student accountable for conduct on the way to and from school, on the school grounds, and during breaks from classroom activities. Any certified employee is given the right to exercise reasonable control over a student in order to protect property, ensure the safety of others, or to maintain conditions conducive to learning. Willful violation of teacher authority by students is grounds for suspension or expulsion (California Teachers Association, 1992).

The part of the school code that focuses on conduct on the way to school and on the way home has brought to the forefront issues such as student harassment that may occur off school grounds. How can teachers and administrators monitor the actions of all students coming to and leaving school? Some parents have even called on the schools to put a stop to cyberbullying that occurs on home computers.

The responsibility of the schools for behavior coming and going from school basically requires that school officials have a duty to act if they know, or should have known, of acts such as bullying and harassment that threaten the physical or emotional well-being of students. What this means is that, if it is brought to the attention of a teacher that harassment is taking place on the way to or from school, action must be taken. It simply cannot be ignored. If teachers become aware of problems like this, they should contact the school administration and follow up to make sure that something is done to remedy the situation.

Legal responsibility in the area of cyberbullying is just emerging. If any cyberbullying takes place at school, then the school is obligated to respond. Students are reporting cyberbullying at increasing rates. In fact, the U.S. Department of Health and Human Services, Health Resources and Services Administration (2008), reports that 30% of teens state that they have received cyberbullying messages at school. The primary burden for addressing cyberbullying outside school, however, must reside with parents.

The operative word in establishing rules is *reasonable*. Arbitrary rules and regulations that have nothing to do with the establishment of a safe school or a climate conducive to learning are not legally protected. If a school attempts to impose or enforce rules that fail to meet the "reasonableness" test, these rules are unlikely to survive a legal challenge.

Not Interfering with the Maintenance of a Safe School Environment   School officials have an obligation to protect the health and safety of those who are present in the school and to maintain a school environment that is conducive to learning. Students have a responsibility to refrain from actions such as bringing weapons or controlled substances that might endanger the safety and health of others. Most states provide for immediate suspension of individuals who violate this responsibility. The increased fear of violence has led many schools to establish a zero-tolerance policy. This means that students do not get a second chance, and any violations result in immediate suspension.

Similarly, threatening violence or harm to another person is grounds for suspension of expulsion. Thus, a student who threatens you or threatens another student with violence can be immediately suspended. In some instances, this has been followed to the letter of the law; even young children pretending to shoot each other with paper guns have been suspended. One of your obligations is to ensure that students understand their responsibilities and realize the serious consequences of such behavior.

Socially Appropriate Behavior   When political and social leaders suggest that one of your jobs as a teacher is to inform young people about the boundaries of socially acceptable behavior, they assume there are restrictions that can be placed on student behavior. This perspective implies that behavior that might be appropriate in other settings may not be acceptable in school. Several court cases have endorsed this view.

In one case, a high school student who was nominating a friend for a school office gave a speech that was filled with sexual metaphor and innuendo. Although the student did not use explicit language, he was suspended from school for three days. The student sued, claiming that his First Amendment rights of freedom of speech had been violated. The court upheld the school district, ruling that the rights of the student were outweighed by society's interest in educating young people within the bounds of socially appropriate behavior (Zirkel & Richardson, 1988). The finding in this case suggests that students must accept that they have responsibilities to behave in ways that permit schools to maintain a productive learning environment.

To summarize, your students do have certain responsibilities that they are required to fulfill. However, you and others in your school must recognize that you face certain constraints in establishing expectations related to student behavior. For example, courts will not be sympathetic if your school adopts and attempts to enforce capricious regulations. Rules and expectations must be reasonable and consistent with defensible educational purposes.

Student Rights

Legal issues relating to the rights of students focus on the concept that students are citizens who enjoy the legal status guaranteed to all citizens by the United States Constitution. Court cases have focused on two key areas. First, there has been litigation concerned with the limits of the power of school authorities to interfere with student actions. Second, cases have considered the appropriateness or fairness of procedures used by school authorities when making decisions affecting students.

In reviewing information related to students' rights cases, you need to keep in mind that each case is considered by the courts on its own merits, as well as in light of laws and decisions in previous, related cases. Laws and precedents change over time. Therefore, you cannot always presume that when courts consider new cases, they will follow the same course of action they have taken in the past. For reasons we cannot predict today, future courts may take quite different views of some issues related to students' rights.

Freedom of Speech and Expression   One of the fundamental rights guaranteed by the U.S. Constitution is *freedom of expression*. This issue continues to be an irritant for some school officials. In the past, school officials were quite free to limit students' freedom of expression. School officials took the position that they had the right to limit what students could say when they were in the school. However, these broad rights of school officials began to change in the late 1960s.

One of the landmark freedom of expression cases was *Tinker v. Des Moines Independent School District* (1969). This important case, while focusing on the issue of freedom of expression, had a wider impact on schools when the Supreme Court ruling stated that neither students nor teachers surrender their constitutional rights at the classroom door. The *Tinker* case evolved out of a situation that developed in Des Moines, Iowa, during the Vietnam War. Children from several families who opposed the war decided to express their opposition by wearing black armbands to school. When school officials learned of this protest, they quickly adopted a school policy forbidding the wearing of these armbands. According to this policy, students would be asked to remove the armbands. Those who refused would be suspended.

Three students refused to remove the armbands and were suspended. The suspension was challenged on the grounds that the regulation was a clear violation of freedom of speech guaranteed by the Constitution. The case ultimately worked its way to the United States Supreme Court. In its decision, the Court viewed the wearing of the armbands as symbolic free speech. The Court stated that students do have constitutional rights in classrooms and that the First Amendment of the United States Constitution protects free speech and expression; it ruled that the wearing of the armbands was protected and that the school authorities had erred in passing the regulation and enforcing it. This Court decision means that if you or school officials wish to limit student freedom of expression, you have to demonstrate that the exercise of unrestricted freedom of speech would result in material and substantial disruption of the educational environment.

During the 2008 presidential campaign, a student wore a T-shirt to school that bore the picture of a political candidate. The school principal required that the boy turn the shirt wrong side out in order to stay in school. When the actions of the principal were challenged, he quickly admitted that he had erred because there was no evidence of a material or substantial disruption of the educational environment.

A school could limit freedom of expression if there was evidence that exercise of the right would result in disruptions such as fights among students. For example, some schools with gangs have prohibited the wearing of certain colors of clothing if they represent membership in a gang.

Another freedom of expression issue that has prompted much interest over the years concerns the authority of school officials to limit what is printed in official school publications as well as in underground, or unauthorized, student publications. In many places, school officials have censored student publications and forbidden unauthorized publications. Some of these actions have been challenged. In general, the courts have determined that school administrators' power to regulate a publication depends on whether the publication in question is sponsored by the school in some official way. Courts have tended to support more administrative control over the content of student publications produced as part of a regular journalism course than publications that are not officially connected with the school.

An important precedent in this area was established in the case of *Hazelwood School District v. Kuhlmeier* (1988). The *Hazelwood* case focused on the actions of a school principal who deleted two articles from the school newspaper. One article referred indirectly to some pregnant students. Though names in the article had been changed to mask the true identities of these students, the principal felt that many readers might be able to identify them. In a second article, a student had written a complaint about her father, but the father had not been given an option to respond. The principal felt the treatment was unbalanced and unfair. In its decision, the court upheld the right of the principal, noting that educators have the authority to exercise considerable control over school-sponsored publications. The courts have generally supported educators' decisions to reject articles that are poorly written, insufficiently researched, clearly biased, vulgar, or otherwise unacceptable for immature audiences. They may prohibit articles that advocate unacceptable (and often illegal) social practices such as alcohol or drug abuse and irresponsible sexual activities.

Authority to limit the content of school publications does not extend to the censorship of controversial issues or views that may be unpopular with administrators, teachers, or parents. If you and others in your school want to place limitations on what students can print in school publications, you must be able to demonstrate that your actions are for valid educational reasons, not for capricious, convenient, or punitive ones.

Underground and other publications that are produced without formal school recognition and support are outside the control of school officials. These publications ordinarily cannot be regulated unless their contents can be challenged on grounds that would invite legal actions against any type of a publication. Although you and your colleagues may find some of these articles to be highly irritating, you generally lack legal grounds for barring publications from the school or for punishing the writers. However, school leaders generally have legal authority to place some limits on how and when these publications can be distributed. The regulations cannot be so restrictive that they prohibit distribution.

In considering cases involving freedom of expression and freedom of speech, most court decisions have supported the idea that students enjoy constitutional freedom of speech rights. Students cannot be censored because they discuss controversial issues or because they criticize school officials. Freedom of expression can be limited only when there is a legitimate educational concern or when students disrupt the orderly operation of the school.

Students' Freedom of Conscience   Legal questions focusing on the issues of separation of church and state and the place of religious expression in schools have generated much controversy. Two basic First Amendment principles are usually the focus in these disputes. One principle guarantees the right to free exercise of religion; the other bars government involvement in establishing or supporting religion.

Courts have consistently affirmed the idea that freedom of religion cannot be abridged unless the state and its officials demonstrate an overwhelmingly compelling need to do so.

This means that school officials cannot arbitrarily require all students to do something that may interfere with their fundamental religious principles. For example, court cases have upheld the right of individual students to refrain from participating in routine Pledge of Allegiance exercises when those students indicate that taking the pledge conflicts with religious beliefs. In Pledge of Allegiance cases, the courts have taken the position that a refusal to recite the pledge does not threaten any major public interest; hence, the state has no compelling interest in requiring all students to participate.

Suppose, however, that you encountered a situation in which a religious group claimed that teaching students to read was contrary to fundamental religious beliefs. It is doubtful the courts would excuse these students from reading instruction because the state does have a compelling interest in the literacy of all citizens.

Courts have ruled that your students' religious views may excuse them from certain parts of the school program. For example, courts have upheld the rights of some students to be excused from activities such as dancing and viewing films. In recent years, there have been numerous challenges from parents about banning the teaching of literary works such as *The Wizard of Oz* and *Macbeth* on the grounds that they promote witchcraft. For the most part, the courts have upheld school officials' contentions that familiarity with literature such as these examples is essential to the complete educational development of students, something in which the state has a compelling interest.

The issue of prayer and meditation as forms of religious expression continues to draw considerable attention. To understand this complex issue, you must remember that the First Amendment states that Congress shall make no law respecting the establishment of religion, or prohibiting the free exercise of religion. Therefore, the schools, as governmental agencies, cannot promote a particular religious belief or impose a particular religious practice on students. However, neither can the school prohibit a student from exercising his or her religious freedom.

Trying to sort out the boundaries between these ideas continues to be a challenge. For the most part, individuals have accepted that practices such as a required morning prayer over the loudspeaker or the posting of certain religious documents seem to further a particular religious belief and are therefore not allowed. However, there is still some ambiguity regarding prayers at events such as athletic games and school graduations.

Student Dress and Appearance The topic of student dress and appearance has resurfaced in recent years as some school districts have considered requiring uniforms for students. Proponents claim that uniforms improve the educational environment and result in a decrease in discipline problems. However, many students and parents have not found this idea appealing, and they have challenged the authority of the school to place restrictions on what students can wear to school.

While the issue of dress and appearance is still one where there is some ambiguity, the courts have generally recognized that schools do enjoy some rights to govern what students wear to school. In one court case, the courts ruled that requiring uniforms is permissible if the requirement meets certain standards, including the fact that the dress code furthers a substantial governmental interest such as reducing discipline problems and it is unrelated to the suppression of student expression (Fischer, Schimmel, & Steelman, 2007). Some court rulings have indicated that the school does have a responsibility to exclude persons who are unsanitary, or obscenely or scantily clad (Fischer, Schimmel, & Steelman, 2007). As a general rule, dress and appearance standards established by schools must bear a reasonable relationship to the educational process or to the health and safety of students.

Hairstyle and grooming standards have also been the subject of several court cases. Some courts have ruled that hairstyle is a more fundamental right than clothing style. The argument has been that a restriction on hairstyle represents an unacceptably intrusive invasion of individual privacy. Upholding hairstyle regulations has usually been on the grounds of student health and safety or a clear and documented interference with the educational process.

Search and Seizure   Concerns about drugs and weapons on school campuses have prompted much interest in the issue of the right of school officials to conduct searches and seize property. For example, school officials may have a desire to search school lockers, automobiles parked in the student parking lot, student possessions such as backpacks and purses, and even students themselves. The need to search for weapons, drugs, and other illegal items that can threaten the safety of the general student population has to be weighed against Fourth Amendment guarantees against unreasonable search and seizure.

In general, court decisions relating to this issue require school officials to apply four basic tests as they attempt to decide whether a proposed search violates Fourth Amendment rights. The first test relates to the *nature of the material or object* they are seeking. The greater the potential danger posed by the material or the object to the safety of the students, the stronger the justification for the search. For example, a weapon or a bomb poses a tremendous threat to the safety of the students and an intrusive search would usually be justified. However, a search for a stolen book does not pose a danger and an intrusive search would probably not be justified.

The second test to be applied in determining the legality of a search relates to the *quality of the information* that has led to the consideration of a search. This means the reliability and validity of the information must be evaluated. If several reliable people provide similar information, a stronger case can be made for the search than if it is based on an anonymous tip.

If the nature of a proposed search is to be potentially invasive (that is, it involves the search of a person or their private possessions), then the search must meet the test of *probable cause*. This requires a very high standard of evidence as a justification for a search and is equivalent to what courts require before issuing a search warrant.

The third test concerns the *nature of the place to be searched*. If the place to be searched is one where an individual has a high expectation of privacy, school officials must have very reliable information to justify the search. This would apply to searches of a person, a person's clothing, a purse, a wallet, or other private possession. However, there is much less of an expectation of privacy in areas such as a school locker or a school desk. Therefore, a search of these places could be justified on less supporting evidence.

The case of *New Jersey v. T.L.O.* (1985) established some important search and seizure precedents. In this case, a vice principal questioned a girl suspected of smoking, a violation of school rules. At the vice principal's request, the girl opened her purse. It contained not only cigarettes but also drug paraphernalia. This led to a further search of the purse. In court, the girl challenged the search on the grounds that it violated her Fourth Amendment rights of freedom from unreasonable searches. The case ended up in the U.S. Supreme Court. In its decision, the Supreme Court stated that the initial suspicions that the girl had been smoking and might have cigarettes in her possession were sufficient reasons to ask her to open her purse. Once this was done, the physical evidence of drug paraphernalia provided sufficient justification for the extensive search of her purse.

The ruling in *New Jersey v. T.L.O.* seems to give school officials considerable latitude in search and seizure. However, there are some important limits. For example, if you want to conduct a search, you must have reasonable suspicion that the student has violated a specific rule. *Reasonable suspicion* refers to the presence of evidence that is sufficiently compelling to convince a prudent and cautious individual that a violation has occurred. General so-called fishing expeditions are not permitted, and when a search is undertaken in the absence of reasonable suspicion, it is likely to be viewed by the courts as an illegal invasion of students' privacy rights.

To summarize, case law relating to search and seizure does not provide you with absolutely clear guidelines. In general, we advise you not to attempt searches on your own initiative. Responsibility for school searches should be left in the hands of school administrators who are in a better position to check the legality of search and seizure procedures.

Due Process   Discussion of student rights and responsibilities inevitably leads to the issue of due process. *Due process* is a principle requiring that certain procedures and safeguards must be followed when students are denied a right such as school attendance.

Until the years following World War II, school attendance was widely regarded as a privilege to be enjoyed by those who were willing to abide by the rules established by the school authorities. Because schooling was not viewed as a fundamental right protected by the Constitution, students had no legal recourse if they were suspended or expelled from school for a rule violation. In this earlier era, lack of schooling or nonpossession of a high school diploma was not viewed as imposing any serious hardships on an individual.

After World War II, however, it became evident that the possession of a high school diploma was important for the future economic well-being of individuals. Thus, to deprive an individual of an education has serious consequences. This view, coupled with the fact that the public schools are tax-supported institutions, soon led to the idea that education was more than a privilege extended to those who were willing to conform to the rules of the school officials. It began to be viewed as a substantial right. This right merited due process protection.

The legal precedent extending due process protection to public schools was established in *Goss v. Lopez* (1975). In its decision, The Supreme Court noted that, while the United States Constitution does not require states to establish public schools, once they are established, the right to attend them is a constitutionally protected property right. Therefore, efforts to deny students access to schooling through suspension or expulsion must be accompanied by due process procedures in conformity with the Fourteenth Amendment to the Constitution.

There are two basic components to due process. The first, or the substantive component, consists of a set of principles on which the process is based. The second, or the procedural component, delineates procedures that must be followed to ensure that due process rights have not been violated. The following are the substantive components of due process:

- Individuals are not to be disciplined on the basis of unwritten rules.
- Rules must not be unduly vague.
- Individuals charged with rules violations are entitled to a hearing before an impartial body.
- Identities of witnesses are to be revealed.
- Decisions must be supported by substantial evidence.
- A public or a private hearing can be requested by the individual accused of the rule violation.

The following steps are consistent with the guidelines to be followed by schools to ensure compliance with the procedural steps component of due process:

- Rules governing students' behavior are to be distributed in writing to students and their parents and guardians at the beginning of the school year.
- Whenever a student is accused of a serious violation of rules that can lead to the loss of a right, charges must be provided in writing to the student and to his or her parent or guardian.
- Written notice of the hearing to consider the alleged violation must be given, with sufficient time for the student and his or her representatives to prepare a defense. However, the hearing must be scheduled within a timely manner (usually within two weeks).
- A fair hearing must include the following:

  Right of the accused to be represented by legal counsel

  Right of the accused to present a defense and to introduce evidence

Right of the accused to face his or her accusers

Right of the accused to cross-examine witnesses

- The decision of the hearing board must be based on evidence presented and must be rendered within a reasonable time.
- The accused must be informed of his or her right to appeal the decision.

The need to comply with due process requirements means that you and others in your school need to exercise great care in initiating actions against a student who is suspected of having violated important rules or regulations that might result in suspension or expulsion. Suspension is defined as a temporary separation from school. A suspension of less than 10 days is considered a short-term suspension. Short-term suspensions require only minimal due process procedures. In these situations, a student must receive (1) at least an oral (preferably a written) notice of the charges that led to the suspension, (2) an explanation of the evidence supporting the action, and (3) the opportunity to provide her or his version of the facts relevant to the situation. Short-term suspension does not require that legal counsel is present to represent the student. A suspension exceeding 10 days in length is considered long-term suspension. Long-term suspension has the potential to interfere seriously with the education of the student and therefore school officials are obligated to follow all due process guidelines.

Expulsion is a more serious action. It separates a student permanently from school. In situations where expulsion is likely to be the end result of a disciplinary action against a student, very strict due process procedures must be followed. Usually, you and the administrators at your school do not, by themselves, have the authority to make an expulsion decision. This tends to be a prerogative of the highest governing officials of the school district. The policy of referring this kind of decision to higher authorities helps ensure that procedures in place to protect and represent the student's interests are followed. If they are not, the student and his or her legal representatives may initiate potentially expensive legal actions against the school district and the school board.

Due process has important implications for you as a teacher. First, you need to recognize that your students have been legally defined as citizens whose rights are protected by the Constitution. This means you must proceed in a fair and appropriate manner in making and enforcing school rules. However, the need to observe due process guidelines by no means diminishes your authority to control students in the classroom. The courts have affirmed your rights, as a teacher, to establish and maintain a safe and orderly educational environment.

Family Privacy Rights   Since the 1960s, concerned citizens have raised questions about potential misuses of school records. Some parents were angered when school records were given to military recruiters and law enforcement personnel. Parents also became concerned about the damage that might occur when students applied to institutions of higher education or sought employment if their student records stigmatized the student or contained personal opinions or unsubstantiated assertions.

In response to these issues and concerns, Congress passed what was originally called the Buckley Amendment in 1975 and later became known as the Family Rights and Privacy Act (1996). This legislation requires schools to protect students' privacy rights by limiting access to their files to those individuals immediately concerned with their education. Files can be opened to others only with the consent of students' parents or, in the case of students who are 18 years old or older, the students themselves. The law also gives parents free access to school files and records pertaining to their children. Students who are 18 years of age or older have similar rights to see this information. After parents, or individuals over the age of 18, have viewed the records, they may request to amend any records they believe to be (1) inaccurate, (2) misleading, or (3) a violation of privacy rights.

The Family Rights and Privacy Act means that you need to exercise care when placing information in student files. Comments you enter should be descriptive rather than

CHECKING THE WEB

TRENDS AND ISSUES: SCHOOL LAW

The following website has excellent articles on a variety of topics relating to school law. It is a good source for keeping current on issues in education.

http://eric.uoregon.edu/issues/law/index.html

judgmental. It is particularly important to avoid malicious or other kinds of general statements that might be considered as a negative summary judgment of a student. Such comments may subject you to legal action (Connors, 1991).

You also need to be careful about the kinds of comments you make to others about individual students. A person who knowingly spreads false information that hurts another's reputation (in this case, a student) has committed slander, a punishable offense. For example, a parent sitting in a lunchroom overheard teachers making unkind comments about a student. Because the parent was friends of the family, she relayed the remarks to the parents. These teachers had unknowingly opened the door to embarrassing and costly legal action.

Emerging Issues   Several current issues are likely to result in legal action in the future. One of the most volatile issues relates to high-stakes testing. There is evidence that students from low socioeconomic communities do less well on these tests. Some legal challenges claim that the school did not provide the student with sufficient opportunity to learn the content. This has the potential to change the way state funds are allocated to school districts. Rather than providing the same amount of money for all students, states may have to provide more funds to provide sufficient opportunities to learn for high-need students. These challenges set the stage for challenges to the validity of the tests. Challenges would appear likely when there is considerable evidence that a given student has performed well on all other indicators of achievement but is denied a diploma based on the outcomes of one test.

Another issue that is generating considerable attention is the issue of computers and free speech, which relates to the issue of censorship. In the past, the courts have ruled that schools cannot remove controversial books or deny students access to ideas and content with which they disagree. However, they have been given the right to remove material that is educationally unsuitable or vulgar (Fischer, Schimmel, & Steelman, 2007). Computer use opens up a whole new set of circumstances that result in a conflict between these rulings. Some individuals are concerned that restricting computer use and access in an attempt to protect students from pornographic and commercial material may violate student rights by arbitrarily denying students general access to important ideas and material. No doubt there will be some interesting cases relating to computer use and censorship.

Legal Issues Affecting Teachers

Legal issues concerned with schools and schooling do not pertain only to students. There are also important legal dimensions related to your rights and responsibilities as a teacher, including areas such as conditions of employment, contracts, freedom of expression, academic freedom, drug and alcohol abuse, copyright, and professional performance of duties.

Conditions of Employment

Generally, a person must possess a valid *teaching certificate* as a condition of employment. Some states prohibit school districts from paying the salaries of teachers who do not hold a valid certificate. Several court cases have declared that people who sign contracts and perform teaching duties without possessing valid certificates are "volunteers" who have donated their services to the district.

Most school districts require you to register your certificate with the personnel office of the school district prior to the issuance of a paycheck. Some states prohibit payment by a school district until proof of certification is provided. It is important when you apply for a teaching position to represent your certification status accurately. If you suggest that you have a certificate when, in fact, you do not, this misrepresentation may eliminate your future prospects not only in the district where you are seeking employment, but elsewhere in the state. You need to make sure you are clear about your certification status before you leave your teacher preparation program.

Certification is a state responsibility. Each state has its own requirements for people who wish to teach in its schools. Because teacher certification requirements vary from state to state, obtaining a teaching certificate in one state may not mean that you have met the certification requirements in another state. If you are interested in teaching in another state, you should contact the teacher certification office in the state department of education in the state where you wish to seek employment. This office will be able to provide you with information about the procedures you need to follow to qualify for a teaching certificate.

CRITICAL INCIDENT

COMPLETING THE EMPLOYMENT APPLICATION

Rodney Harte started a business after he graduated from college. The business prospered, but his day-to-day routines did not satisfy his need to be involved in service-oriented work. Because Rodney always enjoyed being around young people and he had several friends who were teachers, he decided to pursue a teaching credential.

Rodney proved to be an excellent student and earned high evaluations in his student teaching. As a result of his strong performance, he received excellent recommendations and submitted his application to the state for a teaching credential.

When he was completing the application for the credential, he noted a question asking for information about any previous legal problems. He had been caught shoplifting an item in a shopping center many years earlier when he was an undergraduate. He carefully explained the circumstances on the application form and submitted it to the state department of education. After some additional correspondence with the state, he was granted a teaching credential.

In his job search, he was interviewed for a teaching position that he felt was ideal. It was in a good school district close to where he lived, and it offered him an opportunity to assist in the athletic program. On the district application form was a question asking if he had ever been convicted of a felony. He reflected on the matter and concluded that, because he had been cleared by the state for a credential, there was no need to reopen the issue and answered no. He was hired in the school district and began teaching. At the end of September, he received a note requesting him to report immediately to the director of human resources. When he arrived, he was informed that his employment was being terminated because the school district had learned of his earlier conviction and he had entered false information on his application.

■ ■ ■

What do you think Rodney should do? Do you think that, because this issue was cleared by the state and he had been granted a teaching credential, the district had a right to pursue it? Do you think he has any legal recourse? What is the legal principle that should be learned?

Teacher certificates are not guaranteed for the life of the holder. They may be terminated for a variety of reasons, and states can establish conditions that must be met to renew them or keep them in force. In many states, certificates have fixed expiration dates. For example, you may find regulations that require you to meet renewal conditions such as taking additional college courses or participating in other professional development opportunities. Certificates may be revoked for conviction of a felony, public displays of immorality, incompetence, or extreme examples of socially unacceptable behavior.

Teachers' Contracts

Teachers' contracts are important documents. They contain information related to issues such as conditions of employment, salary, sick leave provisions, insurance coverage, and grievance procedures. For a contract to be valid, it must include four basic features:

- Language that reflects a meeting of the minds of the signatories
- Signatories who are competent parties
- Obligations from each of the signatories to the others
- Definite and clear terms delineating what is to be done and by whom (Fisher, Schimmel, & Steelman, 2007)

The phrase *meeting of minds* means that all parties must agree on the contents of the contract. One party must offer the contract and the other must accept it. In the case of teaching contracts, the formal process of offer and acceptance is not over until the contract is approved by action of the school board. The school board is the only body that can legally hire or dismiss a teacher.

For a contract to be valid between competent parties, the individual signatories must be of legal age and be legally and intellectually able to engage in and conclude needed negotiations. As a prospective teacher, you must have a teaching certificate (or be eligible to receive one before you begin work) to be competent to enter into a contract. Therefore, if you enter into a contract with a school district and are not eligible for a teaching credential, you do not have a valid contract and the school district has no obligation to pay you for your services. The courts have generally ruled that individuals who are not eligible for a credential are volunteers.

Teaching contracts are legal documents. When a contract is breached or broken, the other party is entitled to a legal remedy that will compensate for the injury the breaching party causes. For example, a school district may sue to collect monetary damages if you sign and break a contract. A few years ago, a school district with a good reputation received an infusion of funds and opened several new teaching positions during the summer. A number of teachers from surrounding districts applied for the jobs. However, they were prevented from taking the jobs because they had valid contracts and the districts refused to release them.

You can seek damages from a school district if it fails to honor a legal contract. In general, a teacher is entitled to damages that equal the salary described in the contract minus any money the teacher may have earned if he or she was able to obtain employment somewhere else. Individuals may also collect additional damages related to the costs of seeking another teaching position (Fisher, Schimmel, & Steelman, 2007). However, a person must look for other teaching positions. If the school board can demonstrate that other teaching jobs were available, and the person did not seek them, the amount of damages can be reduced.

In addition, some states have regulations regarding the breach of contract by teachers. These regulations call for the suspension or revocation of the teaching credential of a teacher who breaches a contract. Therefore, the signing of a contract to teach is a serious issue that should be done only with careful consideration. If you have a compelling reason to be released from a signed contract, the appropriate procedure is to make a formal request to the school district requesting a release from the contract. There is no legal obligation on the part of the school district to grant your request. However, if it is based on a solid reason, such a request is often honored. For example, school boards often release a teacher from a contract if a spouse is transferred out of the region. However, they may charge an individual for the cost of implementing a job search. As a practical matter, school districts do not want people who would really prefer to be somewhere else working for them.

There are several types of teachers' contracts. Typically new teachers are offered a term contract, a contract that offers employment for a specific period of time, usually for one school year. Near the conclusion of the term of the contract, a decision is made about renewing the contract. The term contract allows either party (the school district or the teacher) to negotiate new terms of employment or to terminate the relationship at the end of the contract period. No reason for terminating the contract needs to be provided. In some places, term contracts are issued to all teachers. In others, regulations require that term contracts be issued only to new teachers. Usually after they have taught for a number of years, teachers must be offered a different type of contract.

A second type of contract is the continuing contract. Unlike term contracts, basic provisions of the contract do not have to be renewed after a specified term (ordinarily there are allowances for adjustments of salaries). This type of contract is renewed automatically at the end of each year. Before a district can make a decision not to renew a continuing contract, it must provide specific and legal reasons for the termination, and it must follow strict procedural guidelines. This means that teachers holding continuing contracts enjoy more employment security than do teachers who hold term contracts.

A third type of a contract is the tenure contract. Tenure provides teachers with the most job security of any contract. Tenure was instituted decades ago for a couple of reasons. One reason was that it provided teachers with freedom from pressure and intimidation. For example, teachers could be threatened with termination if they did not bow to political pressure by administrators or parents to include in or omit from the curriculum certain content or particular values. This helped protect academic freedom. Indeed, there have been cases of nontenured teachers being terminated because they belonged to the "wrong" church, campaigned for the "wrong" school board member, refused to omit content about controversial events, or expressed public opinions different from those of administrators or school board members. Another reason for offering tenure was that it was an incentive for individuals to stay on the job because it offered a high element of job security to compensate for lower salaries.

Like a continuing contract, a tenure contract remains in force from year to year. A key difference is that a person with tenure can be removed from his or her teaching position only when it can be proven that the person has violated tenure provisions. In addition, the burden of proof for termination is placed on the school administration. This places more responsibility on the school district and is a stricter standard than what is usually contained in a continuing contract. This means that due process must be followed, and the school district must present evidence that the teacher is guilty of violating one of the tenure provisions. This procedure is usually time consuming and costly, so many school administrators do not attempt to remove tenured teachers.

Tenure contracts are generally not awarded to teachers until they have worked successfully in a given district for several years. A typical probationary period is three years. During their initial years of service, teachers are issued term contracts.

Some critics have attacked tenure contracts because they are perceived as guaranteeing lifetime employment for teachers and thus protecting incompetent teachers from dismissal. This is a misconception. Tenure does not guarantee lifetime employment. What it does guarantee is that due process procedures will be followed in any proceedings that might lead to a dismissal and that dismissal will occur only when certain conditions have been met. Some reasons for the dismissal of tenured teachers include (1) evidence of gross incompetence, (2) physical or mental incapacity, (3) neglect of duty, (4) immorality, (5) unprofessional conduct, and (6) conviction of a crime.

In recent years, contracts often followed a standard form. In many places, what is included in the contract is dictated by the state or agreed upon by the school district and the local teacher association. Therefore, you do not need to be too concerned about the type of contract or what is included in the contract. However, you should carefully read the contract to make sure you understand your responsibilities and obligations.

Teacher Dismissal and Due Process

There is no general answer to the issue of whether you, as a teacher, always have the right to challenge nonrenewal of your contract or actions undertaken to dismiss you from your teaching position. Legal discussions of this matter have focused on two basic rights: liberty rights and property rights.

Liberty rights free individuals from having personal restraints imposed on them. These rights give them, among other things, opportunities to engage in the common occupations of life (*Meyer v. Nebraska,* 1923). Some court decisions relating to this issue have established that school districts cannot use unconstitutional reasons to deny teachers employment. As a result, you cannot be dismissed because of things such as age, gender, religious beliefs, or association with groups like unions or clubs.

Property rights give individuals, among other things, rights to enjoy the benefits associated with employment. Courts have wrestled with the question of whether teaching, as defined in a teacher's contractual agreement with a school district, is a property right. In general, the answer depends on the type of contract a teacher holds and the specific language it contains. Sometimes the issue becomes murky. For example, term contracts ordinarily terminate a teacher's employment on a given date. On the surface, it appears that the teacher has no property rights after the termination date of the contract. However, in places where it has been customary for districts to reissue new term contracts to teachers automatically, teachers may enjoy some property rights to employment even beyond the strict terminology in their contracts. The courts tend to weigh questions about such matters in terms of the specifics in the particular case.

In circumstances where there is agreement that the teachers have either liberty rights or property rights that merit legal protection, actions undertaken by school districts to interfere with these rights (typically actions taken to dismiss teachers) must follow strict due process guidelines. If you are in such a situation, you have to be given a notice of charges against you, provided with an opportunity to state your position in a hearing, given a chance to respond to charges made against you, and allowed to be represented by legal counsel. Some states with stricter due process procedures also require the district to provide you with an opportunity to remediate any deficient skills before a formal dismissal proceeding can be initiated against you.

Reporting Suspected Child Abuse

Child abuse has been a major concern in the past couple of decades. As a result, all 50 states now have legislation requiring people in certain positions to report suspected cases of child abuse. You, as an educator, are included among the group of people with special legal obligations to report suspected abuse. No state requires a teacher to know beyond a reasonable doubt that a child is being abused before reporting suspicions to authorities. All you need is reasonable suspicion of abuse (Monks & Proulx, 1986).

Each state has a set of specific procedures that are followed when reporting suspected cases of child abuse. Some states have established a 24-hour telephone hotline to make it easier for suspected cases to be reported. These reports need to be made with Child Protective Services. In most cases, there is a requirement that an oral report be followed by a written report within a few days (often about three days). Many school districts provide teachers with forms they can use in preparing reports of suspected child abuse.

All states provide teachers with some immunity from lawsuits for reporting suspected child abuse. This offers protection to individuals who may otherwise hesitate to file a report for fear of reprisal. Immunity from lawsuits is not unlimited. Immunity is guaranteed only when reports are filed in good faith. For example, if you are found to have filed a report maliciously for the purpose of "getting even" with the parents, you may find yourself facing a lawsuit.

Many states have established penalties to be levied against required reporters of suspected abuse who fail to do so. Penalties range from fines up to about $1,000 to jail terms of up to one year. These penalties and the long-term negative consequences of abuse on the development of a student make it imperative for you to learn how to recognize signs of potential abuse and to become familiar with the required reporting process in your state.

Legal Liability

There are number of grounds for lawsuits against teachers. One major category of liability lawsuits against teachers is tort liability. A tort is a civil wrong against another that results in either personal injury or property damage. There are many categories of torts, including negligence, invasion of privacy, assault, and defamation of character. The areas that draw the largest number of lawsuits against teachers are (1) excessive use of force in disciplining students, and (2) negligence.

Excessive Use of Force   Many court cases have focused on the issue of using physical punishment as a means of disciplining students. In the landmark case of *Ingraham v. Wright* (1977), the United States Supreme Court held that teachers could use reasonable but not excessive force in disciplining students. The justices further noted that corporal punishment did not constitute cruel and unusual punishment and therefore was not a violation of a student's constitutionally protected rights.

Some individuals mistakenly conclude that this makes the use of corporal punishment legal. This is not the case. Because of the national concern for child abuse and the message that is conveyed by hitting students, numerous states and school districts have prohibited corporal punishment. Even in those places where it is still allowed, teachers must follow strict guidelines before administering corporal punishment. For example, they may be required to have an administrator or some other designated person act as a witness. Even then, legal action is possible if the punishment worsens a student's preexisting health condition. This is the case even if the person administering the punishment was unaware of a preexisting health condition. In addition, allegations of excessive force by students or their legal representatives may result in criminal assault and battery charges. In such situations, juries often decide cases on the basis of whether the teacher acted as a prudent parent would have acted.

Corporal punishment or the use of force in disciplining students is a very controversial topic. In light of concerns about child abuse and the possibility of legal action against teachers who are judged as having used excessive force, we subscribe to the view that the risks associated with corporal punishment outweigh any potential benefits. It is a practice you should avoid.

Negligence   Negligence is a failure to use reasonable care and/or take prudent actions to prevent harm from coming to someone. There are three basic types of negligence:

- Nonfeasance
- Misfeasance
- Malfeasance

Nonfeasance occurs when an individual fails to act and when there is a professional responsibility to do so. Many lawsuits filed against teachers fall into this category. These acts of nonfeasance frequently occur when a teacher is absent from his or her place of assigned responsibility and an injury occurs. For example, nonfeasance might occur when you are assigned the responsibility of supervising students boarding or leaving the buses. However, you are not present and a student is injured. Another example might be when you slip out of your classroom while students are present and an injury occurs.

By no means does this imply that there are no circumstances that can justify your absence from your designated area of responsibility. There can be compelling reasons for being away from your designated area. For example, if an incident or an event outside the classroom poses potential harm to students, your absence from the room would be justified. However, you should avoid the practice of one secondary school teacher we know who regularly leaves his classroom and walks into the hall to visit with other teachers!

Misfeasance occurs when a person fails to act in a proper manner to prevent harm. In misfeasance, a person acts but she or he acts in an unwise or an unprofessional manner. Misfeasance might occur in the classroom if proper precautions and instructions are not given when students work with potentially dangerous material or equipment or when they engage in potentially harmful activities. Thus, misfeasance might occur in a science classroom where students are allowed to handle a dangerous substance without instruction, in a shop class where students are using potentially dangerous equipment without appropriate supervision, or in a physical education class where students are not taught a proper technique. For example, one teacher was charged with misfeasance when a student was injured during wrestling practice. The assertion was that the teacher had not given proper instruction about a particular wrestling hold. However, misfeasance can also occur in other classrooms where students are using paper cutters, or electronic equipment or tools.

An important step in avoiding many lawsuits based on misfeasance is to make sure that clear and specific instructions are provided to students regarding issues such as the safe use of equipment and the proper uses of tools and chemicals. You must also provide proper supervision when students are working with potentially dangerous materials or equipment.

Malfeasance occurs when a person deliberately acts in an improper manner and thereby causes harm to another. One example might be a situation where a teacher becomes angry with a student and gives her or him a shove that results in a fall or an injury. The actions of the teacher would be interpreted to mean that he or she intended to cause harm to the student.

Academic Freedom and Freedom of Expression

Academic freedom issues for teachers often involve conflicts between (1) teachers' rights to conduct their classes according to their best professional judgment and (2) school authorities' responsibilities to make sure the prescribed curriculum is taught. Court decisions in this area do not reflect a consistent pattern.

One principle that has often been supported by the courts is that school officials have the right to expect that the prescribed curriculum is taught and to require you to teach the subject-matter content of the class you have been assigned. For example, if you have been assigned to teach mathematics, you cannot avoid teaching the content prescribed for this particular class and instead spend time promoting your personal political views on the grounds that you are protected by academic freedom. In other words, academic freedom does not give teacher total freedom to teach and say whatever they please.

However, the courts usually have ruled that districts cannot require you to avoid dealing with controversial issues or prohibit you from teaching certain topics that are a legitimate component of the subject you teach. An example is the case of an American history teacher who used a simulation activity that evoked strong racial feelings. The school district informed the teacher she was not to continue using the simulation. However she continued to do so. The courts upheld the rights of the teacher on the grounds that it was a legitimate part of the curriculum (*Kingsville Independent School District v. Cooper,* 1980). In another case, the courts supported a teacher who challenged an administrative ruling that forbade her from using a particular book. In this decision, the court ruled that the book was appropriate for high school students, contained nothing obscene, and the administration's decision to ban its use had violated the teacher's academic freedom rights (*Parducci v. Rutland,* 1979).

In the *Parducci* case, the court noted that the right to teach, evaluate, and experiment with new ideas is fundamental to a democratic society. In other cases, however, courts have upheld the rights of the school boards to prohibit use of certain books, even literary classics. Decisions in this area have tended to be responsive to specific characteristics of the work in question, the age and sophistication of the students, and the nature of the local community.

Freedom of expression refers to the rights of individuals to state their views on a subject without fear of reprisal. Court cases in this area that involve teachers have often arisen from situations in which school authorities have attempted to punish teachers for out-of-classroom speech. A landmark freedom of expression case is *Pickering v. Board of Education of Township School District 205, Will County* (1968). Pickering, a teacher, wrote a letter to the editor of the local newspaper criticizing the way school funds were being allocated. Members of the school board were outraged. They claimed Pickering had made untrue statements in the letter and had thereby damaged the reputations of school board members and leading school administrators. The board took action to dismiss Pickering. Pickering protested and challenged the dismissal action in court. The case ultimately made its way to the United States Supreme Court.

In arriving at its decision in the *Pickering* case, the High Court considered two key issues. The first focused on whether a teacher can be dismissed for making critical comments about the school district and district policies in public. On this issue, the Court ruled that teachers have a right to speak out on school issues as part of a general effort to provide for a more informed public. The second issue the Court considered had to do with whether a teacher could be dismissed for making false statements. In this particular case, the Court found that Pickering had made only one false statement in his letter. In the absence of any information that Pickering knowingly or deliberately made the false statement, the Court ruled in favor of Pickering. In other cases, dismissal actions taken against teachers have been upheld when evidence has been presented that they knowingly made false statements with a clear understanding that they were recklessly disregarding the truth.

These rulings by no means suggest, however, that you, as a teacher, have a right to complain about everything. Some activities of schools and school districts may not be seen as matters of public concern by the courts. In addition, the style and manner of your complaints is important. Complaints cannot be made at a time or in a manner that interferes with the operation of the school or the responsibility of the administrators to perform their assigned responsibilities.

Copyright Law

Copyright law seeks to protect the works of authors and artists. Federal copyright law covers the use of material copied from books, journals, computer programs, CDs, DVDs, and videotapes.

The doctrine of fair use is an exception to copyright law that has implications for you as a teacher. Fair use seeks to balance the rights of a copyright owner with the public's interest in having easy access to new ideas and information. The fair use doctrine makes it permissible for you to make single copies of book chapters, articles from journals, short stories or poems, and charts and graphs for your own scholarly research or as part of your preparation for teaching lessons. Multiple copies (not to exceed one for each student in the class) may be made if guidelines related to (1) brevity, (2) spontaneity, and (3) cumulative effect are met (Committee on the Judiciary, 1976).

Brevity (as the term applies to fair use) for different kinds of material is defined as follows:

- A complete poem may be used if it is not more than 250 words and not more than two pages in length.

- An excerpt from a longer poem may be used consisting of no more than 250 words.

- A complete article or story may be used that is less than 2,500 words long.

- From a larger work, an excerpt may be used that is less than 1,000 words in length or that consists of no more than 10 percent of the length of the total work, whichever is less.

- One chart, diagram, picture, or cartoon per book or periodical may be used.

The spontaneity criteria refers to situations when you need to use the work is so close to the time it must be provided to students in your class that it would be unreasonable or impossible to request and receive permission. If this is the situation, then you would be allowed to use the material one time and then would be expected to seek permission for continued use.

Cumulative effect is defined as the following:

- The material is used for only one course.

- Not more than one short poem, article, short story, or essay or two excerpts from works by the same author and not more than three excerpts from the same collective work or periodical volume may be used without permission.

- There are no more than nine instances of such multiple copying for one course during one term.

Unless these fair use guidelines can be met, you are obligated to secure permission from authors, artists, or other copyright holders before making and distributing copies. If you fail to do so, you may face legal action brought by copyright holders or their representatives.

It is also important to note that computer software programs are not covered by fair use doctrine. It is illegal to make copies of commercially produced programs and to use them on different computers in the classroom unless specific permission has been granted. Many software vendors will sell a site license to a school or business authorizing the purchaser to make and distribute a given number of copies of a specific program.

Special copyright provisions apply to videotaping for educational purposes. A copyrighted program may be recorded and used for instructional purposes, provided that you use it within 10 days and keep the videotape for no more than 45 days. The only legal use that can be made of the videotape between the tenth and the forty-fifth day is evaluating its content. If you wish to keep a given program for some time and to use it repeatedly in your classes, you need to secure written permission from the copyright holder.

Failure to abide by copyright regulations can result in significant penalties. There can be an award to the copyright holder equivalent to the loss of profits resulting from the illegal use or an amount of money determined by the court ranging between $500 and $20,000. If the court determines the violator acted willfully, it can increase monetary damage to an amount as high as $100,000. However, if the violator can prove that the infraction was unintentional, the court can scale back damages to a figure as low as $220.

Teachers' Private Lives

Individuals often think that what they do away from the school campus is of no concern to others. However, the courts have held that, because of the unique role of the teacher in working with impressionable youth, they can be held to a higher standard than other citizens.

There have been numerous cases involving allegations of immoral teacher behavior. Typically, the courts have dealt quite harshly with teachers who have been found to be "immoral." The difficulty in deriving general principles from a review of these cases is that the terms *moral* and *immoral* tend to take on different meanings from place to place.

FOR YOUR PORTFOLIO

Your understanding of legal issues can be very important for you as you move toward a teaching career. You might want to gather information regarding what is required to obtain a credential in your state, information regarding tenure and due process for teachers, the process and phone numbers for reporting suspected child abuse, contract information, and recent court decisions in your region regarding student rights and responsibilities. In addition, select at least one activity related to the content of the chapter. Reflect on the importance of this information and how it affects your choices as a teacher, and include it in your portfolio.

Material on the legal issues relates most directly to Interstate New Teacher Assessment and Support Consortium (INTASC) Standard 9 (evaluating the effect of choices and actions on others). However, some legal issues could relate to Standard 10 (fostering relationships with colleagues, parents and agencies in the larger community). Decide how the material in your portfolio relates to each of these standards.

A theme that runs through many of these cases has to do with the perceived impact of a given teacher's behavior on his or her classroom performance and his or her standing in the local community. When a teacher has been dismissed for alleged immoral behavior and there is evidence that the behavior violates prevailing community standards, the courts have tended to support the dismissal. However, if the alleged immoral behavior has been shown to have little impact on the teacher's ability to teach effectively and has elicited little negative reaction in the community, the courts have often ruled for the teacher and against the school officials.

Consequences have been severe for teachers whose immoral behaviors have involved students. Courts have upheld dismissals of a teacher who was found playing strip poker with a student in a car, of another teacher whose offer to "spank" two female students was interpreted as a sexual advance, and of a teacher who tickled and used suggestive language to female students on a class field trip.

In still another case, a teacher was dismissed when a high school girl he had been dating became pregnant. He admitted having an affair with the student, but contended that since the girl was not a student at the school where he taught that there was no adverse impact on his teaching. The teacher felt he should be reinstated. The court disagreed, stating that in situations like this, no evidence of interference with the classroom performance of the teacher was needed (*Denton v. South Kitsap School District No. 402*, 1973). The court ruled that the relationship between the teacher and any student constituted sexual misconduct that was inherently harmful to the school district.

Other cases in which teacher dismissal actions have been upheld have involved situations where teachers have been arrested for public intoxication, had repeated drunk driving convictions, shoplifted, lied about being sick in order to collect sick leave, taken school property, engaged in welfare fraud, and allowed students to consume alcohol in their home. Conviction of any serious crime, such as a felony, ordinarily is grounds for dismissal.

To summarize, because of the sensitive role that you, as a teacher, play as a nurturer of young people, you are expected to reflect standards of personal behavior that are higher than those expected of average citizens. Hence, you have to be a careful monitor of your own behavior. In particular, you have to avoid personal behaviors that interfere with your ability to function as an effective teacher or that clearly conflict with standards of morality prevalent in your community.

Key Ideas in Summary

■ Students not only have rights, they have responsibilities. Among those responsibilities are following reasonable rules and regulations, attending school regularly, refraining from the possession of unsafe articles such as weapons and controlled substances, and behaving in socially acceptable ways.

- Students enjoy considerable freedom of expression rights. Administrators have limited rights to oversee the contents of student publications that are produced as part of the regular school program. However, they may not censor materials simply on the grounds that they are controversial or on other grounds that clearly violate students' constitutional rights. Administrators have even less authority over student publications that are not produced under the auspices of the school. Students also enjoy constitutional protection of oral speech.

- In general, the courts have allowed students' religious beliefs as grounds for excusing them from school activities that cannot be demonstrated to be essential to their health or welfare or essential to the welfare of the state. In practice, this means that religious reasons have been viewed as grounds for excusing students from activities such as the Pledge of Allegiance but not from basic school subjects such as reading.

- Regulations regarding dress and appearance have been reported most frequently when the courts have found a demonstrable connection between a student's dress or appearance and (1) the safety or health of the student body or (2) disruption of the instructional process. Recent cases have also supported decisions to ban items of dress associated with gang membership.

- The Fourteenth Amendment to the United States Constitution guarantees due process rights to citizens. These guarantees provide certain procedures or safeguards that must be followed whenever a person is denied a constitutionally protected right.

- Search and seizure cases have considered the authority of school officials to search students, their property and areas such as school lockers. In determining the appropriateness of a search, the courts have generally considered (1) the nature of what is being sought, (2) the quality of the evidence leading to the decision to conduct a search, (3) the degree of the expectation of privacy associated with the place to be searched, and (4) the intrusiveness of the search.

- The federal Family Educational Rights and Privacy Act gives parents and students who are 18 years of age or older the right to look at school records. The law prohibits the records from being shown to anyone not immediately concerned with the students' education. Requests can also be filed to amend records that are identified as (1) inaccurate, (2) misleading, or (3) in violation of privacy rights. Individuals who have entered defamatory comments on student records can be sued.

- Teachers' contracts are legal documents that establish a working relationship between the individual and the school district that employs her or him. For contracts to be valid, they must be approved by the school board. There are several types of contracts, including term contracts, continuing contracts, and tenure contracts. Penalties are attached whenever either party violates a contract.

- Dismissal procedures must be followed when a school district decides to release a teacher with a continuing or a tenure contract. Dismissal actions against a teacher with a term contract cannot be initiated for reasons that are inconsistent with constitutional rights.

- All states have laws requiring that teachers report suspected child abuse. These laws also protect teachers who make such reports in good faith from reprisals. Penalties are associated with failure to report suspected cases of child abuse.

- Teachers may be held liable for certain types of actions. Many teacher liability suits have resulted from charges of (1) excessive use of force in disciplining students or (2) negligence. Negligence cases have often focused on nonfeasance (a failure to act when there is a duty to do so), misfeasance (a failure to act in a proper manner), or malfeasance (acting to harm another deliberately).

- In considering issues of academic freedom, courts have weighed both teachers' rights to conduct their classroom according to their own professional judgment and the needs of school officials to make sure that the prescribed curriculum is taught. In general, the courts have supported the actions of administrators to ensure that the mandated curriculum is taught; they have supported teachers in cases where administrators have attempted to stifle the study of controversial or embarrassing content that is directly related to the content being taught.

- Copyright regulations are designed to protect the interests of the developers of intellectual property such as books, music, works of art, radio and television programs, and computer programs. In general, teachers must request and receive written permission for making and distributing multiple copies of copyrighted material. Fair use guidelines allow some limited classroom use of copyright material without securing permission.

- Actions teachers take in their private lives sometimes come to the attention of the courts. The courts have declared that, because of their potential influence on young people, teachers can be held to higher moral and behavioral standards than citizens in general. Dismissal actions against teachers have frequently been upheld when courts have found their actions to undermine their credibility in the community and to make them ineffective as instructional leaders.

Learning Extensions

1. Survey recent articles that have appeared in the press for articles on legal issues relating to education. Identify the legal principles that were applied to the situation.

2. Interview a local high school principal on the procedures followed when it becomes necessary to suspend or expel a student. Pay particular attention to how due process guidelines are implemented.

3. Interview the human resources director of a local school district and discuss the various elements of a teaching contract.

4. Obtain information regarding the laws about reporting suspected child abuse. This information should be filed so that you will have easy access to it when you begin teaching and should be updated regularly as laws and regulations change.

References

California Teachers Association. (1992). *Guide to school law.* Burlingame, CA: Author.

Committee on the Judiciary, H.R. No 94-1476, 94th Congress, 201 Sess. 68–70 (1976).

Connors, E. (1991). *Educational tort liability and malpractice.* Bloomington, IN: Phi Delta Kappa.

Denton v. South Kitsap School District, No. 402 516 P2d 1080 (Wash. 1973).

Fischer, L., Schimmel, D., & Steelman, L. R. (2007). *Teachers and the law* (6th ed.) Boston: Allyn and Bacon.

Goss v. Lopez, 419 U.S. 565 (1975).

Hazelwood School District v Kuhlmeier, 484 U.s. 260 (1988).

Ingraham v. Wright, 430 U.S. 651 (1977).

Kingsville Independent School District v. Cooper, 611 F2d 1109 (5th Cir. 1980).

Meyer v. Nebraska, 262 U.S. 390, 399 (1923).

Monks, R., & Proulx, E. (1986) *Legal basics for teachers.* Fastback No. 235. Blomington, IN: Phi Delta Kappa.

New Jersey v. TLO. 105 S.Ct. 733 (1985).

Parducci v. Rutland, 316 F. Supp. 352 (m.d. Ala. 1979).

Pickering v. Board of Education of Township School District 205, Will County, 225 N.E. 2d 1 1967); 391 U.S. 563 (1968).

Schimmel, D. (2006). Classroom management, discipline, and the law: Clarifying confusions about students' rights and teachers' authority. In C. M. Evertson & C. S. Weinstein (Eds.).

Classroom management: Research, practice, and contemporary issues (pp. 1005–10018). Mahwah, NJ: Lawrence Erlbaum.

Tinker v. Des Moines Independent Community School District, 393 U.S. 513 (1969).

U.S. Department of Health and Human Services, Health Resources and Services Administration. (2008). *Cyberbulling.* Retrieved March 29, 2008, from http://www.stopbullyingnow.hrsa.gov/adult/index.Adult.asp?Area=cyberbulling

Valente, W. (1994). *Law in the schools* (3rd ed.). Upper Saddle River, NJ: Merrill/Prentice Hall.

Wisconsin v. Yoder, 406 U.S. 205 (1972).

Zirkel, P., & Richardson, S. (1988). *A digest of Supreme Court decisions affecting education.* Bloomington, IN: Phi Delta Kappa.

15

Career-Long Professional Growth

Objectives

This chapter will help you

- understand your need for career-long preparation and development

- define characteristics of professionalism as they apply to teaching

- identify teachers' professional growth stages

- state the purposes of teacher evaluation

- define different types of teacher evaluation

- find some alternative approaches to acquiring additional expertise as you work throughout your career to be a more effective teacher

- distinguish between general organizations and specialty organizations for teachers

- describe the advantages for beginning teachers of joining a professional group

- identify career options that may be open to you as someone who has a background in classroom teaching

Bob Daemmrich Photograph

Graphic Organizer: Chapter 15

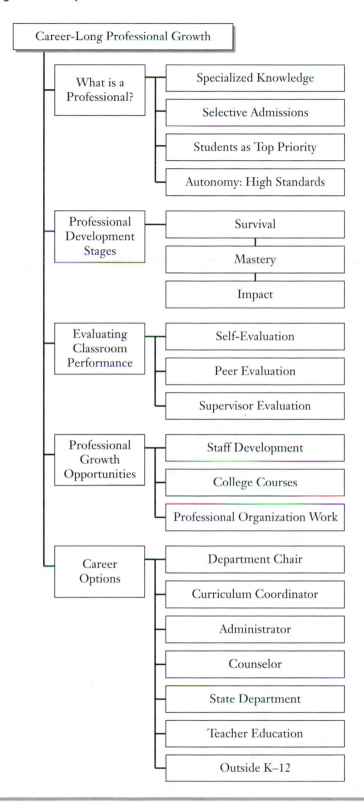

Introduction

Although you are almost at the end of this text, most of you are just in the beginning phases of your professional preparation. When you complete your studies, we hope you will be a highly talented beginning teacher. However, your preparation does not end with the conclusion of your teacher credential program. To reach a high level of professionalism and obtain the rich personal satisfaction that accompanies a successful teaching career, you will need to engage in career-long professional growth.

When you survey the contemporary world of education, you may be struck by the complexity of the changes taking place. You should take some comfort in knowing that change has always characterized our profession. Current change is somewhat different because education has been discovered as a political issue. Therefore, proposals for change are now coming from sources that have the power to change secondary schools significantly. The likelihood is high that throughout your career, you will face proposals for change that include some of the following:

- The curriculum
- School choice
- Basic processes of teaching and learning
- Uses of technology
- High-stakes testing
- Teacher and school accountability
- Performance standards and merit pay for teachers
- Changes in school governance

If you are the type of individual who desires predictability and a career that will remain relatively unchanged for the next 10 to 20 years, you should consider a career other than teaching. Successful educators understand that change is a constant professional companion. The expertise you have earned at the conclusion of your preparation program is something you should see simply as the end of the beginning phase of your professional preparation.

Throughout this text we have emphasized the importance of reflective practice. This approach to teaching can provide you with the basis for establishing a career-long professional growth agenda. Reflective teaching encourages you to accept responsibility and to be open-minded—attitudes that are essential if professional improvement is to occur.

You need to embrace the idea that what you do as a teacher makes a difference and that your actions have consequences. This means accepting responsibility for your actions and avoiding any temptation to blame difficulties on external factors, such as parental indifference, negative student attitudes, or administrative decisions that conflict with your beliefs. While certainly not all conditions you face will please you, it is important to avoid falling into the trap of assuming these circumstances can overwhelm your ability to adjust and respond in ways that provide sound educational experiences for your students. You need to remain open, flexible, and committed to responding proactively to the special situations you will face. That is what professionals do.

What is a Professional?

As you consider a career in teaching, you may find it useful to reflect on the definition of the term *professional*. Education specialists John Jarolimek and Clifford Foster (1996) state that professional teachers are individuals who

- possess specialized knowledge and skill

- have been admitted to a professional development program after having met specified criteria
- place students as their number one priority
- exercise a certain amount of autonomy and set high standards for their own professional practice

Specialized Knowledge and Skill

The value of professional knowledge in education is often questioned. There are several reasons for this. Some see teaching as an art, not as a science. If it is an art, then some people have the skill and some do not. If it is an art, then there is little specialized knowledge relating to teaching and learning.

Some members of society do not view teaching as an especially difficult task. They see teaching as little more than common sense and thus requiring little specialized knowledge beyond what an average person would know. Their contention is that "good" people with strong academic qualifications are all that is needed to have excellent teachers.

How can you tell if a given occupation demands professional preparation? The basic measure is to look for answers to this question: Can a person be successful without specialized knowledge and formal preparation? The question is not so easily answered in teaching. Yes, there are examples of individuals who have become successful with minimum prior preparation. However, there are also numerous examples of strong, academically qualified individuals who have failed.

A growing body of research attests to the fact that a solid preparation in professional education is important. As you will recognize when you begin to work in the classroom, you need a depth of knowledge in the subjects you teach, an understanding of the developmental dimensions of those you teach, as well as sound professional knowledge related to instructional design and delivery issues. Experts suggest that specialized expertise acquired in areas related to transmitting what you know (as opposed to simply acquiring this kind of knowledge yourself) correlates highly to the quality of instruction you are likely to provide your students (Darling-Hammond, 2000). Yet another factor lending support to the idea that specialized knowledge is important is the high attrition rate of individuals who enter the teaching profession without adequate professional preparation.

We need to be clear, however, that good teaching, like most other professions, requires more than just specialized knowledge. In other words, successfully completing a teacher preparation program will not guarantee success. There is something of an art in knowing when and how to apply the specialized knowledge that you have. In essence, there is a scientific basis to the art of teaching.

Acquisition of specialized knowledge will not end when you meet qualifications for a degree or a teaching license or credential. Remember, you are dealing with one of the most complex and sophisticated organisms, the human brain. How the brain develops and how learning occurs is still largely a mystery. To make things even more complicated, you are dealing with a whole room full of these complex organisms and they are all programmed differently! In addition, the students you teach are influenced by their culture and their background. As the world changes, culture will change and so will students. Thus, as society changes and as we learn more about how individuals learn, professional knowledge will change. Therefore, you and your professional teaching colleagues will need to be involved in a career-long process of professional development. If you reach the point where you feel you have nothing more to learn, then it is probably time to consider another profession.

Selective Admission to Preparation Programs

Teacher preparation programs are "professional," in part, because candidates selected meet specified criteria. These criteria seek to identify people with the knowledge and attitudes that are necessary for successful professional practice. Not everyone meets these requirements; not everyone should be a teacher.

It should also be clear to anyone who has been a student that more than subject matter and pedagogical knowledge is required for a person to be a successful teacher. Good teachers also need to have personality characteristics and emotional dispositions that allow them to achieve success in the school environment. As a teacher, you will find yourself interacting with a wide array of people. You need to be able to establish good working relationships with students, other teachers, administrators, parents, and members of the general community. Some individuals simply do not have the values and the interpersonal skills needed to facilitate the establishment of these important personal relationships. Thus, good teacher preparation programs consider characteristics beyond just academic success in selecting individuals who complete the teacher preparation program.

Students as a Top Priority

Professionals in all fields accord a high priority to providing service to clients. As a teacher, your "clients" are your students. When you become a teacher, you accept responsibility for one of our society's most important obligations—educating young people. The importance of this role has been recognized for centuries. For example, the great Roman orator Cicero remarked that there is no nobler profession than teaching the youth of the [Roman] Republic (Clark & Starr, 1996).

In practice, "putting students first" means that professional teachers place service to students higher than competing interests and obligations. There will be occasions when you spend time with individuals far beyond the end of the regular school day, and there will be times when you willingly listen to students' concerns even when you have stacks of paperwork to review. You will devote extra time outside class to ensure that the lessons you provide are responsive to your students' needs. You will spend some of your own money to purchase instructional resources that will help your students learn. In summary, everything you do is framed by a commitment to helping the young people under your charge grow into secure, informed, and contributing members of our society.

An additional dimension of this priority requires you to express informed judgments about policies and practices that involve students. In the contemporary world, people with little knowledge about students and schools often feel free to make proclamations and decisions regarding what should be done to educate our youth. Unfortunately, some of these proposals have the potential for harming the educational development of some students. Because your students do not vote and may have limited political power, your role as a professional educator obligates you to speak out against policies and practices that are potentially detrimental to students.

Autonomy and High Standards

As a professional, you will exercise a certain amount of autonomy and need to accept responsibility for setting high standards of professional practice. Although adopted curriculum requirements and other rules and regulations give some external direction to what you can do, you still have a certain amount of authority as a teacher to decide exactly what you will do each day. As a professional, you will not be subject to minute-by-minute scrutiny and your lessons are generally your own creations that involve your professional knowledge and your creativity.

Along with this autonomy comes responsibility. You need to be a thoughtful decision maker who constantly seeks to improve your professional expertise. Teachers who resist change are insensitive to the unique needs of a given class of students, and simply repeating the same units or lessons from year to year is unprofessional. This kind of behavior diminishes the profession and invites intervention by dissatisfied external authorities.

Professional Development Stages

As you enter the field of teaching, you must realize that you will experience different stages as you continue to grow professionally. You need to understand the dimensions of each of these stages in order to cope with them. The sad fact is that many new teachers do not cope well. As stated in Chapter 1, there is a high attrition rate for teachers during their first five years of teaching. Typically, about 15% leave after the first year, and another 15% leave after the second year (Kronowitz, 1999).

Much of this high attrition rate can be ascribed to what is called reality shock. Reality shock is what happens when an individual experiences unexpected events during the early years at a job. Everyone experiences some unease upon undertaking a new responsibility. There is evidence, however, that this problem is especially acute among new teachers. People who have studied this problem note that part of the difficulty is the disconnect between what new teachers remember about their own school days and what they encounter when they begin teaching (Ryan et al., 1980). Consider your own situation. You spent many years sitting in school classrooms. You may have had contact with 50 to 100 teachers by the time you graduated from high school. Some were good, some were poor, and many fell somewhere in between. You have clear memories of the sights, the smells, and the pace of daily life in secondary schools. In short, we think we have a clear understanding of schools and teaching. One of the frustrations many of us in teacher preparation programs face are those students who enter our programs with absolute certainty that they know exactly what they need to know and be able to do as a teacher. Many of these individuals are not open to new learning that is important for their success.

You may well begin your work in the profession feeling confident that you really understand what your life as a teacher will be like. However, your confidence may be shaken once you have your own classroom and begin teaching. For the first time, you will be viewing education exclusively from the perspective of the teacher. In your former student days, you may have been largely unaware of those students who were not enthusiastic about school and had only the vaguest understanding of the behind the scenes issues and problems your teachers faced on a regular basis.

Even the experiences you will have as a student teacher may not prepare you for the fact that some (often quite a large number) of your students, initially at least, may be indifferent to the subjects you are teaching. You may also find that large numbers of students do not have as much background information as you imagined they would have. You may also be surprised at how much work is required to motivate students and to maintain good order in the classroom. Finally, you may not initially be prepared for the huge time investment required to handle out-of-school responsibilities, including lesson planning, correcting papers, attending meetings, and supervising student activities.

Do not be surprised if some of these realities overwhelm and concern you when you accept your first teaching position. As we have worked with new teachers during their induction phase, we have laughed, and cried, along with them as they face issues ranging from "unwritten rules" for teachers in their school and lesson "disasters." The good news is that thousands of teachers have successfully made the adjustment to their new professional roles and take great personal and professional satisfaction in their ability to promote the educational development of young people.

For years, researchers have been interested in how new teachers adjust to the profession. Experts who have studied this issue have identified three important teacher growth and development stages:

- The survival stage
- The mastery stage
- The impact stage

(Fuller, 1969).

Survival Stage

Given the discussion so far in this chapter, it should come as no surprise to you that the initial stage of development is called the survival stage. When you first begin teaching, you are likely to be worried about your adequacy as a teacher. You may well be concerned that problems will arise for which you are not prepared. It would not be unusual for you to worry about whether your students and professional colleagues will like and respect you. Initially, you are likely to focus on surviving each period, getting through the day, and making it to the next break in the school calendar.

The survival stage may vary in length. Some people quickly solve their survival problems and begin to develop confidence in their ability to handle the multiple dimensions of their teaching. You may be one of these individuals who develops a strong sense of teaching efficacy within a few months and completes your first year of teaching eagerly anticipating the next group of students. However, others who start at the same time as you do may struggle. They may have a difficult time adjusting and they may experience frustration and failure. By the end of the first year, some of these individuals may well decide to leave the teaching profession. Others will persist and return for a second year with the hope that things will surely improve. For many, the second year will prove to be more satisfying. Others, however, will continue to find it difficult to deal with all the problems and frustrations involved in teaching and will remain in the survival stage. Many of them will leave at the end of the second or third year. A few people remain in the survival stage for a large portion of their careers and go on to become unhappy, even bitter, teachers.

CRITICAL INCIDENT

"I Just Wasn't Prepared for This"

Arlene Newby has been struggling through her first year of teaching mathematics to eighth-graders at King Middle School. She teaches a pre-algebra course to some of her students and a regular algebra class to the others. After a particularly difficult day, she made her way into the faculty lounge. Her friend, Veronica Linn, was sitting on one of the battered couches.

"So, another day in the bag, Arlene. Get some coffee and sit down. What's new with you?" asked Veronica.

"My day . . . my week . . . they've just been the pits," Arlene replied. "Even my best algebra kids have been on a tear. As for the rest of them, well, I just feel I'm barely keeping the lid on."

"Well, eighth-graders will be eighth-graders. Remember you've got all those surging hormones and the football game with Madison coming up tomorrow night. I mean the Pied Piper and Mother Theresa combined would have a hard time convincing these kids that quiet attention to mathematics should be their top priority."

"That's fine for you to say. You've been here for years. The principal thinks you're great. Parents support what you're doing. But what about me? I'm the new kid on the block. I feel like I'm really under the microscope. I've had several parents make a big point of telling me that they expect their kids to become engineers or scientists and that they want them to 'really be prepared' for their high school math classes. If the kids thought math was half as important as their parents do, my job would be a breeze."

"Anything else on your mind?" asked Veronica.

"Well, since you asked, yes. These pre-algebra classes are driving me nuts. The students just don't have the basics. I mean, some of them don't even know their multiplication tables. What did those elementary school teachers teach these kids? Not much. Sometimes I wonder why I struggled through all of those calculus classes only to be given a bunch of students who hate math and who can't even manage basic arithmetic. I just wasn't prepared for this."

"All right, so some of your kids don't think the sun rises and sets on math. And you think this wasn't true when you were in school? Give me a break." Veronica continued, "Do you think all my kids love English? Do you think Mr. Harmon's students turn hand-flips at the prospects of studying science? Are Ms. Knight's kids just lusting to study history? No way. That's not how the world is. Part of our job is seeing to it that kids tolerate our instruction. Beyond that, we try to motivate them to like it. Enthusiasm doesn't come from any inherent interest in the subject itself; it comes from what we do. You've got to get beyond this idea that these kids are just going to sit there and let you build on enthusiasm and interest that are already there. Won't happen."

"Well, thanks a lot, Veronica," sputtered Arlene, "you've just made my day. Now even you don't think I'm being professional. I'm so frustrated right now I can't believe it. I feel like a real square peg in a round hole. I'm working hard, getting by on less sleep than I need, and for what? I can't seem to please anybody . . . least of all myself. I just don't know what I'm going to do."

■ ■ ■

What did you learn about some things that are important to Arlene? What aspects of her teaching responsibilities seem to challenge some of her values? What are her assumptions about how students and schools ought to be? What discrepancies exist between her assumptions and what she encounters?

How do you explain the differences in the perspectives revealed in Arlene's comments and in Veronica's comments? What do these reveal about differences in values and in other priorities? What might account for these differences?

What kinds of personal responsibilities does Arlene have in trying to respond to the problems she feels she is facing? Has she assumed that professional development ceased before she began her first teaching job? Does she have an obligation to take specific actions that might lead to different patterns of behavior and to different expectations of students? Does she have a place in education, or should she pursue a different career option? What should her next steps be?

Your focus during the survival stage should be on mastering the basics of teaching. Develop routines for predictable and recurring events. Make sure that you have completely thought through your daily lessons. Have rules and clear expectations for your students. Make sure you have all your material ready to go before the school day begins. Working on these basics will allow you to focus your energy on those unpredictable events that are bound to occur. You need to seek out "older hands" who can give you advice. You will find most of your colleagues to be highly sympathetic to the stresses and challenges you will be experiencing. Remember that even the most confident teachers in your building were, at one time, newcomers to the profession.

When you begin teaching and are at the survival stage, you can do several things to make your life more manageable. First, have realistic expectations. Developing excellence in teaching takes time. Don't feel bad if every lesson does not work out well. Avoid negative self-judgments. You need to understand that even highly experienced teachers have forgettable days. The concept of reflection introduced in Chapter 5 is critical at this stage. When your lessons go well, ask yourself why they went well. When they do not go well, again ask why, then identify what you might do differently next time.

Second, if your school does not assign newcomers an official mentor, seek out experienced people on the faculty. They will likely remember the adjustments they had to make as newcomers to the profession. Many of these people will reach out and befriend a beginner. Their support can be invaluable as you work to retain and extend your self-confidence. One of us remembers an experienced teacher who reached out and gave advice concerning school procedures and expectations, working with parents, and the handling of discipline problems.

You also need to think about how people-intense the activity of teaching is. Prolonged interactions with others on a daily basis can produce stress. To counteract this situation, consider developing outside activities that you particularly enjoy. Many teachers find that exercise programs and other activities that free the mind from job-related concerns add a much-needed dose of psychological serenity.

Finally, remember that the first year of teaching is a unique time. Even if you were fortunate enough to have experienced an exemplary preparation program, you still have much to learn. You will find that much professional development occurs during your first year on the job. In fact, the benefits of this early, on-the-job learning are so great that we often counsel frustrated beginners who want to leave the profession to wait at least two years before making a decision.

Mastery Stage

After you solve issues at the survival stage, you will move on to the mastery stage. Once you have arrived at this stage, you will have developed confidence in your ability to deal with your students and in delivering the curriculum. You will understand how to plan and use time wisely. You will have confidence that you can handle unpredictable events. Your concerns now will turn away from worrying about getting through the day or the week and become more focused on your skill as a teacher.

You will pay more attention to mastering the fundamentals of teaching, and you are likely to develop interest in approaches that promise to enhance your instructional effectiveness. You are also likely to look more carefully at the contents of the curriculum and to consider ways to augment basic information you have been sharing with your students. Basically you are seeking to become a master teacher. You want to use the latest and the best approaches and stay current with new approaches.

If you are typical of teachers at this stage, you will be eager to seek professional development opportunities. You will want to learn more about your subject area and about new approaches to teaching and learning. This phase of your professional development can last a long time. Learning new ideas and developing increased confidence in your teaching can generate great personal satisfaction. During this time of your professional life, you may well become interested in serving as a mentor for new teachers.

Impact Stage

The third stage that you are likely to enter as your career progresses is the impact stage. Once you have developed a strong repertoire of teaching skills and have developed confidence in your teaching abilities, your concerns are likely to turn from how to master more teaching approaches to a focus on the impact you are having on students. To be sure, you will have some concern about your impact even during the survival and mastery stages. During earlier stages, however, it is a secondary concern. During the impact stage, this concern assumes a position of primacy.

This priority will be reflected in several ways. For example, when a new teaching approach is promoted, you will not be inclined to adopt it simply to expand your repertoire of techniques. Rather, your first question will be: What do we know about how this approach affects students and their learning? Your acceptance or rejection of approaches will depend on your relative confidence that new ways of doing things have excellent potential to help students learn.

Your life as a teacher can be highly satisfying when you arrive at the impact stage. Seeing students grow and change and being able to adapt your instruction to meet the needs of individuals can be highly rewarding. At the same time, your concern for impact can produce some personal frustration as you witness adoption and implementation of policies that, in your view, may interfere with your ability to have a positive and lasting influence on students.

Jackson (2009) has recently reexamined these stages. She presents a master teacher trajectory that, if followed, has the potential of moving you from a novice to a master teacher. This trajectory includes the following steps:

- Novice to apprentice (acquire)
- Apprentice to practitioner (apply)
- Practitioner to master teacher (assimilate)
- Becoming a better master teacher (refine and reflect) (pp. 196–199)

She cautions that moving from step to step takes time. You should not expect to acquire all skills at once. As a novice, your goal is to learn principles and focus on how you might use them in your classroom. You will know you have become an apprentice when you begin to try different approaches and are willing to experiment. As a practitioner, you will feel comfortable using a variety of strategies. Finally, as a master teacher you are able to assimilate these strategies effortlessly into your instruction.

Jackson says, "[T]he road to mastery isn't easy. There will be missteps and struggles along the way" (p. 199). Allow these missteps and struggles to be learning experiences so that you can become the master teacher you want to be.

Teacher Development Stages—Summary You need to understand that teachers do not necessarily move through these stages in either of the examples that we described in lockstep fashion. At various times during your career, you may find yourself moving back and forth through the categories. In general, these changes occur when you face significant and expected personal and professional circumstances. For example, if you change schools at some point in your career and find conditions drastically different from where you previously were employed, you may shift back (initially at least) to the survival stage. There can also be unexpected stresses in your personal life that affect your abilities to cope with challenges at school, and these events can cause a backward developmental-stage shift.

Thinking about these stages can assist you in several ways. First, they can help you understand that these are stages that all teachers experience. At one time or another, every teacher in your building will have gone through the survival or novice stage. Knowledge about these stages will help you appreciate that feelings of being overwhelmed during your first year are not signs of personality flaws or professional failings. You are merely experiencing a normal stage of professional development. You should also understand that the survival phase will pass and that, in time, you will move on to professional stages you are likely to find more satisfying.

Second, you can use these stages to evaluate your own growth. If you are struggling to get through the day, you will know that you are in the survival stage. You may then turn your attention to the kinds of professional growth opportunities that will allow you to master tasks that are challenging you and that will help you to move on to the next stage.

Finally, an understanding of the development stages can help you better understand your colleagues. Without understanding these stages, you might find yourself intimidated when you see some of your fellow teachers getting excited about a new program or growth opportunity that you see as a threat because you are still struggling just to get through the day. But knowing what you now know about patterns of teachers' development, you should feel secure in understanding that these teachers have moved beyond the survival stage and have arrived at the point in their careers where they are concerned with expanding their instructional capacities and increasing their impact on students' lives.

Evaluating Classroom Performance

Productive growth as a teacher requires useful data on which to base your reflections and your professional growth plans. Good teacher evaluation can supply data that can serve this function.

There are basically two purposes for teacher evaluation. One is what might be called quality assurance. The public demands that each classroom is taught by a quality teacher. This has received more emphasis in recent years as the concept of teacher quality and accountability has been given more importance in educational policy. Today, almost everyone recognizes that the quality of an individual teacher matters (Danielson, 2001).

A second purpose of teacher evaluation is to provide the basis for making decisions about professional growth. This purpose has also been recognized in recent years. However, many point out that teacher evaluation for the purposes of growth and for quality assurance may be incompatible. For example, evaluation for growth requires trust between the individuals involved in the process and requires that the person being evaluated be open and honest in discussing his or her strengths, weaknesses, and concerns. However, evaluation that carries the possibility of serious consequences can lead to a lack of trust between those involved in the evaluation process, and those being evaluated may be reluctant to share their concerns for fear that they will be held against them on the evaluation. As a result, three different types of evaluations have emerged: self-evaluation, peer evaluation, and supervisor evaluation.

Self-Evaluation

Self-evaluation requires more than merely guessing about your instructional skills and your teaching effectiveness. During self-evaluation, you need to consider how you can gather information about your teaching and reflect on the meaning of that information. You can use your own creativity in identifying ways of gathering information that will inform your teaching. If meaningful professional growth is to occur, you need to be open to the possibility that you will find areas where growth is needed.

Several arguments support self-evaluation as an important professional growth tool. First, it is something that you can do to generate information about your teaching more frequently than supervisor or peer observations. This means that you can use the approach to fill any information gap that results from infrequent peer or supervisor observations.

A second reason for self-evaluation is that you will be more inclined to change your behavior when you personally identify something you do not think is satisfactory (Airasian & Gullickson, 1997). When you make changes based on self-evaluation, you gain a sense of personal control over your needs and how they should be accommodated (Rodriguez & Johnstone, 1986).

Third, self-evaluation is a nonintrusive way of gathering information and making judgments. When it is used, you don't have to do anything that interferes with your normal classroom procedures. Because self-evaluation preserves a normal teaching environment, the information you gather may be a better reflection of how you teach under typical classroom conditions than information gathered by others who visit your classroom (and thereby alter the normal classroom environment).

Finally, self-evaluation can build your confidence. Over time, modifications in your teaching behavior adopted as a result of your own personal reflections will be changes you believe in. If your self-evaluation information is compelling enough to commit you to make changes, it is typically a rationale you can use to explain your teaching to others.

You will discover a few negatives associated with self-evaluation. If you don't implement self-evaluation carefully, you may be gathering information in a haphazard, unsystematic manner so that it is of little value. To be effective, self-evaluation should be based on the systematic gathering of data about those teaching dimensions that are of interest or concern to you.

Researchers have discovered that teachers who are unable to describe and defend the procedures they used in gathering information about their teaching often draw conclusions about their teaching that correlate poorly with the observations of others (Brown, 1983). This suggests that poorly conceived self-evaluation is not very helpful in providing the basis for instructional improvement.

Another difficulty with self-evaluation is that it is difficult to make accurate records of what goes on in the classroom. Classrooms are fast-paced environments. So much happens that you will find it impossible to reconstruct the lesson from memory. In addition, you may be so focused on your concerns that you miss significant events that occur during the lesson. One method that is useful in overcoming this problem is the use of CDs, DVDs, and videotapes to capture your teaching. Although this can be threatening, making a recording and viewing it in the privacy of your own classroom can be very beneficial.

When using recordings of lessons, it is helpful to develop a checklist or a rating scale of items you want to observe in the lesson. This will help you focus on the specifics and help you pinpoint behaviors. It is not necessary for you to record an entire lesson every time. You might find it useful to focus on small pieces of your lesson. For example, you might record just the beginnings of lessons to see how you capture attention and get lessons started. Or you might focus just on the directions you give to make sure they are clear and concise. These "samples" are often easier to record and do not require large amounts of time to analyze.

Borich (2008) suggest eight "lenses" that you might use to observe your own teaching:

- Learning climate
- Classroom management
- Lesson clarity
- Instructional variety
- Task orientation
- Student engagement
- Student success
- Examples of higher thought processes (pp. 16–17)

Consider selecting one or more of these to observe each time you watch a recording of yourself. By focusing on one or two at a time, you will provide yourself with a structure that can help you make significant improvement over time.

Your professional portfolio can be another source of information that can be used for evaluation. It can serve as a repository for ideas about teaching, as well as a basis for both self-and supervisor evaluation.

When you use a portfolio either as part of a self-evaluation process or as a data source for others who will be evaluating you, you need to pay particular attention to how you organize materials. If others are going to review your portfolio, you need to have a clear understanding of their assessment standards. Portfolio evaluators often use clear sets of standards, or rubrics, to enhance their ability to make consistent judgments. These rubrics are often based on descriptions of good teaching. They address questions such as: What should a good teacher know and be able to do? Does the teacher have a clear understanding of the content? Does the teacher know how to communicate clearly? How does the teacher assess student learning? You want to make sure that you understand the rubrics and the types of evidence that would be useful in demonstrating your knowledge and skill. You should then make sure the items in your portfolio address these rubrics and standards, and you can use the rubrics as a basis for your self-evaluation. You can ask yourself, Where would I place myself on the scale of descriptors provided on the rubric?

Consider the advantages to your being evaluated based on information contained in a portfolio you have assembled. More traditional evaluation schemes depend on data gathered during one or two classroom observations. Information in a portfolio, on the other hand, includes items you have gathered over a considerable period of time from a variety of sources. The portfolio can provide a more comprehensive picture of what you know and are able to do than information gathered during a couple of classroom observations. In addition, because you assemble the portfolio, you are in a position to play an active role in the evaluation process by selecting items to be included. This gives you some ownership of the evaluation process (Painter, 2001).

Another useful tool for self-evaluation is the reflective journal, a journal where you keep a record of classroom events and your reactions and thoughts. One of the serious problems in promoting teacher growth is that teachers get so busy that they rush from one thing to the next and seldom have time to pause and reflect. Choosing a regular pattern of writing in a reflective journal can provide you with some useful benefits that help overcome the disadvantages of the hectic life of a teacher.

When using a reflective journal, you want to look for recurring patterns or themes. It might be helpful to generate questions that you want address when you read through your reflective journal. Are there recurring patterns or themes? What does the journal indicate about your decision-making? Does the journal reflect growth or change over time? What might account for the change or the lack thereof? These questions will help you move beyond superficial reading and analysis.

You may also include student achievement data in your self-evaluation. Rather than looking at student scores on daily work and tests as just a measure of assigning grades, look at them as indicators of your teaching effectiveness. Are students growing in understanding as the year unfolds? Where are they having difficulty? Why might they be having difficulty? These are often difficult questions for us to ask about our students because sometimes we find that we are part of the problem.

Peer Evaluation

Collaboration with a respected peer can help you gain insight into your behaviors and can give you a glimpse of your teaching performance through a different set of eyes. When a colleague observes your work, you have an opportunity for a rich discussion that allows both individuals to gain insights and to grow. Basically, data gathered from multiple perspectives is more comprehensive than data gathered from one source (Dyer, 2001). This provides a good rationale for having others observe your teaching and work with you.

In recent years, a major emphasis has been on peer coaching, a situation in which two or more individuals voluntarily work together to help each other solve problems and grow professionally. In peer coaching, no person is regarded as superior to another. The purpose here is not quality assurance but professional growth and change. This requires that the two people who work together have a high degree of mutual respect and trust.

It is best to begin the peer coaching relationship by discussing perspectives about teaching and sharing ideas. In time, peer coaching teams begin observing lessons and sharing insights and ideas. The approach should be a positive one that helps individuals build confidence and enhances a sense of professional self-worth.

The normal cycle of activity during a peer coaching observation is a preconference, the observation, and a postconference. During the preconference the purpose is to share information about the lesson that will be taught. Together the team members then plan the observation and make decisions about the primary focus. This is the phase during which you might identify some of the "lenses" (Borich, 2008) mentioned earlier in this chapter. For example, if you are having significant issues with classroom management, you might ask your observer to look at this exclusively. During a subsequent visit, he or she can focus on another "lens" but comment on the classroom management, particularly noting improvements or digressions.

The postconference is the time when the information is shared in a nonjudgmental fashion. A good peer coach will present the data and then ask the observed individual to look for patterns and draw conclusions. This is also a time to affirm what was done well and to suggest what to try in the future. Ideally, the postconference is a two-way discussion between equals.

Another form of peer evaluation involves mentoring. Mentoring is different from peer coaching because it is more of a superior–subordinate relationship. It is a more experienced or skilled person helping a less experienced or skilled person. The mentor serves as a guide, adviser, role model, or consultant. In many places, mentors have become a regular part of the induction process for a new teacher. When you are hired, a person might be appointed as your mentor. This person has the responsibility of serving as your guide and adviser through the difficult beginning stage of teaching.

If you take a position in a school district with a formal mentoring program, the benefit you derive from the program will depend on the mutual trust and respect between you and your mentor. One of the problems associated with formal mentoring is that, because it is prearranged by administrators, the two individuals working together may not be philosophically or interpersonally compatible. This incompatibility then leads to a lack of openness that hinders professional growth.

If your school does not have a formal mentoring program, we recommend that you try to identify a more senior faculty member with whom you feel comfortable. Then try to develop an informal mentoring relationship with that person. Many experienced teachers are willing to serve as informal mentors to new teachers. However, be cognizant of the fact that they also have responsibilities and demands on their time. So carefully choose the times to discuss questions with your mentor, or work out a schedule that suits both of you for addressing questions.

Supervisor Evaluation

Supervisor evaluation occurs when someone in a position of authority is given the responsibility of evaluating your performance. Although professional growth has long been a major thrust of supervisor evaluation, the basic purpose of supervisor evaluation is quality assurance. School leaders are increasingly being held accountable for how well teachers in their schools perform. Many school districts require a supervisor evaluation process, and results of supervisor evaluations can have serious consequences relating to personnel decisions such as retention or tenure.

Because supervisory evaluations have important consequences, they are often accompanied by high levels of anxiety. Thomas Sergiovanni (1994), a scholar who has studied these relationships, argues that the traditional supervisor–subordinate relationship often results in negative outcomes because new teachers are unwilling to share concerns and problems out of fear that these will be used against them when personnel decisions are made. Sergiovanni advocates replacing traditional supervisor evaluation with a conception of schools as communities where the status relationships among people are minimized and interpersonal communication is enhanced. While this is a worthwhile concept, it is unlikely that the role of supervisors in quality assurance and accountability will disappear anytime soon.

Even though you might have concerns about supervisor evaluations, researchers have found that, in general, teachers want and value this type of assessment (McLaughlin & Pfeifer, 1988). This is especially true if the supervisor is perceived as knowledgeable, credible, and trustworthy. One teacher who reflected on this finding indicated general agreement but also noted an important condition: "We need people to come in and check on us just like anybody else. As long as it is done in a positive and constructive manner, all it can do is benefit education" (McLaughlin & Pfeifer, 1988, p. 63). When supervisors provide constructive and positive feedback, they can help you overcome any fears you have about the evaluation process.

Supervisor evaluation tends to be done more systematically than peer evaluation. For example, supervisors often use formal observation/evaluation instruments that have been developed by specialists and are used for evaluating all teachers in the district. When preparing for supervisor visits to your classroom, you will find it useful to review the observation instruments. This will provide you with an understanding of the behaviors that will be assessed and the expectations of the supervisor.

If possible, it is useful to follow the sequence of a preteaching conference, observation, and a post-teaching conference. This allows you to share with the observer your objectives and what you plan to do. It also provides time to try and find out the focus of the observer. This helps both you and the observer during the observation phase. The post-teaching conference allows both of you to share your observations and develop an understanding of strengths and area of needed improvement.

Whether supervisors see a truly representative sample of teachers' work is a matter of debate. When a supervisor comes into your room, the classroom environment is altered. The changes can be positive and negative. Sometimes your students will behave better and be more responsive than usual. On the other hand, the presence of the supervisor can make you nervous, and this may significantly alter your normal teaching style.

In summary, evaluation is likely to be an important component of your teaching career. Currently, there is considerable attention to making sure that teacher evaluation is directed toward significant dimensions of teaching. You need to understand that teacher evaluation can be productive and is an important component in helping you improve and make choices for your professional growth.

Professional Growth Opportunities

Regardless of the excellence of your teacher preparation and regardless of where you begin teaching, you are likely to recognize early in your first year of teaching that there are some gaps in what you need to know to become an effective teacher. This situation is inevitable given the tremendous differences among students, physical facilities, materials availability, levels of parental involvement, and administrative support from one school to another. You will have a number of options available to you as you seek to extend your levels of understanding. For example, you may wish to pursue one of the following:

- Staff development activities, including meetings sponsored by the school or school district
- College and university courses
- Professional organization work, including special programs sponsored by professional education associations
- Webinars, podcasts, and e-workshops

Staff Development Activities

Many school districts provide development activities for their teachers. These are part of a larger effort to improve the overall quality of the educational program. Sometimes staff development activities for teachers are referred to as in-service education. In many districts, the school calendar is developed so that students are dismissed from school on several days throughout the year to enable teachers to participate in professional development opportunities.

Attendance at district-sponsored staff development is often required for new teachers. When you begin to teach, you should inquire about the professional growth opportunities available in the school district. In some places, teachers receive staff development credits for their participation; when teachers accumulate enough of these credits, they qualify for salary increases.

Staff development takes a variety of forms. Sessions sponsored by school districts often feature speakers, workshops led by teachers with special expertise, and sharing sessions that allow teachers of common subjects to exchange ideas. As a newcomer to the profession, you may find these staff development sessions an excellent source of information for improving your instruction and your approaches to classroom management.

College and University Courses

You may also want to take some college and university courses while you are teaching. To serve this market, many institutions offer courses at night so local teachers can attend. In some places, Saturday classes are available. You may find yourself working in a school district that places limits on the number of courses teachers can take during the school year. This requirement has been adopted in some places out of a concern that teachers may not leave themselves enough time to plan adequately for their teaching responsibilities.

In addition to adding to your knowledge, college and university courses may help you move to a higher level on the salary schedule. In many places, salaries go up as (1) the number of years a teacher has taught increases and (2) the total number of academic credits the teacher has earned past the time of initial certification increases. This scheme is built on the idea that your expertise will increase in tandem with years of experience and additional college-level study.

Taking college courses may also be applied toward an advanced degree. Teachers often qualify for a master's degree after taking courses for several years in the evening and attending several summer sessions. We caution against using applicability toward a degree as a reason for selecting any college courses you might take during your first year or two in the classroom. Advanced degree programs often prescribe specific programs of study. These courses may not meet the kinds of needs you face every day in your classroom. We think it makes much more sense for you to select courses that will be of immediate help in your day-to-day work. After these initial knowledge gaps have been filled, there will be plenty of time for you to enroll in a more formal program of study leading to an advanced degree.

Professional Organization Work

Professional organizations regularly sponsor events that include sessions designed to improve teachers' levels of expertise. They provide opportunities for teachers to interact with others who share similar interests. This is important in a profession where individual practitioners do not come into much direct contact with other professionals during the major part of their workday. An affiliation with professional groups can help you to appreciate the bonds that join all who teach.

This kind of involvement can give you access to information through several channels. Professional organizations sponsor meetings that almost always feature presentations and workshops that allow participants to gain up-to-date information about content and instructional methodologies. Many of them also publish journals and newsletters with helpful information. Simply coming into contact with others who share your professional concerns can be a confidence builder as you come to recognize that many others share an interest in issues that are important to you.

Two broad types of professional organizations serve educators: general organizations and specialty organizations. The two largest general organizations, the National Education Association (NEA) and the American Federation of Teachers (AFT), seek their members from the total national population of teachers. Members include teachers working at all grade levels and in all subject areas. Specialty organizations seek members from among teachers who are interested in specific subject areas or certain categories of learners. Both of these types of organizations provide professional growth opportunities for teachers.

General Organizations   The NEA and AFT are particularly interested in issues associated with teachers' working conditions. In many parts of the country, local affiliates of these groups represent teachers in negotiating salary and working conditions with representatives of the school board and administration. At the state and national levels, representatives of these organizations work to support passage of legislation of interest to teachers.

Representatives also serve as members of accrediting agencies that are responsible for examining and certifying the adequacy of practice within individual school districts. Sometimes they also serve as members of bodies considering curriculum changes. In general, representatives of the major general professional organizations are involved in almost all situations when issues of great concern to teachers are considered.

Teachers who belong to these groups are in a position to keep informed about issues affecting the profession. For more information about these groups and their programs, visit their websites:

The National Education Association
1201 16th Street NW
Washington, DC 20036-3207
http://www.nea.org/

American Federation of Teachers
555 New Jersey Avenue NW
Washington, DC 20001-2029
http://www.aft.org/

Specialty Organizations There are dozens of specialty organizations in the field of education. Affiliation with one will give you opportunities to exchange ideas and share perspectives with others who share your interests and who work with similar kinds of students. Thousands of teachers belong to these groups.

Specialty organizations provide numerous services to their members. Most of the large ones have annual meetings. These meetings bring together educators from throughout the country to share ideas and discuss issues. Many national organizations also have state and local affiliates that sponsor meetings. Typically, these meetings include presentations that inform teachers of promising approaches to instruction and issues of special interest in that particular state.

Most of the national specialty groups publish professional journals for their members. Articles often focus on up-to-date research findings, descriptions of innovative teaching practices, and discussions of other relevant issues. Many new teachers find these journals to be an excellent place to discover new teaching ideas.

Many specialty groups encourage people who are preparing to become teachers to join. We think this is a good idea. If you join and become active in one of these organizations, you will have opportunities to become acquainted with employed teachers and gain insights on some aspects of their professional lives that may not have received much attention in your education courses.

Box 15-1 introduces a number of specialty groups. This listing is by no means comprehensive. We have selected these organizations to illustrate the broad range of those that invite secondary school teachers to join. We encourage you to visit those sites that are of particular interest to you, particularly the one affiliated with your content field.

Organizations profiled in Box 15-1 typify those that draw much of their membership from teachers. These groups help members build communities of shared concern. Many of the groups also have state and local affiliates that provide easy access for local teachers.

Finally, they function as catalysts for political action. Many federal and state laws that influence schools began as lobbying efforts of educational specialty groups. For example, present laws about serving students with disabilities can be traced to pressures first brought to bear on legislatures by organizations committed to better serving the needs of these young people.

You may wish to visit the websites of some additional specialty organizations. The home page at http://www.ed.gov/ titled "Educational Associations and Organizations" is a good place to start. You will find links here to many public and private groups with interests in education. For example, you will find sites for groups such as Achieve (an organization

Box 15-1

American Alliance for Health, Physical Education, Recreation, and Dance (AAHPERD)
http://www.aahperd.org/

American Council on the Teaching of Foreign Languages (ACTFL)
http://www.actfl.org/

Association for Career and Technical Education (ACTE)
http://www.acteonline.org/

Association for Supervision and Curriculum Development (ASCD)
http://www.ascd.org/

Council on Exceptional Children (CEC)
http://www.cec.sped.org/

International Reading Association (IRA)
http://www.reading.org/

International Society for Technology in Education (ISTE)
http://www.iste.org/

Modern Language Association (MLA)
http://www.mla.org/

Music Teachers National Association (MTNA)
http://www.mtna.org/

National Art Education Association (NAEA)
http://www.naea-reston.org/

National Association for Gifted Children (NAGC)
http://www.nagc.org/

National Business Education Association (NBEA)
http://www.nbea.org/

National Council for the Social Studies (NCSS)
http://www.ncss.org/

National Council of Teachers of English (NCTE)
http://www.ncte.org/

National Council of Teachers of Mathematics (NCTM)
http://www.nctm.org/

National Middle School Association (NMSA)
http://www.nmsa.org/

National Science Teachers Association (NSTA)
http://www.nsta.org/

---

that draws together governors, business leaders, and others interested in improving students' achievement levels), the American Educational Research Association (a group dedicated to promoting research on topics related to education), the Council of Great City Schools (a group dedicated to improving the education of inner-city youth), and the National Rural Education Association (a group interested in improving education in rural areas). Here is the URL that will take you to the Web page with links to these and other education-related associations and organizations: http://www.ed.gov/

Webinars, Podcasts, and e-workshops   The newest venue through which you can receive professional development is through online workshops. Many of the associations listed in Box 15-1 provide webinars, podcasts, or e-workshops (occasionally all three). Typically you will find them listed under the professional development link. Even though they usually charge a fee (often reduced for association members), it is often small compared to the fees and travel expenses related to conferences. You don't receive the same social interaction, but it is an alternative worth exploring because you can access the workshop from the comfort of your own home. Some of the organizations suggest that several teachers pool their resources and take the workshops together. This allows for discussion about how the ideas can be implemented in your own classrooms. On occasion you will find free workshops. The quality of the content varies on these free workshops, so don't use these as a judge of others for which you must pay.

A quick search of some of the organizations identified the following workshops either currently available or upcoming:

NMSA—Motivating Young Adolescents

NCTE—(1) Literature Circles: Focusing on Differentiated Instruction; (2) Critical Literacy

NCTM—Integrating Writing and Mathematical Understanding

NSTA—An entire series on climate change

ASCD—How Can I Motivate My Students?

These workshops change on a regular basis but this list gives you a flavor of what you might find. Many of the associations archive the presentations; if you are looking for a particular topic, don't forget to check the archive list.

Finally, many of the associations now have a presence on Facebook and Twitter. If you are a loyal participant on either of these sites, you can follow your professional organization there, too.

Career Options

As you have been working to complete your preparation program, you may not have thought much about the wide range of career options in education. Many of these options will be open to you only after you have spent some time actually working as a classroom teacher. A few require you to leave classroom teaching entirely.

Department Chair

The department chair in a secondary school is the person designated to exercise leadership in a specific subject area (English, social studies, mathematics, science, and so forth). Duties vary, but often they include responsibilities in areas such as evaluating new faculty members, coordinating staff development opportunities, disseminating information about school policies, and ordering supplies for department members. In general, the department chair functions as a liaison between school administrators and faculty members in the department.

Typically, department chairs are selected from among the most experienced teachers in their respective departments. They tend to be individuals who have credibility both with their teaching colleagues and with school administrators. Often, department chairs teach a reduced load to allow them time to perform other assigned duties. They sometimes receive extra salary and often they must work more days each year than regular classroom teachers.

Opportunities for people to become department chairs are limited. Only one chair is appointed for each department. In some schools, many years go by before a new chair needs to be appointed. One potential advantage of the department chair's role is that it allows an individual to assume some administrative and supervisory responsibilities while continuing to teach. Elevation to the position of department chair is one of the few promotions in education that does not remove a teacher completely from the classroom.

Curriculum Coordinator

This position often goes by one of a number of titles other than curriculum coordinator. Among them are curriculum director, curriculum supervisor, and curriculum leader. By whatever title it is known, this position requires the designated individual to assume leadership in areas such as curriculum planning, in-service planning, and instructional-support planning. In small school districts, the curriculum coordinator may have responsibilities for several subject areas and may even continue to teach part-time. In larger districts, curriculum coordinators do not teach. Typically curriculum coordinators have their offices in the district's central administrative headquarters.

Curriculum coordinators are individuals with a great deal of knowledge about up-to-date trends in the subject area (or areas) for which they are responsible. They are in a position to influence the nature of the instructional program throughout the district in their areas of responsibility. Many curriculum coordinators hold advanced degrees. Curriculum coordinators often work a longer school year than teachers, and they are paid more. Their primary audience is teachers in the district. Especially in medium-size and large districts, curriculum coordinators only infrequently work with students in the classroom.

School Administrator

Nearly all school administrators begin their work in education as classroom teachers. By taking advanced courses, often including completion of at least a master's degree and relevant administrative certification requirements, they qualify for administrative positions. These positions exist both at the school level and at the central district administrative level. Some typical administrative positions at the school level are assistant principal and principal. Positions often found in central school administrative headquarters are director of personnel, assistant superintendent, and superintendent.

Administrators have responsibilities that require some skills that are different from those required of classroom teachers. Much of their work involves preparing budgets, planning, scheduling, supervising noncertified personnel, filling out paperwork related to state and federal guidelines, and completing evaluation reports on teachers.

Administrators function as official representatives of the schools to the community; hence, they must have good public relations skills. School administrators almost always work a longer school year than classroom teachers and are paid higher salaries than teachers. Because demands of administration are quite different from those of teaching, some individuals who are outstanding teachers may not much care for administrative positions.

School Counselor

Many school counselors begin their careers as classroom teachers. In most parts of the country school counselors must take additional graduate training to qualify for a counseling certificate, usually by completing master's degrees with a school-counseling emphasis. Counselors typically work a longer school year than teachers, and they are paid more.

In addition to personal and academic counseling, many school counselors also are expected to perform a number of administrative tasks. Sometimes counselors are responsible for establishing the master teaching schedule for a school. Often they are in charge of all standardized testing. They must spend a great deal of time attending special meetings. Time available for working with individual students often is surprisingly limited.

State Education Agency Employee

All states have education departments or agencies that are staffed primarily by professionals with backgrounds in education. State education agencies hire people with a variety of backgrounds and for diverse purposes. There often are subject-area specialists who are charged with coordinating curriculum guidelines and in-service training throughout the state for teachers in specific subjects, and assessment specialists who coordinate statewide testing programs. Teacher education specialists work with colleges and universities to ensure that teacher preparation programs are providing new teachers with appropriate backgrounds.

Employees of state education agencies often have had considerable prior experience working in the schools. Most of these positions require people to have at least a master's degree, and some of them require a doctoral degree. Considerable travel is often required. Employees of state education agencies work all year long. Levels of remuneration typically are considerably higher than those of classroom teachers.

Teacher Educator

Individuals who have taught successfully sometimes seek opportunities to share their expertise with future teachers. One way for them to do this is to become a teacher educator. Most teacher educators are faculty members of colleges and universities. A few are employed by large school districts. Almost always, teacher educator positions require a doctoral degree. Because most teacher educators are members of college and university faculties, this degree is essential for the teacher educator to meet employment and tenure standards at most institutions of higher learning.

The role of the teacher educator is more varied and complex than is sometimes imagined by those viewing it from the outside. Although exemplary teaching certainly contributes to success as a faculty member in teacher education, still more is necessary. Faculty members must also demonstrate initiative in improving preparation programs, keep up to date on findings of researchers, conduct research, write for publication, seek opportunities to make presentations at regional and national meetings, maintain good working relations with other departments and with the schools, serve on large numbers of committees, maintain good links with state education agencies, and counsel students. All of these obligations require processing of massive quantities of paperwork.

A person who enters a doctoral program must devote considerable time to intensive study. About three years of full-time study after the award of the master's degree is typical. Many institutions require that prospective doctoral students spend at least one full year as resident, full-time students on the campus. This means that a teacher interested in doing this must leave his or her teaching position for at least one year. Many who decide to pursue a doctorate resign their positions to devote their full attention to their studies. Most universities have graduate assistantships and fellowships that provide modest financial support to individuals doing advanced doctoral work.

Teacher educators typically are employed for nine months out of the year. Many of them also have opportunities to work during the summer months, too. Salaries are not particularly high. In fact, some beginning teacher educators are paid less than some experienced public school classroom teachers. Although beginning salaries of teacher educators tend to be modest, top salaries for experienced teacher educators tend to be higher than those paid to classroom teachers.

Individuals considering pursuing a doctoral program and becoming a teacher educator should seek information from reputable and accredited universities that offer doctorates. Some universities that offer doctorates are not widely respected, and an individual holding such a degree is going to have difficulty finding employment as a teacher educator. Discussions with practicing teacher educators can provide useful information. Once several possible universities have been identified, it makes sense to write to them for information about the specific features of their doctoral programs in education. There are important differences among institutions, and someone considering advanced study should look for one that is compatible with his or her own objectives. For example, one university may have an outstanding program in mathematics education, and another may have special strengths in social studies education.

Opportunities Outside Education

For a variety of reasons, some teachers decide to leave the classroom after teaching for just a few years. If you decide to do this, does it mean that your time spent preparing to teach was wasted? Not at all. There are employment options outside the K–12 classroom for individuals with backgrounds in teaching.

Many large firms employ people with good teaching and curriculum development skills to work in their employee training programs. Education in industry is becoming big business. Many large corporations have special training divisions. The term *human resource development,* often abbreviated HRD, is frequently used to describe the corporate training function. There is a large national professional organization, the American Society for Training and Development (ASTD), devoted exclusively to promoting the interests of its members who are educators in industry. The group produces a fine journal titled *Training and Development.* People interested in the possibility of working as an educator in industry should look through several issues to get a feel for what corporate trainers do.

In addition, individuals with skills developed in education find work in the human services sector. Positions in this sector involve working in places such as museums or youth organizations such as the scouts or the YMCA and the YWCA.

Some individuals with educational backgrounds have also found employment working as educational material salespersons. The types of communication and interpersonal relations skills typically developed in education can also be transferred to success in other occupations that demand face-to-face contact with the general public.

Final Comments

The teaching profession is complex. Changing student populations, federal and state education regulations, public expectations, and knowledge about what works in the classroom require a commitment to career-long professional development. It is a process that may take unexpected twists and turns but that, despite these surprises, promises to go resolutely onward. If you embrace the idea that change is going to be a regular feature of the life of a teacher, you probably will be satisfied with your career choice. If you expect to enter an ordered and predictable world that will be in the future much as it was in the past, you will be disappointed.

When you teach, you will find yourself making dozens of decisions each day. Our intent in this book has been to provide you with some principles that have been followed by successful teachers. We know that a good part of teaching is unpredictable. However, if you have a set of guiding principles and have learned how to routinely handle most tasks, the unpredictable nature of teaching will not overwhelm you. We hope that some of the material we have presented will be of help to you.

We also recognize that teaching is not for everyone. Our intent has not been to try and convince all readers that they should be a teacher. Rather, we have attempted to provide you with information that will assist you in making an intelligent decision.

For those who do decide to teach, we hope you will enjoy some of the same exciting moments and rewards we have experienced as teachers. We are proud of what we do, and we look forward to welcoming you to one of civilizations proudest callings: teaching.

FOR YOUR PORTFOLIO

Interstate New Teacher Assessment and Support Consortium (INTASC) Standards 9 and 10 both relate to the content of this chapter. Standard 9 indicates that a professional educator is one who continually evaluates the effects of his or her actions and constantly seeks to grow professionally. Standard 10 indicates that professional educators participate in the professional community and foster relationships with colleagues, agencies, and parents. With that in mind, identify two or three entries for your portfolio.

1. Reflect on the items you chose for the portfolio. Why did you choose them? Write a reflection cover for each entry that describes the entry and what it indicates about you and your teaching.

2. How do these entries communicate how you profit from evaluation?

3. How do these entries communicate your involvement in the professional community of educators?

Key Ideas in Summary

- You will be involved in professional development throughout your career. Conditions change over time, as will your professional interests and needs. You cannot expect to have mastered all you need to know during your teacher preparation program.

- Teaching is a profession. This means you need to be prepared to accept special responsibilities. Professionals are individuals with specialized knowledge who have met selection criteria for entry and place service to their clients as a priority. They have a high degree of autonomy and responsibility.

- At least three distinct growth stages have been observed in the professional development of teachers. The first stage is that of survival, where the concerns are focused on self and being able to get through the day or the week. The second stage is mastery, where the concerns are still on self but are focused on becoming an expert or master teacher. The third stage is impact, where the concerns now shift from self to that of the impact on students.

- There are two basic purposes of teacher evaluation. One purpose is for accountability and quality assurance. There is much public interest in making sure that there are quality teachers in every classroom. The second purpose is to provide a database for professional growth and development.

- There are three types of evaluation that can be performed. Perhaps the most powerful type of evaluation is self-evaluation. Self-evaluation needs to be done systematically and with care.

- Peer evaluation has been emphasized in recent years as a way of bringing about growth and development. One type of peer evaluation is peer coaching, in which individuals are considered to be equals and they share ideas. The second type is mentoring, in which a more experienced and skilled individual helps a beginning teacher.

- Supervisor evaluation is focused on accountability and quality assurance. The results of this type of evaluation are usually used for retention and tenure. Although this type of evaluation can be threatening, it can be useful if the supervisor is knowledgeable, credible, and trustworthy.

- Many kinds of staff development activities are available to classroom teachers, including school-based development activities, college courses, and participation in professional organizations.

- There are two types of professional organizations. General organizations represent the interests of the entire teaching profession. Specialty organizations serve the interests of teachers working in a specific subject area or with a specific type of student.

- Although many individuals who choose teaching as a career do so because they want to work in classrooms with students, career opportunities exist beyond the classroom. Career opportunities outside the classroom include department chair, curriculum coordinator, state agency employee, and teacher educator. These roles often require additional preparation.

- Some individuals with backgrounds in education do not work in K–12 schools. Some work in training departments in industry or in human services organizations. The skills acquired in teacher education program are transferable to other occupations that need individuals with good organization and human relations skills.

Reflections

1. This chapter emphasized that a person in education must be prepared to accept and adapt to change. How do you react to change and unpredictable events?

2. Debate continues about whether teaching is a profession. Using the standards discussed in this chapter, do you think teaching is a profession? Why or why not?

3. One of your obligations as a professional is to speak out against actions and policy decisions that might not be in the best interest of students. Are there some actions now that you see as detrimental to students? What could you do about them?

4. How do you react to supervision and evaluation? What would be your reaction to the prospect of entering a mentor relationship and to supervisor evaluation?

5. Where do you see yourself five years after entering teaching? Ten years after entering teaching? What will it take for you to accomplish these long-term goals?

Learning Extensions

1. Interview some first- and second-year teachers. Ask them to describe their first year. What surprised them? Did they experience reality shock? How did they cope with the survival stage? What contributed to their growth to the next stage?

2. Begin the process of self-evaluation by taking the time to evaluate honestly your growth toward successful teaching. What have you learned? What do you need to learn? What actions and responsibility can you take to make sure you can assume responsibility for a classroom?

3. Visit some local school districts or go online to see what types of professional growth opportunities are provided by different school districts.

4. Conduct some research on career opportunities outside education for people who have completed teacher education programs. What do these positions entail? How do salaries compare to those in schools? What do you think would be the professional and personal satisfactions and frustrations of these positions?

References

Airasian, P., & Gullickson, A. (1997). Teacher self-evaluation. In J. Strong (Ed.), *Evaluating teaching: A guide to current thinking and best practice* (pp. 215–241). Thousand Oaks, CA: Corwin.

Borich, G. D. (2008). *Observation skills for effective teaching* (5th ed.). Upper Saddle River, NJ: Pearson/Merrill Prentice Hall.

Brown, R. (1983). Helpful and humane teacher evaluations. In W. Duckett (Ed.), *Teacher evaluation: Gathering and using data* (pp. 9–26). Bloomington, IN: Phi Delta Kappa.

Clark, L., & Starr, I. (1996). *Secondary and middle school teaching methods* (7th ed.). Columbus, OH: Merrill.

Danielson, C. (2001). New trends in teacher evaluation. *Educational leadership, 58*(5), 12–15.

Darling-Hammond, L. (2000). Teacher quality and student achievement: A review of state policy evidence. *Educational Policy Archives, 8*(1). Retrieved May 21, 2004, from http://epaa.asu.edu/epaa/v8n1/

Dyer, K. (2001). The power of 360-degree feedback. *Educational leadership, 58*(5), 35–38.

Fuller, F. (1969). Concerns of teachers: A developmental conceptualization. *American Educational Research Journal, 6,* 207–226.

Jackson, R. R. (2009). *Never work harder than your students & other principles of great teaching.* Alexandria, VA: Association for Supervision and Curriculum Development.

Jarolimek, J., & Foster, C. (1996). *Teaching and learning in the elementary school* (6th ed.). Columbus, OH: Merrill.

Kronowitz, E. (1999). *Your first year of teaching and beyond* (3rd ed.). New York: Longman.

McLaughlin, M., & Pfeifer, R. (1988). *Teacher evaluation: Improvement, accountability, and effective learning*. New York: Teachers College Press.

Painter, B. (2001). Using teacher portfolios. *Educational leadership, 58*(56), 31–34.

Rodriguez, S., & Johnstone, K. (1986). Staff development through collegial support groups. In K. Zumwalt (Ed.), *Improving teaching: 1986 ASCD yearbook* (pp. 87–99). Alexandria, VA: Association for Supervision and Curriculum Development.

Ryan, K., Newman, K., Mager, G., Applegate, J., Lasley, T., Flora, R., & Johnston, J. (1980). *Biting the apple: Accounts of first year teachers*. New York: Longman.

Sergiovanni, T. (1994). Organizations of communities? Changing the metaphor changes the theory. *Educational Administration Quarterly, 30*(2), 214–226.

Name Index

Subject Index

Positive interdependence, 250
Poverty, success at school and, 42–43
Power
  coercive, 294
  expert, 295
  legitimate, 294
  referent, 295–296
  reward, 294
Practice, 198–199
Praise, 89
Prereading strategies, 270–271
Prerequisite skills, teaching, in small-group learning, 244–245
Prior knowledge, importance of, 198–199
Problem solving, 230–231
  in higher-level thinking, 232–233
Professionalism, 81–82
Professional knowledge, 84
Professional organization work, 351–354
Professionals
  autonomy and high standards, 340
  selective admission to preparation programs, 339–340
Project-based learning, 117
Project Follow Through, 194–195
Proximity control, 301
Psychomotor domain, 118–119
  instructional objectives in, 116

QAIT Model, 196

Racial diversity, 41–42
RAFT, 279–281
Rate of learning, altering, 173–175
Readability, 270
Reading
  analyzing material, 269–270
  creating conditions to stimulate, 267–268
  framework, 268
  independent levels, 269
  instructional level, 269
  diagnosing of, 268–269
Reading across curriculum, 267–268
Reading framework
  assistance phase, 275
  preparation phase, 268
  reflection phase, 278–279
Reciprocal questioning, 272
Referent power, 296
Reflective decision making, 78–79
Reflective journal, 348

Reflective teaching
  context considerations, 79–80
  critical incident, 80–81
  decision-making, 78–79
  defined, 76–77
  fluid plans, 89–90
  growth opportunities, 91–93
  knowledge, 82–83
Reform movement trends, 10, 14–16, 18, 42, 106
Reform proposals, 13, 15, 19, 31–32
ReQuest, 272
Research-on-teaching studies, 85–86
Research reports, 278
Responding, 117
Review of Educational Research, 85
Reward power, 294
Routines, establishing, 213
Rubistar for Teachers, 141
Rubrics, 138–139
  analytic, 138

Same-age peer tutoring, 184
Scholastic Achievement Test (SAT), 251
  scores, 233–234
School administrator, 7, 9, 39, 103, 305, 307, 318, 355
School counselor, 355
Schools
  attendance at, 315–316
  as context variable, 79
  following reasonable rules at, 315–316
  maintenance of safe environment at, 316
  poverty and success at, 42–43
Search and seizure, 320
Secondary education, 4, 10
  historical development of, 10–12
  improving teacher quality in, 19–20
  race to the top (RTTT), 20–21
  reform trends in, 15–19
Selected response items, 131, 133, 135, 145
Self-advocacy, teaching, 59
Self-concept, 5, 12, 65, 86
Self-control, 292–293, 306
Self-esteem, 53, 59, 87, 89, 252, 263, 305–306
Self-evaluation, 346–348
Self-monitoring, 86
Senior high school, 10–12
Sensory perceptions, 199
Sexual assault, 302
Sexual metaphor, 316
Sheltered instruction, differentiation through, 184–187
Short-term memory, 199